POWER AND THE NATION IN
EUROPEAN HISTORY

Few would doubt the central importance of the nation in the making
and unmaking of modern political communities. The long history of
'the nation' as a concept and as a name for various sorts of 'imagined
community' likewise commands much acceptance. But when did the
nation first become a fundamental political factor? This is a question
which has been, and continues to be, far more sharply contested.
A deep rift still separates 'modernist' perspectives, which view the
political nation as a phenomenon limited to modern societies, from
the views of scholars concerned with the pre-industrial world who
insist, often vehemently, that nations were central to pre-modern
political life also. This book represents the first attempt to engage
with these questions by drawing on the expertise of medieval, early
modern and modern historians.

LEN SCALES is Lecturer in Medieval History at the University of
Durham. He has written articles for various journals such as *Past and
Present* and the *Transactions of the Royal Historical Society*.

OLIVER ZIMMER is Reader in Modern European History at the
University of Durham. His previous publications include *A Contested
Nation: History, Memory and Nationalism in Switzerland 1761–1891*
(2003) and *Nationalism in Europe, 1890–1940* (2003).

POWER AND THE NATION IN EUROPEAN HISTORY

EDITED BY
LEN SCALES AND OLIVER ZIMMER

CAMBRIDGE
UNIVERSITY PRESS

CAMBRIDGE UNIVERSITY PRESS

Cambridge, New York, Melbourne, Madrid, Cape Town, Singapore, São Paulo

CAMBRIDGE UNIVERSITY PRESS
The Edinburgh Building, Cambridge, CB2 2RU, UK
Published in the United States of America by Cambridge University Press, New York

www.cambridge.org
Information on this title: www.cambridge.org/9780521608305

First published 2005

Printed in the United Kingdom at the University Press, Cambridge

Typeset in Adobe Garamond 11/12.5pt   *System* Advent 3B2 8.07f [PND]

A catalogue record for this book is available from the British Library

Library of Congress Cataloguing in Publication data

Power and the nation in European history / edited by Len Scales and Oliver Zimmer.
p.   cm.
Includes bibliographical references and index.
ISBN 0-521-84580-7 – ISBN 0-521-60830-9 (pbk.)
1. Europe – Politics and government.   2. National state.
I. Scales, Len, 1961–   II. Zimmer, Oliver, 1964–
D31.P68 2005
940–dc22   2004062837

ISBN-13 978-0-521-84580-9 hardback
ISBN-10 0-521-84580-7 hardback
ISBN-13 978-0-521-60830-5 paperback
ISBN-10 0-521-60830-9 paperback

Patrick Wormald
In Memoriam

Contents

vii

List of Contributors

JOHN BREUILLY is Professor of Nationalism and Ethnicity at the London School of Economics and Political Science, and is one of the leading British historians of modern Germany. His *Nationalism and the State* (1983) belongs to the corpus of classic texts on the subject of nationalism. He has written and edited several books on German history, including *Labour and Liberalism in Nineteenth-Century Europe: Essays in Comparative History* (1992) and *The Formation of the First German Nation-State, 1800–1871* (1996).

SARAH FOOT is Professor of Medieval History at the University of Sheffield, with interests in the development of 'English' identity before the Norman Conquest, and in the role of the Anglo-Saxon Church, particularly monasticism. Her publications include *Veiled Women* (2 vols., 2000) and *Minsters: Reflections on Early English Monasticism* (2002).

ROBIN FRAME, Professor Emeritus of Medieval History at the University of Durham, is one of the leading authorities on the political history of medieval Ireland and Britain. His numerous publications include *The Political Development of the British Isles, 1100–1400* (1990) and *English Lordship in Ireland, 1318–1361* (1982).

ROBERT FROST is Professor of Early Modern History at the University of Aberdeen, and a leading authority on the history of the Polish-Lithuanian Commonwealth. He has published widely on this subject, including *After the Deluge: Poland-Lithuania and the Second Northern War* (1993) and *The Northern Wars. War, State and Society in Northeastern Europe, 1558–1721* (2000).

ABIGAIL GREEN is a lecturer in Modern European History at the University of Oxford, and a Fellow of Brasenose College. She specialises in the political and cultural history of nineteenth-century Germany, with particular reference to the issues of nationalism and German unification. She is the author of *Fatherlands: State-Building and Nationhood in Nineteenth-Century Germany*. Her current interests include work on a biography of Sir Moses Montefiore (1784–1885) and the role of the press in international politics in the nineteenth century.

JENNIFER HEUER, Assistant Professor of Modern European History at Middlebury College, Vermont, specialises in Modern French and European History, Gender History, and European Colonialism. She is the author of *The*

Family and the Nation: Gender, Citizenship, and Nationality in Revolutionary France (forthcoming, 2004).

GEOFFREY HOSKING, FBA, is Professor of Russian History at the School of Slavonic and East European Studies (University College London). He is a leading authority on Russian history and Russian national identity; his numerous publications on these topics include *A History of the Soviet Union* (1985), *Russia: People and Empire, 1552–1917* (1997), and *Russia and the Russians: A History from the Earliest Times to 2001* (2001), as well as several edited works. Professor Hosking was Reith Lecturer in 1988.

PETER MANDLER is a lecturer in modern British history at the University of Cambridge, and Fellow of Gonville and Caius College. His research centres on questions of national heritage and national consciousness and on the relationship between popular and elite cultures. Among his recent publications are *History and National Life* (2002), *The Fall and Rise of the Stately Home* (1997), and *Aristocratic Government in the Age of Reform* (1990).

IAN MCBRIDE lectures in Early Modern History at King's College London, and specialises in the political, intellectual and cultural history of eighteenth-century Ireland, and has wider interests in political thought, religion and national identity in England and Scotland during the same periods. He is the author of *Scripture Politics: Ulster Presbyterians and Irish Radicalism in the Late Eighteenth Century* (1998) and *The Siege of Derry in Ulster Protestant Mythology* (1997).

SUSAN REYNOLDS, FBA, formerly Fellow of Lady Margaret Hall, Oxford University, is a distinguished medieval historian who has worked widely on different forms of community in the medieval West. Her books include *Kingdoms and Communities in Western Europe 900–1300* (1984) and *Fiefs and Vassals* (1994).

LEN SCALES is a lecturer in Medieval History at the University of Durham. He specialises in the political, social, cultural and intellectual history of Germany between the thirteenth and fifteenth centuries. He is the author of *In a German Mirror: Authority, Crisis, and German Identity, 1245–1414* (forthcoming).

ANTHONY D. SMITH, Professor Emeritus of Ethnicity and Nationalism at the London School of Economics and Political Science, is probably the leading scholar of nationalism writing today. His numerous publications on the subject include *Theories of Nationalism* (1983 [1971]), *The Ethnic Revival* (1981), *Ethnic Origins of Nations* (1986), *National Identity* (1991) and *Nationalism and Modernism* (1998).

TIM THORNTON, Senior Lecturer in History at the University of Huddersfield, works on the late medieval and early modern political and social history of the British Isles (c.1400–1650), concentrating particularly on the non-English territories of the crown. His publications include *Cheshire and the Tudor State, 1480–1560* (2000).

STUART WOOLF, Professor of Contemporary History at the University of Venice, is a leading authority on nationalism and has published widely in other fields of comparative European history. His numerous publications include *The Italian Risorgimento* (1969), *A History of Italy 1700–1860: The Social Constraints of Political Change* (1979) and *Napoleon's Integration of Europe* (1991). He has edited *Fascism in Europe* (1981) and *Nationalism in Europe 1815 to the Present: A Reader* (1996).

The late PATRICK WORMALD was tutor and university lecturer at Christ Church, Oxford, and was among the most distinguished historians of law and political culture in early medieval Europe, with a particular focus on England. His numerous publications in the field include *Legal Culture in the Early Medieval West* (1999) and *The Making of the English Law: King Alfred to the Twelfth Century* (1999).

OLIVER ZIMMER is Reader in Modern History at the University of Durham. He specialises in the political and cultural history of nineteenth-century Europe. He is the author of *A Contested Nation: History, Memory and Nationalism in Switzerland 1761–1891* (2003) and *Nationalism in Europe, 1890–1940* (2003).

Introduction

Len Scales and Oliver Zimmer

Something more than discontent and speculative ingenuity is needed in order to invest a political idea with power over the masses of mankind.
Lord Acton, 'Nationality' (1862)

The long history of 'the nation' as a concept and as a name for various sorts of 'imagined community' commands much acceptance. But when did the nation first become a fundamental *political* factor? This is a question which has been, and continues to be, far more sharply contested. A deep rift still separates 'modernist' perspectives, which view the political nation as a phenomenon limited to modern societies, from the views of scholars concerned with the pre-industrial world who insist, often vehemently, that nations were central to pre-modern political life also. Yet the engagement of these two broad camps with each other's distinctive viewpoints has often resembled a dialogue of the deaf. All this has favoured the perpetuation of an increasingly repetitive discussion about the origins of nations and nationalism.

This unfortunate state of affairs could only be improved, we were convinced, by bringing together specialists in the history of the pre-modern and the modern nation to scrutinise the nation's historical relationship with political power. A number of more specific questions appeared to flow naturally from this theme. When, and under what historical circumstances, did the nation become constitutive, rather than simply descriptive, of state power and legitimacy? Can the nation attain political importance only when mature state institutions exist, requiring participation, as against mere acquiescence, from members of the putative national community? Does the seeming relative unimportance of national bonds in some premodern societies – certain states of the European *ancien régime* come to mind – preclude the nation *ever* having political importance in such societies? Should key concepts, such as 'nation' and 'state', be ascribed fixed, trans-historical, meanings, or is a flexible approach more illuminating – one allowing, for example, for the possible existence of distinctive 'pre-modern nations', with political qualities and implications different from those associated with modernity?

Our aim was not to encourage a search for a consensual answer to all or even some of these questions. To do so would have been neither possible nor desirable in our view. The real motivation behind the organisation of a conference on 'Power and the Nation in History' was the conviction that it was high time that these questions be addressed. The wide-ranging nature of the topic suggested that this could best be achieved by a group of scholars who were willing to place their own contributions in a wider comparative and conceptual context. The concentration on power was to provide our enterprise with the necessary thematic focus. It was not designed to marginalise the cultural and symbolic aspects of the nation as a historical phenomenon; but it does reflect our preference for a cultural history that seeks to demonstrate how particular symbols, myths or narratives helped to shape the political communities we call nations. Thus in a sense, the question that is at the heart of all the essays in this volume concerns the ways in (and extent to) which the national idea began to permeate political institutions (such as states, representative assemblies, churches, dynasties and so on) across historical epochs and geographical spaces in Europe's past.

The communication between different period specialists has proved both challenging and rewarding, and we hope that the present book will inject new life into a debate that seems to have grown more than a little stale in recent years. This, after all, is its declared objective. Although it is difficult to judge the degree to which the contributors to this volume influenced one another's thinking during those two April days in Durham, the essays suggest that not a few revisited their original arguments in light of the discussions which we led. We gained the impression, for example, that some of the hard-nosed modernists left as qualified modernists. The past may well be a foreign country, but this is not to say that the splitting of the history of the last two thousand years into two unconnected parts – 'modernity' versus 'pre-modernity' – is a persuasive, let alone productive, proposition. The visible flexibility on the part of the modernists made it easier for medievalists and early modernists to concede the existence of important qualitative differences between pre-modern and modern manifestations of the national idea. The purpose of this Introduction is to revisit some of the central themes in the scholarly controversy over nations and nationalism, and to highlight how the essays in this volume can add to our understanding of this important subject.[1]

POWER AND THE NATION IN THE PRE-MODERN WORLD

The keen interest which students of the ancient, medieval and early modern periods have in recent years taken in the matter of the nation has without doubt extended our picture of the history of collective cultures and institutions. But one consequence has been more ambiguous. In a kind of conference-podium ethnogenesis of their own, scholars of the nation have been led, through heightened awareness of each other's approaches and theories, not on the whole to deeper mutual engagement and benefit, but rather to the excavation of more elaborate historiographical trench-systems and a polarisation of debate around 'us and them' distinctions, replete with *topoi* to mark and stigmatise the 'other' beyond the ramparts. Admittedly, the gulf of perception is not wholly new. Indeed, the chronology of the nation and its historical importance were dividing opinions among German sociologists even before the First World War.[2] Nonetheless, the proliferation in recent times of writings on the nation from both sides of the current scholarly divide – or 'schism', as one writer terms it – has sharpened the denunciations, heard in some pre-modernist quarters, of the misleading 'sociological stereotypes' being peddled by 'social scientists' on the subject.[3] The modernist bogeyman's teachings have not, it is true, fallen wholly on deaf ears, and certain limited but significant elements of his concerns have (by design or default) been assimilated by students of the pre-modern nation. A degree of convergence is particularly detectable in interpretations of the role of *power* in making and sustaining pre-modern 'national' identities. The pre-modern nation is now routinely treated as an essentially artificial, constructed – indeed, with many an approving nod to Benedict Anderson, 'imagined' – community, of a fundamentally political nature, made within history.[4] Modernists and their adversaries, then, seem increasingly to have in mind at least the same *kinds* of forma-tion, and to envisage comparable social and political processes for their making. This does not, however, mean that consensus is at hand: on the contrary, by claiming the specifically *political* nation for themselves, stu-dents of pre-modern societies have only thrown into sharper relief those elements which still divide them from the modernists – whose models, they claim, are now unmasked more starkly than ever as 'somewhat weak on hard history'.[5]

Often it is medievalists who in recent polemics have cast themselves in the role of beleaguered and misunderstood truth-tellers. In part, perhaps, the role has been thrust upon them. Social and political scientists have a habit – ultimately grounded in the rhetorical distinctions of the

Renaissance, though today shared by 'quality' journalists and headline-hungry politicians – of fashioning the European Middle Ages as a singularly quaint, repellent, and deliberately alien backdrop onto which to project their favoured versions of 'modernity'. Jürgen Habermas, for example, judged the medieval centuries to be uniquely bereft of a 'public sphere' of political culture.[6] In such accounts of the modernising process, 'the Middle Ages', with their 'private', 'feudal' political world, serve as a functional antithesis – one which, in its strangeness and artificiality, evokes on occasion the imaginative flights of literary Romanticism. But medievalists, in their turn, have hardly been reluctant to take up the cudgels against the modernist position. Perhaps there are elements in the European Middle Ages themselves, and in the approaches adopted in recent times to their study, that help to explain why that should be.

A few self-evident truths about the 'medieval' epoch perhaps bear reiteration here. Striking first of all is its sheer length: between Constantine and Luther lie a full twelve centuries. Over such a vast period, across the richly varied landscapes of continental Europe and its appurtenant islands, we must expect to find an immense variety of forms of political and social life. Yet, amid this variety, there are clear long-term patterns of change too. In the fifth century urban life was mostly confined to the heartlands of the disintegrating Roman Empire; by the fifteenth, towns – some very large – were to be found throughout Europe, from Ireland to Lithuania, from Norway to Sicily. In the early Middle Ages, much of the continent was wilderness; by the later medieval centuries, patterns of human habitation had been established which in many regions broadly anticipated those of the nineteenth and twentieth centuries. The population of Europe as a whole experienced massive growth over the medieval period – checked, but not ultimately reversed, by epidemic disease in the late Middle Ages. Core technologies and organisational forms, particularly in agriculture, were transformed; and over the course of several centuries western Europeans migrated in substantial numbers into neighbouring and more distant lands, where they reproduced their indigenous social, economic and political formations. In a related process, the Middle Ages saw Europeans forge new, often violent and exploitative, relationships with non-European peoples, their cultures and civilisations. A range of different communications channels and technologies emerged, stimulated partly by the development of trade and commerce, partly by the needs and resources of the Church and secular government. Catholic Christianity carried Latin literacy to the remotest corners of the continent; by the end of the Middle Ages, writing in the various European vernaculars was also commonplace.

The intellectual, legal and cultural inheritance of Antiquity was likewise disseminated far and wide, a resource for rulers and their educated champions and opponents. The social and institutional contexts within which education and higher learning were pursued changed fundamentally, becoming over the course of centuries more diverse and, in many regions, more widely accessible. A pattern of discrete political communities, among them many new kingdoms, gradually formed, which in much of Europe was destined to endure in broad outline down to modern times. Institutionalised, literate and intrusive secular government, in the fifth century a decaying remnant of Roman imperialism, had by the fifteenth become general in Europe – resting upon explicit, ambitious and complex ideological foundations. All these long-term developments (and others besides), medievalists contend, had a hand in the formation and consolidation in Europe of self-conscious ethno-political communities – of 'nations'.[7]

The significance of these observations becomes clearer when we notice another salient characteristic of the European Middle Ages: their relative proximity, taking a broad view of the nation in history, to those very societies on which modernists habitually focus. The France of Villon and Joan of Arc had substantive elements – social, economic, cultural, religious, even political, not to mention geographical, topographical and climatic – in common with the France of 1789, or even of 1848 or 1871, that none of those societies shared with, let us say, Davidic Israel or the Egypt of Ramses II. The broad distinction between 'modern' and 'pre-modern' epochs and societies has its legitimate uses: it is, indeed, drawn repeatedly by contributors to the present volume. But it runs the risk of obscuring things that should not be obscured. Not every component of the relationship between nations and power can be made to turn on a historical hinge marked with the date 1789 (or with any other 'milestone' date or period on the road to 'modernity'). Not all the factors which constitute the political stature of this or that modern nation are likely be unambiguously 'modern'; and not everything that commands our attention in a given pre-modern nation will necessarily be characteristic of 'pre-modern' nations as such. Typologies properly have their part in the study of the nation in history; but so too does an awareness of the contingencies of time, place and circumstance, and of the conditioning role of specific, unique common pasts. No one, indeed, has grounded the making of nations more firmly within concrete processes of historical change than have the modernists themselves. Kedourie's nationalism was famously 'invented *in Europe* at *the beginning of the nineteenth century*' (my italics).[8] The nation, in this view, first attained importance in a specific place – Europe – at a particular time, within definite, identifiable historical processes. If such a contention poses a challenge to medievalists, it also presents them with an opportunity. For medievalists too are concerned, on a long view, with the development of just those European polities which, in modernist accounts, gave birth to the politicised nation. Who, then, is to say precisely when those crucial formative processes first reached fruition? There is clearly room for more than one viewpoint.

No one is more aware than the medievalist of the sheer magnitude of those processes of historical change that lie concealed beneath the bland label 'medieval'. He or she is unlikely to be persuaded that Europe in 1500 – with its crowded towns, mobile goods and wealth, demanding princes, assertive burghers, periodically vocal peasantries, parliaments and estates, (potentially 'total') wars, pogroms and uprisings, universities, print shops, newsletters, vernacular religious and political cultures – in its capacity for imagining and politicising the nation axiomatically shared more in common with the Europe of AD 500 (not to speak of yet more remote 'premodern' worlds) than with that of 1800. Such a viewpoint also puts into a fresh perspective the 250–300 years of the 'early modern' period – which, for all their own distinctive developments, on a long view of the European past become less obviously distinct from, on the one hand, the later centuries of the long 'Middle Ages' and, on the other, the early decades of European 'modernity' proper. It is not hard, then, to understand why some medievalists have been such strident critics of the modernist paradigm. The important question, however, is whether they have been *persuasive* critics.

Modernists could, after all, in their turn legitimately retort that it is all well and good to detect 'medieval people' describing their world in terms of *naciones* and *gentes*;[9] but did such terms really constitute a fully functioning doctrine of nation, comparable to the modern one? If an identifiable conception of the nation did exist, how did it relate to other ideas about community, allegiance and power? How relatively *important* was it? And who were these 'medieval people' anyway? Just the (untypical?) literate minority who have left a record of their thought? Is there any reason to suppose that such beliefs were more widely held? If so, *how* widely? To what extent were they sustained by institutional structures, 'public' spaces, roles and obligations, and by communications media comparable to those judged so important in the modern period? If belief in the nation was widespread, was it more than just a passive assumption? Did it cause people to behave in specific, identifiable ways? Did it serve merely to elucidate and legitimise existing political arrangements, or could it be invoked to challenge or change them? These are important and difficult questions – ones that medievalists, and students of the pre-modern nation more generally, do not always confront squarely enough. Some of them are, as pre-modernists occasionally concede, in many cases impossible to answer from the surviving evidence. Nevertheless, a brief survey of some of the answers that *have* in recent times been supplied, both by contributors to the present volume and by others, should provide at least a glimpse of the kinds of political substance which the nation in pre-modern societies could command, as well as highlighting those aspects of the problem where further work is needed.

Even as a concept, the existence of the national political community in the Middle Ages does not appear secure. Eric Hobsbawm has written that 'in its modern and basically political sense the concept *nation* is historically very young'.[10] It is certainly not hard, by perusing some of the best-known studies of medieval political thought, to form such a view, since few of them find much to say about the nation.[11] Such volumes are not, however, a trustworthy guide, tending as they traditionally have to privilege the abstract, the demanding and the novel. The idea of nation was none of these things. Instead, it was deeply rooted in classical and biblical ethnography and belonged, as Susan Reynolds insists, to the mostly unexamined, yet highly influential, subsoil of commonplace belief and assumption.[12] Not only, in Reynolds's view, was the medieval concept of nation political; it was *distinctively* so – a community of shared allegiance which, by that fact, came over time to be conceived as a unit of common blood, descent and destiny too (Reynolds). While all communities, down to the village, could be imagined as descent groups, kingdoms had a distinctive status as (imagined) ethnic unities, with the result that 'medieval ideas about kingdoms and peoples were very like modern ideas about nations'.[13] This pattern of interconnected political assumptions ultimately matters more for our view of the concept of the medieval nation than does the existence (or not) of a contemporary array of terms precisely and unambiguously matching modern ones in this area. A medieval vocabulary of 'nation' there certainly was, and it was quite articulate and extensive; yet most of its component words were notoriously capable of bearing a range of other meanings too, depending on context. Nevertheless, in many cases at least, terms like *populus* and *natio* were clearly deployed to signify communities understood simultaneously as political and ethnic unities.[14] They tended, moreover, to become fortified over time by a growing array of supporting terms and concepts, expressive of increasingly explicit and absolute ties between power and common belonging. The 'native' (*naturalis*), 'true-born' (*verus*) member of the commonality (*regnum, res publica*) naturally longed to be ruled by native princes, not foreigners (*alienigenae*); in return, however, he or she could by the later Middle Ages be summoned, in a revived language of Roman patriotism, to bear burdens and make sacrifices 'for the father-land' (*pro patria*).[15] The same period saw the language of blood and power joined to classical ethnography to form an offensive rhetorical weapon, justifying colonial rule and expropriation by certain self-styled medieval master-peoples, at the expense of their allegedly less advanced ('barbar-ian') neighbours.[16] The language of nation in the Middle Ages was therefore political in a two-fold sense: not only did it describe fundamen-tally political relationships, its emergence and development also mapped the consolidation of stable, sophisticated and domineering political communities.

Medievalists argue persuasively for the significance of ideas of common ethnicity in medieval political culture, and for the existence of deep-rooted similarities between pre-modern and modern conceptions of the nation (Reynolds). They cannot, however, afford to rest their case there, since modernist accounts of the nation in history deal with more than just ideas. Indeed, one of the strengths of modernist approaches lies in the rigour with which they have examined the social foundations and consequences of nations and nationalism. In these fields, students of the pre-modern nation face sterner challenges. Ernest Gellner's famous diagram of the working of 'power and culture in the agro-literate polity' portrayed a world in which 'almost everything ... militates against the definition of political units in terms of cultural boundaries'.[17] Ruling elites in pre-modern societies were, in Gellner's view, both rigidly stratified internally and fundamentally set apart from the peasant majority of the population. The nation had no role in such societies; only under the conditions of modernity did it become functionally necessary. Medievalists can of course reply that, as a matter of plain fact, their sources quite routinely define 'political units' in terms of 'cultural boundaries'. But that does not exhaust the challenge posed by Gellner's model. Is the map of 'lines of cultural cleavage', that Gellner believed fractured and fragmented pre-modern societies from within, an accurate one?[18] If so, then, even if it is allowed that the nation existed as *idea* in such societies, it is hard to see how it could ever be a materially *important* idea.

But in fact, however faithfully Gellner's diagram might depict other 'agro-literate' societies, as a portrayal of the varied and changing cultural landscapes of medieval Europe it must be deemed crude to the point of caricature. It is also misleading, exaggerating as it does the homogeneity and distinctiveness of the groups comprising the 'ruling class', overstating the absoluteness of the cultural barriers between different social strata, and underestimating the penetrative capacities of medieval political ideas. Precisely where, in medieval societies, lay the (often fluid) boundary between rulers and ruled, between those embraced by and those shut out from the 'political nation' is seldom easy to judge.[19] What we can say is that medieval political 'elites' were commonly larger, and more diverse in composition, than modernist – and, indeed, some medievalist – generalisations often allow. In particular, from early England or colonial Ireland to Lithuania, a broad, numerous – though not necessary wealthy or well-connected – stratum of secular arms-bearers appears to have been prominent in sustaining notions and sentiments of political solidarity (Wormald, Frame, Frost).

The political culture of the Middle Ages, it is now clear, was in general more participatory, less apt to exclude people on principle, than Gellner's view suggests. Nor was it, as modernist accounts tend to assume, overwhelmingly concerned with 'private' relationships within the 'feudal' elite. The routine assumptions underpinning medieval political life, though without question profoundly hierarchical, also gave more emphasis to broad political involvement, and to 'public' rights and duties, and showed less concern with enforcing absolute internal social divisions, than is commonly supposed.[20] Each of these, traditionally underrated, tendencies appears potentially favourable to a political role for the concept of nation. Reynolds has pointed to an ingrained habit among scholars of emphasising vertical at the expense of horizontal bonds in medieval society.[21] Yet often these were communities deeply imbued with both the principle and the practice of collective action – in law, in local self-government, and in dealings with the political 'centre'. The parliaments and estates that were such a pronounced feature of the late medieval and early modern periods were merely a particularly large-scale and formalised expression of more ancient, pervasive and routine habits of association, consultation, and common judgement and decision-making.[22] Such assemblies were evidently capable of bringing together large and relatively diverse groups of people in regular, politically significant, association and common action – even in the absence of visible formal structures (Wormald). Their origins, where we can glimpse them, appear on occasion remote indeed.

Yet despite all this, it seems hard to imagine how medieval societies could have sustained a genuinely and self-consciously 'national' political culture. Did not intense localism, and the meagreness and fragility of the channels available for transmitting ideas, guarantee that pre-modern European political discourse was every bit as sharply truncated and parcelled-up as Gellner's neatly ruled horizontal and vertical lines suggest? Perhaps we should at least hesitate for a moment before answering this question in the affirmative. First of all, we should not underestimate the capacity of government, its structures and its demands, to forge and sustain common political identities – fashioning on occasion new, self-conscious, composite ('national') political communities out of previously discrete and disparate ethnic groups (Frame, Frost, Thornton). How did this come to pass? What resources did pre-modern structures of power bring to bear? Medievalists must, of course, curb any innate over-eagerness to trace in remote societies the precocious lineaments of political unification (Foot). Nevertheless, they are entitled occasionally to remind their modernist counterparts of just what government might do, even without the advantages of an industrial society.

Even 'dark-age' kingdoms could on occasion manage impressive organisational feats – exacting general oaths of allegiance, for example, or completing ambitious, labour-intensive 'public works' projects.[23] Duties of service in royal armies could be extensive, penetrating deep into the countryside – though the social reach of military obligations did vary widely between different places and times, another reminder of the hurdles in the way of blithely generalising about the scope of 'pre-modern' political culture.[24] Pre-modern realms also gathered taxes: by the late Middle Ages they were doing so systematically, frequently and, in many a hard-pressed subject's view, extortionately. But by this time, the institutional channels of command and demand were carrying a two-way traffic. If governments grew increasingly adept at hectoring and coercing, they also learned to listen and persuade.[25] By the late Middle Ages, the persuasive and consultative channels at the disposal of some European regimes were varied, flexible and far-reaching. Fourteenth-century English sheriffs were instructed to publicise royal decrees not only in the shire court (itself the regular meeting-place for a large, diverse political public) but 'in cities, boroughs, market towns and other places where you shall see fit'.[26] Social and economic changes over the medieval centuries had greatly extended the number and range of venues in which messages from the 'centre' were received and reflected upon. Their density and interconnections, their scope for nurturing common attitudes, their historical contingency and specificity – such things are elided and lost in schematic visions of 'the agro-literate polity'.

Political culture was not sustained only by strictly political institutions. The ('universal') Church too had a prominent part (Frame). It could even, in special circumstances, perform some of the intrusive, identity-shaping roles of 'the state', where this was impaired (Scales). Church councils witnessed on occasion debates and struggles invoking 'the nation', and provided a forum for the exchange of ideas within a surprisingly broad and varied political public.[27] Travel was a more routine feature of life in pre-modern Europe than is sometimes realised. People of diverse background took to the roads in substantial numbers, and their journeys – whether as traders, migrants, pilgrims, soldiers, scholars, officials or in other capacities – and their sojourns far from home allowed common ties to be affirmed, ideas exchanged, enmities cultivated, distinctions drawn and stereotypes honed.[28] Alongside the princely courts mentioned by Gellner, a range of other locations – towns and their markets, religious communities, and, in the later Middle Ages, universities – provided venues for association and for a politicised sociability not always obviously distinct from the sort discerned by Habermas in the 'public sphere' of modernity.

On some of the contrasts detectable between the political qualities of pre-modern and modern nations there has been more consensus. Before the nineteenth century, it is widely accepted, the main political role of the nation was to gloss and legitimise the prevailing political order.[29] This helps explain why medievalists, for all their impassioned claims to 'the nation' itself, seldom seek with any conviction to make the concept of national*ism* their own.[30] 'Nationalism' seems to presuppose an organised movement with an explicit ideological programme, committed to re-shaping the political order where necessary in the name of an abstract ideal (Zimmer).[31] All this looks far too systematic and ambitious to fit the Middle Ages. The medieval nation may have followed along faithfully in the wake of political change; but it does not appear to have been its agent. Yet, while this observation holds true generally, two qualifications must be entered. First, we should remind ourselves that smooth consensus was no more characteristic of political life in medieval times than in later centuries. The idea of nation may broadly have endorsed the established order; but how that order should be constituted might become on occasion a matter for dispute. Gellner's pre-modern 'ruling class' was by no means invariably of one mind on the subject. Access to court, and to the ear and favour of the prince, was an advantage well worth fighting for, and the concept of nation was periodically a weapon in the hands of those who deemed themselves wrongfully excluded. Demands were then loudly put about, to the effect that the 'aliens' around the throne should be made to pack their bags, giving way to the ruler's native-born, and thus 'natural', companions and counsellors.[32] This sort of clamour naturally did not seek the fundamental overthrow of the existing order; but it did desire, and from time to time achieve, changes in the distribution of power within it. These changes tended to be described by contemporaries as the outcome of (natural, inevitable) inter-ethnic struggles.

More radical programmes of political activism in the nation's name were rare – but (to come to our second qualification) not wholly unknown. Owain Glyn Dŵr's uprising in Wales early in the fifteenth century married a programme of political independence to appeals – sustained both by the native bardic elite and by the institutionalised church – for national mobilisation and solidarity.[33] For a time at least, Glyn Dŵr's call evoked a ready, socially diverse response. Just a few years later, on the other side of Latin Europe, the Hussite movement rallied Bohemians in substantial numbers behind a programme which, whatever its religious objectives and roots in social conflict, was also explicitly national.[34] If the Dutch Revolt, to which Philip Gorski ascribes such significance, anticipated 1789, it had in turn its own precursors in popular movements with a broad social base and distinctly national flavour to be found in Europe around the end of the Middle Ages.[35] To state that the pre-modern European nation was seldom an agent of fundamental challenge or change is surely true; to suggest that it *never* was, or by its nature never *could* have been, goes too far.

Whither, then, from here? While medievalist enthusiasts for the nation unquestionably have important things to contribute to the larger debate, they also have unfinished business of their own to attend to. They will need, first of all, to beware of responding to modernist caricatures and distortions with equally self-serving, one-size-fits-all counter-visions of their period. The modernists' favourite categories for envisaging medieval life – the local, the face-to-face, the hierarchical, the 'private', the supra-national, even the 'universal' (whatever that means) – are far indeed from being the whole story; but they are no mere phantoms either. Sprawling, 'multi-national' dynastic empires were indeed an established feature of the landscape, as were, at the other end of the spectrum, regions of bewildering political fragmentation. The hurdles which such formations cast in the way of pre-modern nation-making are not to be conjured away in comforting images of holistic unity. So have medievalists, and pre-modernists gen-erally, been guilty of making too much of too little? One thing at least seems undeniable: getting to the bottom of the relative *importance* of the pre-modern nation – relative to other kinds of identity and association at the time, and relative, too, to the nation's importance in modernity – is, to say the least, never other than a hard and a speculative task. Medievalists should come clean about this. At the same time, modernists will do well to heed Patrick Wormald's warning against the 'historical fallacy' that 'nothing happens before we know about it'. The problem of evidence is a real one; but, wielded as a polemical weapon, it has a habit of cutting both ways.

POWER AND THE NATION: CONNECTING THE PRE-MODERN AND THE MODERN

As we move on from the medieval and early modern to the modern period, the question that assumes central importance concerns the relationship between an existing national consciousness and (modern) nationalism. Under what conditions do pre-modern forms of national identity facilitate, or even accelerate, the genesis of modern nationalism? Can the presence of pre-existing national sentiment increase the chances of success for modern nation-state formation? Or does the bulk of the evidence suggest that modern nationalism can do without such antecedents?[36]

So far no consensual answer to these questions has emerged. At one end of the explanatory continuum are those who refrain altogether from distinguishing between the national idea and nationalism. For Ernest Gellner, for example, nations (conceived as modern, language-based high cultures that industrial societies need to function effectively) and nationalism (defined as the doctrine which holds that the political and national unit should be congruent) essentially arose together.[37] Gellner even went so far as to argue that it is 'nationalism which engenders nations, and not the other way round'.[38] A few years later he was seconded by Eric Hobsbawm, who wrote that 'Nations do not make states and nationalisms but the other way round.'[39]

While the assertion that nationalism creates nations in the modern period has proved influential, unlike the general proposition commonly referred to as modernism it has not solidified into a scholarly orthodoxy. Many historians in particular subscribe to a version of modernism that is predicated on a distinction between national consciousness (which may pre-date the magic date of 1789) and nationalism, attributing the latter to the politicisation of the national idea in the eighteenth century, particularly in the wake of the French Revolution. An early formulation of this argument can be found in Lord Acton's famous essay on 'Nationality' (first published in 1862). It was the partition of Poland, an 'act of wanton violence', that in Acton's view had 'awakened the theory of nationality in Europe, converting a dormant right into an aspiration, and a sentiment into a political claim'.[40] Hence what for Acton turned the idea of nationality 'from a dormant right into an aspiration' was an abuse of power by Europe's leading absolutist states. The consequence of this act of injustice was not just the dismantling of Poland, but the destruction of the dynastic state system and the birth of nationalism in Europe. As Acton concluded: 'Thenceforward there was a nation demanding to be united in a State, a soul, as it were, wandering in search of a body in which to begin life over again; and, for the first time, a cry was heard that the arrangement of States was unjust, that their limits were unnatural, and that a whole people was deprived of its right to constitute an independent community.'[41]

What makes Acton's explanation of nationalism interesting – and, certainly by the standard of current scholarship on the topic, unconventional – is that it combines an emphasis on power politics with an appreciation of the 'nation' as a pre-existing concept, idea and sentiment. Thus Acton did not believe that an event, even one as dramatic as the partition of Poland-Lithuania, could in itself have produced nationalism as an ideological movement. Rather, he saw nationalism as the outcome of a complex *interaction* between, on the one hand, existing ideas, identities and sentiments which resonate among important sections of a community, and, on the other, the transformation of given political institutions and arrangements. It is during such moments of institutional rupture that political activists embrace the national idea to legitimate an alternative blueprint for social and political organisation. What was crucial in Acton's view, however, was that the nationalism of the Poles could build on pre-existing patterns of thought and argument – he mentions a 'theory of nationality', a theory that corresponded with manifestations of 'national sentiment'. In other words, the national idea, elevated to new heights by a number of nationalist activists, served as a cognitive and moral framework through which many Poles experienced the partitions.

More recently, several authors have explored the relationship between pre-modern forms of national identification and modern nationalism in a more systematic fashion. One of them is Eric Hobsbawm, a scholar commonly identified with the radically modernist point of view. In his standard account of the subject, Hobsbawm uses the term 'proto-nationalism' to refer to 'certain variants of feelings of collective belonging which already existed and which could operate, as it were, potentially on the macro-political scale which could fit in with modern states and nations'.[42] Of special significance for modern nationalism, he writes, are 'political bonds and vocabularies of select groups more directly linked to states and institutions', because they 'are capable of eventual generalization, extension and popularization'.[43] Where proto-national bonds existed, he asserts in a key passage, 'they made the task of nationalism easier ... insofar as existing symbols and sentiments of proto-national community could be mobilized behind a modern cause or a modern state'.[44]

In his book *The Ethnic Origins of Nations* (1986), as well as in several of his more recent contributions, the most prominent critic of radical modernism, Anthony D. Smith, has advanced an argument that at first glance appears remarkably similar to Hobsbawm's notion of proto-nationalism. According to Smith, nationalism and modern national identities have stronger roots in pre-modern ethnic communities than modernists like Gellner and Breuilly are prepared to concede. In particular, he has emphasised the role of *ethnies* in the formation of nationalism and modern national identities. The former he defines as 'named human populations with shared ancestry myths, histories and cultures, having an association with a specific territory, and a sense of solidarity'.[45] Such communities, Smith insists, often functioned as bearers of communal values and myth–symbol complexes. Through institutions such as the Christian Church, kingdoms with their lateral *ethnies*, communal treaties, cults and customs, these myth–symbol complexes are often preserved and transmitted over centuries, thus facilitating the formation of nations in the modern period.

As far as nationalism is concerned, Smith and Hobsbawm are not really so far apart. Above all, both regard nationalism as a genuinely modern historical phenomenon. Their major disagreement concerns the ways in which such pre-modern forms of national identification influence the formation of modern nationalism. Hobsbawm conceives of proto-national formations in terms of a toolkit from which modern political actors (and particularly nationalists) select certain elements depending on their situational needs. Even though he points out possible connections between proto-nationalism and modern nationalist ideology, his argument does not therefore fundamentally alter his essentially modernist interpretation of nationalism. By contrast, Smith's ethno-symbolic approach represents an explicit critique of certain modernist accounts of nationalism. Although he does not claim direct or determinate links between pre-modern *ethnies* and modern nations – what distinguishes the latter from the former, he has repeatedly emphasised, is that modern nations possess legal, political and economic unity as well as a mass public culture – he insists that nationalists have to operate within cultural and institutional *structures* that evolved over the *longue durée*. Their ideological activities are constrained not only by the basic norms of nationalist doctrine, but also by existing 'scientific evidence'. Most importantly for Smith, the ideologies which nationalists create are unlikely to resonate among the broader population if they remain wholly detached from existing ethnic myths, symbols and memories. For it is via these ethno-symbolic structures that nationalists communicate with their target audience.[46]

Smith's argument in particular has provoked a number of criticisms. John Breuilly, for example, has expressed strong reservations about what he perceives as the implication of Smith's argument, namely, that 'the stronger and more persistent such [ethnic] identities, the more successful will be modern nationalism'. For Breuilly, this perspective assigns rather too much weight to pre-modern ethnic identity in the formation of modern nationalism. What distinguishes pre-modern forms of ethnic or national consciousness from modern ones, he argues, is that the former 'have weak institutional force in the pre-modern period'.[47] It is precisely the three elements that Smith admits are absent in pre-modern *ethnies* – legal, political, and economic identity – which Breuilly deems vital for the formation of modern national identities. He concedes that there are cases where pre-modern ethnicity is embedded in important institutions, particularly the Church and the dynasty. The problem here, however, is the lack of affinity, or fit, between these institutions and modern nationalism. Institutions such as the Church or dynasty, Breuilly claims, 'carry at their heart an alternative, ultimately conflicting sense of identity to that of the ethnic group'.[48]

Ernest Gellner expressed similar reservations about Smith's insistence on the significance of pre-modern ethnicity for modern nationalism. His main point was that 'ethnicity' and 'ethno-symbolism' may well have some role to play in certain cases, but that on the whole they are not 'determinative'. Unlike the structural transformation brought about by industrialisation – the central thrust of Gellner's own theory of nationalism – such ethno-symbolic patterns and resources do not represent causal forces but at best provide cultural resources for modern nationalist rhetoric. Where such pre-modern manifestations of national identity (as represented in a repertoire of myths, symbols and memories) were absent, nationalism would create nations where they did not exist. As he put his criticism in a characteristically trenchant passage: 'My main case for modernism that I'm trying to highlight in this debate, is that on the whole the ethnic, the cultural national community, which is such an important part of Anthony's case, is rather like the navel. Some nations have it and some don't and in any case it's inessential. ... So I would say there is a certain amount of navel about but not everywhere and on the whole it's not important. ... The cultural continuity is contingent, inessential.'[49]

Breuilly's and Gellner's critique of ethno-symbolism undoubtedly points to the central issue in the debate about the relationship between pre-modern forms of group consciousness – whether we describe these through terms such as ethnicity/ethnic groups or national identities/ nations – and modern nationalism. The question is, however, whether their argument holds water – or rather, to what extent. It seems that their basic point – that it is difficult to establish a causal link between pre-modern nations/national identities and the modern nation-state/nationalism – is very persuasive. It is one thing to identify proto-national forms of identity and loyalty that had formed before the eighteenth century. It is quite another to correlate the successful transition to nation-statehood of certain societies with such cultural and symbolic antecedents. It is indeed difficult to attribute the genesis of nationalism and early nation-statehood to the objective importance of such myths and symbols. Even in those cases where rich myth–symbol complexes existed prior to the eighteenth century, this did not in itself guarantee the formation of powerful national movements (let alone nation-states) later on. Although the image of self-evident continuity between pre-modern and modern nationhood has been a stock item of nationalist historiography, historical reality is too contingent and unpredictable to lend much plausibility to such views.

One wonders, however, whether it is helpful to take a cause–effect relationship as the benchmark from which to judge the process of nation formation. It may admittedly be nearly impossible to argue for causal links between pre-modern national identity and modern nationalism. But does this mean that we should not explore the relations that may link them in complex ways? After all, no single theory of nationalism can claim universal applicability. To be sure, some cases reveal a conspicuous *affinity* between industrialisation and nationalism, or between print-capitalism and the spread of national identity. But as long as there are so many cases refusing to fit these ambitious theoretical models – the emergence of nationalism in the pre-industrial society of revolutionary France or in polyethnic Switzerland represent two very obvious, but by no means the only, misfits – we must refrain from positing a causal link between these factors and modern nationalism. Even the grand theories of Gellner and Anderson provide ideal types rather than universally applicable explanations – no more, and no less.

Equally unwarranted is the restriction, characteristic of most modernist theories of nationalism, of institutionalised national identity to the apparatus of the modern nation-state – above all, an education system, a common legal code, and an institutionalised public culture. We may readily accept that these genuinely modern institutions were essential to heightening national awareness across a large spectrum of a given population. In terms of the means of communication it was able to command, the nineteenth-century state was undoubtedly superior to even the most developed communities of the early modern period. But, at least in principle, pre-modern political institutions could fulfil the same function, if perhaps somewhat less effectively than the nineteenth-century state. The Council of the Marches and the courts of Great Sessions in Wales (Thornton), the Polish-Lithuanian Commonwealth (Frost), and the Holy Roman Empire of the German Nation (Green) offer instructive examples of institutional structures that facilitated the formation of a sense of Welsh, Polish and German nationhood between 1500 and 1800.[50] To be sure, these early modern institutions did not cause the modern nations of Wales, Poland and Germany to emerge, let alone make their emergence inevitable or predictable. Even so, they provided nineteenth-century nationalists and nation-builders with a stock of cultural codes and historical memories which they could use to legitimate their cause and gain a wider following for it.[51]

Nor are the Church and the dynasty, as far as their normative outlook and political aims are concerned, necessarily irreconcilable with ethnic or national forms of identification and loyalty. In several other pre-modern societies, including England and the Netherlands, as well as in Catholic ones like Poland (Frost) and Ireland (McBride), medieval Germany (Scales) or in Orthodox Russia (Hoskings), religion in general and the Church in particular often functioned as an incubator of national sentiment, particularly where religion served as a vehicle to accentuate national differences.[52] This is not to say, of course, that the existence of a national Church in the early modern period did guarantee a successful transition to modern nation-statehood.

Nor should we quickly discard as non-institutional and therefore irrelevant what Hobsbawm calls 'proto-nationalism', embodied in memories of former statehood and the concept of a political 'historical nation'. To be sure, such proto-nationalisms are not the same as modern nationalism. In terms of both their 'ideological quality' (demands for popular sovereignty and self-determination were usually absent) and their social and political scope (their appeal was frequently confined to the literate elites) there are significant differences. The assumption of strict continuities between

proto-nationalism (let alone pre-modern ethnicity) and modern nationalism is therefore highly questionable in most cases. The same caution is
warranted with regard to alleged continuities between pre-modern manifestations of patriotism and modern nationalism. 'Patriotism' – whether defined
as 'love of country' or 'loyalty to one's fatherland and institutions' – undoubtedly represents a sentiment much older than nationalism. But certainly
before 1800, such sentiments were often (though by no means always)
focused on a particular town or region rather than on an entire 'nation'.
Nationalism was not simply a continuation of patriotism with other
means, although in late eighteenth-century Europe the two movements
were often closely interlinked.[53]

Perhaps the cardinal reason why some of us think it necessary to explore
the links between pre-modern and modern nationhood concerns the
question of public resonance. Although it would undoubtedly be naïve
to argue that modern nationalists and nation-builders invariably captured
the attention of the masses, a non-negligible number of them did launch
highly successful political campaigns. How can this be explained? It is here
that the problem of public resonance becomes central, at least for those
who doubt that references to the functional needs of modernisation or to
political interests always offer the most satisfactory explanation for nationalism's public appeal. Is it not conceivable that part of the explanation for
this appeal may lie in the fact that nationalist activists often render their
arguments meaningful to themselves as well as to others by connecting
them to pre-modern national idioms?

A few recent studies suggest that such idioms may have served to
legitimate nation-centred programmes and actions – both 'internally'
and 'externally'.[54] Internally, they helped to inspire the aims and ambitions
of nationalist circles and movements and make them morally acceptable
to those who took part in them. (To visualise the average member of a
nationalist group as a cynic driven by instrumental reasoning appears
both crude and implausible, not least because the formation of interests
does not occur in a culture-free vacuum.) Even more important when it
comes to explaining the political significance of the national idea is the
way in which such pre-modern idioms enabled national movements to
communicate with a larger public. For if the national messages that
nationalists construct have to serve as an effective device for interest
co-ordination, political legitimation and popular mobilisation, which
John Breuilly rightly identifies as three of the key functions of modern
nationalism, then they have to be understood within an existing context of
meaningful communication.[55]

NATIONALISM AND THE TRANSFORMATION OF NATIONAL
IDENTITY IN MODERN EUROPE

Finally, we need to ask ourselves how specifically modern developments transformed the national idea. It is here that the modernist account of nations and nationalism proves indispensable. As communities of collective loyalty and identification, nations, we have said, were rarely invented by modern nationalism. But it would be unreasonable to deny the extent to which nationalism, from the 1780s or thereabouts, transformed the nature and scope of national identity. In ideological terms, modern nationalism dynamised the idea of the nation and turned it into an explicit programme based on new ideas of popular government and of the Rights of Man (Reynolds). From the late eighteenth century onwards, reform movements of various kinds referred to these ideas to justify calls for the construction of new political communities. The emergence of modern nationalism was also linked to the view, prevalent at least among European elites, that nations were actors in an international system of states (McBride). Governments began to use nationalist arguments to legitimise their actions both internally and externally.

The spread of nationalism was of course itself inextricably linked to a variety of processes that are commonly associated with modernisation: the formation and extension of a public sphere; the struggle over political participation; the expansion of communication networks within civil society (through the proliferation of associations, newspapers and public transport as well as popular festivals and rituals, etc.); and the institutionalisation of compulsory elementary education. As John Breuilly rightly insists in his essay in this volume, these processes unfolded at different speeds in different societies; they were also more or less pronounced, or were even absent in certain cases. These variations explain why nationalism came in different shapes and sizes. Most importantly, the formation of nationalist movements from the 1830s invariably politicised the nation to an unprecedented degree. It was nationalism, to use Acton's words, which invested the national idea with 'power over the masses of mankind'. This all sounds reasonably familiar. Yet here too the contributions to this volume offer a number of fresh insights that can take the debate further.

At the most general level, the essays collected here reinforce the impression that a particular variant of the modernist account – namely, that which emphasises the significance of political power struggles whose participants almost invariably draw on nationalist arguments – proves more persuasive than those which prioritise economic factors. While the extension of industrial production and the creation of a new communications infrastructure (railways, roads, schools, etc.) were undoubtedly conducive to the spread of national messages, much of Europe did not experience sustained and widespread industrialisation (the sort of high industrialisation Gellner had in mind) until the second half of the nineteenth century. Until that time, moreover, most of eastern and southern Europe, as well as displaying substantial degrees of illiteracy in certain of its regions, was still overwhelmingly agricultural. And yet, there is much evidence of significant nationalist movements in western and central Europe from at least the 1830s onwards, even if it would be another three decades on average until they turned into a mass phenomenon. It is now generally acknowledged that nationalist arguments of various kinds played a central role in the Europe-wide revolutions of 1848 – not only in France, Germany, Switzerland and Italy, but also further to the east, in Bohemia, Hungary and Poland. By the middle of the nineteenth century, the national idea had become the central political category in public contests over the shaping of the social and political order.[56]

Yet while nationalism had become clearly visible by the 1840s, there can be little doubt that, until the last third of the nineteenth century, the state of existing communication infrastructures and of levels of literacy imposed limitations on the spread of the national idea. By the outbreak of the First World War, and partly due to the efforts of nationalising states, the nation had become a mass phenomenon, which ought not to be confused with a consensus regarding the meaning of national identity. The nation's meaning was contested from the moment it acquired political significance. But there remains the question of what prompted nations to become mass communities whose moral authority was increasingly taken for granted. What explains the nationalisation of entire societies, defined as the process by which people came to identify with a particular nation or nation-state? Whereas many of the classic works on nineteenth-century nationalism concentrate on political elites, the state, anonymous structures or civic associations,[57] the essays in this volume see the driving force of nationalisation as the complex interaction of state and civil society.

That the nation-state was often central to the nationalisation of nineteenth-century European society can hardly be denied. Yet this process is more complex, unpredictable, and protracted than is sometimes suggested. In Britain, for example, the state was conspicuous by the discrete part which it played in the fostering of national awareness via mass schooling (state schools did not exist until the 1860s) or the promotion of national symbols. The British state could stay aloof because by 1800 Britain was a monoglot society that displayed an extraordinary degree of geographical mobility (Mandler). The situation was clearly different on the Continent. But here too the essays in this volume challenge the view that the nationalisation of nineteenth-century societies was essentially the work of a strong nationalising state (Green, Woolf, Zimmer). To begin with, in Germany, Italy and Switzerland the process of nationalisation got under way well before the creation of a central nation-state (which occurred, respectively, in Switzerland in 1848, Italy in 1861/66, and Germany in 1871). Secondly, in all three cases a central state had to be created against strong regional interests and identities. Its strength rested on a set of political institutions that had evolved during the early modern period in the German states, the Swiss cantons and the historic city-states of the Italian peninsula. These political communities provided the focal point for a distinct cultural identity. If this identity went far beyond a vague sense of regional difference, and if it survived (albeit transformed) into the era of the modern nation-state, this was because it was embedded in political institutions. Thirdly, in none of these societies did the 'nationalisation of the masses' proceed in a straightforward fashion from the centre to the periphery, let alone from the top to the bottom of society. Instead, it took the form of an interaction between the federal state and its constitutive parts. The latter – the states, cantons, regions, localities or city-states – did not supply the passive audience in the drama of modern nation formation. In order to defend their historic status and prestige within the nation-state framework, the German states, Swiss cantons and Italian city-states had to engage with the institutions and rhetoric of modern nationhood, thus making an unintended yet decisive contribution to the nationalisation of these societies.[58]

Finally, the nineteenth-century nation-states transformed the definition of insiders and outsiders, and thus of membership of the national community.[59] These definitions and their legal institutionalisation in citizenship law were partly inspired by nationalist assumptions, albeit of different kinds, and in part driven by the perceived interests of the states in question. In more general terms, as Timothy Snyder has recently argued, modern nations are simultaneously more inclusive and more exclusive than their predecessors.[60] They became more inclusive because nineteenth-century nationalism often involved an element of democracy, or at least a demonstrative populism, which served to undermine the association of nationhood with the nobility or aristocracy that had been characteristic of some medieval and early modern societies. The national activists of the early nineteenth century (with the exception of the moderate liberals whose vision of national progress included economic and administrative yet excluded extensive democratic reforms) put political participation at the core of their programmes.

But if modern nations became more inclusive politically, the nationalist preoccupation with cultural or ethnic homogeneity also turned them into more exclusive communities. This is highlighted in all the contributions that address the modern period, but it comes out most clearly in the essays on Poland (Frost), France (Heuer) and Germany (Green). The ubiquitous use of the 'nation' as a concept during the Jacobin Terror signalled the vertical extension of the French polity in the name of the moral regeneration of an entire people. At the same time, faced with external threats and domestic opposition, the Jacobins embarked on a crusade whose aim was the separation of true citizens from foreigners whose loyalty to the revolutionary cause they doubted. In Germany, too, the vertical extension of the nation from the 1840s unleashed a fierce and protracted debate about the boundaries of a German nation-state. This became particularly obvious in the revolution of 1848, when the Frankfurt Parliament became the scene of a fierce controversy between the champions of a multi-national *Reichsnation* and the proponents of a smaller Germany based on an ambivalent mixture of shared ethnicity and power politics. These tensions and conflicts intensified further after 1871, aided by the introduction of universal suffrage at national level and by the general expansion of communication networks.

'Nations', wrote Ernest Renan in his justly celebrated article *Qu'est-ce qu'une nation* (1882), 'are not something eternal.' And he continued: 'They began, so they will come to an end. A European confederation will probably replace them. But such is not the law of the age in which we live.'[61] Renan was remarkably accurate in his prediction. A European Community did in fact take shape after the Second World War, but it has not replaced the nation, let alone its modern institutional form, the nation-state. More troubling is the fact that excessive, violent forms of nationalism are still very much part of contemporary political reality, as the fall of the Soviet Union and of former Yugoslavia reminded the world. This book's primary objective is to breathe new life into the scholarly debate surrounding nations and nationalism. Beyond that, we hope it may also contribute to a historically grounded understanding of the Europe of nations in which we all live – one that takes us beyond the prevalent rhetorical choices of polemical anti-nationalism, idealist Europhilia, or the irrational veneration of nations as eternal and natural communities.

NOTES

1 Bracketed names in the following pages refer to contributions to this volume.
2 See Walter Schlesinger, 'Die Entstehung der Nationen: Gedanken zu einem Forschungsprogramm', in Helmut Beumann and Werner Schröder (eds.), *Aspekte der Nationenbildung im Mittelalter: Ergebnisse der Marburger Rundgespräche 1972–1975*, Nationes, vol. 1 (Sigmaringen: Thorbecke, 1978), pp. 29–30.
3 For examples of such denunciations, see Keith Stringer, 'Social and political communities in European history: some reflections on recent studies', in Claus Bjørn, Alexander Grant and Keith J. Stringer (eds.), *Nations, Nationalism and Patriotism in the European Past* (Copenhagen: Academic Press, 1994), esp. p. 11; Edward Peters, ' "The infancy of celebrated nations": folk, kingdom, and state in medieval Europe', *Medieval Perspectives* 3,2 for 1988 (1991), esp. 19. The 'schism' image is invoked by Adrian Hastings, *The Construction of Nationhood: Ethnicity, Religion and Nationalism* (Cambridge University Press, 1997), p. 2.
4 Benedict Anderson, *Imagined Communities: Reflections on the Origin and Spread of Nationalism*, rev. edn (London: Verso, 1991).
5 Hastings, *Construction of Nationhood*, p. 2.
6 Jürgen Habermas, *The Structural Transformation of the Public Sphere: An Inquiry into a Category of Bourgeois Society* (Cambridge, MA: MIT Press, 1989), p. 5.
7 For a broad survey of the development of medieval Europe, covering the whole period, see Jacques le Goff, *Medieval Civilization* (Oxford: Blackwell, 1988); for medieval colonisation and its ideological foundations, see Robert Bartlett, *The Making of Europe: Conquest, Colonization and Cultural Change 950–1350* (Harmondsworth: Penguin, 1993); for the development of medieval political communities, and the assumptions underpinning them, see Susan Reynolds, *Kingdoms and Communities in Western Europe 900–1300*, 2nd edn (Oxford: Clarendon, 1997).
8 Elie Kedourie, *Nationalism* (Oxford: Blackwell, 1994 [1960]), p. 1.
9 R. R. Davies, 'The peoples of Britain and Ireland 1100–1400. I. Identities', *Transactions of the Royal Historical Society* 6th ser., 4 (1994), 3.
10 E. J. Hobsbawm, *Nations and Nationalism Since 1780: Programme, Myth, Reality*, 2nd edn (Cambridge University Press, 1993), p. 18.
11 For example, the nation is barely mentioned in the monumental study by the Carlyles, though kindred ideas, such as representation and sovereignty, are discussed: R.W. Carlyle and A. J. Carlyle, *A History of Mediaeval Political Theory in the West*, 6 vols. (Edinburgh: Blackwood, 1909–36). For further thoughts on this matter see John Breuilly's comments in his essay in the present volume.

12 Reynolds, *Kingdoms and Communities*, p. 320; eadem, 'Medieval *origines gentium* and the community of the realm', *History* 68 (1983), 375–90.

13 Reynolds, *Kingdoms and Communities*, p. 8.

14 See Bernard Guenée, *States and Rulers in Later Medieval Europe* (Oxford: Blackwell, 1985), p. 219. For the changing meanings of *natio*, see Hans-Dietrich Kahl, 'Einige Beobachtungen zum Sprachgebrauch von natio im mittelalterlichen Latein mit Ausblicken auf das neuhochdeutsschen Fremdwort "Nation"', in Beumann and Schröder (eds.), *Aspekte der Nationenbildung*, pp. 63–108.

15 For examples of these forms, see M. T. Clanchy, *England and its Rulers 1066–1272* (London: Fontana, 1983), p. 242; František Šmahel, 'The idea of the "nation" in Hussite Bohemia', *Historica* 16 (1969), 179; Leonard E. Scales, 'At the margin of community: Germans in pre-Hussite Bohemia', *Transactions of the Royal Historical Society* 6th ser., 9 (1999), 337 n. 51; Gaines Post, *Studies in Medieval Legal Thought: Public Law and the State, 1100–1322* (Princeton, NJ: Princeton University Press, 1964), pp. 435–52; Ernst H. Kantorowicz, *The King's Two Bodies: A Study in Medieval Political Theology* (Princeton, NJ: Princeton University Press, 1957), pp. 232–72; Guenée, *States and Rulers*, p. 55.

16 Bartlett, *Making of Europe*, chs. 8, 9. For the medieval barbarian, see W. R. Jones, 'The image of the barbarian in medieval Europe', *Comparative Studies in Society and History* 13 (1971), 376–407.

17 Ernest Gellner, *Nations and Nationalism* (Oxford: Blackwell, 1983), p. 11. For his diagram, see p. 9.

18 Ibid., p. 10.

19 For a striking example of the possible breadth of the medieval 'political nation', see D. A. Carpenter, 'English peasants in politics, 1258–1267', *Past and Present* 136 (1992), 3–42.

20 Two studies arguing, from different perspectives, for the centrality of 'public' elements in medieval political culture are Alfred Haverkamp, '"... an die große Glocke hängen": Über Öffentlichkeit im Mittelalter', *Jahrbuch des Historischen Kollegs 1995* (Munich: Oldenbourg, 1996), pp. 71–112; Bernd Thum, 'Öffentlichkeit und Kommunikation im Mittelalter: Zur Herstellung von Öffentlichkeit im Bezugsfeld elementarer Kommunikationsformen im 13. Jahrhundert', in H. Ragotzky and H. Wenzel (eds.), *Höfische Repräsentation: Das Zeremoniell und die Zeichen* (Tübingen: Max Niemeyer, 1990), pp. 65–87.

21 Reynolds, *Kingdoms and Communities*, p. 1.

22 See generally: A. R. Myers, *Parliaments and Estates in Europe to 1789* (London: Thames & Hudson, 1975); Wim Blockmans, 'Representation (since the thirteenth century)', in Christopher Allmand (ed.), *The New Cambridge Medieval History*, vol. VII (*c. 1415–c. 1500*) (Cambridge University Press, 1998); Guenée, *States and Rulers*, chs. 10, 11. For an example of an earlier assembly, see Thomas N. Bisson, 'An early provincial assembly: the general court of Agenais in the thirteenth century', in Thomas N. Bisson, *Medieval France and her Pyrenean Neighbours: Studies in Early Institutional History* (London: Hambledon, 1989).

23 Oaths: Patrick Wormald, '*Engla Lond*: the making of an allegiance', *Journal of Historical Sociology* 7 (1994), 7; 'public works': James Campbell, 'The late

Anglo-Saxon state: a maximum view', in James Campbell, *The Anglo-Saxon State* (London: Hambledon, 2000), pp. 6, 9.

24 Specific examples: Alexander Grant, 'Aspects of national consciousness in medieval Scotland', in Bjørn, Grant and Stringer (eds.), *Nations, Nationalism and Patriotism*, pp. 90–5; Kare Lunden, 'Was there a Norwegian national identity in the Middle Ages?', *Scandinavian Journal of History* 20 (1995), 31.

25 Guenée, *States and Rulers*, pp. 25–31 (persuasion), 96–105 (taxation).

26 J. R. Maddicott, 'The county community and the making of public opinion in fourteenth-century England', *Transactions of the Royal Historical Society* 6th ser., 28 (1978), 35.

27 See, e.g., L. L. Loomis, 'Nationality at the Council of Constance', *American Historical Review* 44 (1938–9), 508–27. For attendance at Constance, see W. T. Waugh, 'The Councils of Constance and Basle', in C. W. Previté-Orton and Z. N. Brooke (eds.), *The Cambridge Medieval History*, vol. VIII (Cambridge University Press, 1936), p. 3.

28 For travel, see Norbert Ohler, *The Medieval Traveller* (Woodbridge: Boydell, 1989). For the role of such unstructured contacts with 'the other' in shaping medieval collective identities, see Ludwig Schmugge, 'Über "nationale" Vorurteile im Mittelalter', *Deutsches Archiv für Erforschung des Mittelalters* 28 (1982), 439–59.

29 This is the view, for example, of Reynolds, *Kingdoms and Communities*, p. 302, and eadem, 'Medieval *origines gentium*', 390.

30 Though a case for the term's applicability to the sixteenth and seventeenth centuries – and perhaps to earlier epochs also – is made in some detail in Philip S. Gorski, 'The mosaic moment: an early modernist critique of modernist theories of nationalism', *American Journal of Sociology* 105 (2000), 1428–68.

31 For a definition, insisting on nationalism's modernity, see Anthony D. Smith, 'National identities: modern and medieval?', in Simon Forde, Lesley Johnson and Alan V. Murray (eds.), *Concepts of National Identity in the Middle Ages* (Leeds: University of Leeds, 1995), pp. 24–5.

32 Examples of such struggles, and of the sentiments of 'nation' to which they gave rise: Clanchy, *England and its Rulers*, ch. 10; Scales, 'Germans in pre-Hussite Bohemia', 342–5.

33 R. R. Davies, *The Revolt of Owain Glyn Dŵr* (Oxford University Press, 1995).

34 Šmahel, 'Idea of the "nation"'. The concluding part of Šmahel's essay appeared in *Historica* 17 (1970), 93–197.

35 See Gorski, 'Mosaic moment', 1434–52 for his interpretation of the Dutch Revolt.

36 For two critical discussions of the main theoretical approaches, see John Breuilly, 'Approaches to nationalism', in G. Balakrishnan (ed.), *Mapping the Nation* (London: Verso, 1996), pp. 146–74; Anthony D. Smith, *Nationalism and Modernism* (London: Routledge, 1998). For concise introductions that combine conceptual and historical discussions, see Geoff Eley and Ronald Grigor Suny (eds.), *Becoming National: A Reader* (Oxford University Press, 1996), 'Introduction'; Stuart Woolf (ed.), *Nationalism in Europe 1815 to the Present: A Reader* (London: Routledge, 1995), 'Introduction'.

37 The viewpoint which holds that nations and nationalism arose together is shared by the historical sociologist Philip Gorski, an explicit critic of classical modernism. See Gorski, 'Mosaic moment'. The same assumption informs Anderson, *Imagined Communities*, chs. 2, 3. For a critique of the tendency to conflate 'diverse matters such as national consciousness, nationalist doctrine, and nationalist politics', see John Breuilly, 'Reflections on nationalism', in Woolf (ed.), *Nationalism in Europe*, pp. 146–174. See also Breuilly's discussion of Gorski's argument in this volume.

38 Gellner, *Nations and Nationalism*, pp. 55–56.

39 Hobsbawm, *Nations and Nationalism*, p. 10.

40 Lord Acton, 'Nationality', cited here from Balakrishnan (ed.), *Mapping the Nation*, p. 21. The French Revolution occupies a central place in most classic accounts that tend to treat nationalism primarily as a political doctrine. See, for example, Hans Kohn, *The Idea of Nationalism*, 2nd edn (New York: Collier-Macmillan, 1967). Elie Kedourie, in his *Nationalism*, advances an argument that is very Actonian in its basic tenets; yet, unlike Acton, Kedourie attributes the responsibility for nationalism to the three German philosophers Immanuel Kant, Johann Gottlieb Fichte, and Johann Gottfried Herder.

41 Acton, 'Nationality', p. 21.

42 While Hobsbawm is habitually depicted as an arch 'modernist', one can hardly fail to notice that there is an interesting tension running through his œuvre on nationalism: between, on the one hand, his chapter on 'Popular proto-nationalism' in his book *Nations and Nationalism Since 1780* and, on the other, the decidedly presentist perspective he adopts in *The Invention of Tradition*. Ironically, his chapter on 'proto-nationalism' has received much less attention than the rest of his book, which deals with the elaboration and dissemination of nationalism in the course of the long nineteenth century. The most obvious explanation for this selective reading seems to be the prevalence of what one might term unqualified modernism in the wider scholarly community.

43 Hobsbawm, *Nations and Nationalism Since 1780*, pp. 46–47.

44 Ibid., p. 77. Although the term 'proto-nationalism' carries teleological implications, Hobsbawm does not use it in this way.

45 Anthony D. Smith, *The Ethnic Origins of Nations* (Oxford: Blackwell, 1986), p. 32.

46 See in particular Anthony D. Smith, 'Gastronomy or geology? The role of nationalism in the reconstruction of nations', *Nations and Nationalism* 1 (March 1995), 19.

47 John Breuilly, 'Approaches to nationalism', in Balakrishnan (ed.), *Mapping the Nation*, pp. 146–74.

48 Ibid. In his contribution to this volume, John Breuilly has re-formulated his original argument somewhat in light of some of the recent criticisms raised against it. While still insisting on the quintessential modernity of nationalism, he now concedes that national identity became politically significant in the

confessional conflicts of the sixteenth and seventeenth centuries, particularly in England and the Netherlands.

49 Ernest Gellner, 'Reply (to Anthony D. Smith): do nations have navels?', *Nations and Nationalism* 2, 3 (1996), 367, 369. John Breuilly makes the same point in his contribution to this volume when he argues that modern nationalism appropriates pre-modern national idioms where they exist, and creates them where they don't.

50 There is now a considerable comparative literature on early modern conceptions and uses of the national idea. See, for example, Orest A. Ranum (ed.), *National Consciousness, History and Political Culture in Early-Modern Europe* (Baltimore: Johns Hopkins University Press, 1975); Tony Claydon and Ian McBride (eds.), *Protestantism and National Identity: Britain and Ireland, c. 1650–1850* (Cambridge University Press, 1998); Dieter Langewiesche and Georg Schmidt (eds.), *Föderative Nation. Deutschlandkonzepte von der Reformation bis zum Ersten Weltkrieg* (Munich: Oldenbourg, 2000).

51 For the selective appropriation of the cultural and historical legacy of the early modern Commonwealth of Poland-Lithuania by late nineteenth-century Lithuanian and Polish nationalists, see Timothy Snyder, *The Reconstruction of Nations: Poland, Ukraine, Lithuania, Belarus, 1569–1999* (New Haven: Yale University Press, 2003), chs. 1–2. On Germany see, for example, Jörg Echternkamp, *Der Aufstieg des deutschen Nationalismus 1770–1840* (Frankfurt: Campus, 1998); T. C. W. Blanning, *The Power of Culture and the Culture of Power: Old Regime Europe 1660–1789* (Oxford University Press, 2002), ch. 6. On France, see David A. Bell, *The Cult of the Nation in France: Inventing French Nationalism 1660–1800* (Cambridge, MA: Harvard University Press, 2001).

52 We may also note in passing that the Polish case (as well as the Kingdom of Poland-Lithuania more generally) also poses the strongest challenge to what might be called the Protestantism thesis of early modern nation-formation, which takes such a prominent place in many of the key texts on nationalism.

53 On patriotism as a historical phenomenon, see Maurizio Viroli, *For Love of Country: An Essay on Patriotism and Nationalism* (Oxford University Press, 1995), ch. 1; John Plamenatz, 'Two types of nationalism', in Eugen Kamenka (ed.), *Nationalism: The Nature and Evolution of an Idea* (London: Edward Arnold, 1976), pp. 23–7; Bell, *The Cult of the Nation*; Oliver Zimmer, *A Contested Nation: History, Memory and Nationalism in Switzerland 1761–1891* (Cambridge University Press, 2003), ch. 2.

54 This seems to us to be a fruitful yet still largely uncharted territory for future research. Although the (mostly descriptive) concern with symbols and cultural representations of the nation has become a highly fashionable topic in recent years, few have asked how existing (rather than invented) symbols and cultural idioms may have shaped the communication between national activists and the wider public. The problem is addressed, in different ways, in some of the following works: Snyder, *The Reconstruction of Nations*; Bell, *The Cult of the Nation*; Echternkamp, *Der Aufstieg des deutschen Nationalismus*; Linda Colley,

Britons: Forging the Nation 1707–1837 (London: Vintage, 1992); Zimmer, *A Contested Nation.*

55 Skocpol's distinction between 'ideology' and 'cultural idioms' could provide a most fruitful analytical tool for those investigating the links between national identity and nationalism. As she explains their relationship: 'Cultural idioms have a longer-term, more anonymous, and less partisan existence than ideologies. When political actors construct ideological arguments for particular action-related purposes, they invariably use or take account of available cultural idioms, and those idioms may structure their arguments in partially unintended ways.' Cited in Theda Skocpol, *Social Revolutions in the Modern World* (Cambridge University Press, 1994), p. 204.

56 See, for example, Dieter Langewiesche, *Nation, Nationalismus, Nationalstaat: Deutschland und Europa* (Munich: Beck, 2000); Lucy Riall, *The Italian Risorgimento: State, Society and National Unification* (London, 1994); Alena Šimůnková, *'BÖHMISCHE SKIZZEN:* reflections on social space and nationhood in nineteenth-century Prague', *Nationalities Papers* 30, 3 (2002), 335–50; Karl F. Bahm, 'Beyond the bourgeoisie: rethinking nation, culture, and modernity in nineteenth-century Central Europe', *Austrian History Yearbook* 29 (1998), 19–35.

57 For two classic examples of this view, see Eric Hobsbawm and Terence Ranger (eds.), *The Invention of Tradition* (Cambridge University Press, 1983); Eugen Weber, *Peasants into Frenchmen: The Modernisation of Rural France, 1870–1914* (London: Chatto & Windus, 1976). The study of particular regions has led to important qualifications and revisions of their arguments. See in particular Celia Applegate, *A Nation of Provincials: The German Idea of Heimat* (Berkeley: University of California Press, 1990); Alon Confino, *The Nation as a Local Metaphor: Württemberg, Imperial Germany, and National Memory, 1871–1918* (Chapel Hill and London: University of North Carolina Press, 1997); Caroline Ford, *Creating The Nation in Provincial France: Religion and Political Identity in Brittany* (Princeton University Press, 1993); James Lehning, *Peasants and French: Cultural Contact in Rural France during the Nineteenth Century* (Cambridge).

58 This is why the insistence on 'multiple identities' by some students of particular regions in the nineteenth century, however plausible it may seem, is something of a cop-out. In particular, it fails to address the dynamic and competitive interaction between the nation-state and its parts (regions, localities, individual states or cantons) and its pivotal role for the rise of the modern mass nation.

59 The most influential work on this theme is Rogers Brubaker, *Citizenship and Nationhood in France and Germany* (Cambridge, MA: Harvard University Press, 1992). See also Andreas K. Fahrmeir, *Citizens and Aliens: Foreigners and the Law in Britain and the German States, 1789–1870* (New York: Berghahn, 2000); Dieter Gosewinkel, *Einbürgern und Ausschliessen: Die Nationalisierung der Staatsangehörigkeit vom Deutschen Bund bis zur Bundesrepublik Deutschland* (Göttingen: Vandenhoeck & Ruprecht, 2001).

60 Snyder, *Reconstruction of Nations*, pp. 23–4.

61 Cited in Woolf (ed.), *Nationalism in Europe*, p. 59.

PART I

Approaches and Debates

CHAPTER I

Were there nations in Antiquity?

Anthony D. Smith

Did the ancient Egyptians constitute a 'nation', and was ancient Egypt an early form of 'nation-state'? This question, rarely raised by Egyptologists, let alone by modern historians and social scientists schooled in the post-war modernist orthodoxy of the study of nations and nationalism, is, nevertheless, one that is worth posing for the questions of conceptualisation and comparison that it raises – that is, the problem of the nature of our conceptual categories of human community and identity, and their historical and sociological applicability. Certainly, it is in that spirit that the question is posed here.

Nevertheless, we do well to start with the case in hand, because of its special features. After all, the designation of 'ancient Egypt' refers to a population subsisting over at least three thousand years in a particular location, one that possessed a collective proper name and self-definition, and whose territory, at once compact and straggling on both banks of the Nile, known to the inhabitants as *Kemet*, the Black Land, undoubtedly helped to preserve the special character of an Egyptian culture and religion, despite periodic incursions by neighbours from the south or north-east. Add to this the uniqueness of language and of hieroglyphic script, the distinctive repertoire of myths, symbols and memories, and the peculiar position of the head of the Great House, or Pharaoh, as god-king on earth, who together with a centralised bureaucracy ruled most of Egypt from a single place for long periods of time, and a *prima facie* case for embryonic nationhood becomes apparent. But in what sense of 'nationhood'? Can there be any use in comparing an ancient Egyptian nation with a modern French or Polish nation? And, if so, in what respects, and why does it matter?[1]

The problem is not simply the vexed question of definition, though that is part of it. Nor simply of the status of particular theories – in this case, the various versions of the modernist paradigm of nations and nationalism, which tend to rule out the possibility of nations existing before nationalism, and of nations before modernity. More important, the question about

Egypt forces us to enquire into the nature of forms of human community and categories of association that are cross-cultural and cross-temporal; and it raises the problem of whether we can and should speak of different types or forms of the concept of the nation. That is why an examination of the evidence for the existence of a concept of nation, and of the corresponding form of collective cultural identity, in the ancient world is pertinent.

In what follows, I shall concentrate on the question of the presence or absence of nations in Antiquity. I shall not address questions of ethnic or national continuity beyond late Antiquity, nor will I deal with the ideology of nationalism itself. My view on this latter issue is the opposite of the late Adrian Hastings's thesis. Nationalism, he argued, is a reaction of a nation under threat and as such can be found long before modernity – among the later Anglo-Saxons, for example. The theory of the nation may be modern, he concedes, but theory is unimportant. I take the view that, though nationalism is more than a theory or even an ideology, it is a modern phenomenon, emerging in the eighteenth century and coming to fruition under the aegis of Romanticism's cult of authenticity. That which Hastings terms 'nationalism' I regard as a more or less fervent 'national sentiment', and hence always particularistic, even solipsist; whereas modern national-ism is, by definition, universalistic as well, since in its perceptions there are always other nations.[2]

THE WESTERN MODEL AND ITS USES

If nationalism is at one level a modern ideology and movement which marries ethno-cultural unity to popular sovereignty in an ancestral home-land, what of the nation whose cause it seeks to promote? The nation, surely, is also modern, a territorial and legal community of participant citizens with membership by birth and residence and a distinctive public culture. Indeed, in the modernist paradigm there can be no nations before nationalism because they are creations of nationalists and the state. In Eric Hobsbawm's words: 'Nations do not make states and nationalisms but the other way round.'[3]

It is worth spelling out the features of the modern nation in more detail, in order to clarify the differences between it and comparable pre-modern collective cultural identities. In this widely held view, the nation refers to an ideal-type of a named human community with the following features:
(1) the nation is a geographically bounded community, with clear and recognised borders, within which the members reside, and with a clear centre of authority;

(2) the nation is a legal community, that is, its members have common rights and duties as members under a single law code;

(3) as a result, the nation is a mass participant community, with all classes participating in politics and society;

(4) the culture of the nation is equally a mass, public culture, with culturally distinctive elements inculcated through mass educational institutions;

(5) the nation is an autonomous community, and the members are accordingly citizens of a national state;

(6) the nation and its state are part of a wider inter-national system of national states, of which they are sovereign members;

(7) the nation is a human community that owes its conception and legitimation to nationalism, the ideology.

Of course, individual cases differ in certain respects from this ideal-type, to which they approximate; but the above provides a summary of the main features of the concept of a nation as a modern phenomenon.

Now, measured against the yardstick of this ideal-type, ancient Egypt clearly fails to qualify as a nation. Not only does it lack many of the features of the ideal-type nation, it also exhibits features that are not part of that type – for example, a theocratic and dynastic ideology in place of nationalism. It appears to lack legal rights and duties common to all members of ancient Egyptian society, since they were specific to particular classes, and we cannot speak of mass participation of all classes except in the corvee and army. Egyptian culture, albeit quite distinctive and very public, could hardly be described as a mass culture and education system, and though there were diplomatic relations with other states, certainly at the time of the New Kingdom, it is doubtful how far we can speak of political membership in an 'international system', even in the Tell-el-Amarna epoch of the second millennium BC.[4]

Much the same might be said of the ancient Persians. It is true that the Persians had a clear sense of themselves as a distinct community of language and religion, as much as did the Egyptian elites, and that on the staircase of the Apadana in Persepolis we may still see the sculptured reliefs of various peoples of their empire bearing gifts for the Persian New Year. But the Persians too were class divided; there was no sense of popular participation in politics, no common rights and duties for all Persians and no nationalist legitimation. Nor is it clear where the borders of the Persian community ran, both before and after the acquisition of an empire by the Achaemenids, even after their migration to the Iranian plateau.[5]

Much the same can be said about the Hittites and other peoples of Antiquity. True, the Old Kingdom of the Hittite nobles had its centre in the bend of the Halys river, and Hittite kings consulted a *pankush*, or assembly of notables, but this is hardly evidence of common rights and duties, let alone mass participation. As with many other early peoples of the ancient Near East, such as the Elamites or the Kassites, the record is insufficient to allow any inference about the intensity or diffusion of a sense of collective cultural identity beyond a very small ruling class. There is slightly more evidence for the sentiments and conduct of city-states like those of the Sumerians, Phoenicians and Philistines, but earlier theories of a primitive form of Sumerian democracy seem to have been misplaced, and the fierce rivalries of many of these city-states seem to have prevented any attempt or even desire to give unitary political expression to their sense of common ethnicity based on myths of common origin, language and customs, though Nippur did serve as a religious centre for the Sumerians, and the Philistine lords did manage to field joint armies against external foes.[6]

I shall not run through the gamut of possible candidates for nationhood in the ancient world, but, given its enduring legacy to the modern West, the 'failure' of ancient Greece to constitute itself as a political nation needs to be recalled. For Moses Finley, Friedrich Meinecke's familiar distinction between a *Staatsnation* and a *Kulturnation*, a distinction that made sense in nineteenth-century Germany, was also true of classical Greece. For there, the panhellenic dreams entertained by a small minority around Isocrates continually stumbled on the rock of loyalties to the *polis*, with the result that cultural identity centred on Hellas or its ethno-linguistic subdivisions (Ionians, Dorians, Aeolians etc.) remained, for the most part, apolitical. 'Hellas' remained a cultural network of common religion, languages, customs, calendars, artistic styles and the like. Of course, many Greeks did recognise that there was a political dimension to Hellas; Pericles' Funeral Oration can be read, *inter alia*, as an Athenian bid for political as well as cultural leadership of 'all-Greece'. But, even under dire Persian threat, some *poleis* medised; and if Edith Hall is right, the idea of Hellas really gained currency only as a result of the Persian Wars.[7]

TOWARDS AN ALTERNATIVE DEFINITION

Must we then accept the argument of Ernest Gellner that the ancient world had no trace of, and no place for, nations?[8]

That conclusion seems to be altogether too categorical and too neat. It assumes that the ideal-type I have delineated is a pure analytic construct, whereas it is clearly the product of a particular ideology and milieu. That ideology is itself a specific version of nationalism, the civic-territorial version, and the milieu is eighteenth- and nineteenth-century Western Europe. Hence, what we have right from the outset is not a general definition of the nation, but a partial one: a modern, western, civic-territorial nationalist, ideal-type of the nation. There are three points to note about this particular definition. The first is the pivotal nature of one particular feature, that of mass participation. Nationalism, as Walker Connor repeatedly avers, is a mass phenomenon; it appeals to 'the people'. But so, he continues, is the nation. If that is the case, if we cannot speak of a nation until the great majority of its population participates in its political life, which in democracies means voting rights, then we cannot really identify nations until at least after the First World War, because women were not enfranchised in Europe and America until after 1918. What then shall we call the societies of these states before that liberating dawn? Must we dismiss their national self-appellations as no more than wishful rhetoric? Can't people feel they belong to a 'nation' without participating in its political life? And what, in this context, constitutes a great majority? What of the many classes of second-class citizens, denizens, asylum-seekers and the like? Shall we say that because a significant minority of the population fails to be given equal citizenship rights, we cannot describe that particular community as a nation?[9]

The second point is one we have touched on, namely, the very western and Eurocentric nature of the civic-territorial nationalist version of the ideal-type of the nation. As Stein Tonnesson and Hans Antlov have pointed out, in the introduction to their *Asian Forms of the Nation*, other, non-western forms do not fit easily into this western model. In the Asian cases of the nation, the emphasis falls less upon territory and residence, legal community, mass citizenship and civic culture, though these are important, than upon fictive genealogical ties, vernacular culture and religion, nativist history and popular mobilisation. A similar theme has been developed by Yasir Suleiman, who has sought to show that western conceptions of the nation do not square with Arab ideas of an Arab nation, with its emphasis on high linguistic culture, Islam and classical Islamic history. The effect of such critiques is to underline the specificity of the modern western nationalist model of the nation, both in time and place, and its lack of easy applicability outside that context.[10]

The final point is more controversial. But we cannot overlook the fact that concepts of the nation, like those of *ethnie,* have a long history of usage prior to its specific, modern nationalist meaning. I am not thinking so much of the ways in which the term *natio* was used to designate geographical

subdivisions of medieval church councils and universities, but of its frequent use in Latin and vernacular European languages in the Middle Ages
and in the early modern epoch, including in translations of the Bible.
These purveyed the rough-and-ready division between *am* and *goyim* in the
Hebrew Old Testament text to distinguish Jews from neighbouring peoples, and of *laos* and *ethne* in the Greek New Testament text to distinguish
Jews and then Christians from the Gentiles. This must alert us to the
importance of the pre-nationalist history of usages of the concept to refer to
certain pre-modern collective cultural identities, and that raises the possibility that some of these collectivities might be described as 'nations', at
least in some sense of that elusive term.[11]

But, in what sense? Clearly, not in the sense demanded by the
Eurocentric and nationalist ideal-type of the nation, with all its biases
and limitations. Can we perhaps frame a different ideal-type, one that is
not embedded in nationalist ideology, and that might therefore be free of
its western limitations? If not, we are doomed forever to judge and measure
every other cultural collectivity by the yardstick of a conception peculiar to
a particular place and time, and find each and every case doubly lacking:
first, in one or more of the features intrinsic to the time-specific ideal-type,
and secondly, in the peculiar power and dynamism that the presence of
these features ensures and which we associate with the concept of 'nation'.
The result, as Bruce Routledge argues, is to create the past as an implicit or
explicit 'mirror' of the present, that is, of western modernity, usually by
way of contrast, and so fail to argue the case on its own merits and in its
own context.[12]

I am more optimistic in this regard. I think we can, and should, try to
offer different ideal-types of the nation, at least in some respects. What
distinguishes them from the western type is their dissociation from the
world-view of nationalism; yet their features when combined produce a
similarly powerful effect.

I start from the premise that the nation, unlike the state, is a form of
human community which is conceptually a development of the wider
phenomenon of ethnicity, and that particular nations originated as specialised and politicised subvarieties of one or more ethnic categories, networks
and communities (or *ethnies*). The latter, in turn, may have derived from
smaller clan-based groupings, but by the time they became ethnic networks
or communities, they had lost any earlier kinship elements, except in their
myth of origin and descent. *Ethnies* can be defined ideal-typically as named
human communities, with myths of common descent, shared memories
and one or more elements of common culture such as language, religion

and customs, and a sense of solidarity, at least among the elites. While they are often linked to specific territories, *ethnies* may continue to function outside any homeland as diasporas, and remain resilient over centuries.[13]

Though the concept of the nation shares certain elements with that of the *ethnie*, the emphasis falls elsewhere. For example, fictive descent myths play a much diminished role in nations, except in the nationalist rhetoric of blood and perhaps in times of extreme danger. Instead, nations are distinguished by a panoply of shared memories, myths, symbols and traditions, including foundation myths; but the cultivation of shared memories, myths and symbols is only one of the processes of nation-formation that endow it with such power. Conversely, where a link with a given territory may have been present in the case of the *ethnie*, if only symbolically, that link turns into occupation and possession of a homeland and comes to occupy centre stage in the concept of the nation.[14]

Here I can only briefly enumerate the main elements of an alternative ideal-type, which, as the nation is a 'moving target', are better conceived as generic processes of nation-formation. They include:
(1) the discovery and forging of a common self-image, including a collective proper name, which symbolises 'us' as opposed to others around us;
(2) the cultivation of distinctive shared memories, myths, symbols and traditions of the historic culture community formed on the basis of one or more ethnic categories and communities;
(3) the occupation, residence in and development of a common ancestral homeland with clear and recognised borders;
(4) the creation and diffusion of a distinctive public culture for the members of the collectivity;
(5) the observance of distinctive common customs and the framing of common laws for the members.
Of course, these processes vary in duration and extent, and their development can be reversed. Collective self-definition, myth and memory cultivation, territorialisation of ancestral memory, creation and diffusion of public culture, and development of law and custom: these are the essential processual elements of nation-formation, and they are simultaneously subjective and objective, a mixture of unplanned development and conscious intervention. Analytically separate, they develop historically in different ways and at varying rates, depending on a host of economic, political and cultural circumstances. If and when they combine to an observable extent, the result is the creation of what we term nations out of pre-existing ethnic and cultural elements. Ideal-typically, then, a nation would be a named and self-defined human community whose members

cultivate shared memories, myths and symbols, occupy and develop an ancestral territory, create and spread among themselves a distinctive, public culture, observe common customs and are bound by common laws. It is to this pure type that given instances of communities termed 'nations' (by themselves or others) approximate.[15]

NATIONALITIES AND ETHNIES

With this simpler, and more generic, ideal-typical definition of the nation in mind, let us return to the initial question of the relations between 'nations' and the various kinds of collective cultural identity found in the ancient Near East and the classical world.

Steven Grosby, in a series of articles now collected in a book entitled *Biblical Ideas of Nationality*, is concerned to distinguish the various types of cultural collectivities in the ancient world, including tribal confederations, city-states, empires and what he calls 'nationalities'. Though he does not supply a definition of this latter term, he finds that the three vital characteristics of national communities are: first, a stable spatial extent that is at once translocal and bounded, and possesses a clear centre; second, the presence of a single cult and pantheon headed by a supreme deity, with a common law for members; and third, a sense of collective self, of the unity of the collectivity against outsiders. Of course, there may be other features in the case of particular national collectivities; in fifth-century Armenia, for example, Grosby stresses the importance of a separate language and script for the demarcation and self-consciousness of the community. As for a myth of common origins and descent, Grosby concedes its importance, but argues that it derives from the belief in a bounded territory and in members' birth in that territory.[16]

It is clear from Grosby's account that nationalities are not simply cultural categories or ethnic networks, as in the case of Hellas. They are centres of what Herder called *Kraft*, combining what we would term political will with cultural intimacy. Grosby supplies a 'primordialist' explanation for their power: people attribute to their national collectivity life-enhancing functions connected with the soil and its nurturing products. We need not follow him in this, to recognise that in highlighting the widespread belief in the close connection of peoples with their ancestral lands and the 'god of the land', Grosby has drawn attention to a powerful nexus of beliefs and attachments in all epochs. Speaking of these beliefs, he contends that 'The existence of the nation, whether ancient Israel or the modern nation-state, is predicated upon the existence of a collective consciousness constituted by a belief that there is a territory which belongs to only one people, and that there is a people which belongs to only one territory.'[17] Grosby attributes much importance to self-definition and self-assertion, and they are clearly vital elements of collective cultural identity. But we should be cautious about over-emphasising collective self-affirmations, not only because voluntaristic definitions bring us close to Renan's 'daily plebiscite', but also because they tell us little about the cultural collectivities that affirm themselves as nations, and which could in principle include other kinds of cultural collectivity, such as city-states and tribal confederations. Hence the importance of Grosby's other characteristics, such as a growing attachment to a stable, bounded, translocal territory, and to a single cult, god and law code. To these we should add the development of a distinctive public culture and education system, and the cultivation of a corpus of shared memories, myths, symbols and traditions peculiar to that group of people.

How far were these processes developed in the ancient Near East and to what extent were they combined in such a way that we may begin to speak of nations in Antiquity? Grosby examines three possible cases: Edom, Aram and Armenia. All three appear in our extant sources as translocal, bounded units. As regards the first, in the Book of Numbers (20:21), we read: 'Thus Edom refused to give Israel passage through his border'; a little later we meet the phrase (20:23) 'at the border [*gebul*] of the land [*eres*] of Edom'; and much later Edom was conquered by the Hasmonean kings.[18]

It is also possible that Edom had become a monolatrous society under its local god, Qaush, by the late eighth century, as had Judah under Yahweh. But we know nothing of other relevant processes: no myths of origin nor historical memories, no distinctive public culture nor laws and customs, only references in the Hebrew Bible to *kol-Edom* (all Edom) and *edomi* (the Edomites).[19]

The case of Aram is more complex and intriguing. The treaties on the Sefire Stele of c. 745 BC contain the following clauses:

> and the treaty of KTK with [the treaty of] Arpad; and the treaty of the lords of KTK with the treaty of the lords of Arpad; and the treaty of the un[ion of . . .]W with *all Aram* and with <the kings of> Musr and with his sons who will come after [him], and [with the kings of] *all Upper-Aram and Lower-Aram* and with all who enter the royal palace.[20]

After an involved discussion, Grosby concludes that, with the city-kingdom of Arpad at its head, Aram was in the process of nation-formation:

> This common designation of 'Aram' in the terms 'all Aram', 'Upper Aram' and 'Lower Aram' would appear to indicate the developing sociological uniformity of a

collective self-consciousness of a nation. An element of this uniformity may also be seen in the fact that Hadad appears to have become the leading god of the Aramean pantheon.[21]

This conclusion is supported by the wide diffusion of the Aramean language throughout its city-kingdoms and a probable sense of common ethnicity, expressed in the very names of the Aramean states: the Bible speaks of Aram-Naharaim, Aram-Zobah, Aram Beth-Rehob, and Aram-Damascus, and Tiglath-Piliser III speaks of 'The kings of the land of Hatti (and of) the Aramaeans of the western seashore'.[22]

Do we have here another *Kulturnation*? Grosby is unhappy with the term, and with Benjamin Mazar's 'ethnic-territorial' collectivity, as neither term can distinguish between empire, nation and city-kingdom and their different territorial referents. But can we accept his own designation of all-Aram as a 'nation'?[23]

My own preference here would be to treat the Arameans as a large-scale ethnic network, divided, in the manner of Hellas, into a series of rival, but culturally similar, city-kingdoms whose jurisdiction waxed and waned as a result of intra-ethnic wars and of encounters with external powers, notably Assyria. In this, they conformed to a well-known pattern of development with a long history in the area, including the Phoenician, Philistine and Canaanite city-kingdoms whose members shared elements of culture such as language and religion, but retained separate political identities. The isolation of this pattern allows us to discriminate between looser ethnic city-kingdoms and confederations with shared culture and more compact *ethnies* and ethnic territorial kingdoms in which processes of nation-formation begin to be visible, in which we can also observe the links between such ethnic networks and *ethnies*, on the one hand, and the formation of nations, on the other.[24]

NATION-FORMATION IN ANTIQUITY

Steven Grosby's third example, Armenia in the fourth and fifth centuries AD, may help us to clarify the distinction and illuminate some of the processes involved.

The period commences with the conversion to Christianity of King Trdat III and his family by Gregory around 314 AD, and sees a remarkable flowering of religious activity, language reform, art and epic history writing. The self-definition of Armenia and Armenianness was no longer purely ethnic – stressing the myth of Haik and early Armenian migration – nor purely territorial-political – a relatively autonomous province of

Achaemenid Persia and then Parthia, with a temporary period of greatness as an independent state under Tigranes the Great in the first century BC. Now the emphasis shifted to culture, and more specifically to the Gregorian version of Monophysite Christianity and the Armenian language, the latter soon to be reinforced by the deliberate invention in the fifth century by Mesrop Mashtots of a separate script both to secure internal cohesion and to aid external missionary activity. Missionary activity by Gregory and his successors in Iberia and Albania to the north stimulated the parallel growth of the Georgian Church and kingdom, and compensated in no small measure for the depressing political situation of Armenia, with the mountain kingdom being a regular battleground for Roman and Sasanid Persian armies. By 387, the Armenian kingdom had been partitioned, but this did not end the succession of revolts followed by repression or the need to invoke Roman/Byzantine aid against the Sasanid threat.[25]

In many ways, Armenia possessed an orientalising culture, much influenced by Persian Zoroastrianism, and her social structure mirrored that of Sasanid society. But, as Nina Garsoian points out, the conversion to Christianity, perceived as a western Roman religion, together with unbending Sasanid hostility, pushed Armenia towards Rome and the West, though never to the point of accepting the Chalcedonian position adopted by Byzantium in 451. The myth of Armenia as the 'first Christian nation', and in time the one truly Christian nation, became a source of pride for subsequent generations, as did its missionary record.[26]

Equally important for self-definition was the glorious defeat of Avarayr in the self-same year of 451. In fact, the defeat was not comprehensive, and was one of a series of battles with the Sasanids, in much the same way as the later Serbian defeat by the Ottomans at Kosovo Polje in 1389 was one of a series of battles. But because, like the Serbian king Lazar, the Armenian commander, Vardan Mamikonian, and many nobles with him fell heroically on the field, this battle has been commemorated throughout the centuries as a saints' day, and has continued to inspire resistance. Even more potently, it was quickly embedded in the collective historical memory retailed in the flowering of epic histories from the late fifth to the eighth centuries, from the histories of Agat'angelos and Paustos Buzand to those of Elishe and Mouses Xorenatsi. Thus Paustos' *Epic History* proclaims that the 'pious martyrs [who] strove in battle... died so that iniquity should not enter into such a God-worshipping and God-loving realm... [so] let every one preserve continually the memory of their valour as martyrs for Christ for... they fell in battle like Judah and Mattathias Maccabei...'[27] By the

fifth century, Armenian elites were provided with a providentialist reading
of their history and situation, through the cultivation of myths, symbols
and memories. Equally important, that reading placed the ancestral homeland, *erkir Hayoć* (land of Armenia), at the centre of their self-understanding,
and it is clear that for the Christian historians its boundaries were well
known. For example, Agat'angelos' *History* recounts in great geographical
detail the missionary travels of Gregory throughout the length and breadth
of Armenia. There is also a much greater cohesion in terms of a distinctive
public culture. This is partly the result of the adoption of a unique script,
but even more because of the influence of a particular religious culture and
its theological concepts. Through the institution of the Church and its
scriptures, liturgy and clergy, Armenians became party to a covenant with
Christ, and thus subject to its laws and regulations. Here, too, we find some
movement towards a greater legal uniformity and cohesion, at least in
theory.[28]

At the same time, this process should not be exaggerated. Armenia was a
semi-feudal peasant society, divided into regions dominated by great noble
families or *Naxharars*, as well as lesser nobility or *azats*; even the Church
was a feudal appanage. Armenia was also divided into Roman Lesser
Armenia and partitioned Greater Armenia, so that the picture of unity
given by the Christian historians was considerably idealised. Nevertheless,
there was a supreme noble family, that of the royal dynasty, to which the
church leaders in fact belonged, which acted as a restraint on the
Naxharars. Moreover, the spirit of martyrdom for the holy covenant of
the Armenian Apostolic Church united the aristocracy to a clear conception of the Christian nation of Armenia. Lazar P'arcepi's sixth-century
History speaks of the valiant princely men 'who gave themselves in countless
numbers to martyrdom on behalf of the covenant of the holy church . . .'.[29]
Elishe, too, according to Robert Thomson, argues that the reason for the
covenant, which he thinks was modelled on the *brit qodesh* of the
Maccabees, was to preserve the Armenians' 'ancestral and divinely-
bestowed *awrenk'*, a term that embraces more than religion to include
customs, laws and traditions, a whole way of life that characterised
Armenians as Armenians.'[30] In other words, though the fragmented social
structure appeared to deny the possibility, a conception of nationhood
made its appearance and received expression in the distinctive institution of
the Armenian Church and its covenant. This is something more than the
vague relationship of 'all-Aram', or the separate territory of Edom. There
are even references in Paustos' *Epic Histories* to the gathering of an
Armenian 'council (*zolov*)', which included 'even [some/many?] of the

ramik (ordinary people) and *sinakan* (peasantry)', though we should not make too much of this.[31]

Once again, the evidence for processes of nation-formation is uncertain and conflicting. Centrifugal and unifying elements appear side by side. But for students of modern nations this should come as no surprise. Well into the nineteenth century, the aristocracy dominated political life and assemblies, even in western national states and even when their estates no longer afforded a base for separate political activity; and large sections of the population remained disenfranchised into the twentieth century, with little protection from the law. Instead, we should look for parallels in an earlier period: Armenia was closer to early modern nations in absolutist states, with their great nobles competing with the court and bureaucracy, but with a clear sense of a shared origin and history, the growth of a distinctive public religious culture, a growing attachment to an ancestral land, and the appearance of laws and customs specific to the inhabitants of that land.[32]

Similar centrifugal and centripetal forces can be discerned in ancient Israel and Judah. Leaving aside the ongoing debates about early Israelite tribal assemblies reflected in the relatively egalitarian laws of the Mosaic code, and the lack of evidence for a strong united monarchy, there is little doubt that by the eighth century BC, clear self-definitions of 'Israel' and 'Judah' as related sociological communities had taken hold among many people in both the northern and southern kingdoms. But, despite the efforts of certain prophets such as Amos and Hosea, following in the traditions of Elijah and Elisha, to insist on the exclusive worship of Yahweh and popular obedience to His laws, the ruling elites of the materially more advanced northern kingdom of Israel were much more powerfully influenced by the pagan Phoenician and Aramean cultures than were the rulers of its poorer southern neighbour. For all that, the destruction of the kingdom of Israel by the Assyrians in 721 BC and the deportation of its elites did not entail the destruction of the northern religious traditions. Rather they seem to have been incorporated into the Deuteronomic, and other, editings of the much older Israelite laws, histories and prophecies that appear to have achieved their present biblical form in Judah and Babylon from the seventh to the fifth centuries.[33]

For Steven Grosby, the Judaites of the time of King Josiah in the later seventh century BC possessed the characteristics of a 'nationality'. By that time, they appear to have had a clear self-designation and a sense of their collective existence as a people under threat, as well as an exclusive devotion to a single God of the land. They were also in the process of collating the many traditions, memories and myths of their ancestors in a fixed religious centre, Jerusalem, and they had a clear attachment to the God-given land of Eretz-Israel, which they claimed to have fixed boundaries which they were intent on reoccupying in the wake of the Assyrian withdrawal. But the extent to which the reforms of Kings Hezekiah and Josiah, and the laws of the Deuteronomic code, were observed and accepted by non-priestly segments of the Judean population is uncertain. The facts that pagan *asherot* (sacred trees which came to be regarded as idolatrous by Judaite leaders) had to be destroyed in the high places throughout the land, that a Book of the Law was 'discovered' in the Temple around 621 BC, and that it had to be publicly promulgated in the purified Temple by Josiah, suggest that we are witnessing only the beginning of a process of observance of common laws.[34]

It was really only after the reforms of Ezra and Nehemiah that a restored Judean community committed to the worship of Yahweh and the observance of His laws, and centred on Jerusalem and the Second Temple, seems to have been able to persist as a separate ethno-religious community first under Persian, and later under Ptolemaic and then Seleucid, protection. Though there were schisms – between hellenisers and traditionalists and then between Sadducees, Pharisees and Essenes – they do not appear to have undermined the sense of a separate Judean ethnicity, or the boundary introduced by the exclusive worship of Yahweh, the importance of Shabbat and the annual festivals, and the observance of the Mosaic law code throughout the whole community, right into the period of Hasmonean and Roman rule. Indeed, it may be that, as Shaye Cohen has so fully and vividly documented, it is in this latter period that the creation of a Jewish ethnicity vis-à-vis Edomites and others can be traced.[35]

But does all this allow us to characterise ancient Judea as a 'nation' in this period? For Doron Mendels in his provocatively titled *The Rise and Fall of Jewish Nationalism*, the Jews are indeed a nation, and one of many cases of 'nationalism' in the Hellenistic and early Roman world. This term, Mendels makes clear, actually signifies 'ethnicity'; it is quite unlike the modern usage of the term. But, then, says Mendels, historians of Antiquity frequently make use of anachronistic terms like 'imperialism' and 'utopia'. In fact, Mendels is really concerned with the *ethne* (peoples) of the Hellenistic world, though, like S. G. F. Brandon before him, he is happy to speak of nationalist feelings or nationalistic traits such as 'language', 'territory', 'history', 'culture', and 'religion'. Indeed, on the same page we read that Alexander the Great, for all his ideas of the unity of mankind, failed to abolish the existence of nations, just as Napoleon, with similar 'universalist' ideas, actually aroused nationalistic feelings among some of his subjects. Yet, in this modern sense of the term, there is little evidence of 'nationalism' in Maccabean or even Zealot circles.[36]

All this seems to me to be a far cry from the penetrating sociological enquiry of Steven Grosby into the presence or absence of constitutive elements of nationality in Judah and other collectivities in the ancient world. On the other hand, one must admit that Mendels's choice of epoch is a more likely milieu for the generation of nation-forming processes in Judea. As I indicated earlier, it is unclear to what extent the Mosaic code had a deep impact in the seventh or sixth centuries BC. But it clearly became much more widely observed in the late Second Temple epoch, as well as in the Mishnaic period, when, as Jacob Neusner documents, a much more participant synagogal Judaism had replaced the Temple hierarchy and when the rabbis sought to create a largely self-governing community, mainly in Galilee, based on the needs and circumstances of the *Am-haaretz*, the common man of the land. Here, I would argue, we have the nucleus of a nation operating according to its own religious laws, even though it was at the time under Roman/Byzantine occupation and suzerainty. In this respect, we should recall that not all nations have sought outright independence, even in the modern world, as the cases of modern Scotland, Catalonia and perhaps Quebec remind us, but they have nevertheless exhibited all the processes of nation-formation that I enumerated earlier.[37]

Both in Armenia and Judea, the emergence of a national community took place in the crucible of pre-existing states in which political action appeared as the main factor in ethno-genesis. In other words, kingdoms helped to forge these nations by providing the arena and impetus for those processes of self-definition, myth and memory cultivation, territorial development, the diffusion of public culture and legal standardisation that together constitute the bounded sociological and cultural community we call the nation.

But this is only one aspect of the matter. For all their importance as impetus and arena, political action and the state require other non-political sources and factors to galvanise the processes of nation-formation, in particular shared origin myths, historical memory and culture (mainly language and religion). In both Judea and Armenia, these factors, and especially those of religious belief, sacred law and clerical institutions, were able to 'carry' the sense of common ethnicity and the memory of nationhood into exile and diaspora. While it is possible to argue that, unlike most ethnic categories, networks and communities in Antiquity, Judea and Armenia exhibited a balance between state and nation, and this was significant for survival, it was ultimately the strong territorial attachments, distinctive scriptures and messianic beliefs of their members that enabled these ethnic communities to persist through the vicissitudes of diaspora and to nurture over the *longue durée* the dream of collective territorial restoration to an ancestral homeland.[38]

CONCLUSION

With Armenia and Judea in mind, we can return to our original question. In some ways, ancient Egypt exhibited the processes of nation-formation. After all, it had a clear name and self-definition, a consciousness of being a separate community and a suspicion of outsiders like the Nubians and the Hyksos. When King Kamose of Thebes around 1570 BC exclaims

I should like to know for what purpose is my strength. One prince sits in Avaris, and another in Nubia, and here sit I with an Asiatic and a Nubian, each having his slice of Egypt ... I will grapple with him, and rip open his belly. My desire is to save Egypt which the Asiatics have smitten ... Your counsel is wrong and I will fight with the Asiatics ... Men shall say of me in Thebes: Kamose, the protector of Egypt[39]

he is surely referring to a wider collectivity than Thebes or Upper Egypt. There is also much evidence of territorial attachments in ancient Egypt, as for example in the Song of Sinuhe, who had fled Egypt and become prosperous in Palestine (Upper Retenu), but felt a foreigner there and desired to be buried 'in the land wherein I was born'. There was also, of course, a rich corpus of myths and symbols, including Creation myths, widely disseminated by priests and scribes and enacted in temples, together with a considerable repertoire of historical memories recorded in both inscriptions and papyri. We may also discern the growth of a distinctive religious public culture perpetuated in powerful priesthoods and scribal institutions, in whose culture all upper-class Egyptians were educated. Finally, there is little doubt about the high degree of legal regulation by the well-developed state bureaucracy, and its penetration of the countryside.[40]

But this is where the problem lies. We can certainly point to a relatively powerful, and enduring, Egyptian state and its culture, but can we equally speak of a sense of Egyptian nationhood? In terms of rights and duties, Egypt was a very unequal society, even if there were links and pathways from commoners to scribes and even nobles; but then that is true of a great many other, modern societies. More important, there was nothing like a pact or covenant between the Pharaoh and his people such as we have seen in the case of fifth-century Armenia or of first- and second-century Judea. It is also difficult to know to what extent Egyptians were imbued with the scribal culture or were inculcated with its values. The public culture was that of the state and the priesthoods. So when Kamose claims the title of 'protector of Egypt', is it the nation he desires to liberate, or the state and its territorial integrity? It may be difficult, given the nature of the sources and the dynastic monopoly on inscriptions, to go behind royal propaganda, but we should attempt to ask these questions, if only to clarify our own conceptual categories and test the limits of comparison.

In this connection, it is interesting that, while a clear sense of common Egyptian identity persisted through the Saite and Persian periods (witness the serious revolts against the Assyrians and Persians) and into the Ptolemaic and Roman periods, to re-surface subsequently in more than one period, it was less marked than that of Armenians and Jews in their diasporas, at least before the modern epoch. Perhaps the processes of nation-formation had gone much further among ancient Jews and Armenians, and while all three cases had been formed in the chrysalis of the state, an emergent Egyptian sense of nationhood was more tied to the success of an all-powerful and all-pervasive bureaucratic state. The latter's fragmentation signalled the reversal of nation-forming processes among the Egyptians.

But, in the absence of sufficient data, all this is necessarily speculative. What I hope this brief and schematic enquiry into the presence or absence of 'nations' in Antiquity shows is both the difficulty and the possibility of distinguishing categories of collective cultural identity, in all periods of human history, through the use of the ideal-type method. This allows us to distinguish ethnic and national types from other kinds of collective cultural identity, but it also reveals the ways in which often fluid ethnic identities overlap with more compact and clear-cut national communities.

Here, I have tried to give some examples of this fluidity and the processes involved from Near Eastern Antiquity. This can only be done if we separate the ideal-type of the nation from the specific framework of modern nationalist ideology. Not to attempt to do so is to further entrench the concept of nation in the modern epoch and the western world, thus leaving in outer darkness all those cases that crystallised in quite different milieux and circumstances. To rule these out as not conforming to the modern, western type appears arbitrary, if not myopic.

NOTES

1 See A. Rosalie David, *The Ancient Egyptians: Religious Beliefs and Practices* (London, Boston and Henley: Routledge and Kegan Paul, 1982), pp. 4–5.

2 See Adrian Hastings, *The Construction of Nationhood: Ethnicity, Religion and Nationalism* (Cambridge University Press, 1997). On ideologies of nationalism, see Anthony D. Smith, *Nationalism: Theory, History, Ideology* (Cambridge: Polity Press, 2001), chs. 1–2.

3 Eric Hobsbawm, *Nations and Nationalism Since 1780* (Cambridge University Press, 1990), p. 10.

4 For the social structure and history of ancient Egypt, see B. G. Trigger, B. J. Kemp, D. O'Connor and A. B. Lloyd, *Ancient Egypt: A Social History* (Cambridge University Press, 1983).

5 See Richard Frye, *The Heritage of Persia* (New York: Mentor 1966), and J. M. Cook, *The Persian Empire* (London: J. M. Dent & Sons, 1983), especially ch. 1 for theories of Persian migration.

6 For the Hittite *pankush* (the 'whole assembly' was confined to the nobles and priests), see Sabatino Moscati, *The Face of the Ancient Orient* (New York: Anchor Books, 1962), ch. 5; O. R. Gurney, *The Hittites*; see Samuel Kramer, *The Sumerians* (Chicago University Press, 1963). On the Philistines and other peoples, see D. J. Wiseman (ed.), *Peoples of the Old Testament* (Oxford: Clarendon Press, 1973).

7 See Moses Finley, *The Use and Abuse of History* (London: Hogarth Press, 1986), ch. 7; Edith Hall, *Inventing the Barbarian: Greek Self-Definition through Tragedy* (Oxford: Clarendon Press, 1992).

8 See Ernest Gellner, *Nations and Nationalism* (Oxford: Blackwell, 1983).

9 See Walker Connor, *Ethno-Nationalism: The Quest for Understanding* (Princeton University Press, 1994), ch. 8; for a critical discussion, see Anthony D. Smith, *Nationalism and Modernism: A Critical Survey of Recent Theories of Nations and Nationalism* (London and New York: Routledge, 1998), pp. 161–5. On Connor's criterion of mass political participation, neither ancient Greece nor Persia would constitute nations, but neither would some modern states like Switzerland until well after the Second World War.

10 See Stein Tonnesson and Hans Antlov (eds.), *Asian Forms of the Nation* (Richmond, Surrey: Curzon Press, 1996), especially Introduction. On the special place of the Arabic language in Arab national identity, see Yasir Suleiman, *The Arabic Language and National Identity* (Edinburgh University Press, 2003).

11 The distinction between *am* and *goyim* was not as clear-cut as that between *populus* (Romanus) and *nationes* (distant, barbarous tribes) in Latin authors, as Patrick Geary (*The Myth of Nations: The Medieval Origins of Europe* [Princeton University Press, 2002], ch. 2) appears to think. See on this Steven Grosby, *Biblical Ideas of Nationality: Ancient and Modern* (Winona Lake, IN: Eisenbrauns, 2002), p. 15. On classical usages, see under *ethnos* in H. G. Liddell and R. Scott (eds.), *A Greek–English Lexicon*, 6th edn (Oxford: Clarendon Press, 1869); and under *natio* in C. T. Lewis and C. Short (eds.), *A Latin Dictionary* (Oxford: Clarendon Press, 1955 [1879]).

12 Bruce Routledge, 'The antiquity of nations? Critical reflections from the ancient Near East', *Nations and Nationalism* 9, 2 (2003), 213–233.

13 On 'state' and 'nation', see Connor, *Ethnonationalism*, ch. 4; and more normatively, Maurizio Viroli, *For Love of Country: An Essay on Nationalism and Patriotism* (Oxford: Clarendon Press, 1995). For the definition of *ethnie*, see Anthony D. Smith, *The Ethnic Origins of Nations* (Oxford: Blackwell, 1986), ch. 2; on its kinship basis, see Donald Horowitz, *Ethnic Groups in Conflict* (Berkeley and Los Angeles: University of California Press, 1985), chs. 1–2, and Pierre van den Berghe,'Does race matter?', *Nations and Nationalism* 1, 3 (1995), 357–68. On diaspora ethnies, see John Armstrong, 'Mobilised and proletarian diasporas', *American Political Science Review* 70 (1976), 393–408.

14 On territory and nation, see David Hooson (ed.), *Geography and National Identity* (Cambridge, MA and Oxford: Blackwell, 1994); Mark Bassin, 'Russia between Europe and Asia: the ideological construction of social space', *Slavic Review* 50, 1 (1991), 1–17; Eric Kaufmann and Oliver Zimmer, 'In search of the authentic nation: landscape and national identity in Switzerland and Canada', *Nations and Nationalism* 4, 4 (1998), 483–510. For discussions of traditions of poetic landscape and the territorialisation of memory, see Simon Schama, *Landscape and Memory* (London: Harper Collins Publishers, 1995), and Anthony D. Smith, *Chosen Peoples: The Sacred Foundations of National Identity* (Oxford University Press, 2003), ch. 6.

15 For fuller discussion of these processes, see Anthony D. Smith, 'When is a nation?', *Geopolitics* 7, 2 (2002), 5–32; also Gordana Uzelac, 'When is the nation? Constituent elements and processes', *Geopolitics* 7, 2 (2002), 33–52, and other essays in the same Special Issue. For some measures of these processes of ethnic and national formation, see Eric Kaufmann, 'Modern formation, ethnic reformation: the social sources of the American nation', *Geopolitics* 7, 2 (2002), 99–120.

16 Grosby, *Biblical Ideas of Nationality*. Whether his criteria derive ultimately from his reading of modern nationality, or are grounded in ancient Near Eastern contexts, is a moot point.

17 Ibid., p. 27. On primordialism, see Smith, *Nationalism and Modernism*, ch. 7.

18 Grosby, *Biblical Ideas of Nationality*, p. 124. On the later conquest and forced conversion of the Edomites, see Shaye Cohen, *The Beginnings of Jewishness: Boundaries, Varieties, Uncertainties* (Berkeley, CA: University of California Press, 2000), ch. 4.

19 Grosby, *Biblical Ideas of Nationality*, citing , for example, II Samuel 8:14.

20 Ibid., p. 127 (Grosby's emphasis), citing Sefire Stele I, face A (ll. 3–6).

21 Ibid., pp. 135–6.

22 Ibid., p. 135, citing Stele IIIA of Tiglath-Piliser III from Iran.

23 It is interesting that in these passages Grosby equates the concepts of 'nation' and 'nationality'.

24 See the critique by Routledge, 'The antiquity of nations', and, for Canaanites, Philistines and others, Wiseman, *Peoples of the Old Testament*.

25 For a detailed history of early Armenia, its myth of origins and its conversion to Christianity, see Anne Redgate, *The Armenians* (Oxford: Blackwell, 2000), especially chs. 1, 4–6. On the dating of the conversion, the debates about

Chalcedon and the missionary efforts, see Vrej Nersessian, *Treasures from the Ark: 700 Years of Armenian Christian Art* (London: The British Library, 2001), chs. 1–3. On early Armenian literature and script, see David Lang, *Armenia: Cradle of Civilisation* (London: George Allen and Unwin, 1980), ch. 7. For a more general discussion of pre-modern Armenian ethnicity and modern Armenian nationalism, see Razmik Panosssian, 'The past as nation: three dimensions of Armenian identity', *Geopolitics* 7, 2 (2002), 121–46.

26 Nina Garsoian, *Church and Culture in Early Medieval Armenia* (Aldershot: Ashgate Variorum, 1999), ch. 12.

27 Ibid., p. 128, citing Paustos Buzand, *Epic Histories* III, xi, 80–1.

28 On the boundaries of Armenia at the time of the missions, see Nersessian, *Treasures from the Ark*, ch. 1. On the religious culture of Christian Armenia and its combinations with earlier Sasanid Zoroastrian beliefs and rituals, see Anne Redgate, *The Armenians*, chs. 6–7. On the Armenian Monophysite religion and Church, see A. S. Atiyah, *A History of Eastern Christianity* (London: Methuen, 1968), Part IV, and K. V. Sarkissian, 'The Armenian Church', in A. J. Arberry (ed.), *Religion in the Middle East: Three Religions in Concord and Conflict*, vol. I: *Judaism and Christianity* (Cambridge University Press, 1969).

29 Nina Garsoian, *Church and Culture*, p. 128, citing Lazar P'arcepi's *History* (LPI, ii, 2(34)).

30 Robert Thomson (ed.), *Elishe: History of Vardan and the Armenian War* (Cambridge, MA: Harvard University Press, 1982), p. 10. Thomson's Introduction places Elishe's *History* in the context of the wars and martyrdom, and of the new history writing of the period.

31 Grosby, *Biblical Ideas of Nationality*, p. 145, citing Paustos Buzand, *Epic Histories* III, xxi, and indicating the parallel with Josiah's council in II Kings 23. Once again, I am sceptical of the power and composition of such councils, as we saw in the case of Sumer and among the Hittites. It is rather in the enduring institution of the Armenian Church and its regulative influence that we may perhaps discern a movement towards nationhood.

32 For national sentiment in early modern Europe, see the essays in Orest Ranum (ed.), *National Consciousness, History and Political Culture in Early-Modern Europe* (Baltimore: Johns Hopkins University Press, 1975).

33 On early biblical history, see *inter alia* Martin Noth, *A History of Israel* (London: A. & C. Black, 1960); G. W. Anderson, *Tradition and Interpretation* (Oxford: Clarendon Press, 1979); Irving Zeitlin, *Jesus and the Judaism of his Time* (Cambridge: Polity Press, 1988); Gosta Ahlstrom: *Who Were the Israelites?* (Winona Lake, IN: Eisenbrauns, 1986); and from an archaeological perspective, Israel Finkelstein and Neil Asher Silberman, *The Bible Unearthed: Archaeology's New Vision of Ancient Israel and the Origin of its Sacred Texts* (New York: The Free Press, 2001).

34 On the Josianic reforms, see Finkelstein and Silberman, *The Bible Unearthed*, ch. 11.

35 See Shaye Cohen, *The Beginnings of Jewishness: Boundaries, Varieties, Uncertainties* (Berkeley: University of California Press, 2000), chs. 3–4. See

also Martin Hengel, *Jews, Greeks and Barbarians* (London: SCM Press, 1980), Parts II and III.

36 See Doron Mendels, *The Rise and Fall of Jewish Nationalism* (New York: Doubleday, 1992), p. 14; cf. S. G. F. Brandon, *Jesus and the Zealots* (Manchester University Press, 1967), ch. 2.

37 See Jacob Neusner, *Max Weber Revisited: Religion and Society in Ancient Judaism* (Oxford: Oxford Centre for Postgraduate Hebrew Studies, 1981).

38 On the importance of institutions in 'carrying' ethnicity and ensuring its persistence, see John Breuilly, 'Approaches to nationalism', in Gopal Balakrishnan (ed.), *Mapping the Nation* (London: Verso, 1996). For the Armenian case, see Ronald Suny, *Looking Towards Ararat: Armenia in Modern History* (Bloomington and Indianapolis: Indiana University Press, 1993), and Panossian, 'The past as nation'. For the case of the Greek diaspora and the Orthodox *millet* under Ottoman rule, see G. Arnakis, 'The role of religion in the development of Balkan nationalism', in Barbara and Charles Jelavich (eds.), *The Balkans in Transition* (Berkeley: University of California Press, 1963). For a critique, see Paschalis Kitromilides, '"Imagined communities" and the origins of the national question in the Balkans', *European History Quarterly* 19, 2 (1989), 149–92. On national restoration movements among Greek, Armenian and Jewish diasporas, see Anthony D. Smith, 'Zionism and diaspora nationalism', *Israel Affairs* 2, 2 (1995), 1–19.

39 Grosby, *Biblical Ideas of Nationality*, p. 31, citing A. Kirk Grayson and Donald B. Redford (eds.), *Papyrus and Tablet* (Englewood Cliffs, NJ: Prentice-Hall, 1973), p. 22.

40 Grosby, *Biblical Ideas of Nationality*, p. 31. On Egyptian myths, see A. Rosalie David, *The Ancient Egyptians*; J. A. Wilson, *The Burden of Egypt* (Chicago University Press, 1951).

CHAPTER 2

The idea of the nation as a political community

Susan Reynolds

The object of this chapter is to persuade those who need persuading, or are willing to be persuaded, that the concept of the nation that lies at the heart of all forms of nationalism was widespread long before the eighteenth century. This concept, as I understand, is the idea or assumption that nations are natural, given, objectively existing human communities, each of which is assumed, generally in a vague and unreasoned way, not only to have its own common culture, myths, history, and destiny, but also to be a political community with a right to what is now called self-determination. This definition is derived from that given by Anthony Smith in 1973, which lit up the subject for me in a flash and still seems to me a masterpiece of clarity.[1] He was setting out what he saw as the basic doctrine of nationalism, so that his definition was in effect a nationalist one. That seems to me inevitable, because nations are hard to identify and define except in terms of the beliefs about them held by those who think of them as real objective entities. I shall refer to this way of thinking about nations as 'nationalist', but that does not mean that I suggest that all who thought like this in the past had the same aims and policies as have those who are called nationalist today. Not that modern nationalism is at all uniform, but one thing all its varieties seem to have in common, and, as I argue, share with people in many pre-modern societies, is this idea of the objective reality of nations or peoples as communities with collective political rights as well as shared histories and cultures.

My argument is not that nationalism as it is generally understood was already rising in the Middle Ages. The whole idea of its 'rise' in any period may be misleading insofar as it subsumes the appearance of the idea of the nation into the appearance of the nationalist movements of the eighteenth and nineteenth centuries. The conflation of the two derives, I suggest, from an assumption that the only true nations that could arouse true nationalism are the nations of today, reflecting a fallacious teleology that assumes a single linear development towards the modern world. This assumption can be maintained only by ignoring anything beyond textbook knowledge about pre-modern ideas on government and practices of government. That does not mean that I argue that nothing has changed. Although the idea of nations as political communities looks to me much older than most students of modern nationalism assume, its impact was changed when it came to be associated with other quite different ideas about the structure of society and government, as well as with different economies and different technologies. What I argue is that it was those external factors, not a change in the basic idea of nations or peoples as political communities, that produced modern nationalism.

Whether or not one chooses to call the concept of the nation that I am discussing a form of nationalism seems to me unimportant. If modernists want to reserve the word to the kind of nationalist movements that appeared in their period, that is fine. The earlier ideas about nations or peoples that I shall describe were not part of anything like a movement: though they were sometimes deliberately used to fortify existing polities, they seem to have been for the most part uncontroversial assumptions. If, on the other hand, modernists want to make the concession of calling these pre-modern ideas proto-nationalist, that is fine too, except that 'proto' always seems a little teleological. Words, however, seem to me to matter less in this context than the concepts or notions in the heads of those who use them, and the external phenomena to which they seem to be referring.[2]

I shall therefore not waste time arguing about words – nation, people, *gens, populus*, nationality.[3] Fewer writers on nationalism now say such nonsensical things about the use or non-use of *natio* in the Middle Ages as used to be common, and anyway the particular words used in any particular language are irrelevant. What matters is the concepts or notions in the heads of those who use whatever words they use – which may not have been the same as the notions we have in our heads when we use those words. The notion or concept that I am concerned with is that of a natural community of descent and culture that is also a political community with political rights, even if it is not actually independent, that is, whether or not it is a state or (if the word is thought unsuitable for pre-modern polities) some other more or less independent polity.[4] Since people do not always agree about which communities are nations or who belongs to which, it is difficult – unless one adopts a nationalist point of view – to see nations as objective phenomena. States or polities, on the other hand, however loose and variable the concept or notion of them may be, are easy to recognise as phenomena. They are facts: we live under them. The phenomenon of the practice of government in pre-modern societies suggests that the notion of the nation as a natural political community reflected the phenomena of the collective nature of much government and its need of voluntary submission. The concept of the 'imagined community' that we call the nation and the phenomenon of the power structure were thus closely related, irrespective of whatever words people used for either in whatever language they spoke or wrote. The frequent use nowadays of the word 'nation' as a synonym for 'state' reflects some of the same assumptions.[5] Analytically, however, the distinction between state and nation seems important.

In trying to trace the history of the concept or notion of the nation as a community of descent and culture that is also a political community we have to pay attention to the words used in our sources because they are all we have. But what we are really concerned with is the notions in the minds of people in the past, so far as we can deduce them from what they wrote, and the phenomena of government and politics to which they seem to have been referring. When I decided to use the word 'regnal' instead of 'national' in discussing medieval loyalties it was not, as Smith thought, because I thought medieval kingdoms were 'not nations in the modern sense',[6] but because the word 'national' seems to make others focus on the modern 'nation-states', with their modern boundaries.[7] Looking both at the phenomena of medieval power structures and at the ideas they seem to reflect suggests to me that medieval kingdoms were quite often perceived as something very like 'nations in the modern sense', as defined by Smith in 1973. They would not, I admit, qualify according to his later definitions that introduce 'common rights and duties for all members',[8] but then, if women count as members, neither would the nineteenth-century collectivities that historians of nationalism count as nations.

In many societies and periods it has been taken for granted, however mistakenly, that areas under separate governments are also collective, corporate units of culture and descent: kingdoms in medieval Europe, for instance, were perceived by their own inhabitants not just as the territories that happened to belong to kings, but as territories that also belonged to the collective or corporate groups of their peoples.[9] Medieval Europeans seem to have thought of kingdoms as the highest and most important units of government. Forget the old textbook idea of universal empire, which was used in polemics between pope and emperor but was never a serious threat to the supremacy of kings as the archetype of rulers and kingdoms as the archetype of political communities. Forget too that other textbook idea of medieval loyalties as exclusively local and fragmented by 'feudalism', which I have discussed elsewhere.[10] Even when kingdoms were weak and divided they remained the model for the other, lesser units that are often called feudal lordships. In the standard medieval view, government was the primary responsibility of kings and lords, but it was never their responsibility alone. All government was supposed to depend on custom. Custom implies a community that makes and follows it. Kingdoms were perceived as belonging not just to their kings but to the communities of their peoples (in Latin, *gentes, nationes,* or *populi*). All government rested, in both theory and practice, on the advice and consent of its greater subjects, who were supposed to represent the rest. Government came in layers (as it does today, most noticeably in federal states), but at every level units of government were perceived as communities bound by custom and mutual obligation, each of which depended on a lot of collective activity. At every level there needed to be what A. B. White called 'self-government at the king's command'.[11] He was talking about England, but he could have made much the same point about other polities. At every level people of higher status, the richer and more noble, were supposed to take the lead and bear responsibility, but they were also supposed to rule justly in the interests of the community of those under their authority and to consult with its senior members. Of course they did not always do either, and of course politics and law did not always fit the model of harmonious hierarchy and consensus. They never do conform to the ideals of their respective societies.

Kingdoms or other units of government in medieval Europe were also perceived as natural units, bound together not just by their present political unity but by their common descent. This was not argued about: it was just assumed, and myths were elaborated to express the assumption. In the seventh century a Frankish monk borrowed the Roman story of the descent of the Romans from the Trojans who left Troy after their defeat by Homer's Greeks. This was taken up by others so that the Franks, or the more literate among them, came to think of their people as descended from the Trojans. So did many other groups that formed political units. Descent from Trojans was claimed by the inhabitants of many cities and was attributed at one time or another to all the inhabitants of Britain. Others claimed to be descended from people in the Bible, and some mixed both Trojans and Bible characters into their collective genealogies. This may look silly to us, but it was perfectly rational at the time: both sets of stories had high authority, and without more archaeological and other information than people then had, it would have been difficult to show that either story was untrue or that the two were incompatible.[12]

Though all these ideas were too much taken for granted to be much, if at all, argued about, medieval governments sometimes used them to mobilise

support for their own purposes. One of the most eloquent pieces
of propaganda I have ever read is the letter known as the Declaration
of Arbroath, which seems to have been drafted by the servants of the king of
Scots to be sent to the pope in 1320 in the name of the barons, freeholders
and the whole community of the kingdom. According to the letter, the
nation of the Scots (*natio Scottorum*) had come from Scythia and through
the Pillars of Hercules to settle, after many troubles, in poor little remote
Scotland. Despite many attacks from outside the Scots had lived in freedom under their own kings ever since until they were cruelly assailed by
Edward I of England. We may doubt whether all of them were as determined to carry on their war of independence, irrespective of whether their
king did so, as the splendid rhetoric of the letter maintains, but like all
propaganda, it was presumably designed to appeal both to the barons who
sealed it and to the pope. The ideas it articulates are therefore likely to have
been around both in Scotland and at the papal court at Avignon.[13]

There are four points about all this that need emphasis.

First, most of the myths of collective origins that were told in medieval
Europe were told about the inhabitants of kingdoms or other polities who,
like the fourteenth-century Scots, were extremely unlikely to have had a
long common descent. As political facts changed, stories were adapted to fit
them. Because people in the Middle Ages assumed that the inhabitants of
kingdoms formed peoples united by custom, law, descent, and sometimes,
if language happened to fit, by language, old stories about kingdoms went
on being told as the kingdoms or other units of government were altered.
Provided a name went on, the story was assumed to fit the new or expanded
polity. For instance, the story that the seventh-century Franks were descended from the Trojans was still told in the fourteenth century about the
inhabitants of the kingdom of France, who were not all descended from
those who had called themselves Franks in the seventh century and did not
occupy the same territory. People just assumed that the inhabitants of the
fourteenth-century kingdom were the same as the seventh-century Franks
and used the old story to fortify the solidarity of the changed unit. The
same goes for other groups. The perception of the inhabitants of kingdoms
and other polities as political communities, and as enduring political
communities, identified with the territories of those polities, looks to me
very like the perception of the nation as a people identified with the
territorial nation-state that historians of modern nationalism date from
the French Revolution.[14]

The second point is that, though historians sometimes trace the origins
of modern nationalism to the late Middle Ages and, in particular, to the

rise of what they call the 'national monarchies' of France and England, that does not do justice to the medieval evidence. Though these two so-called 'national monarchies' are often seen as the forerunners of their respective 'nation-states', neither kingdom was anything like coextensive with the modern state. It is, moreover, only by looking through the spectacles of modern nationalism that these two kingdoms appear to have had more national solidarity in the Middle Ages than had other polities that did not survive as independent states into modern times or bequeath their names to modern states. Saxony in the eighth century, Flanders and Normandy in the eleventh, and Venice throughout the Middle Ages may have been fortified as units of government by ideas of common culture and descent that were at that time just as widely and firmly held. Teleology is a bad guide to understanding the past. It is true that many polities that were envisaged as nations in the Middle Ages were smaller than most modern states, but if one thinks of nations as defined by being *perceived* as communities of descent, culture, and politics, it is not rational to disqualify medieval Venice or indeed ancient Athens because they were too small. Size seems to me relevant only if it is so great as to impede communication and solidarity.[15]

The third point about medieval ideas and assumptions about peoples that I want to note is that they combine cultural features – customs, language and religion – with genetic or biological features. Before the rise of modern genetics it was assumed that the two went together. Of course to some extent they do. People who form one society and are governed together tend to share at least some customs and they may become one linguistic group too in the long run (though, interestingly, not always). People living in one country and under one government also marry among themselves more than they marry outsiders and may in the long run therefore develop physical peculiarities that mark them off from people in other societies with whom they don't intermarry. In other words, cultural groups may correspond roughly to breeding populations. But the inhabitants of nation-states or those who wish to form a nation-state are not races insofar as races are understood to be groups with common and distinctive physical characteristics. Talking of 'races' at all may be misleading, since most geneticists now do not think that human beings can be divided into separate, nameable categories; but medieval people, in any case, seem to have noticed inherited physical differences much less than we do. They were, however, not in a position to distinguish physical inheritance from cultural transmission, for the distinction between them did not become obvious until the twentieth century, and even now is often not recognised. Some scholars in the later nineteenth century began to worry about it, but it was only after Mendel's work was re-discovered in 1900 that the difference between racial or physical characteristics on the one hand and cultural characteristics on the other began to be worked out. Until then, the distinction between races and nations, racism and nationalism, could not be drawn.

The last point I have to make about the European Middle Ages is that the evidence does not seem to support the argument, most fully worked out by Anthony Smith, that ethnic solidarities came first and true political nationalism came later. According to this argument, groups before, say, the eighteenth century might have myths of common descent, a sense of a common culture, and a link with a particular territory, and their elites might have a measure of solidarity, but these characteristics had no real political content.[16] But some of the communities that are allowed this kind of ethnic solidarity, as it is now called, had been independent polities at some point, or formed subordinate units which participated collectively in their own government within larger states. This seems to apply even in at least some parts of central and eastern Europe where significant cultural differences resulting from migrations or conquests survived into modern times, so that students of nationalism have tended to stress the detachment of ethnic loyalties from political structures.[17] The medieval evidence suggests that ethnicity, the belief in common descent and customs and so on, was then quite often the result, rather than the cause, of political unity. That is not surprising. Ethnic groups do not have clear boundaries: it is hard to draw lines round cultures, and in medieval Europe custom and law did not fit political boundaries much better than cultures did. A shared history is generally not much more than a myth which can be easily adapted or re-written, while the distinction between a language and a dialect is as much a matter of politics as of the relative difficulty of communication. Although it is often difficult to tell which kind of solidarity, ethnic or political, came first, the evidence from medieval and early modern Europe suggests that, by and large, to borrow a phrase recently used by Colin Kidd, the 'ill-defined facts of "ethnicity" were shaped by the gravitational pull' of politics.[18]

To judge from my reading, such as it is, of non-European history and social anthropology, I suspect that, although one of the great myths of European history is that European political arrangements and social solidarities are unique, some of the same ideas about governments and communities as I have sketched were to be found in other, non-European societies, particularly where custom was the basis of law, long before opposition to European imperialism provoked newer forms of national-ism.[19] The new nations that have now emerged from colonial empires also illustrate the way that being governed together has stimulated political solidarities within colonial boundaries.[20] Often, of course, these new solidarities have to compete with those of pre-colonial units within or overlapping the colonial boundaries, but insofar as those were once more or less independent polities, they once again suggest that association under government prompts the kind of solidarities that find expression in claims both to common culture, history, and descent, and to collective self-determination.

By the later Middle Ages, the traditional idea of kingdoms and lesser units of government as communities of custom and descent was being undermined by two new ideas.[21] Class distinctions became more fixed from the twelfth century and found expression in new myths by which separate origins were found for different classes. Rather later, a new political theory of absolutism began to emphasise rulers at the expense of their subjects, so that by the seventeenth century it was possible, at least for rulers and some intellectuals, to envisage a kingdom as merely the territory that its ruler ruled, with no identity or community apart from him. In practice govern-ments remained rather more reliant on collective support and solidarity than was suggested by those who looked back on the *ancien régime* with horror. Historians sometimes stress the restricted nature of the 'political nation' or *Adelsnation,* but participation in politics in the supposed heyday of nationalism was not always much wider than it had been in the early modern period. However that may be, it was perhaps partly in reaction against theories of absolutism that another new set of ideas began to be worked out from the late seventeenth century on from a genuinely new set of premises: namely, ideas of popular government of a new and different kind, based not on old ideas of custom and law and community, but on the Rights of Man – individual natural rights independent of community or government. The stages by which these became combined with the old idea of existing, given political communities need further investigation by historians of eighteenth-century thought.[22] In the meantime I submit tentatively two early examples of the way that the old ideas of nations came to be combined with the new individualist ideas.

First, Rousseau's ideas about the state of nature and the social contract, however idiosyncratic, clearly derive from the new paradigm. His ideas about nations clearly do not. He thought that peoples or nations had originated as communities of custom and way of life – what might be called merely ethnic communities, though they were now under governments that he thought quite wrong. Nevertheless, the actual nations or peoples he mentioned by name or seems to have had in mind were all long-established units of government. That includes Poland, even if it was now in trouble, and Corsica, even if it had been passed around between different states like a parcel: it remained a single parcel and one whose inhabitants, or some of them, had ideas about their own collective rights.[23] Rousseau's nations, in other words, were what would have been assumed within an older kind of politics to be political communities. My other example is the Declaration of Independence. Its first two paragraphs offer a clear and concise combination of the old and new sets of ideas. Jefferson's belief in peoples with political rights looks as if it reflected the old assumptions and needed no justification or explanation, even though his 'people' had hitherto been connected by 'political bands' with another. What belonged unambiguously to the new ideas and needed formal statement, even though he claimed they were self-evidently true, were the equality and rights which men had had before the institution of government.

Popular government needs cohesive units in which to work. If one is going to make decisions by finding a majority of equal individuals one needs a collectivity in which votes can be counted and which is cohesive enough to hold together when opinions differ and after votes have been counted. Those who took up the new ideas of popular government found the cohesive collective units they needed in what they generally called nations.[24] Where a new nation had to be formed, such as that which comprised the thirteen American colonies or states, then the process, as they found, might be complicated and controversial;[25] but the important point I want to make is that, whether the political units were new or old, the basic ideas about nations or peoples were not new. They were old ideas even though, combined with new ideas about individualism and political equality, they now formed a significantly new form of nationalism that became much more explosive. Now the myths were not just universal assumptions: they were ideas that were consciously worked out and developed.

The way that they were worked out owed much to Germans who argued that people who spoke German, and were therefore a nation of common descent, ought to have some kind of political unity. The new philological nationalism they created was different from the old, not only because of the new emphasis on language, or because it came to be combined with new ideas of popular government which were of quite separate origin, but because it was articulated and rationalised in a way that the old assumptions had not been. Instead of validating existing states it became a movement – a programme for creating new states. Both new and old states came to be called nation-states, and both new and old were different from the old states, but not because they were now thought of for the first time as political nations. The novelty was that they were based on a conscious ideology of nationalism which governments used as a means of internal control and of mobilisation for external conflicts. All the anomalies hidden in the old easy assumptions about nations were thus much more likely to be revealed and to fuel conflicts: disagreements about who formed a nation, about the boundaries of nations, all mattered much more now that nations came to be thought of as composed of equal individuals with equal rights to share in their governments.

The changes in the nature and conduct of politics during the past two hundred years were thus, I suggest, not the result of new ideas about nations as such but of other, quite separate political ideas about the structure of society and government within nations or states and – obviously – of new technologies of agriculture, industry and communications. All these brought changes in structures and methods of government, new methods of communication and control, the provision of mass education, the development of economic policies, and so on. These, however, were changes in states rather than in ideas about nations, even if nationalist thought and expression confuse the two and governments use the language of nationalism to muster mass support. Modern technology needs big states, and big states need more glue to hold them together. Ideas about the reality and rights of nations could provide the glue, just as they had done through simpler forms of communication with the smaller populations of the past. In earlier times most people may not have felt very involved most of the time, but nor do they now. In peaceful times loyalties to smaller groups take precedence and need not conflict with loyalties to the state or nation. The difference is that the articulation and fostering of nationalist ideas, combined with ideas of democracy, mean that, when smaller groups within states feel discontented, the same ideas also offer a solvent to dissolve the old glue.

In conclusion: of course there have been great changes. But one cannot argue that the idea of the nation as a political community as well as a unit of ethnic solidarity was new at any point in time without looking at the evidence of ideas before that point. All I argue is that the great changes sometimes lumped together as 'the rise of nationalism' did not include the idea of the nation as a natural human community – a 'self' – with its own common culture, myths, history and destiny, which by its very existence has the right to self-determination. Looking more closely at earlier ideas about politics and the earlier practice of government would help to distinguish what was really new about modern nationalism and what came from other strands of thought. It might also help to achieve what John Breuilly has called 'a more explicit and selective view of the modernity/nationalism relationship'.[26]

NOTES

1　Anthony D. Smith, 'Nationalism' (= *Current Sociology* 21/3, 1973), pp. 9–10.

2　What I call words, concepts, and phenomena are discussed in Charles K. Ogden and I. A. Richards, *The Meaning of Meaning* (London: Kegan Paul, 1923), pp. 13–15; further discussions in e.g. John Lyons, *Semantics* (Cambridge University Press, 1977), vol. I, pp. 95–119, 175; Raymond Tallis, *Not Saussure: A Critique of Post-Saussurean Literary Theory* (Basingstoke: Macmillan, 1988), pp. 114–16. As applied to medieval history: Ruth Schmidt-Wiegand, 'Historische Onomasiologie und Mittelalterforschung', *Frühmittelalterliche Studien* 9 (1982), 49–78; Susan Reynolds, *Fiefs and Vassals: the Medieval Evidence Reinterpreted* (Oxford: Clarendon Press, 1994), pp. 12–14.

3　Hugh Seton-Watson, *Nations and States: An Enquiry into the Origins of Nations and the Politics of Nationalism* (London: Methuen, 1982), p. 147, is useful on *Nationalität*.

4　On the use of 'state' in medieval history see S. Reynolds, 'The historiography of the medieval state', in Michael Bentley (ed.), *Companion to Historiography* (London: Routledge, 1997), pp. 117–38.

5　This seems to go back at least to Louis XIV: Hubert Méthivier, *Le siècle de Louis XIV* (Paris: PUF, 1988), p. 3.

6　Anthony D. Smith, *Myths and Memories of the Nation* (Oxford University Press, 1999), p. 31, n. 25.

7　S. Reynolds, *Kingdoms and Communities in Western Europe, 900–1300* (2nd edn, Oxford: Clarendon Press, 1997) pp. 253–4.

8　E.g. Anthony D. Smith, *Nationalism: Theory, Ideology, History* (Cambridge: Polity Press, 2001), p. 13.

9　The following paragraphs are based on Reynolds, *Kingdoms and Communities*, pp. xlv–lxii, 250–61, where fuller references are given.

10　Reynolds, *Fiefs and Vassals*.

11　Albert B. White, *Self Government at the King's Command: A Study in the Beginnings of English Democracy* (Minneapolis: University of Minnesota Press, 1933).

12　S. Reynolds, 'Medieval *origines gentium* and the community of the realm', *History* 68 (1983), 375–90, repr. in Reynolds, *Ideas and Solidarities of the Medieval Laity* (Aldershot: Variorum, 1995).

13　Archibald A. M. Duncan, *The Nation of Scots and the Declaration of Arbroath* (London: Historical Association, gen. ser. 75, 1970).

14 Stuart Woolf (ed.), *Nationalism in Europe, 1815 to the Present: A Reader* (London: Routledge, 1996), p. 2. Cf. F. Graus, 'Die Entstehung der mittelalterlichen Staat', *Historica* 10 (1965), 5–65.

15 Cf. Anthony D. Smith, *Theories of Nationalism* (2nd edn, London: Duckworth, 1983), p. 188.

16 Anthony D. Smith, *The Ethnic Origins of Nations* (Oxford: Blackwell, 1986), pp. 23–30; with slightly varying definitions in *Myths and Memories*, p. 127; *The Nation in History* (Cambridge: Polity Press, 2000), p. 65; *Nationalism: Theory, Ideology, History*, pp. 12–13.

17 František Graus, *Die Nationenbildung der Westslawen im Mittelalter* (Sigmaringen: Thorbecke, 1980); B. Zientara, 'Nationale Strukturen des Mittelalters', *Saeculum* 32 (1981), 301–16; L. E. Scales, 'At the margin of community: Germans in pre-Hussite Bohemia', *Transactions of the Royal Historical Society*, 6th ser., 9 (1999), 327–52.

18 Colin Kidd, *British Identities before Nationalism* (Cambridge University Press, 1999), p. 287. Cf. Max Weber, *Economy and Society*, ed. and trans. G. Roth and C. Wittich (Berkeley: University of California Press, 1978), p. 389 (*Wirtschaft und Gesellschaft* [5th edn, Tübingen: Mohr, 1976], p. 237); Margaret Canovan, *Nationhood and Political Theory* (Cheltenham: Edward Elgar, 1996), p. 53; Roger Just, 'Who are "we"?', *Times Literary Supplement*, 8 May 1998, 11.

19 On stories of collective origin and history as reflecting current political situations see R. Finnegan, 'A note on oral tradition and historical evidence', *History and Theory* 9 (1970), 195–201; Jan Vansina, *Oral Tradition as History* (London: James Currey, 1985), pp. 19–24, 103–7; David P. Henige, *The Chronology of Oral Tradition* (Oxford: Clarendon Press, 1972), pp. 47–8, 54–5, 105–18, 163–5. On the identity of people and territory see e.g. Raymond Firth, *Primitive Polynesian Economy* (2nd edn, London: Routledge and Kegan Paul, 1965), p. 39; and of people, territory and kingdom see Max Gluckman, 'The Lozi of Barotseland', in Elizabeth Colson and M. Gluckman (eds.), *Seven Tribes of British Central Africa* (London: Oxford University Press, 1951), pp. 1–93, at pp. 19–21.

20 E.g. A. Seal, 'Imperialism and nationalism in India', in John Gallagher *et al.* (eds.), *Locality, Province and Nation: Essays in Indian Politics 1870 to 1940* (Cambridge University Press, 1973), pp. 1–27; John Iliffe, *A Modern History of Tanganyike* (Cambridge University Press, 1979), pp. 8–10, 318–41, 485–90.

21 S. Reynolds, 'Our forefathers? Tribes, peoples and nations in the age of migrations', in Alexander C. Murray (ed.), *After Rome's Fall: Narrators and Sources of Early Medieval History. Essays Presented to Walter Goffart* (Toronto: University of Toronto Press, 1998), pp. 17–36, with references.

22 Hans Kohn, *The Idea of Nationalism* (New York: Macmillan, 1945), pp. 227–325. Despite his teleological concentration on the past of modern 'nation-states' and the unreality of his picture of the Middle Ages, which for long led me to discount him, Kohn seems to have treated this subject more seriously than later writers on nationalism.

23 *Œuvres complètes*, vol. III, ed. Bernard Gagnebin *et al.* (Paris: Gallimard, 1964), pp. 169 (*Discours sur l'origine de l'inegalité*, pt 2), 381–3, 386, 391 (*Contrat social*,

2.7, 8, 10); F. M. Barnard, 'National culture and political legitimacy: Herder and Rousseau', *Journal of the History of Ideas* 44 (1983), 231–53.

24 Canovan, *Nationalism*, pp. 14–22, 101–2.

25 Cf. Oliver Zimmer, *A Contested Nation: History, Memory and Nationalism in Switzerland, 1761–1891* (Cambridge: Past & Present Publications, 2003).

26 J. Breuilly, 'Reflections on nationalism', *Philosophy of the Social Sciences* 15 (1985), 65–73, repr. in Woolf (ed.), *Nationalism*, pp. 137–54.

CHAPTER 3

Changes in the political uses of the nation: continuity or discontinuity?

John Breuilly

INTRODUCTORY REMARKS*

In this essay I consider the claims that nations existed in pre-modern history and that political arguments appealing to such communities were significant. I argue that the limited evidence available from the pre-modern period suggests two principal ways in which the term 'nation' was used: ethnographically, to describe 'barbaric' societies, and as political self-description, usually of a territorial kingdom. The nation was subordinated to values associated with civilisation and monarchy. Strong claims for the nation as a 'whole society' with a widespread and continuous sense of national identity elide this ethnographic/political distinction and ignore the subordinate value nation plays in both kinds of discourse. Furthermore, those arguing for a significant pre-modern sense of nation-ality conflate fragmented pieces of evidence in which 'nation' and cognate terms are used, investing these with a coherence, continuity and political importance they did not possess.

I argue that national identity, understood as the processes of maintaining, reinterpreting and transmitting the values associated with the nation, has weak force in the pre-modern period because it operates discontinuously and does not fuse cultural identity with political interest, and its impact – often highly opportunistic and contingent – is confined to court, noble and Church elites. Finally, in this critical part of the essay, I suggest that nation and national identity (though not nationalism) become significant in specific parts of Europe during the confessional disputes of the early modern period but that this can be accommodated within a modernist framework.

In the second part of the essay I briefly outline the transformations of modernity which radically alter the concept of the nation, strengthen

* My thanks to Nicholas Brooks, Len Scales and Oliver Zimmer for their comments on drafts of this chapter.

national identity and generate nationalism. This contrasts sharply with what can be reliably established about nations, national identity and nationalism in the pre-modern period. It supports the argument that there is no significant continuity between pre-modern and modern national identity and that such connections as do exist are contingent, arising out of nationalist myth-making.

In the first section where modernists (including myself) have normally made sweeping and often misleading assertions, I focus on two cases for which very strong arguments in favour of pre-modern nations and even nationalism have been mounted: medieval England and Reformation Netherlands. If these arguments can be refuted, *a fortiori* so can those for weaker cases. The second section works more by general assertion as I can draw upon detailed modernist arguments.

DEFINITIONS

It is important to define key terms. I start with definitions of *nation, national identity* and *nationalism* proposed by Smith:[1]

NATION: 'a named human population occupying an historic territory and sharing common myths and memories, a public culture, and common laws and customs for all members'.

NATIONAL IDENTITY: 'the maintenance and continual reinterpretation of the pattern of values, symbols, memories, myths and traditions that form the distinctive heritage of the nation, and the identification of individuals with that heritage and its pattern'.

NATIONALISM: 'a *political* movement for the attainment and maintenance of autonomy, unity and identity on behalf of a population, some of whose members deem it to constitute an actual or potential "nation"'. [Smith uses the term 'an ideological movement'. For reasons which will become clear I replace 'ideological' with 'political'.]

Some writers have objected that such definitions are too precise and already load the dice in favour of modernist arguments. Thus Blanning suggests that Smith's definition of nation puts 'any investigation into lead boots before the start-line has been reached.'[2] I note two points about such objections. First, these definitions were devised by a leading critic of modernist interpretations and deliberately avoid building modernist features into the definitions. Second, like so many critics of this ilk, Blanning hints instead at a vague and inoperable 'definition', quoting with approval an eighteenth-century writer: 'the native inhabitants of a country in so far as they have a common origin and speak a common language, whether they constitute a single state or are divided into several'. Notions like 'common origin' and 'language' beg more questions than they answer. Blanning considers any xenophobic expression as a form of nationalism, exemplified by the standard quotations from Shakespeare's *Henry V*.[3] 'Nation' becomes so loose a term as to render impossible any discriminating and analytical approach to the subject. It is up to such critics to propose more useful definitions rather than to object to such a necessary first step.

WHEN WAS THE NATION?

The perennialist claim

Recently medieval and even ancient historians have insisted on the existence of nations in their period.[4] These claims have been taken up in general works and presented as an important objection to modernist views of nation and nationalism.[5] I call arguments asserting the significant existence of pre-modern nations 'perennialism'. Perennialists do not claim that nations have a continuous or universal existence, only that there have been occurrences of the nation as a significant human group in pre-modern times.

If this perennialist claim is accepted, one could infer that pre-modern national identity also existed. It would be difficult to see how a nation could exist in the absence of processes which maintain, reinterpret and transmit values associated with it. The processes which maintain and transmit national identity are precisely what produces nations. In principle one could identify such processes and deny the existence of nations on the grounds that these processes had an extremely limited impact. I will suggest that perennialists have jumped from apparent national identity processes identified in fragmented discourses to construct an over-coherent idea of the nation. I will stress the need to establish *processes* of producing national identity which go beyond demonstrating that 'nation' and cognate terms are found in texts.

MEDIEVAL ENGLAND[6]

Introductory points

The perennialist argument is at its strongest in the case of medieval England. Key texts and events are Bede's *Ecclesiastical History of the*

English People, the Anglo-Saxon Chronicle, the achievements of Alfred of Wessex, the bringing together of much of England under one government in the late Anglo-Saxon period, the rapid acceptance of English identity by Normans after 1066, the elaboration of notions of English superiority from the early twelfth century, the growth of central government from the thirteenth century, the fourteenth-century emergence of an English written vernacular, and the national(ist) propaganda deployed during the Hundred Years War against France.[7]

I am not competent to debate with specialists who have researched difficult sources, textual and other, to construct a perennialist argument. However, these specialists insist on the implications of their arguments for an understanding of national identity and nationalism in the modern period.[8] Generalists like Hastings and Smith draw upon such medievalists to support their criticisms of modernists. So modernists (whose expertise is usually confined to the modern period) cannot ignore these arguments. Fortunately, there is no consensus amongst medieval historians, some of whose arguments are supportive of modernist approaches.[9] This emboldens me to engage with medieval and early modern historiography. That engagement has led me to revise but not abandon my modernist position.

The 'English' project before 1066

In both title and language the *Ecclesiastical History* asserts the identity and mission of the English against other inhabitants of Britain. The first thing that strikes a modern historian is the paucity of other evidence. We depend upon Bede for the context within which we situate his text.[10] The danger is obvious: if one accepts Bede's view of his world, his national terminology will seem appropriate to understanding that world. However, when there is non-textual evidence showing that 'British' cultural traits continued after their supposed destruction by the 'English', this suggests that the sharp distinction Bede draws between the two groups is problematic.[11]

It is now generally agreed that we should read Bede as a project, not a description. Bede pressed the claims of Roman Christian against Celtic Christian and pagan rulers; more specifically he supported Northumbrian rulers against their enemies. Bede's shift in usage from 'Saxon' to 'English', for example, makes sense in terms of the timing of Pope Gregory's mission to the English and the conversion work of Augustine. It has no ethnic or linguistic meaning.

The term 'English' therefore is subordinate to a primary Roman Christian and a secondary Northumbrian dynastic value. The promotion of Roman Christianity proceeds by conquest (one ruler replacing another) and conversion (missionaries working on rulers). Much of the *Ecclesiastical History* is concerned with the conversion of pagans to Christianity and the acceptance by Celtic Christians of Roman Christian practices such as the dating of Easter.[12] Conversion was a top-down process of which Bede provides wonderfully vivid accounts. The 'Anglicisation' of the British Isles consists of removing or converting rulers.

One finds modern missionaries taking the same line. (Admittedly 'conversion from below' was another option.) There is abundant evidence that such conversion was superficial and fragile. The chief often 'lapsed'.[13] Bede reports chiefly conversions to Roman Christianity as the spreading of Englishness. We know that such conversions in nineteenth-century Africa were episodic, potentially reversible and did not signify ethnic transformation. Why should we assume anything different for eighth-century England? Bede seems to make an ethnic/religious equation, inviting the English to see themselves as the new Israelites, but we have no evidence that the invitation was understood, let alone accepted.

Bede's text at best is an agent in the *later* making of English national identity, influencing the way subsequent writers used national terms. As Nicholas Brooks puts it:

Bede's Ecclesiastical History of the English People provides many of [the] crucial components necessary for ethnogenesis: it asserts a common history and origin myth for the English; it emphasises the enmity (both military and ecclesiastical) of the Britons and thus justifies their forfeiture of most of the island of *Britannia*; and it gives only the slightest glimpses of an earlier Roman and British Christian history – the minimum necessary to provide a credible context for the conversion of the pagan Anglo-Saxons.[14]

Brooks goes on to trace Bede's influence in the use of the term 'English' upon Boniface and Alcuin, who wrote later in the eighth century.[15] But Bede's text on its own does not support perennialist claims for eighth-century England.

The claim looks stronger for Alfred, who wielded more power than a monk in Northumbria. Alfred drew upon the *Ecclesiastical History* (which he had translated into English, thereby promoting its 'ethnogenesis' function) as well as the *Anglo-Saxon Chronicle*, and framed justifications for his territorial claims in national terms. However, if we accept the point made by Reynolds,[16] that it was normal for regnal claims to be justified by claims of affinity with a territory or its inhabitants, one can see why an 'English' argument made sense in Alfred's disputes with other Anglo-Saxon as well as Danish rulers.

Alfred shifted from projecting his realm as 'Saxon' to 'Anglo-Saxon' or even 'English' (*Angelcynn*) as he extended his power over Mercia and Kent. Later, in the 890s, Alfred's court stressed that the language into which Gregory, Boethius, Bede, parts of the Bible and other writings were translated was *English*.[17] Educating 'free-born' men in reading and writing English was an aristocratic project to construct cultural, linguistic and legal unity within the different territories ruled or coveted by Alfred. His challenge to Danish control in northern England was, in a way directly influenced by Bede, framed in terms not of conquest but of unifying the English. Selecting the name 'English' helped justify his expansionist ambitions.

Alfred's achievement lay in his realisation that by harnessing and focusing these three forms of identity [cultural, linguistic, legal] through an appeal to a common memory, and by imposing a cultural hegemony he was able to provide a retrospective and self-consciously historical explanation for the creation of a fourth, national consciousness. In that sense, while Bede invented the English as a people in the sight of God, they were made one nation by 'Alfred of the English . . .'.[18]

However, it is doubtful whether this justification made sense beyond the claimant and members of the small elite Alfred tried to educate in being English. Mid-ninth-century land charters in northern England acknowledged a plurality of identities: Anglo-Saxon, Northumbrian, pagan and Briton.[19]

'England' and the English was first a local Christianising (Bede) and then a dynastic (Alfred) project. If this changing project had been pursued energetically, consistently and successfully it might be argued that it would eventually have actually produced an English nation. However, one must not confuse the early project with one possible long-run outcome. Very different, and more extensive, kinds of evidence are needed to argue this latter case. Even if the usage of the term 'English' spread and its meaning stabilised from the late ninth century, that would tell us only that subsequent political actors who followed Alfred found the same value in his 'instrumental ethnicity'.

In fact, over the next couple of centuries the meanings shifted. The Danish rulers who established political unity in the early eleventh century might find some use in national terms when responding to external threats from Scandinavia and Normandy, but did not deploy the name 'English' in internal conflicts as Alfred had. The Normans who arrived in 1066 had no interest at all in sustaining the name of the English. So thorough was their displacement of pre-Conquest elites that Henry of Huntingdon, writing in the middle of the twelfth century about the situation in 1087, judged that the 'English people' had been destroyed.[20] He meant that the elite male figures of pre-Conquest England had been divested of their land and power by Norman conquerors. Why descendants of those conquerors, including Henry himself, re-named themselves 'English' is another story to be explained in new ways. It certainly is not a continuation of an earlier story as the perennialists would have it.[21]

The name 'English' before 1066 related to expansionist religious and political projects, not ethnographic categories. One does not find cultural stereotyping in Bede, e.g. Britons against English, pagans against Christians, civilised against barbarian – in contrast to certain twelfth-century texts.[22] Neither Bede nor Alfred understood Anglicisation as ethnic transformation. They use the name 'English' in ways which make sense to a biblical scholar and an ambitious king, but its meaning does not include that of a whole people with a common language, historic territory or shared culture.[23]

The construction of a political nation

By the late Anglo-Saxon period the projects of Christianisation and political unification had achieved a degree of success. Common administrative units and institutions such as shires and shire courts were established. This construction of a national system of government was continued and consolidated by Norman rulers after 1066.[24] 'England' and 'English' became names for this system of rule and the territory to which it applied.

If one assembles claims about the consolidation of shires and their courts, familial continuities among the landowners using such institutions, the national scope of parliaments from the thirteenth century and the consolidation of a national Church system, one could argue that from the late Anglo-Saxon period there developed self-conscious elites with extensive and continuous institutions which embodied and reproduced ideas of the English nation.[25]

Well – *possibly*. There are important qualifications and counter-arguments. First, this is a process over time. What may be the case in the fourteenth century cannot be read back into the tenth. The continuity of the name 'English' does not mean continuity in the meaning of the name. Second, the existence of an institution does not produce some determinant, matching consciousness. We may regard the shire courts as a national institution, but we need independent evidence to show that people using such courts thought about them like that. Combining these two points, the

longevity of certain institutions does not imply some constant and matching group identity over that whole period.

Take the example of shire courts. As I understand it, these came to be
established over much of England by the late Anglo-Saxon period.
Presumably they took time to embed themselves in areas where they had
been most recently established, and varied in how they functioned according to local circumstances.[26] They met twice a year and were largely
confined to adjudicating disputes within the county. Why should infrequent meetings of local institutions, even if organised along (roughly)
similar lines and under one royal authority, be assumed to have induced
a sense of national identity? In the absence of *direct* evidence of such a
shared sense of identity I do not see the justification for such an assumption. Indeed, it is more plausible to assume the opposite, namely that most
people using these institutions cared or thought little about their national
significance and regarded them primarily as instruments for the resolution
of local disputes.

As for longevity, institutions change their purposes and the constituencies they serve. Thegns using shire courts in late Anglo-Saxon England
have few connections or affinities with the early modern gentry for whom
we do have evidence of a sense of national identity.[27] I am not persuaded –
and will not be unless presented with good, direct evidence – that
substantial landholders attending a court in Wiltshire once every six
months had any sense of 'imagined community' with their counterparts
in Cheshire. For Anderson such a capacity for imagination requires not just
similarity but communication.[28] Clearly there was some communication;
shire courts were established by and answerable to royal authority. To that
extent these were national institutions but that had an impact only on the
consciousness of an extremely small elite consisting of the king and his
officials.

Furthermore, especially for the period c.1066–1300, one can find very
local and contingent explanations for the use of national language. William
of Malmesbury's assertions about the English served the interests of a
particular group of second- or third-generation elite Normans against
magnates with still-powerful ties back in Normandy, rather than indicating
the absorption of a new elite into the group identity of older elites.[29] The
same point explains the apparent contradiction of Henry of Huntingdon
mourning the destruction of the 'English people' by 1087 but affirming
their existence by the time his story ended in 1154.[30] These assertions of
Englishness differed between an earlier generation of 'English' resignation
to marginalisation by newly arrived Normans and a subsequent generation

which, as Normandy and other continental possessions were lost, identified themselves with the polity of England.[31] Incidentally, the occasional
argument about 'British' identity could be explained in similar fashion.
One reason Geoffrey of Monmouth objected to the stereotyping of the
Welsh as barbarians was that his patron, Robert of Gloucester, had formed
alliances with Welsh chiefs in his conflict with King Stephen (see below,
'The civilised and the barbaric').[32]

The consolidation of a single system of government over much of
England gave to the terms 'England' and the 'English' a new force,
referring to the territory ruled by this government, the institutions it
used and the elites which ran these institutions. However, these names
were institutional, not ethnic ones. There was no effort to persuade the
majority of subjects to identify themselves with this system of rule and its
names. The project of using English, begun under Alfred, was abandoned.
Latin was the principal written language. When a written vernacular
developed in the thirteenth century, it was *French*. English as a written
vernacular prose form only starts to become important in the fourteenth
century.[33] Any argument that the Normans understood themselves as
English[34] in any ethnic sense requires that 'ethnicity' be sharply separated
from language for some two hundred years.[35] Any attempt to locate
'ethnicity' instead in elite customs and manners founders on the 'supra-
national' ethics of chivalry and piety which came to dominate amongst
Western European elites in this period.

The achievement of strong national government, coupled with a weak-
ening hold on continental territories, ensured that the names 'England' and
'English' used by Bede and those influenced by him were taken up by rulers
of Norman descent as a political self-description but with new, often
highly instrumental and rapidly changing meanings.[36]

'England' as the name of a territorial polity became more fixed and
significant. A comparison can bring out how this influences political
language. Second- or third-generation Norman elites in England called
themselves English, often to assert themselves against Norman magnates
now acquiring an interest in the rich pickings of England. Second- or
third-generation English elites settled in Ireland called themselves English
too, even as they in turn grumbled about the lack of truly English qualities
back in the home country or amongst new arrivals, whether settlers or
administrators. There is a compelling parallel with modern examples:
Algerian French, British Rhodesians. The asymmetry in this comparison –
Normans become English in England but English stay English in Ireland – is
best explained by the centrality of the rule of the English monarchy and the

marginal positions in relation to that power of both Normandy and Ireland. As a territorially centred monarchy becomes increasingly powerful and stable, it provides the language of political identity for its elites. To that extent the increased salience of 'national identity' is to be expected in England from c.1300 onwards.

The civilised and the barbaric

Historians have argued persuasively that from the middle of the twelfth century there developed an ethnic discourse of the Irish and Welsh (rather less the Scots) as barbarians compared to the civilised English, even if these views were expressed in Latin and French.[37] Such texts, and supporting evidence for the greater importance of towns, money and arable farming in southern and central England compared to Wales, Ireland and highland Scotland, connect ethnic stereotypes to distinct ways of life which extend well beyond elite institutions.

This discourse is less about national differences and more about the revival of a classical ethnography There is an affinity between how Herodotus writes about Scythians or Tacitus about Germans and how William of Malmesbury writes about the Welsh. There is an implication that arable farming, market towns, civilised conduct of warfare and much else would turn barbarians into civilised people.[38] The contrasts are between elites and are based on ways of life, the civilised and the barbaric; they are not national contrasts. Tribal chiefs, their retinues and holy men, are compared to the English king, landowners and clergy, as is clear when comparison touches upon subjects such as literacy or table manners.[39]

Gillingham has argued that such ethnographic contrasts underpin what he calls a project of 'English imperialism'.[40] However, this language is distinct from that used in disputes with the Scots and the French, the principal enemies of this period. The Scottish crown and the society it ruled in the lowlands was not dissimilar to that of England in language and customs. Ethnographic distinctions played little role in Anglo-Scots and Anglo-French disputes (except when Scottish Gaeldom was involved). The most serious threats to England came from the arable and commercial kingdoms of Scotland and France, not the poorer, pastoral societies of the Welsh and the Irish. Therefore, the language of nationality used in disputes with the Scottish and French shifted from the ethnographic to the political. I will focus on the use of national terms in conflicts with France.[41]

Invoking the nation in inter-state conflict

The Hundred Years War is often cited as proof positive of the importance of national identity, even of nationalism. French and English kings appealed to the nation and depicted themselves defending national territory. The English crown commanded that sermons be preached in churches in support of war. The figure of Joan of Arc served as a focus of patriotic feeling at the time; she was not just a myth constructed much later.

There are changes in how the idea of the nation was used during this prolonged conflict. It is the work of centralising monarchy which accounts for the changes. As monarchies increased their authority over a given territory, so they identified themselves increasingly with that territory, what Reynolds calls the 'regnum':[42]

In France the thirteenth century had witnessed a gradual advance in what was regarded as a vassal's obligation, from defence of his lord (the king) to defence of the crown (the *corona*) and, by the end of the century, defence of the kingdom (the *regnum*).[43]

Increasing demands placed by the crown on those it ruled made direct relations between kings and subjects more important:

In 1439 the English Parliament moved with the times when it passed legislation making desertion, even when no war was being fought, the breaking not simply of a private contract between soldier and captain but, more important, the breaking of a formal undertaking in which both soldier and captain were the servants of a greater, public good.[44]

The nation is coterminous with the polity: territorially through the kingdom, politically through the public good as defined by the crown.

The national idea could be deployed only in certain ways and situations. The English crown could not persuade its English subjects that defence of Aquitaine – an Angevin legacy – was a defence of part of the realm of England. War had to be justified either as a pre-emptive move against possible French attack or as a source of profit. Invoking the nation correlates directly with increasing dependence on taxation falling upon ever larger segments of the population. This is a measure of both centralising royal authority and the need to sell royal policy to tax payers.

The national idea remained largely monarchical. Learned treatises argued claims in terms of lineages. Sometimes royal genealogies were posted on church doors. Myths of common descent, such as that from the Trojans, were elaborated but this was an aristocratic rationalisation, declining in meaning with the rise of powerful and impersonal territorial polities. Such myths were purely genealogical; issues of language and custom were absent. Celebrating military success and mourning defeat focused on the king and knightly warriors (Joan of Arc is a notable exception). Two centuries later Shakespeare would depict Henry V on the eve of Agincourt moving in disguise amongst common men, ethnic stereotypes of Scot, Irishman and Welshman (but not English), but such imagery was not deployed at the time.[45]

Other, often more important identities and interests were involved. The English crown held on to Aquitaine and more short-lived occupations in other parts of France by incorporating (and sometimes importing) landed elites. When the French crown gained control of these areas, it had to come to a similar understanding with local elites, including recent immigrants from England. Much of the war effort must be seen in these local terms:

> not all public expenditure related to war was the direct result of centralised intervention or initiative. French historians have ... stressed ... that in their country there existed two financial systems, one national, the other local, which worked side by side, and which were built up together ... Opposition to the raising of taxes which might be spent in another part of the kingdom militated against involvement in a war being fought perhaps hundreds of miles away. Equally, only when their region and, consequently, their common profit was threatened, were people ready to act. Indeed, it can be argued that the piecemeal and local nature of war dictated by both the English (the enemy from without) and by the Companies (the enemy from within), to say nothing of the very local character of the civil war which dominated so much of Charles VI's reign, encouraged people to see war in local, rather than national, terms, and that this led naturally to the need for the reaction to come from local initiatives and to be based on local wealth.[46]

Even while writing this Allmand cannot resist placing these local concerns into a national framework. However, for some inhabitants of 'France', the enemy 'without' was the *French*, not the English crown.

If the crown defined the nation and claims to authority were justified by royal lineage arguments, the 'English' king could claim the 'French' crown and *vice versa*. By the Treaty of Troyes (1420) Henry V was designated next king of France, an agreement which presumably would have come into operation had Henry not died in 1422 shortly before Charles VI.[47] It is difficult to reconcile this with the claim that national identity was politically significant. The agreement of 1420 worried 'English' elites, but this was due to anxiety about Henry acquiring powers and commitments which might conflict with their interests rather than to any sense that 'their' king could not also be the ruler of another 'nation'. This was why monarchs undertaking personal unions had to make elaborate promises to respect the customs and laws of their different kingdoms. This does demonstrate a capacity to separate 'kingdom' (= country) from 'king', but it also shows a simultaneous incapacity to oppose nation to monarchy.[48]

From the 1290s in England, and for both the English and the French crowns during the Hundred Years War, royal propaganda appealed to the national idea.[49] Documents such as royal writs and requests to the Church to say prayers for the king and preach patriotic sermons suggest that the crown sought to address the nation as a broad community extending beyond elites. The idea that authority was legitimate only if it served the common good was central to medieval political thought.[50] The immediate reasons for such appeals are also clear: the costs of war necessitated higher taxation and other impositions. These were unpopular and could provoke resistance, as in 1381. It was vital for the crown to persuade people that the wars were not narrowly royal affairs but in defence of broader English interests.

However, to interpret these appeals as evidence of nationalism or wide-spread national identity, or as a project to construct a favourable 'public opinion', goes further than the evidence allows. Such appeals were infrequent. During the Hundred Years War, most of them were concentrated into the first decade and there was little or nothing for years at a time. It is difficult to see how a public culture of national consciousness could be produced and transmitted by these episodic efforts. We do not know if and how local churches implemented royal commands for prayers and sermons, let alone their impact on congregations. There was no ethnic component to the addressees of these appeals: the English. The English people *are* the subjects of the English crown. The principled case, for example the claim to the French crown, was made entirely within a monarchical frame of reference and the 'nation' subsumed within that frame. There is another argument about 'defence of the realm'. Insofar as the realm is England and its population the 'English' people, this could be construed as an argument about defending the national interest. But this is an inference from the arguments deploying the non-ethnic terms of 'crown', 'realm' and 'subjects'.

Where ethnographic language bolstered dynastic claims and counter-claims, it was used in two ways. First, the enemy could be ethnically stereotyped. Thus the French were sometimes presented as effeminate, the Scottish as savage. Such stereotypes drew upon the tropes of the civilised and the barbaric. However, the specific referent was the political opponent: 'French' and 'Scottish' were often shorthand for French or Scottish kings. This language never acquired the strength and stability of that used to characterise the Welsh and Irish, because it was a matter of occasional political manipulation rather than part of a continuous process of comparing different ways of life.

The absence of nation in political thought

In studies of medieval political thought, one rarely encounters nations, national identity or nationalism. None of these words can be found in the index of Gordon Leff, *Medieval Thought*. The index to John Bowle's *Western Political Thought* has many entries under 'natural law' but none under 'nation'. Even where the term is encountered it is not of central, conceptual importance. Antony Black entitles one chapter in his *Political Thought in Europe* 'Empires and nations'.[51] However, so far as explicit political theory is concerned, that chapter divides into sections on theories of universal monarchy ('empire') and state sovereignty. There is an intermediate section (pp. 109–113) which touches upon the subject of nations, but it consists of the author's reflections on the subject and does not involve analysis of contemporary political texts and ideas.[52]

If nations mattered, why did political thinkers not write about them? There are four possible answers. One is that they failed to confront this subject, despite its significance.[53] A second is that the failing rests with historians of medieval political thought. The third one is that nations were so *implicit* in the thought of the day that they never became an object of explicit political argument. The fourth and simplest is that nation was not a significant political concept. Invoking William of Occam, unless the more complex arguments offer some advantage over the simplest one, the latter should be preferred.

A closer look helps explain why the 'nation' is marginal. Medieval thinkers regarded secular government as a necessity arising from the fallen, sinful nature of man. It was recognised, particularly through the influence of Aristotle, that the state (*civitas*)[54] has purposes apart from the defence and promotion of Christianity, that this justifies temporal autonomy from the Church, and that existing rulers can be judged by their subjects to have failed these purposes. Some writers, most notably Marsiglio of Padua, expressed what could be taken as a 'democratic' view. He argued that people are the best judges of their own interests, that majority views are superior to minority ones, that government should be judged by how far it serves the people, and that temporal power in the form of coercion is not subject to spiritual power (if anything, the opposite is the case). This all suggests that there should be institutional provision for enabling the view of 'the people' to be ascertained and brought to bear upon rulers. However, Marsiglio was unusual. Insofar as he had any conception of the people and how they could express their views, it was derived from the city-state, which had a role for citizen assemblies and could connect directly to the political writings of Aristotle. Even in Marsiglio's writings this 'democratic' conception was qualified by such phrases as 'the weightier part of the population' along with notions of 'tacit consent'. [55]

Thus there was no place for a *political* conceptualisation of the subjects of a state as an ethnic collectivity. There was a concept of the body of citizens in a city-state, but this collective had no ethnic or national quality. As for the states which we might call 'national' by the fifteenth century, such as England or France, there is no suggestion that the term implies the existence of a 'nation' consisting of citizens, more or less widely defined by certain collective characteristics (language, customs, manners) and whose interests and will must be taken into account by princes if their actions are to be regarded as legitimate. There is a body of political thought on the functions and powers of certain assemblies such as parliaments in territorial monarchies or general councils in the Church. Sometimes the term 'nation' can be linked to such bodies, such as the subdivisions within the early fifteenth-century Council of Constance. However, this was a *territorial* not an *ethnic* concept (the English were the delegates who were subjects of the English crown), and was accorded political meaning only in terms of formal, abstract reasoning about the nature of government.

The nation and 'public culture'

Smith's definition of the nation, quoted at the start of this essay, includes the term 'public culture'. However, what does 'public' culture mean in medieval England? There were few fixed points of monarchical government, few permanent physical structures which displayed the crown to its subjects. Access to these places was confined to elites or, at best, imposed restrictions on most people, as the layout of medieval churches and cathedrals makes clear. [56]

Beyond Sunday worship, with visual images for a non-literate congregation, royal faces on coins, images on bridges and other large structures and the occasional display of a royal tour, there was little in the way of symbols which might portray a public, national culture to most people. There is little evidence about the reception of these symbols.

Elites had many more possibilities for communicating ideas and values: the circulation of manuscripts amongst clerics, the rituals and imagery of royal courts, the trappings associated with the opening and closing of legal institutions. However, this sustained specific group cultures, what in modern parlance we might call private cultures. Were images of the nation important in these enclosed elite cultures? I doubt it – and even if they were, they were always subordinate to other images.

Just to take examples of claims to a 'British' past. In the late thirteenth century one of the illuminations in a manuscript of *Flores Historiarum* was an image of King Arthur; in the early fifteenth century another image of Arthur was included in windows for the library at All Souls' College, Oxford. In both cases Arthur is placed in a selective lineage of kings of England.[57] These images were only accessible to a small part of a narrow elite and any notion of ethnicity is submerged in a royal line (which in the manuscript goes back to Troy and in the windows includes the Roman Emperor Constantine). This hardly qualifies as an element of a public culture maintaining, re-interpreting and transmitting national identity from one generation to the next.

Popular culture in this world was oral. We know virtually nothing about it. Were villagers in Kent and Warwickshire relating similar stories? Did these stories tell of wise and just national rulers, stereotypical foreigners and glorious exploits of English warriors? Did one set of villagers, as they told their national stories, imagine that they *were* just one such set, and that villagers like them all over the country were telling similar stories, as Anderson suggests happens when a thousand or a million people all sit down at breakfast to read the same newspaper? We do not know; we have too little evidence. The most plausible speculation is that there was no such imagining, that these oral cultures were tied to their localities, that even the exotica of travellers' tales were transformed by local context, and that even if – which I think unlikely – similar and national stories were told from one place to another, there was no consciousness of that happening.

The nation in medieval culture

Lack of evidence can encourage boldness of argument. I am interested in how far there existed a significant sense of national identity, even if confined to elite level, amongst late eighteenth- and early nineteenth-century 'Germans'. Compared to what is available to medieval English historians, there is an abundance and variety of evidence, though thin compared to that for twentieth-century Germany. Yet gaps in the evidence make historians cautious about claims for a widely shared sense of national identity underpinning war against Napoleon in 1813–15. What evidence there is suggests conflicting forms of national identity and the importance of other, competing senses of loyalty, such as to region, religion, monarch and social estate. Precisely because the evidence is *not* confined to elites in power but includes dissident intellectuals, local assemblies and even, occasionally, rank-and-file soldiers, the historian becomes circumspect about discerning any one central or authoritative meaning for the nation. Furthermore, other evidence such as conscription lists or measures against deserters points to the limited appeal of the national idea.

Apart from this range of material I would like to see evidence for medieval England pointing to the formation of a national elite (e.g., through geographical mobility, inter-marriage, common education and cultural tastes, economic transactions, concerted political action) capable of producing, using and sustaining a sense of national identity. For nine-teenth-century Germany one can trace the formation of a *Gymnasium-* and university-educated bourgeoisie whose members cross state and regional boundaries to participate in a common culture mediated through the German language and communicated through newspapers, journals and cultural associations such as choirs and gymnastic associations. Even then there is lively debate about the role of the national idea. Perhaps the confidence with which claims about national identity in medieval England are made is helped by the *absence* of evidence which might complicate, or even undermine, such claims.

If national values mattered politically I would expect *contention* over them. In the modern period, as soon as the language of nationality becomes politically important it is contested. Consensus suggests unimportance. In medieval sources 'nation' and cognate words are used as terms of art (e.g. of classically based ethnography) in Latin manuscripts with a limited readership linked to an often local, even personal agenda on the part of the author and his patron, or intermittently and manipulatively deployed by rulers to justify dynastic claims and policies. In this second context appeals to the nation are occasional (there are many dynastic claims which would be undermined by national arguments) and subordinate to dynastic interest.

In both its ethnographic and political uses, the term 'nation' is not disputed. The nation is not used to justify political opposition to con-stituted rule.[58] In politics the nation is conceived of as the passive addressee of dynastic action, not an autonomous political actor.[59] What makes nationalist ideology special is that the nation, as a 'whole society', becomes the *source* of legitimacy, not an instrument deployed or appealed to by an authority legitimised in other ways.

England was precocious in constructing a common set of legal, political and religious institutions which exhibited great continuity from the late Anglo-Saxon period onwards. Furthermore, the separation between local and central institutions breaks down earlier in England than anywhere else, above all with the growth in the significance and functions of parliament from the 1530s. However, we must not project the later meanings of this institution into earlier periods (even if that was what apologists for seventeenth-century parliaments did). An institution that looks national from outside is not necessarily seen like that from inside. Ancient origins do not denote ancient consciousness. Too many historians create an over-coherent picture in time and space, arbitrarily juxtapose fragmentary pieces of evidence, and conflate ethnographic discourses about barbarians with political arguments proffered by monarchs and their followings to justify their pursuit of power.

We should not return to the misleading simplicities of Gellner's model of 'agrarian empire' with its fragmented rural communities and its horizontally separated castes of craftsmen, merchants, landowners and clerics.[60] There *is* a language of nationality in late medieval England, which became institutionalised in Church, royal courts and parliament. But we do not know whether this penetrated below the elites which ran those institutions; we cannot equate elite structures and institutions with some 'matching' sense of national identity in the absence of direct evidence; and political arguments couched in Christian and dynastic terms mattered far more than national arguments, which were set aside if they did not serve religious or dynastic purposes.

Strong perennialist claims have been made for medieval England. Yet one is entitled to feel sceptical about many of these. National identity existed only at elite level, in discontinuous and fragmented forms, in two different worlds of meaning (ethnographic and political) which were casually connected, subordinate to Christian and dynastic values, and with no 'public culture' which could maintain, reinterpret and transmit national identity on a sufficiently extensive scale and stable basis as to enable one to claim that a nation existed.

EARLY MODERN EUROPE AND THE PERENNIALIST ARGUMENT

Changes in Europe from the early sixteenth century made national identity more important. These include the development of a print culture and an accompanying expansion of literacy, and the emergence of popular movements which challenged established institutions.

However, one must be cautious about projecting back later developments. Parliament is seen as central to the development of an oppositional sense of nationality in England. However, Elton has argued that parliament in the sixteenth century was an event rather than an institution, an instrument of royal rule rather an autonomous institution with national goals.[61] The 'national' arguments deployed in the early phase of the English Reformation come from the court and royal servants, for example, when making claims about a national church with a history pre-dating the connection to Rome.[62] Insofar as members of parliament had autonomous goals, these concerned local disputes over property and offices. It is vital to the precocious formation of a national state in England that local goals were pursued through a national institution rather than local institutions – but that is another matter.[63]

There are good arguments to support the idea that the Protestant and national values of those who pushed through reform under Henry VIII and Edward VI represented a fragile, minority zealot view which rooted itself in a broader consciousness only in the early seventeenth century (if then). The work of a regime and a small minority dispersed across the country laid the foundations for a widespread sense of national identity, but that work is not to be confused with the later achievement. Furthermore, there was much continuity with the 'old religion'.[64]

Let me take one example. Generalists arguing for a strong sense of national identity in sixteenth-century England frequently cite the high circulation figures and numerous editions of Foxe's *Book of Martyrs*.[65] The popularity of this powerful litany of Protestant martyrdom under Catholic rule, especially the Marian regime, is taken as evidence of a widespread national and Protestant sense of identity. However, a closer look indicates something rather different. It was the regime which decided to publish the book in large numbers in an expensive format. The command that all churches must keep a chained copy was an attempt to ensure sales and defray costs. Many churches resisted the order precisely because of that cost. Foxe writes about *Protestant*, not *English*, martyrs, including Scottish, German and Dutch figures. To turn Foxe's *Book of Martyrs* into an index of a popular sense of national identity in Elizabethan England is like inferring widespread Christian belief from the ubiquity of Gideon Bibles in modern hotel rooms.[66]

Nevertheless, national arguments took on a new intensity and significance when the struggle for reformed Christianity became associated with rebellion and civil war. A recent essay by Gorski focusing on the Dutch revolt against Habsburg rule presents a strong and cogent argument for the existence of nationalism, not merely national identity.[67]

Gorski provides a penetrating and fair account of modernist views of nationalism. He makes a useful distinction between content (nationalist claims), scope (the social support nationalism mobilises) and politics (specific nationalist political goals). For modernists nationalism is an ideological movement mobilising multi-class support in pursuit of political autonomy for the nation: 'I will try to show that *some instances of early modern national consciousness must be counted as instances of full-blown, modern nationalism by the very criteria set forth by modernists* [author's own emphasis]'.[68] However, Gorski has already narrowed the focus to 'national consciousness', meaning claims made in nationalist texts and images. He distinguishes four strands: Hebraic, classical (Batavian), monarchist, popular (republican). The Batavian idea derives from Tacitus' *Germania*. The Hebraic notion is of the elect nation which has made a covenant with God. Monarchical nationalism supported the House of Orange. Republican nationalism took two forms: oligarchic, associated with wealthy cities hostile to Orange rule; radical, appealing to the 'people'.

Gorski identifies these ideologies in many sources: treatises, pamphlets, images on coins, woodcuts. He shows how they were elaborated between 1620 and 1670 and used in conflicting ways in the struggle for power. The extensive circulation of printed and visual materials suggests popular resonance.

Before looking at Gorski's extension of his argument beyond seventeenth-century Holland, we need to see what he has established for his principal case.

Gorski does not go beyond analysing uses of the 'category' (his term) nation in various sources. His argument would be stronger if connected to 'proto-nationalist' movements, as has been done for English Puritanism and French Calvinism.[69] That would lead to a search for specific explanations for this cluster of cases. I would note the importance of Calvinism, even if there are similar Catholic and Lutheran cases, using a theology which justified collective resistance to authority by the people or their representatives. In territorial kingdoms, the theology could identify a chosen nation in revolt against foreign rulers and false churches.[70] Extensive print propaganda in the vernacular was vital, linked to Protestant insistence on the need to encounter the 'Word of God' as *written*. These movements flourished in commercialised regions – lowland England, Holland, lowland Scotland, the north-eastern seaboard of North America – centred on cities like London, Edinburgh, Antwerp and Boston. All this suggests a modernist interpretation.

There are severe limitations to Gorski's argument. There are three authentically 'national' arguments: Hebraic, Batavian, popular republican.[71] None possesses ethnic content. The Hebraic argument easily took on an internationalist form under Calvinist leadership. The Batavian idea was an erudite conceit and its fragility makes clear that nations cannot be invented out of nothing. Radical republicans equated the common people with the nation. Meanwhile, politics remained largely confined to elites, their interests and institutions, above all the balance of central against provincial, monarchical against urban oligarchical power.

Gorski also makes three expansionist moves beyond his Dutch case. First, he argues that there are similar features in other cases at the time, citing Portugal, Hesse, England, Scotland and North America. Ignorance prevents me commenting on Hesse and Portugal (Gorski provides no detail). I agree in the other three cases but see these in modernist terms.

Gorski's second expansionist move is back in time, citing examples of medieval kings using the language of a chosen people. I have already dealt with the strongest such case, medieval England. His third move is forward in time, suggesting that nationalism in the French Revolution is similar to his Dutch case. He does concede a greater role for secular argument. That is a significant concession: freeing the concept of the nation from Christian and monarchical associations is a radical change, not a minor alteration. More importantly Gorski's exclusive focus on discourse overlooks the point that this change in language accompanies fundamental changes in political goals and social mobilisation. An Estates-General becomes a National Assembly, drawn from constituencies across the country. Organised political parties use the term 'nation' in contested ways. The king is executed for betraying the nation. Declarations of rights invoke the nation as the bearer of those rights. National constitutions are drawn up. Some of the linguistic shifts had been anticipated in *ancien régime* France[72] but were transformed in meaning by the part they played in new types of political opposition, popular movement and state organisation. Only a narrow focus on nation as 'discourse' can ignore these fundamental changes and sustain Gorski's generalisations across different historical periods. Remove that and what remains persuasive in Gorski is that too exclusive a focus on modernity as something starting in the middle of the eighteenth century obscures significant precursors of modern national identity and even nationalism in the Reformation.

Gorski's generalisations are meant to promote not perennialism but what he calls the post-modern case.[73] Perennialists and modernists debate on the same ground. Modernists claim that nations, national identity and nationalism are peculiar to the modern period; perennialists argue they are also significant in the pre-modern period. The post-modern argument is of a different order.

POST-MODERNISM: THE NATION AS DISCOURSE

Post-modern scepticism about how easily we can jump from discourse to the apparent referents of that discourse, and post-modern alertness to the changeable, contingent and constructive role of language in shaping what it purports to reflect or express, have had a salutary impact. It is important to look closely at discourses of nation and nationalism in their own right and not to assume that such discourse reflects in any simple or direct way the existence of nation and nationalism in any broader or more 'real' sense. Examination of the English medieval case makes it clear that there are complex discourses about the nation and modernists cannot simply deny or ignore this. The same point applies even more emphatically to the early modern period.

Difficulties arise when one tries to contextualise discourse by relating it to non-discursive actions such as mobilising a crowd or organising a faction and seeking evidence for the scope and intensity of such actions. I borrow these two terms from Gorski, who agrees that one must find ways of gauging the broader significance of discourse. By 'intensity' Gorski refers to a continuum which extends from discourse to movements, then political parties, and finally to regimes. The point is a good one, though I would place 'regimes' second on that continuum. 'National' monarchies avail themselves of national language under specific and controlled conditions before movements beyond governmental control take up such language.[74] I would also conflate movements and parties; the latter are often best understood as movements shaped by specific institutional constraints such as parliamentary elections. The last term in the continuum should be 'state', meaning not the intentional values of those holding governmental power but the ways in which state institutions are described and legitimised.

By 'scope' Gorski means a continuum stretching from intellectual elites through social elites and 'middling groups' to the 'common people'. Again I accept the general idea but modify specific terms, moving from establishment to oppositional elites to middling groups and finally to common people. In the pre-modern period 'intellectuals' were part of a clerical-aristocratic elite associated with the ruling order; 'intellectuals' in the modern sense of the term are linked to the emergence of oppositional elites.[75]

Having outlined these useful ways of contextualising national discourse, Gorski abandons them and focuses entirely on discourse, using elaborate analogies about how discourses are 'woven' and employing Foucauldian terms of analysis. However, what happens if one introduces into the analysis the notions of intensity and scope Gorski had earlier considered important?

I will crudely create two indices on a 1–4 basis, using my modified version of Gorski's scales of intensity and scope. The weakest form of nationalism has a score of 2: pure discourse confined to establishment elites. The strongest form of nationalism has a score of 8: state institutions described and legitimised in a national language which appeals to the common people.

There are many weak cases in the pre-modern period. In a few pre-modern cases, like late medieval England, where national language appealed to middling groups, the score might occasionally rise to 3, even 4. Only in the Reformation are national ideas taken up by movements which occasionally mobilise non-elite support. The index might rise to 4 or 5. Only after the post-1789 period do we obtain higher scores of 6 to 8.

This *is* crude. Sometimes, however, there is virtue in crudity. Sophisticated analyses of texts displaying the 'discourse' of nationalism can overlook the point that we study nationalism because of its *political* significance.[76] To be politically significant such discourses must be taken up by movements, appeal to different social groups and help re-order political power. Cases which score 2 on this crude index do not qualify as politically significant. The clustering of higher scores for the post-1789 period demonstrates that modernists are right to insist against post-modernism on the need to contextualise national discourse and against perennialism on the modernity of politically significant national discourse.

CONNECTING THE PRE-MODERN TO THE MODERN

Nothing is completely new or the same as what went before. In this sense arguments about 'continuity' and 'discontinuity' are vacuous. No political concept is constructed *ab nihilo*. This seems especially true of nationalist discourse which draws on past motifs to insist on the historicity of the nation. Looked at in this way it is impossible to dispute perennialist or ethno-symbolic arguments. There will always be *something* in the pre-modern period – language, rituals, names, customs – which resembles or is continuous with national language, rituals, names and customs in the modern period.

The real issue is that of *connection*. *How* do pre-modern discourses, forms of action, senses of identity, relate to modern ones? It is insufficient to consider each of these elements in isolation. People use language as part of some larger project; they acquire a sense of themselves in relation to roles they play and interests they pursue. To detach discourse from action, identity from role, is to mystify. One must start with one subject – say the use of national terms in certain documents or the function of appeals to the nation in political movements – but to make sense of that subject one needs to go beyond it. So my question becomes: how do pre-modern uses of terms like 'nation' connect to modern uses? In particular, given the central concern of this book, my question is: how do pre-modern uses of the term 'nation' relate to the project of gaining or using power and how does that connect to modern uses of the term for the same purpose?

To answer this question one must make clear the significance of the pre-modern/modern distinction. Just to select a moment (the middle of the eighteenth century, 1789, the start of the nineteenth century) and connect that to some event (industrialisation, the French Revolution, reaction to Napoleon) is insufficient. The particular event can never bear the weight of explanation placed upon it. My point of departure is rather to see these various events within the context of a societal transformation which I call modernisation.[77]

Modernisation re-orders the institutional means by which societies carry out the operations which enable them to survive and replicate. Producing and raising children, making and exchanging goods and services, exercising political and military power, creating and communicating agreed know-ledge of society and nature: these tasks are taken up by more functionally specialised institutions than existed in pre-modern societies. Such institutions include the nuclear family; the market-oriented firm; the elected parliament and/or professional bureaucracy; armed forces based on profes-sional volunteers or universal conscription; universal and compulsory schooling; universities with research and teaching functions; print media extending from mass circulation newspapers to specialised journals. These replace, marginalise or transform such institutions as guilds; corporations; manorial and common lands; personal monarchy; monopolistic estab-lished churches; peasant armies officered by aristocrats.

This is not a simple, instantaneous or invariant transformation but a complex, protracted and variable one. In some cases there is an extensive period of gradual institutional change; in others such change comes about rapidly. Usually one or another element of modernisation takes the leading role: rapid mechanisation in parts of England; the sudden emergence of mass politics in France; the imposition of bureaucratic rule in Napoleonic Germany. As a consequence, the way in which nationalism develops varies.

Such a transformation alters the way political power is understood and justified. The state becomes an impersonal set of institutions controlling a sharply defined territory which is legitimated in terms of the interests and views of those it rules. Between the middle of the eighteenth century and the late nineteenth century the idea of democracy moved from the political margins to become the dominant political creed, the fiction to which states must subscribe. States enveloped those they ruled with border controls and surveillance techniques.[78] The idea of the nation ceased to be an ethnographic label for barbarians or the political self-description of kingdoms. It became the claim that whole societies were nations entitled to their own states. This idea was used by oppositions claiming to represent the nation and demanding institutional and/or boundary changes. Specialised institutions, such as political parties and a political press, appealed to a broad range of social groups, addressing them as the 'nation'. States took up the call, using new mass institutions such as schools to present their version of the idea.

Precisely how the doctrines, politics and sentiments of nationalism developed in particular cases requires specific investigation. The concept of modernisation is not a formula which can dispense with historical research; rather it is a framework to enable research into particular cases as well as systematic comparison between cases.

No one seriously disputes that much of modern nationalism is peculiar to the modern period. The question is rather of how far modern nationalism builds upon earlier ideas of the nation. Once one is clear about the scale and kinds of difference between pre-modern and modern ideas of the nation, it is easier to focus on this question.

We need to consider principally what political uses the idea of the nation serves and how the idea can be produced and diffused and transmitted from one generation to another.

I have argued that the pre-modern national idea, insofar as it was an idea with political significance, operated in two different ways: ethnographic and political. The first use developed on the borders between different societies, framed as the contrast between civilised and barbaric. It was sustained through continued separation. If and when English-origin settler groups began to inter-marry with indigenous Welsh or Irish groups, and the two groups began to imitate each other's ways of life, so the contrasts would diminish. In Ireland, for example, the development of 'old English' institutions could lead to political uses of the idea of the nation, now portrayed as 'Ireland'.[79] There was a constant tendency for the ethnographic contrast to become weaker. In the modern era nationalists would return to these earlier ethnographies and appropriate them for contemporary usage but this followed a period of diminished usage.

The political concept was different. As a monarchical idea it served as a political self-description. Courts, parliaments and established Churches proclaimed the idea. One can see how this idea could be transmitted institutionally across generations. The idea could even become contested, as when aristocratic elites defended their prerogatives on 'national' grounds against the crown, and the crown justified its attempts to overcome such prerogatives by appealing to subjects beyond the elite. Nevertheless, the idea remained political and subordinate to the institutions associated with monarchy: courts, aristocrat-dominated assemblies, territorial Churches.[80]

A rupture with these political patterns came with the Reformation, in particular with appeals to the 'people' as the collective bearer of true Christian values, the new Israelites in a world of corruption and sin. The crushing of the radical Reformation stopped this notion of the Elect Nation providing a political alternative to monarchical rule, although there remained a significant, often underground legacy. Echoes of the radical idea were taken up by existing regimes: for example, the conceit of a Protestant British nation fighting against foreign Catholic powers.

The modern and enduring transformation of the national idea into one of a 'whole society' understood not as ethnographic category but as political actor was usually the work of political opposition. This involved detaching the national idea from dominant institutions. This new idea combined national labelling with demands for reformed political institutions.

The results are complex. Attempts to distinguish between civic and ethnic or cultural and political nationalism fail in the face of this complexity.[81] Political groups tried to retain older associations of the national idea, combining these with new arguments about language or customs having a political significance. The range of possible combinations is bewildering, and any coherent political ideology had to ignore or marginalise most possible associations.[82] What remains common to all modern nationalist discourses is that the nation is a 'whole society' and is no longer ideologically subordinate to any other idea. That is linked to its appeal for popular support, if necessary directed against existing authority, and to the claim that the nation can provide the justification for reformed political institutions.

These new ideological uses of the concept of the nation are taken up by a broad range of institutions, including elite institutions of the pre-modern period, a popular print media, specialised political movements, schools and cultural associations, town councils and economic interest groups. Such institutions may seize upon some earlier names and practices but they do so in transformative ways. Equally they may repudiate earlier ideas, as in revolutionary France. Perennialists stress *similarity* as the principal form of *connection,* ethno-symbolists stress *continuity.* The modernist emphasis is upon *transformation* and connection is understood as *appropriation.* That one nationalist movement is dominated by a rhetoric of modernity and another by a rhetoric of the archaic does not suggest to the modernist an essential difference, but rather poses the question of why similar movements take up different postures to an imagined past. Clearly the 'real' nature of that past matters in the sense that (modern) notions of evidence and reason impose limits on what can be claimed. It is important that there were earlier usages of national terms, ethnographic and political. But that is all. Just as building materials limit the range of possible buildings but do not determine (or make it possible to predict) just what building will be constructed, so do historical legacies relate to political ideologies.

The recurrence of particular words in pre-modern and modern discourses does not establish significant similarities or continuities between those discourses. Similarities in the *functions* of words are what matter. Words associated with the idea of the nation were deployed in various discourses in medieval England and Reformation Europe and modernists, including myself, must recognise this. There are interesting and important accounts to be written about pre-modern notions of national ideas which can tell us much about the mentalities and politics of the societies involved. Many of the essays in this book do precisely that.

However, only by ignoring the limited, distinct, changing and discontinuous uses to which those words were put, and paying insufficient attention to the institutions and interests which produced and reproduced those ideas, can one simply match words in the pre-modern discourses with the same or similar words in modern discourses to produce false notions of similarity and continuity. Matching does not establish comparability of meaning or significance of national terms or of the institutional processes of transmission of such terms. Under conditions of modernity these are transformed. Connection with pre-modern usages takes the form of appropriating old terms for new purposes, not of repeating or building upon the earlier meanings of those terms. Furthermore, where a demand for modern national terms exists, it can be supplied even if there are no older terms conveniently available.

The modernist approach to nationalism remains the most effective one. However, modernists have been too sweeping in their dismissal of the significance of pre-modern ideas of the nation. The major contribution perennialists and ethno-symbolists have made to the study of nationalism is that of compelling modernists to improve upon their arguments.

NOTES

1 I take these quotations from Anthony D. Smith, *Chosen Peoples: Sacred Sources of National Identity* (Oxford University Press, 2003), pp. 24–5.
2 T. C. W. Blanning, *The Culture of Power and the Power of Culture: Old Regime Europe 1660–1789* (Oxford University Press, 2002), p. 17.
3 This is a common and easy approach. Turville-Petre furnishes another favourite 'nationalist' quote, John of Gaunt's speech on 'this sceptred isle' in *Richard II*. Thorlac Turville-Petre, *England the Nation: Language, Literature, and National Identity, 1290–1340* (Oxford University Press, 1996), p. 4, which tells us little about nationalism and nothing about the late fourteenth century.
4 S. Grosby, 'Religion and nationality in Antiquity', *European Journal of Sociology* 33 (1991), 229–65; Patrick Wormald, 'The eternal Angle', *Times Literary Supplement*, 16 March 2001, 3–4.
5 Anthony D. Smith, *Nationalism and Modernism: a Critical Survey of Recent Theories of Nations and Nationalism* (London: Routledge, 1998); Adrian Hastings, *The Construction of Nationhood: Ethnicity, Religion and Nationalism* (Cambridge University Press, 1997).
6 A good recent survey of arguments about English national identity which includes a review of the arguments for the medieval and early modern periods is Krishnan Kumar, *The Making of English National Identity* (Cambridge University Press, 2003), chs. 3–5.
7 Different medievalists place the 'moment' of emergence of national identity in one or other of these periods, for example Wormald in pre-Conquest England, Gillingham in the Anglo-Norman period, Clanchy and Prestwich in the thirteenth century, Jones and Allmand in the period of the Hundred Years War. Predictably, historians tend to make 'their' period the crucial one. For Wormald see his essay in this volume and note 4 above. For the others see: John Gillingham, *The English in the Twelfth Century: Imperialism, National Identity and Political Values* (Woodbridge: Boydell, 2000), esp. the essays in Part 2; M. T. Clanchy, *England and its Rulers 1066–1272: Foreign Lordship and National Identity* (London: Fontana, 1983), pp. 241–62; Michael Prestwich, *English Politics in the Thirteenth Century* (Basingstoke: Macmillan, 1990), ch. 5; W. R. Jones, 'The English church and royal propaganda during the Hundred Years War', *Journal of British Studies* 19 (1979), 18–30; Christopher Allmand, *The Hundred Years War: England and France at War c. 1300–c. 1450* (Cambridge University Press, 1988), esp. ch. 6.
8 See Wormald, 'Eternal Angle', for such an example.

9 For a recent constructionist approach applied generally to early medieval Europe see Patrick J. Geary, *The Myth of Nations: The Medieval Origins of Europe* (Princeton University Press, 2002).

10 D. Rollason, 'Bede's *Ecclesiastical History of the English People*', *The Historian* 73 (2002), 7.

11 Ibid. There is no consensus on just how Bede used his key term 'Angli'. Nicholas Brooks, *Bede and the English*, Jarrow Lecture ([s.l.]: [s.n.], 1999).

12 Bede wrote extensively on the measurement of time, and the construction of calendars, used a single chronological system in his *Ecclesiastical History*, and contributed to the debate on how Easter was to be dated.

13 This happened to the only chief David Livingstone 'converted'. Livingstone subsequently reversed the Bedan approach: make Africans more like the British and Christian conversion could be achieved. Andrew Ross, *David Livingstone: Mission and Empire* (London: Hambledon, 2002).

14 Brooks, *Bede and the English*, p. 5.

15 N. Brooks, 'English Identity from Bede to the Millennium', *Journal of the Haskins Society* 14 (2004), 33–51.

16 S. Reynolds, *Kingdoms and Communities in Western Europe, 900–1300* (2nd edn, Oxford: Clarendon Press, 1997), esp. ch. 8. Nevertheless, I think the claims made by Reynolds for a widespread sense of English identity in late Anglo-Saxon times go beyond what the evidence will reasonably bear.

17 See Sarah Foot, 'The making of *Angelcynn*: English identity before the Norman Conquest', *Transactions of the Royal Historical Society* 6th ser., 6 (1996), 25–49.

18 Ibid., 49. The quotation at the end is from Bishop Wulfsige.

19 Brooks, 'English identity'.

20 The passage merits quoting at length. 'In ... [1087], when the Normans had fulfilled the just will of the Lord upon the English people, and there was scarcely a noble of English descent in England, but all had been reduced to servitude and lamentation, *and it was even disgraceful to be called English*, William, the agent of this vengeance, ended his life. For *God had chosen the Normans to wipe out the English nation*, because he had seen that they surpassed all other people in their unparalleled savagery' (emphases added). Diana E. Greenway, *Henry of Huntingdon: The History of the English People 1000–1154* (Oxford: Clarendon Press, 2002), p. 31.

21 I have not had time to consult Hugh M. Thomas, *The English and the Normans: Ethnic Hostility, Assimilation and Identity, 1066–c. 1220* (Oxford University Press, 2003), but drew much profit from the review of this book by R. R. Davies in *English Historical Review* 118 (2003), 1308–10.

22 I follow John Gillingham, 'The beginnings of English imperialism', in Gillingham, *The English in the Twelfth Century*.

23 Len Scales in his very useful comments on a draft of this essay stressed the importance, throughout the medieval period, of the Old Testament culture of the nation. However, the projects of *conversion* or *expansion* make it difficult to equate Bede and Alfred with the self-centred Old Testament focus on one people seeking to survive and to sustain their faith against permanently alien

and hostile pagans. It is also difficult to equate with the rhetoric of Roman Christianity, a supra-ethnic faith and institution.

24 James Campbell, *The Anglo-Saxon State* (London: Hambledon, 2000). See the essay by Foot in this volume for a criticism of Campbell's use of the concept 'state' in the term 'nation-state'. My concern is with the other half of the term.

25 It is not enough to locate texts with names such as 'English' to support claims concerning national identity; one must also show that these names play a central role in social practices which produce and transmit national identity. If, for example, one found the name 'English' being used at a local level, say in county-level institutions, one would still need to be cautious about claiming that the term indicated a sense of identity above the level of the county. To make that case one would need to show similar usages across a range of such local institutions which also were in communication with each other. There must be tests of this kind or one can make claims for national identity on the basis of any encounter with words like 'nation'.

26 There is a tendency to equate 'England' at any moment with the situation in the south-east of the country. That is not a vice confined to medieval historians.

27 By the seventeenth century there are many more recent developments which could account for such a sense of national identity.

28 Benedict Anderson, *Imagined Communities: Reflections on the Origins and Spread of Nationalism* (revised edn, London: Verso, 1991).

29 Gillingham, 'Beginnings of English imperialism'. Robin Frame, in his essay in this volume, makes a similar point about the 'Old English' in Ireland in a way that suggests parallels with white settlers in modern colonies whose 'national' identity is as much an assertion against the mother country as it is against the indigenous people of the colony.

30 Greenway, *Henry of Huntingdon*.

31 Clanchy, *England and its Rulers*, pp. 241–2. Clanchy's later accounts of the Battle of Lincoln (1217) and the civil strife of 1258–64 show just how 'un-English' was the consciousness of many of those subsequently seen as fighting for national independence or liberty.

32 'The context and purposes of Geoffrey of Monmouth's *History of the Kings of Britain*', in Gillingham, *The English in the Twelfth Century*, pp. 19–40. I accept that such arguments on their own are too narrow to account fully for the national identity arguments encountered in such texts, but they do draw attention to the importance of particular, changing and contingent influences which shape such arguments.

33 The earlier use of English verse form suggests texts designed to be read aloud to illiterate elite figures who spoke English as their native tongue.

34 It would make more sense to imagine that the Normans used the term 'English' in its ethnic sense to refer to those they ruled.

35 Hastings, *Construction of Nationhood*, makes the strong point that a written vernacular is a powerful force for the development of a sense of national identity. It fixes and standardises language; a purely oral language in

pre-industrial societies is bound to diverge into a number of dialects, often mutually incomprehensible. Add widespread literacy and the basis for bringing together popular and oral with elite and written language is created. English is the first language where all of this comes together. However, this only starts to happen at the very earliest in the fourteenth century. This makes it all the more puzzling that Hastings argues for any widespread or significant sense of national identity before the fourteenth century.

36 For one transient meaning, see Clanchy, *England and its Rulers*, ch. 10 on 'English' objections to Henry III's 'foreign' brothers. Clanchy notes that the Latin term used for 'native people' was *viros naturalis*, avoiding the word *nativus* with its connotations of the common or vulgar people. This is a very limited, clique usage.

37 Gillingham, *The English in the Twelfth Century*; R. R. Davies, *The First English Empire: Power and Identities in the British Isles, 1093–1343* (Oxford University Press, 2000).

38 Although the stress is usually upon conquest and subjection and the establishment of enclaves of settlers, rather than a civilising mission.

39 The general organisation of society has implications for the manners and morals of the whole of that society, but explicit comparisons remain confined to elite levels. Norbert Elias saw this period as marking the origins of the notion of elite cultural and moral improvement as a civilising process: Norbert Elias, *The Civilizing Process: the History of Manners* (Oxford: Blackwell, 1978).

40 Gillingham, 'Beginnings of English imperialism'. Davies, *First English Empire*, argues that the political use of ethnographic categories was strongest when English kings sought control over the British Isles as a whole and faded along with that project.

41 These are tendencies rather than separate discourses. Any political propaganda directed against a foreign enemy is bound to emphasise the enemy's foreignness. However, in the case of the French the stress was on 'effeminacy' (an excess of civilisation) rather than 'savagery' (not civilised enough), rather like some of the Scottish images of the English. (The trend continues in recent films like *Braveheart* where most of the English male characters are portrayed as refined, sadistic and gay.)

42 Reynolds, *Kingdoms and Communities*, esp. ch. 8.

43 Allmand, *Hundred Years War*, p. 103.

44 Ibid., p. 115.

45 Shakespeare's characters make sense only in terms of the proto-nationalism of his time and of which he was the greatest exponent. In *Henry V* ethnic stereotyping functions to *deny* links between ethnicity and political loyalty. In the early fifteenth century ethnic stereotypes were terms of abuse applied to enemies, not a positive way of depicting a multi-ethnic nation. These are very different ways of connecting together ethnicity, political allegiance and the common people, both of them in turn unlike modern ethnic nationalist ideology. It is these differences we should explore, not the superficial continuity of using the same names.

46 Allmand, *Hundred Years War*, pp. 109–10.

47 Henry's son, Henry VI, was crowned king of France.

48 Thus an impersonal notion of 'kingdom' developed in hereditary as well as elective monarchies. See the essay by Robert Frost on elective kingship, this volume.

49 Jones, 'The English church and royal propaganda'.

50 I elaborate on this point in the next section.

51 Antony Black, *Political Thought in Europe 1250–1450* (Cambridge: Cambridge University Press, 1992). Len Scales drew my attention to this study.

52 Just one more example. In a major edited work of just over 800 pages, J. H. Burns (ed.), *The Cambridge History of Medieval Political Thought c. 350–c. 1450* (Cambridge University Press, 1988), there are just eight short references to 'nation' and cognate terms. All those for the period before 1100 (pp. 137, 141, 163, 176, 244) are concerned to deny the significance of the national. A couple of passages suggest that the rise of stronger territorial polities *weakened* the role of ethnicity in political identity, by undermining the idea of personal ties between chiefs and their followings which in turn were legitimised by descent myths (p. 244). It is also argued that the term *gens* should not be seen as ethnic (p. 137). Post-1100 references (pp. 351–2, 479, 481–2) do include references to peoples as divided by race, climate and customs (p. 481), but only to add that this was a polemical argument used to fend off English claims to the French crown. Even in a passage arguing for the crystallisation of national identity around certain polities in the thirteenth century (pp. 351–2), the writer states: 'In Europe in the period up to 1450 a genuine relationship between the nation and the state can be found only in England, France and Bohemia' (J. P. Canning, in the essay introducing the section of the book on the period 1150–1450).

53 Black, *Political Thought*, p. 3, suggests why: political theorists were more interested in what should be than what actually was. Nevertheless, they were interested in ideal versions of what actually existed, such as universal monarchy (an ideal version of the Holy Roman Empire), or an ideal solution to the problem of the relationship between the papacy and secular authority.

54 The actual word 'state', used roughly as we use it, was unknown until the late fifteenth century. *Civitas, res publica, regnum*, all with different and varying meanings, were the main terms used.

55 See Black, *Political Thought*, p. 65.

56 Len Scales has pointed out to me the ubiquity of assemblies in medieval Europe, down to the hundred court in England, and the centrality of the urban market place as a site where many people came together and discussed matters of common concern and where public pronouncements were made. Nevertheless, market gossip and grumbles and the work of humble courts are not capable of creating a 'public' culture. In the territorial monarchy (clearly things were different in zones of city-states or peasant republics) authoritative institutions were formal and closed, places of broader and more open participation lacked authority beyond the locality. It is precisely when this division

between central and local power breaks down that the 'nation' becomes a significant political category.

57 Davies, *First English Empire*, pp. 1–3.

58 There may be some examples to the contrary, for example the Hussites, though I think this is the exception which proves the rule. See František Šmahel, 'The idea of the "nation" in Hussite Bohemia', *Historica* 6 (1969), 143–247 and 17 (1970), 93–197; Thomas A. Fudge, *The Magnificent Ride: The First Reformation in Hussite Bohemia* (Aldershot: Ashgate, 1998).

59 I do not mean that the nation is not imagined to 'act', as indicated in the title of a chronicle which Len Scales has drawn to my attention – *God's Deeds Done by the Franks*. But the 'Franks' are an elite, led by a chief or king, and assumed to share the ambitions of their leader. Such a concept cannot be transferred to a stable territorial polity and the subject population.

60 Ernest Gellner, *Nations and Nationalism* (Oxford: Blackwell, 1983).

61 G. R. Elton, 'Parliament in the sixteenth century: functions and fortunes', *The Historical Journal* 22 (1979), 255–78.

62 For the 'invention' of this argument, one incidentally which breaks with Bede's linkage between the English and Roman Christianity, see Edwin Jones, *The English Nation: the Great Myth* (Stroud: Sutton, 1998).

63 I argue this point at length in the Conclusion to John Breuilly, *Nationalism and the State* (2nd edn, Manchester University Press, 1993).

64 I draw especially upon Patrick Collinson, 'England', in R. Scribner *et al.* (eds.), *The Reformation in National Context* (Cambridge University Press, 1994), pp. 80–94.

65 For example, Hastings, *Construction of Nationhood*, pp. 58–59. The most recent citation of this kind I have encountered is Anthony Marx, *Faith in Nation: Exclusionary Origins of Nationalism* (Oxford University Press, 2003), pp. 62–3.

66 Since originally writing this paragraph I attended a session on Foxe at the Reformation conference held in Birmingham in April 2004 at which papers were presented by Tom Freeman, Elizabeth Evenden and John Craig. I drew various conclusions from these papers, including the following: after 1570 the regime did not press churches to acquire copies; the reception history is complex and does not support any 'national' argument; even from the point of view of its 'author' (though Foxe was more a constantly revising editor) the book cannot be construed in 'national' terms. This was a central thesis in William Haller, *Foxe's 'Book of Martyrs' and the Elect Nation* (London: Cape, 1967), on which Hastings and Smith draw. For many of these recent arguments see Patrick Collinson, 'John Foxe and national consciousness', in Christopher Highley and John N. King (eds.), *John Foxe and his World* (Aldershot: Ashgate, 2002), pp. 10–34.

67 Philip S. Gorski, 'The mosaic moment: An early modernist critique of modernist theories of nationalism', *American Journal of Sociology* 105 (2000), 1428–68. Marx, *Faith in Nation*, only came to my attention as I was finishing this essay. This ambitious comparative study of early modern Spain, France

and England argues for the mobilisation of national sentiments, primarily through the exclusionary use of confessional identities. The material on such uses is interesting but I do not find it persuasive to treat measures to enforce unity of *belief* (not language or custom or assumed descent), such as the revocation of the Edict of Nantes in 1685, as examples of national(ist) sentiment.

68 Gorski, 'Mosaic moment', 1433.

69 I use here the term coined by Hobsbawm, another modernist who recognises that aspects of nationalism are to be encountered in Reformation Europe. I argued something similar in Breuilly, *Nationalism and the State*, pp. 76–81.

70 Ethnicity (Dutch against Spanish) was unimportant compared to a political conception of the nation as those who follow the true God.

71 The Orange case is more like the English medieval identification of nation with dynasty which I have already considered.

72 For a recent study on the language of nation in *ancien régime* France, see David A. Bell, *The Cult of the Nation in France: Inventing French Nationalism, 1680–1800* (Cambridge, MA: Harvard University Press, 2001).

73 For a more general treatment of post-modernist approaches to nationalism see Smith, *Nationalism and Modernism*, esp. ch. 9.

74 Len Scales makes the point that this could too easily make monarchs the authors of nations and medieval political cultures into simple representations of monarchical values. I would not seek to argue that every usage of the term nation should be seen in this way; doubtless different writers and interests drawn from the Church, law, the nobility, have their own concerns. However, I do not see these as in any significant way using the nation as a *counter* to monarchy, or deploying it in oppositional movements.

75 On the modernity of such an intelligentsia see Elie Kedourie, *Nationalism* (London: Hutchinson, 1960); Bernhard Giessen, *Intellectuals and the German Nation: Collective Identity in an Axial Age* (Cambridge University Press, 1998).

76 Furthermore, as it becomes politically significant, the discourse of nationalism itself is changed. The development of collective action in pursuit of state power clarifies and institutionally fixes nationalist ideology.

77 I have outlined this argument elsewhere. See, for example, J. Breuilly, 'Napoleonic Germany and state-formation', in Michael Rowe (ed.), *Collaboration and Resistance in Napoleonic Europe: State Formation in an Age of Upheaval, c. 1800–1815* (London: Palgrave, 2003), pp. 121–52.

78 These should not be seen as impositions from above but as part of a broad societal change. Labour movements agitated for factory and other inspectorates; progressive income tax and income redistribution by means of selective benefits require a large amount of reliable information on earnings; compulsory education and universal health care call for massive documentation.

79 See the essay by McBride in this volume.

80 On some occasions the ethnographic and political ideas could be combined, above all when one or other of the parties in an inter-state conflict could draw upon some ethnographic label to apply to their opponents. I sometimes think

that much of the medieval case for nationalism consists of taking these infrequent cases and suggesting they were normal.

81 A fine recent study of the mix of ideas in German nationalist discourse in the middle of the nineteenth century which brings out the inadequacy of these distinctions is Brian E. Vick, *Defining Germany: The 1848 Frankfurt Parliamentarians and National Identity* (Cambridge, MA: Harvard University Press, 2002).

82 This is another way of making Renan's point; nationalists have to forget as well as remember much of 'their' history. Perennialists and ethno-symbolists forget the need to forget.

PART II

The Middle Ages

CHAPTER 4

Germanic power structures: the early English experience

Patrick Wormald

I will begin this paper, and open a conference that seems designed to provoke, as provocatively as I can. This Realm of England is now the most enduring polity in recorded history. Significantly disturbed by a mere two decades of ultimately largely abortive revolutionary change from 1640 to 1660, and as little affected in essence by the additions or subtractions of 1284, 1536, 1603, 1707, 1801, 1922 and 1998, its longevity as such is unmatched even by that of China or Japan. Rather than further defend that proposition, however, I shall devote my time to a no less teasing question: not whether but *how*? Our debate, I take it, is about the way that power was exercised in a series of societies through time and space, and the extent to which this reflected any sort of 'national' will. Regrettably, therefore, my paper must begin by reviewing definitions – or perhaps I should say, understandings – of 'power' in historical study, and I shall in effect leave 'nation' to the others. I only hope that I, and indeed those others, will prove able to contribute a bit more than semantic discussion to this debate.[1]

Power is the staple of modern historical discourse – whether within family, village, religious community, or polity itself. It falls naturally from our lips as a *datum*. Yet, when asked quite what they *mean* by power, historians can look shifty. The answer is clear enough in one sense: power consists in a regime's ability to get people to do what it wants, whether or not *they* want. But granted that, *how does it manage this*? If power is a fact, what *makes* it a fact? Wherein consists the capacity to exert command, to exact obedience? If our answer is force or the threat of force, the blades and projectiles of a government's arsenal or the venom of its inside knowledge, how do we explain their efficacy when no western army or police force from 395 to 1789 (or 1917) had the actual resources to use coercion or intelligence against vastly more numerous subjects? Are we then thrown back on the seemingly lame notion of 'consensus', against which Foucault warned us at such not uncharacteristic length?[2]

I suggest that the levers of power are perceived by historians as broadly three. The first is the one most instantly recognisable to us moderns: institutions. People do things because the structures in which they are voluntarily or involuntarily enrolled expect it of them. In the ancient city-states liable for raising an emperor's taxes, it was not so much the usually distant threat of a legionary visitation as pressure from fellow-citizens on the city council that encouraged delinquents to pay up, in that the relevant burden would otherwise fall disproportionately on them. Importantly, we know this mainly through the fat files of imperial replies to whingeing cities preserved in the late Roman Codes: power was registered in response.[3] Second is patronage: at its crudest, mutual back-scratching. People obey because of what they get out of it from their master. Obedience earns reward, disobedience instant discountenance – or worse.[4] Third, more elusively but nowadays most fashionably, there is charisma. A ruler is obeyed through striking awe – not just fear but majesty, a sense that it is *they who must be obeyed*.[5] In the Middle Ages and often thereafter, saints and indeed their *imagines* of course had this quality too.

There is obviously any amount of overlap between these categories. What was a later Roman emperor if not charismatic, commanding though he did the largest military force seen in history before 'les armées de la Révolution'? Saints, royal or otherwise, had nothing if not charisma, but they had institutional power too, built up from their wealth, which they could use to attract and keep followings. We cannot break down power into my three neat constituents, however the balance between them might vary in any one instance. Nonetheless, I contend that our inimitable legacy from ancient civilisation has formed in our minds a polarity, whereby institutional rule is *modern, efficient*, in a word civilised, whereas patronage and charisma modes are *traditional*, ultimately *inefficient* (and/or corrupt), and so in the last resort 'barbaric'. I shall suggest that the understanding of early English history has been consistently misrepresented as a result. There was always a rigorous (though not rigid) institutional structure in early England – and throughout much of the West – which made its very predatoriness possible, and on which charisma sat like a gloss.

It is all a matter, I think, of angles – or perhaps 'voices'. Start Old English history with Bede, with *Beowulf*, or with the Laws, and you get three very different early Englands: the proof being the vastly contrasting tones of three very great books: Stenton's *Anglo-Saxon England*, Chadwick's *Heroic Age* and Stubbs's *Constitutional History*.[6] My contention is that Bedan and Beowulfian perspectives have eclipsed the less memorably documented structures of Old English government and society. Indeed, historians have hardly known what to *do* with these records, especially (strangely) when they begin to look more familiar after 900.[7] The essential foundation of almost all else is thereby missed. Without his revenues, services and indeed office, Byrhtnoth could have made no 'Last Stand' at Maldon.[8] We would have no New Minster charter, with its unforgettable frontispiece of King Edgar prostrate below Christ in Glory, without the resources ruthlessly harnessed by Bishop Æthelwold of Winchester.[9] Yet it is where wealth and power were garnered and concentrated that historians have looked least hard, because they have either not known what to look for, or hardly dared to believe what they found. They have thus ignored the footings of human history's most enduring – and west of China, arrogant – political culture. We have studied branches and flowers, when we could and should have examined roots.

I must start, however, with a bit more about the other two possible levers of power, and charisma first. The ceremonial of medieval majesty (or saintliness) undoubtedly made a profound impression on the ruled, and had done since way back into Antiquity and before. A triumphal arch, a statue, even an exquisitely etched coin, reminded Roman citizens of what was special about their ruler – as did the furniture, relics included, of the equivalent power of saints and their deputies on earth. These images were created and beautified to mark rulers out from the ordinary, and so to imply (to say the least) the duty and desirability of honouring and obeying them. Ancient Ruler ceremonial was enhanced in the early Middle Ages by emergent rituals of unction and coronation, derived respectively from Israel and from Rome. The inviolability of the 'Lord's Anointed' was stressed in a Franco-English context by the papal legates' 'capitulary' of 786, which can hardly be unconnected with the unction of Offa's son in the following year.[10] At this stage, the headgear was probably a helmet (like the memorable artefact from Sutton Hoo?), but crowns appear by the 920s at the latest. Solemn crown-wearings, as laden with religious ritual as with banqueting and boozing, were a feature of Carolingian, Ottonian and above all Anglo-Norman monarchy, but also go as far back as the earlier ninth century in England, so their appearance coincides with the date of the earliest English coronation *ordo*.[11] We may take it that there was logic in all this: to make a king look more commanding made him theoretically more secure. But before we go too much further down that line, let us pause. However much Kingston coronations boosted Ecgberht's dynasty, Tamworth crown-wearings did not save the Mercian monarchy from political oblivion. Only a few, admittedly politically very important, monks would be lucky enough to catch a glimpse of the glorious New Minster charter. For the rest, there were not even the sort of mass-produced copies in which Romans specialised. Even the most solemn emperor could barely be sighted riding on in majesty from a window or pavement – unless of course one were burdened with the not-always-welcome job of entertaining him and his voracious court: that is *institutionally* obligated. Leyser's idea that 'sacrality was a substitute for inadequate or failing institutions' fits his own superb account of the sheer superficiality of Ottonian institutional apparatus, but the argument frankly does not suit England, where a case can be made that Edgar was the most brutally formidable ruler before Edward I, or even Henry VIII.[12] I suspect that charisma was less a substitute for effective institutional government than, as I say, a gloss: a quality accorded to those whom society desired, even *needed*, to honour and obey, whether or not forced to.

So to my second category of power, lordship and patronage: what was not long ago known as the 'feudal mode' of government, and may be now more familiar as 'sleaze'.[13] Landlords could undoubtedly discipline their tenants or other more or less helpless dependants until yesterday, or indeed today. But what concerns us here is a relationship of kings and lords, or lords and knights/gentry (the *mot juste* is hopelessly elusive) tying people of real social significance into bonds imposing actual obligation. A lord afforded protection in court or social confrontation of any sort; followers (for want of a better word) offered support in the similar confrontations of their lords. Because of the unwarranted centrality of French history to that of Europe overall, this kind of relationship has come to be seen as the primeval feudal sludge from which real (i.e. institutional) royal government emerged. But how can this be reconciled with the evident role of lordship in Carolingian Francia, whose government institutions were no less evidently vigorous? After the emergence of high-quality weaponry and its appendant skills, each passed down a family, so perhaps from the Bronze, and certainly the Iron, Age select persons had the resources to dictate and draw on, by reward and its withdrawal, the behaviour of others with their own, at least local, significance, so carrying political weight both locally and in the realm at large. This would be as true in the age of the Pelhams as in that of the Warennes or Byrhtnoth. The functioning of pre-Gladstonian society is otherwise inconceivable. Lordship need not be 'feudal', i.e. tenurial. We are looking at lordship *tout simple*, with or without tenurial linkage; there need be nothing 'bastard' about it. To deny the importance of power like this, even when barely pre-modern, would be absurd. But we must ask: whence, other than from the strong arms with which to wield their pattern-welded swords, did lords draw their power? What structure upheld a nobility of birth? The answer is local government institutions, whether *pagus* in tenth-century France or shire in later medieval England.[14] Those with most capacity to disrupt or distort institutions were those who implicitly upheld them. Even privatised power arises from, and expresses itself through, 'public' apparatus.

Turning then to institutions, I shall approach from three or four noticeably oblique angles. In the nature of what and when I am talking about, I cannot *show* how things worked, but I can set out a few indications, a summons to contemplate what is implied by what we do know. First, an area far removed not only in time but in space. When the ethnographers and anthropologists of the late nineteenth and early twentieth centuries set out to investigate the social and political cultures of Africa and South America, their near-invariably classical education pre-disposed them to find situations from which European (i.e. Greco-Roman and, all due allowances being made, biblical) civilisation may have emerged but had long since diverged. They made much that was weird, even 'savage', in the world they researched intelligible to a self-congratulatory western culture: Nuer feuding, Shilluk divine kingship, Azande sorcery, 'tribes without rulers', and so on. But they also found what took them by surprise. In introducing their still invaluable anthology of *African Political Systems*, Fortes and Evans-Pritchard distinguished systems they characterised as Groups A and B. Those in 'A' 'have centralised authority, administrative machinery and judicial institutions – in short a government'; whereas those in Group 'B' 'lack centralised authority, administrative machinery, and constituted judicial institutions – in short . . . lack government'.[15] Societies of which educated westerners might expect nothing but 'savagery' (however, maybe, 'noble') can be singularly institution-minded. There is order as there almost always is in human societies, but in 'Group A' it has *form*.

To labour this point a little, I quote some more:

The people belonged to the king and he . . . took the fine in cases of assault or murder.
The dominant values of life were those of the warrior and they were satisfied in service at the king's [court] and in his wars. [Though] supposed to maintain the customary law . . . the king could in deciding a case create new law for what he and his council considered good reason.
The main duty owed the king was military service including labour service . . . In addition, it was customary to give him gifts of grain, beer, cattle and, some say, girls.
[Lords] had certain powers delegated to them by the king . . . [but] were bound to follow laws issued by the king and from them appeal lay to his court.

Orders to mobilise ... projected laws and matters of national import were announced to the people by the king through his [lords].

The State bulked large in people's lives.

The nation was a stable organization, [the king] symbolised [its] identity.

Conflict of loyalties to officials of different rank ... intriguing against one another, came into the open as a check upon misrule. Therefore, despite the apparent autocracy of king and lords, ultimately sovereignty in the state resided in the people.[16]

Again:

[A king] had the right to punish individuals by death, exile, beating, torture and cursing. He could confiscate the property of any of his subjects. He could prevent the execution of his people by his [lords] for criminal offences. In disputes involving two [kins], [he] alone could grant the right of blood revenge.

[At court] was a group of young men ... selected from among the sons of the prominent men in the kingdom [who] followed the [king] [around] the country. It was from these ... that the future [ministers] and [war leaders and tribute collectors] were selected.

Younger men were known as ... singers. They sang praise ... to the [king], amused him by wrestling, and accompanied him when ... hunting. Men older than these ... were known as the ... warriors, who accompanied the [king] on ... raids, acting as body-guard and messengers. Older men who had not received official positions from the king were known as ... councillors.

Near the meeting [hall] was a large beer-store and a number of smaller halls for visitors. When a large raid had been planned, the men who were going to take part in it gathered before the [hall] and swore ... to come back with [loot] or to die in the attempt. It was before [it] that every new [king] was invested with office, [and] cases of murder and treason were tried and punished. All important meetings were accompanied by beer-drinking.[17]

I submit that many historians might need a 'double-take' before realising that these are not accounts of government in pre- (and indeed post-) conquest England. They in fact describe that of the Zulus (who would give the British army its very own Little Big Horn in 1879), and of the Bayankole in Uganda, a not especially powerful people of Nilotic pastoralists. I made just a few verbal changes, such as 'lord' for 'chief' and 'king' for the Bayankole ruler, who is, believe it or not, called the 'Mugabe'. Both were 'conquest states' which did well out of slaving, just like pre-conquest England and its continental counterparts. Now, I am well aware of what 'post-colonial studies' regard as the 'pre-colonial fallacy': that in 'classical' anthropology, student and subject alike conspired to make 'traditional' societies look as European as possible. But that objection is undermined in this instance by the fact that Fortes and Evans-Pritchard described 'Group B' societies in this collection, yet presumably gave an editorial *fiat* to friends and colleagues producing 'Group A' accounts; and it was Max Gluckmann, responsible here for the *very* 'Group A' Zulu, who unveiled the 'Peace in the Feud' to the goggling eyes of the Anglophone legal historical establishment.[18] I deduce that even societies that had not got far if anywhere beyond 'Peace in the Feud' were nonetheless familiar with penal justice. We need not, then, hesitate to suppose that government could have been institutionalised before 1066, with or without written records.

These anthropological directions lead on to a second angle of approach. The landscape of Atlantic Europe is littered with monuments, dating well back into the Neolithic, bespeaking deployment of impressive resources. For reasons unclear to me, archaeologists tend to maintain that the steepling ramparts of Iron Age hill-forts were built by communities pooling their resources of materials and labour to provide refuge for all. I fail to see why they may not be initiatives by ruling lords, as no one doubts for either their post-Roman successors or immediately pre-Roman *oppida*. To go further back, Stonehenge and Newgrange may be just as much manifestations of power as the pyramids of Gaza or Yucatan. If this is not generally envisaged, is that not because we are no more willing to credit sophisticated institutions to Europe's 'savages' than to pre-colonial Africa? Yet Offa's Dyke, an enterprise in many ways comparable to megalithic structures, is unhesitatingly connected with the duty of fortification that first appears in his charters c. 770; and it probably appears then *not* because it was then new, but because churches now demanded documentary proof of exemption from *other* duties, and had the means to preserve parchment for posterity.[19] The historic and indeed prehistoric archaeology of Britain and the West are redolent of government, which is to say of *rules*. But these rules need not have been written down; and by the time we have gone as far back as mid-Iron-Age hill-forts, let alone Stonehenge's late-Neolithic, talk of lost documentation begins to sound rather silly. Enterprises of this order no more needed the (alleged) buttress of bureaucratic record than did the complex regulations of Zulu power. Such assumptions are functions of what I like to call the 'historical fallacy': nothing happens before we know about it, and nothing much happens without some sort of central direction. Since historians are by definition dependent on written evidence, and do much of their work in Record Offices, this is natural enough. But it is for all that another of the biasses we have inherited from our specifically Greco-Roman experience, which is to say the combination of the most actively literate society before modern times with the most effective professional army until no less recently. It should be obvious that it seriously impairs our vision of pre- and proto-historic change. And insofar as we have now learned to privilege the *longue durée*, we should on principle direct our gaze beyond the purely historical horizon, while at the same time accepting that drastic *événements* might in those unrecorded aeons have been occasioned by human agency just as much as by earthquakes, eruptions or asteroids.

In any case, it now looks as if some of pre-modern government's most basic institutions just *have* to be very old. A remarkable line of research by several younger archaeologists and onomasticians draws attention to places suggested by their names and topography, though seldom by actual records, to have been locations of popular (that is, numerically significant) assembly.[20] In England, a number of places are named with *-mot-* (Mutfod) or *-thing-* (Thingwall), each element meaning 'assembly': the latter occurs in Kentish laws (and in *Lex Salica* as *thunginus*, a local court official), as does *mæþl*, whence Matlock (and *Lex Salica mallus*).[21] Many of these elements combine with *low* or the like, meaning 'mound' (Mutlow, Thinghoe), evoking the tendency of assemblies to meet at or in the neighbourhood of a landmark that either was or was thought an ancestral barrow. That recalls the association of numerous Irish places of assembly or solemn political business (like royal inaugurations), with real or artificial tumuli. Emain Macha (Navan 'fort'), near Armagh, was deliberately constructed as a channel from this world to the Other in (dendrochronologically) 95 BC; it was the legendary 'capital' of Ulster, Ireland's northern 'fifth', and surely must somehow be linked with the later ecclesiastical prominence of Armagh. There is evidence that such sites were believed to house sinister forces (like Beowulf's dragon) in early England, as in Ireland they certainly were; hence, the ditch is on the *inside* of Navan's rampart, to keep nasties *in* rather than enemies out. But that did not discourage meetings in their locality. On the contrary, this sort of assembly was also the locale of fairs, racing human and equine (Berkshire's hundred of Ganfield is named from its 'game field', which may be found on a map), marriage marts and general jollification.

To sum up with two especially striking illustrations: a site in North Sweden has (1) a church, (2) a 'king's mound' just behind it, (3) a royal demesne farm, (4) runestones (often elsewhere recording nearby bridge-building – perhaps because the honorand had personally taken responsibility for what would otherwise have been a general burden, just as citizens had their bounty inscribed in Antiquity's cities); and (5) lastly, is connected with an iron ring (perhaps an oath-ring) engraved in runes of c. 800 invoking the *liuprettr* ('people's law'); it was indeed just here that the *thing* of the Hälsingar would pronounce its law code in 1314. The other site is of course the Isle of Man's Tynwald (meaning 'assembly-field'), still the annual meeting place of its authorities and populace. It is a probably pre-Norse focus for Man's government, as it is still, centrepiece of its six 'sheadings' (sixths), each marked by a name somehow indicating assembly (one a Neolithic tomb); and it meets, by the way, on 5 July, which is eleven days on from Midsummer Day, and thus reminds us of the now all-too-familiar calendrical relevance of prehistoric monumentation. To put the lid on all this, the early medieval assembly has a counterpart, recorded c. 1540, in Red Square.

My final angle comes from political vocabulary. At this stage, I can do no more than note (though I shall return to the theme soon) that languages belonging to the 'Indo-European' family share a number of words for political units.[22] Now, philologists are apt to warn us historians off their subject – nor are they a lot more friendly to each other. We do have to take their word for it (in the event that we were not already aware) that words change their meanings. But if we find that the meaning or connotations of what must once have been the same word seem to be similar across a range of languages which cannot have diverged any later than the earlier first millennium BC, it does not seem unreasonable for a mere historian to deduce that the phenomena they collectively represent are at least that old. This is indeed the case for the Indo-European vocabulary of rule. In Table 4.1 I tabulate a choice of words seeming to denote plural political entities.[23]

The first point to note is that only one of these series denotes an even notionally genetic or biological linkage (there are other series but without so significantly wide a spread). Latin *gens*, Old English *cynn* and their ilk would of course have great importance in European history, but *natio* and *patria* appear to be Latin coinages; and we might note, given its current vogue in discussions of these matters, that the same seems to go for Greek *ethnos* (which is also applied to swarms of bees). By contrast, there are three sets that go yet further across the spectrum, and which can only be rendered in terms of their social collectivity. Most interesting of all is a word that must originally have been something like *teuta*: the word that eventually produced *deutsch* (and by a different route *deuten*, 'to mean'). In Latin and a related Italic dialect, it metamorphoses to *tribus*, which *just might* have an Indo-European root in common with Greek *phule*. But it is there in Germanic just as securely as in Celtic, and indeed in Lithuanian (a language that has a gratifying habit of preserving ancient terminology). This word may appear to have no organic associations; if it ever does, they are concepts with a sense of 'growth' or 'swelling'. Emil Benveniste suggests that it 'be explained roughly as "plenitude"'; which is nice,

Table of 'Indo-European' solidarities

	Iranian	Greek	Latin	Gothic	Old Eng.	Old High Ger.	Old Norse	Old Irish	Brythonic	Slav	Lithuanian
kin (clan)	(zantu)	γενος	gens		cynn/**kindins** **cyning**			[fine]			
community		[φυλη] [εθνος]	[tribus/**tribunus**]	þiuda/**þiudans**	þeod	diot *deutsch*/*deuten*	þïöð	tuath	tud	(tuzdi)	tauta
people		[δημος]	populus/publicus		folc/folclic	*volk*	fylkir		[plemx]		
lord (1)		δεσποτης	dominus		[hlaford]			[flaith]			
lord (2)					dryhten	truhtin	drottin				
lord (3)						herro					

Languages are tabled in approximate order of their appearance in extant writing (though **Old Irish** appears earlier than **Old English** and **Brythonic** than **Old Norse**). Square-bracketed are words with similar meanings but apparently from a different IE semantic family; in round brackets are cognate words with (slightly) changed meanings; modern words are in italics, those for rulers in bold.

inasmuch as its Slavic equivalent, *plemx*, shares a root with Lat. *plenus*, 'full' (and not improbably *plebs*), and Greek *plethos*, 'crowd'.[24] In sum, this ancient term must signify a political unit whose common features are no more nor less than that it is not even quasi-biological and that it is not small; which makes it a highly suggestive indicator of the antiquity of what one might call 'merely political' units.

I suggest that it is from this angle that we approach the lack of anything resembling the word 'state' in Old English, or any other European tongue. This is in fact hardly surprising: it did not crop up in Romance languages for some centuries, and when it got into English from French, it was initially with a sense of 'status' or perhaps 'stature'.[25] But it is quite another thing to say that the Early English and their counterparts had no word for a political collective. For one thing, they had *theod*, which (unlike *cynn*) is normative in the Laws.[26] They did not much use the word *populus* or its adjectival derivative, *publicus*, as the Franks did; but they had a perfectly good vernacular equivalent in *folc*, *folclic*, which *may perhaps* have the same etymology, and which in any event means much the same: namely, neither the cosy sense that 'folk' now has in English nor the appalling connotations that *Volk* came to have in German, but simply 'people', 'public'.[27] No less noteworthy is that though an emergent West's word for 'monarch' was 'king', i.e. '*cynn*-based', that is not the word used in Gothic, the earliest extant Germanic vernacular: the Goths' word was *thiudans*, just as the name of Theodoric, their greatest ruler and commissioner of the Bible translation which is almost our sole source for the language, means 'people-ruler' (it is another nice point that 'Tudor' means the same in Welsh). Old English did, moreover, have a word corresponding to it, *theoden*, 'prince'. *Cyning* and its cognates seem to be new words in the post-Roman West and North; or rather old words that got into Finnish with quite a lowly significance, roughly 'boss', and which then found a new role in the new 'nations' forming as their leaders displaced the emperor.[28] In other words, the older word for a ruler was taken from one for a people, even if a different pattern took hold in the emergency conditions of imperial collapse. We may note, by contrast, that none of the words for 'lord' extends widely along the Indo-European range. This is at least an indicator that lordship developed later than more egalitarian groupings. Be that as it may, it is again evident that it was the collective that gave its terminology to the ruler and his associates, not the other way about: *truht*, whence OE *dryhten*, etc., means a warband, and does nothing for the vocabulary of European rule.[29] It seems, anyway to me, to follow ineluctably that, like the words that reflected and distilled them, units which were in essence collective, however relatively small their size, and which expressed a plurality that derived neither from its leadership nor even theoretically from genetic bonding, belong to the very earliest strata of European history, as they certainly do to Africa's pre-colonial phase.

From the angles so far pursued, it emerges that far back into prehistory, Europeans were in the habit of gathering in considerable numbers at regular times and places for broadly political purposes – but not *only* for such purposes, which enhances rather than detracts from their governmental significance; that the sort of units that formed up at these places also have a significant prehistory; that it is along these lines that we can best account for the erection of Europe's most striking prehistoric structures; and that Africa's literally prehistoric (i.e. pre-documentary) experience suggests that cultures with rudimentary technology can and do do these things. But before you conclude that Oxford's school of Anglo-Saxon studies has taken leave of its marbles (or garnets), I shall try to confront our problem head-on by uniting these perspectives into a single focus. The Appendix to this chapter contains a precious and in effect unique record of proceedings between laymen before a shire court in 990.[30] Four things may be noted, each highlighted in bold. First, business was definitely under royal direction (even under such a king as 'Unready' Æthelred): he sent 'his seal', and its conclusion was witnessed by his 'reeve' (sheriff in all but name). Secondly, it is an assembly of the 'whole shire'. The Queen Mother's team of witnesses included some heavyweights, but also many names otherwise unknown, and 'good men' is a literal Anglicisation of *boni homines*, the local worthies who underwrote Frankish legal transactions.[31] Thirdly, prosopography hints that the case had a political agenda, in that a Wynflæd can be located in the royal entourage; neither her support from the Dowager Queen nor her victory is then surprising. Finally, the court met at *Cwichelmeshlæw*. This means 'Cwichelm's burial-mound'; and it is still there, rejoicing in the name 'Scutchamer Knob', though no tomb it seems. The key point is that Cwichelm was a West Saxon king who in the 620s brought disaster on his people by a treacherous assault on King Edwin of Northumbria; we know from a contemporary record in the *Anglo-Saxon Chronicle* of a prophecy that no army which camped there would ever get back to the sea (the Danes proceeded to do so in 1006, and with impunity). Cwichelm's subsequent baptism appears not to have erased the curse on or of this monster in the mound.[32]

I bring these remarks to a close and I hope together with four necessarily quite succinct conclusions. First, as to the shires we have just glimpsed. It is of local, not central, institutions that Old English records tell us, which is important in itself. Also revealing is that some of these records, including two of the most important, seem actually to have been produced by and for local government.[33] Shires were in a real sense the fulcrum of Old English government, as in some sense they long remained: 'self-government at the king's command' was the order of the day, then as for centuries to come. It is a serious possibility that contact was made between community and crown not, as later, in Westminster's Palace, but in the shires themselves, where the king and his lords spiritual and temporal encountered local opinion. The huge eleventh-century gelds were raised by shire courts which distributed the allotted burden among their constituent hundreds; the land-tax that financed the defeat of Louis XIV was collected in much the same way.[34] When we first have attendance figures in the fourteenth century, they run to hundreds; in the tenth we find maybe not merely notional oaths of thousands.[35] Before and after 1066 the shire court was the forum of gentry, some *very* minor, and of mere freeholders: for four hundred years before 1832, its franchise was of course just 40 shillings.[36] The rising prominence of its JPs and MPs best explains the astonishing rebirth of written English in the late fourteenth century. It is more likely than not that the peacetime responsibilities of shires, like the boundaries of many of them, were created by what amounted to a 'Tenth-Century Revolution in Government'. But as military units, they may have been immemorially older. Similar patterns occur in early Ireland and indeed Rome.[37] The English shire, now the world's oldest operating governing body, may be a function of, in James Campbell's marvellous (if unpublished) phrase, 'the grammar of Indo-European lordship'.

That, secondly, accounts for the word 'Germanic' in my title. The word has not yet featured in my paper because in the last resort it is neither here nor there. Nothing has more discredited the sort of notion I have put forward than its 'Germanist' associations, which nowadays conjure up an image every bit as ghastly as those in an Old English grave-mound. Yet this need never have been so. For what Tacitus said of early German government in an all-too-well-known passage could have been said of any society beyond Rome's frontier.[38] That is why this paper, ostensibly about England, has careered all over the Northern World. The critical point is not that this sort of political activity is German but that it is old; to call it Indo-European is to highlight its antiquity, not any element of 'master-racism'. Beyond the stadia where emperors and post-Roman kings met their peoples, so strikingly replicated in the 'theatre' at Yeavering on the Cheviot fells, lies a tradition reaching back to the original Olympiad, itself a religious, and no doubt a political and commercial as much as an athletic, event: such an assembly as we can imagine congregating up on Yeavering Fell, to be baptized in thousands by the Italian missionary Paulinus – who may have given King Edwin the idea of (as it were) inverting the 'tumular' pattern, so that ruler looked up at ruled, rather than *vice versa* as hitherto.[39] That said, the tradition of assembly we meet in the sub-Roman North is much more likely to have been re-introduced by barbarians than to have been a relic of a Roman administration that was uncompromisingly *dirigiste.*

Third, what has power like this to do with 'the Nation'? The answer is simply if crudely put. If a government so comprehensively 'devolved' as this nonetheless exercised power, what, if not something like 'national' feeling along Zulu lines, can explain it? It must now be accepted, however reluctantly, that the sheer power of the first English kings brooks no debate. Their coin circulated, without rival or alloy, to York, Exeter and beyond; their writ ran to broadly similar effect everywhere to the east of the Tamar and to the south of the Humber, or even the Tees. Since they were in no position to dragoon obedience – or not consistently – what alternative have we but to presuppose a level of mass solidarity that it makes sense to call 'national'? Dr Foot and I have now argued *ad nauseam* that a sense of 'Englishness' was remarkably widespread remarkably early. I shall not do so again; but I shall insist that, however much it seems to accord with common sense, we have little warrant to see either the kin-group or St Augustine's robber-band as the primary vehicles of social coherence. If the word 'national' still sticks in the throat, then please be so good as to find another, preferably supported by evidence rather than modernist assumption. Yes, let it be 'ethnic' if you really think that helps; let it even be 'tribal', so long as you have no illusion that bonding overall was perceived as in any way biological. The substantial point here is that before 1066 as for centuries afterwards, the key to the English realm's operation was the mutual dependence of the king and a decidedly broad political nation. The one offered the other a local government role and the security of his courts, in return for revenues which they collected for him. Control of local government, not mastery of the king, was the aim of pre-1066 England's allegedly fissiparous earls; they competed to dominate the shires by inserting trusted followers. Oxfordshire changed hands five or six times under the Confessor. Power at the top subsisted in managing institutions of local order. Shires were at least as centripetal as they were centrifugal.[40]

So fourthly and lastly, where does this leave us with Foucault? One can never, I fear, be quite sure. But as I (if I) understand him, his objection to the notion of 'consensus' as the foundation of power is that it disguises the coercion never far from its exercise. He prefers to think in terms of the 'discourse' that he – or his translators – have made part of the historian's *lingua franca*. That is fine by me, especially if we go back towards Marx to talk of a 'dialectic', of a creative tension. It is in fact what I have been talking about all along. Northern Europe has for an extremely long time espoused a political discourse within local authorities and between them and central power. That did not make rule democratic, nor need it have been in any real sense popular. But it did make politics *pluralist*, across a wide social span and down to relatively low social levels. The point is not that a figure like Æthelred's mother could manipulate shire-court proceedings, but that she had to work politically through an institution that was not hers to direct as of right. I think it not too much to suggest, nor happily am I alone in suggesting, that Northern Europe's on the whole more stable regimes were based not on compromise between barbarian generalissimos and entrenched regional elites surviving the Roman Empire's demise, but on communities built anew and from the bottom up, in a tradition even older than that of Greece and Rome.

APPENDIX

Wynflæd vs Leofwine, Berkshire 990 (P. H. Sawyer (ed.), Anglo-Saxon Charters: An Annotated List and Bibliography, Royal Historical Society Handbooks 8 (London: Royal Historical Society, 1968), no. 1454)

Here is stated ... how Wynflæd brought forth her witnesses at Woolmer before King Æthelred: namely Archbishop Sigeric and Bishop Ordbriht and Ealdorman Ælfric and Ælfthryth the king's mother; and they all bore witness that Ælfric gave Wynflæd the land at Hagbourne and at Bradfield in return for the land at Datchet. Then the king sent ... to Leofwine through the archbishop and those who were witnesses with him, and told him this. But he would not unless one referred it to **the shire court (*to scirgemote*)**. So this was done. ... **The king sent his seal** through Abbot Ælfhere to the meeting at *Cwichelmeshlæwe* and greeted all wise men that were assembled there, namely Bishop Æthelsige and Bishop Æscwig and Abbot Ælfric and **the whole shire (*eal sio scir*)**, and prayed and ordered them that they should reconcile Wynflæd and Leofwine as justly as ever seemed most just to them; and Archbishop Sigeric sent his statement ... and Bishop Ordbriht his. Then they informed Wynflæd that she could establish her ownership of it. So she brought forth her claim to ownership with the support of **Ælfthryth the king's mother: namely** ... **Abbot**

Wulfgar and Wulfstan the priest and Æfic the Æthelings' seneschal and Eadwine and Eadhelm and Ælfhelm and Ælfwine and Ælfweard and Eadwold and Eadric and Ælfgar and Abbess Eadgyfu and Abbess Leofrun and Æthelhild and Eadgyfu of Lewknor and her sister and … daughter and Ælfgyfu and her daughter and Wulfwyn and Æthelgyfu and Ælfwaru and Ælfgyfu and Æthelflæd and **many a good thegn and good-wife** whom we cannot all recall, so that there came forward the total. Then the wise men who were there declared that it were better that one should leave aside the oath than give it, because there would afterwards be no friendship and one would demand of the robbery that he give it up and pay compensation and his wergeld to the king. Then he left the oath aside and gave Æthelsige the land uncontested, that he would thereafter make no claim on it. Then she was instructed to bring all his father's gold and silver that she had; which she did so far as she dared to secure her oath; then he was not satisfied with that unless she should swear that all his property was there; then she said that she could not for her part nor he for his. And the witnesses of this were **Ælfgar the king's reeve** and Byrhtric and Leofric of Whitchurch and **many a good man** besides them.

NOTES

1 It would of course be fatuous to try to cite all the innumerable studies of this theme, especially since the 1980s, which is why these notes are largely restricted to references required by the text or to other work of mine addressing these problems and their literature. I must here acknowledge an abiding debt to Professor James Campbell: especially – but far from exclusively – to his 'Observations on English government from the tenth to the twelfth century', *Transactions of the Royal Historical Society* 5th ser. 25 (1975), 39–54, repr. in his *Essays in Anglo-Saxon History* (London: Hambledon, 1986), pp. 155–70; and latterly his 'The late Anglo-Saxon state: a maximum view', *Proceedings of the British Academy* 87 (1994), 39–65, repr. in his *The Anglo-Saxon State* (London: Hambledon, 2000), pp. 1–30. I must also gratefully recognise the help – and patience – of my editors and fellow-contributors, in particular Dr Susan Reynolds, to whom this essay is respectfully and affectionately dedicated.

2 M. Foucault, 'The subject and power', *Critical Inquiry* 8 (1982), 777–95; and in general, 'Two lectures', in *Power/Knowledge*, tr. C. Gordon (Brighton: Harvester, 1980), pp. 78–108, with Gordon's 'Afterword', pp. 233–6.

3 The breakthrough study (anyway for me) was the magisterial work of F. Millar, *The Emperor in the Roman World (31 BC–AD 337)* (London: Duckworth, 1977).

4 I remember Denis Mack Smith telling a group of young Balliol idealists in the summer of 1968 (of all years) that the *Mezzogiorno* supported the existence of an Italian state because government service was its main employer: corruption itself creates a stake in government.

5 The seminal inspiration, as for so much twentieth-century historiography (mine included), was of course Max Weber: e.g. *The Theory of Social and Economic Organization*, tr. A. M. Henderson and T. Parsons (New York: Oxford University Press, 1947).

6 W. Stubbs, *The Constitutional History of England in its Origin and Development* (revised edn, 3 vols., Oxford: Clarendon Press, 1880); H. M. Chadwick, *The Heroic Age* (Cambridge University Press, 1912); F. M. Stenton, *Anglo-Saxon England* (3rd edn, Oxford: Clarendon Press, 1971).

7 This defect is the target of my *The Making of English Law. King Alfred to the Twelfth Century I* (Oxford: Blackwell, 1999).

8 D. Scragg (ed.), *The Battle of Maldon AD 991* (Oxford: Blackwell, 1991), with authoritative 'facsimile', text and translation by Professor Scragg, pp. 2–36; and further discussion of historical themes in J. Cooper (ed.), *The Battle of Maldon. Fiction and Fact* (London: Hambledon, 1993), particularly by Professor Campbell, 'England *c. 991*', pp. 1–17 (repr. Campbell, *Anglo-Saxon State*, pp. 157–78).

9 Most glowing illustration, perhaps, J. Backhouse *et al.* (eds.), *The Golden Age of Anglo-Saxon Art* (London: British Museum, 1984), pl. IV, no. 26, p. 47.

10 I discuss this episode and its implications in 'In search of King Offa's "law-code"', in my *Legal Culture in the Early Medieval West* (London: Hambledon, 1999), pp. 201–23; see also J. Nelson, 'The earliest surviving royal *Ordo*: some liturgical and historical aspects', in her *Politics and Ritual in Early Medieval Europe* (London: Hambledon, 1986), pp. 341–60; and C. Cubitt, *Anglo-Saxon Church Councils c. 650–c. 850*, Studies in the Early History of Britain (London: Leicester University Press, 1995), ch. 6.

11 Wormald, *Making of English Law*, pp. 445–8.

12 K. Leyser, *Rule and Conflict in an Early Medieval Society. Ottonian Saxony* (London: Edward Arnold, 1979), pp. 77–107, at p. 105, and cf. his 'Ottonian government', *English Historical Review* 96 (1981), 721–53, repr. in his *Medieval Germany and its Neighbours* (London: Hambledon, 1982), pp. 69–101.

13 The demolition of this model as a government 'mode' was the central achievement of Susan Reynolds, *Fiefs and Vassals* (Oxford University Press, 1994).

14 This much at least may be adduced from the emergent critique of the hitherto prevalent 'dislocated *pagus*' model: D. Barthélemy, *La mutation de l'an mil a-t-elle eu lieu?* (Paris: Fayard, 1997); see also n. 40.

15 M. Fortes and E. E. Evans-Pritchard (eds.), *African Political Systems* (Oxford University Press, 1940), pp. 5–6.

16 M. Gluckman, 'The Kingdom of the Zulu', ibid., pp. 29, 31–2, 33, 34, 38, 46, 54.

17 K. Oberg, 'The Kingdom of Ankole in Uganda', ibid., pp. 137, 139, 142–3.

18 S. E. Hutchinson, 'Death, memory and the politics of legitimation: Nuer experiences of the continuing second Sudanese civil war', in R. Werbner (ed.), *Memory and the Postcolony: African Anthropology and the Critique of Power* (London: Zed Books, 1998), pp. 58–70, gives a broadly very similar account of the now traumatised Nuer, though in less evocative language. I owe

this reference to Mr Tom Wormald; and I am also much obliged for generally supportive enlightenment at the symposium itself by Robert Layton. It will thus be evident that I do not entirely share the reservations as to this approach expressed by Professor Patrick Geary, *The Myth of Nations: The Medieval Origins of Europe* (Princeton University Press, 2003), esp. pp. 157–72.

19 N. Brooks, 'The development of military obligations in eighth- and ninth-century England', in P. Clemoes and K. Hughes (eds.), *England Before the Conquest. Studies in Primary Sources Presented to Dorothy Whitelock* (Cambridge University Press, 1971), pp. 69–84; repr. in his *Communities and Warfare 700–1400* (London: Hambledon, 2000), pp. 32–47. Recent work by Professor Brooks, e.g. 'European medieval bridges: a window onto changing concepts of state power', *Journal of the Haskins Society* 7 (1995/7), 11–29, also in Brooks, *Communities and Warfare*, pp. 1–31, in which see pp. 13–21, further opens up these possibilities; and see now his *Church, State and Access to Resources in Early Anglo-Saxon England*, Brixworth Lectures, 2nd series 2 (2002/3). A most important pointer in this direction is J. Campbell, 'The age of Arthur', *Studia Hibernica* 15 (1975), 177–85, repr. in his *Essays in Anglo-Saxon History*, pp. 121–30, at pp. 125ff.

20 I refer particularly to a one-day conference held in Oxford's Institute of Archaeology on 18 March 2000, which I was privileged to chair; its proceedings have been published as A. Pantos and S. Semple (eds.), *Assembly Places and Practices in Medieval Europe* (Dublin: Four Courts, 2002), and I am especially indebted to the papers by Richard Warner, Elizabeth Fitzpatrick, Stefan Brink, and Timothy Darvill, and by Dr Pantos and Dr. Semple themselves. See also n. 39.

21 K. F. Drew (tr.), *The Laws of the Salian Franks* (Philadelphia: University of Pennsylvania Press, 1991), i, xlvi, pp. 65, 110–11; and cf. Paul Barnwell's 'The Early Frankish *mallus*: its nature, participants and practices', in Pantos and Semple (eds.), *Assembly Places.*

22 See my 'Introduction' to S. Airlie, W. Pohl and H. Reimitz (eds.), *Der Staat im Früh- und Hochmittelalter. Traditionen, Konzepte, Legitimationen, Forschungen zur Geschichte des Mittelalters* (Vienna: Österreichische Akademie der Wissenschaften, 2005).

23 The essential introduction to these matters is E. Benveniste (tr. E. Palmer), *Indo-European Language and Society* (Paris, 1969; Coral Gables, FL: University of Miami Press, 1973), esp. Bks 2–4; it is written in 'laymen's language', which has not endeared it to the author's fellow-philologists; it also has an extremely useful etymological index, grouped by language. Professor Colin Renfrew's celebrated assault on Indo-European notions, *Archaeology and Language: The Puzzle of Indo-European Origins* (London: Jonathan Cape, 1987), should be compared with J. P. Mallory, *In Search of the Indo-Europeans. Language, Archaeology and Myth* (London: Thames & Hudson, 1989).

24 Benveniste, *Indo-European Language*, pp. 296–8.

25 I am guided here by my old comrade, Professor Michael Prestwich.

26 F. Liebermann (ed.), *Die Gesetze der Angelsachsen* (3 vols., Halle: Niemeyer, 1903–16), Iii, *Wörterbuch*, pp. 219–20, *s.v.*; and note its compounds. *Angelþeod* was used alongside *Angelcynn*, especially in the Alfred-period translation of Bede: cf. A. Healy *et al.* (eds), *A Dictionary of Old English* (Toronto: Pontifical Institute of Medieval Studies, 1992–), fascicule 'A', *s.v.*

27 *Folclic* glosses *publicus, popularis, vulgaris*, etc., as may be seen in the 'F' fascicule in the Toronto *Dictionary*. It is becoming a nostrum that early medieval westerners made no clear distinction between 'public' and 'private'; I dissent, not least on etymological grounds, in my Introduction to Airlie *et al.*, *Staat in Früh- und Hochmittelalter*.

28 I discuss this at further length in 'Kings and kingship', in P. Fouracre (ed.), *The New Cambridge Medieval History*, vol. I (Cambridge University Press, 2004).

29 Superbly argued out by D. H. Green, *The Carolingian Lord* (Cambridge University Press, 1968), pp. 59–401; and cf. his *Language and History in the Early Germanic World* (Cambridge University Press, 1998).

30 I discuss this text at length in 'Giving God and king their due: conflict and its regulation in the early English state', *Settimane di Studio del Centro Italiano di Studi sull' alto medioevo* 44 (1997), 549–92; repr. in Wormald, *Legal Culture*, pp. 333–57.

31 W. Davies and P. Fouracre (eds), *The Settlement of Disputes in Early Medieval Europe* (Cambridge University Press, 1986), pp. 217–24.

32 *Anglo-Saxon Chronicle*, in D. Whitelock (ed.), *English Historical Documents*, vol. I, *c. 550–1042* (2nd edition, London: Eyre Methuen, 1979), pp. 240–1. For a quite startlingly lurid depiction of such a monster, see P. McGurk *et al.* (eds), *An Eleventh-Century Anglo-Saxon Illustrated Miscellany: BL Cotton Tiberius B.v, Part I*, Early English Manuscripts in Facsimile XXI (Copenhagen: Rosenkilde and Bagger, 1983), f. 87v.

33 Those known as 'VI Æthelstan' and the 'Hundred Ordinance': best consulted in Whitelock (ed.), *English Historical Documents*, vol. I, pp. 423–30; explanation in Wormald, *Making of English Law*, pp. 296–304, 378–9.

34 The process can be seen at work in the 'Northamptonshire Geld-Roll', a post-Conquest document but in Old English and consistently allotting liabilities 'as was the case in King Edward's time': D. C. Douglas (ed.), *English Historical Documents*, vol. II, *1042–1189* (2nd edition, London: Eyre Methuen, 1980), pp. 517–20; cf. (very important, if on some medieval details risible) T. Ertman, *Birth of the Leviathan* (Cambridge University Press, 1997), pp. 216–17.

35 J. R. Maddicott, 'The County community and the making of public opinion in fourteenth-century England', *Transactions of the Royal Historical Society* 5th ser. 28 (1978), 27–43, at 29–30; P. Wormald, 'Charters, law and the settlement of disputes in Anglo-Saxon England', in Davies and Fouracre (eds), *Settlement of Disputes*, pp. 149–68, at pp. 159–60, repr. Wormald, *Legal Culture*, pp. 289–311, at p. 301.

36 J. Gillingham, 'Thegns and knights in eleventh-century England: who was then the gentleman', *Transactions of the Royal Historical Society* 6th ser. 5

(1995), 129–53; repr. in his *The English in the Twelfth Century* (Woodbridge: Boydell, 2000), pp. 163–85. Note that when the franchise was first established, 499 years before the Great Reform Act, the qualification was *lower*: Maddicott, 'County community', 30.

37 I return to this argument in chapter 10 of *Making of English Law*, vol. II.

38 E. A. Thomson, *The Early Germans* (Oxford: Clarendon Press, 1965), pp. 41–8: it should be noted that this thoroughly convincing picture of social and political change in a barbarian society through the first centuries BC and AD was the work not of a 'Germanist' but of a distinguished *Marxist* historian.

39 S. Driscoll, 'The archaeological context of assembly in early medieval Scotland – Scone and its comparanda'; and Barnwell, 'Early Frankish *mallus*', in Pantos and Semple (eds.), *Assembly Places*. See also my 'Kings and Kingship'.

40 This is demonstrated as never before by Dr S. Baxter– like Dr Driscoll a pupil from whom I have learned much – in his soon-to-be-published Oxford doctoral dissertation, 'The Leofwinesons. Power, Property and Patronage in the Early English Kingdom' (2002).

CHAPTER 5

The historiography of the Anglo-Saxon 'nation-state'*

Sarah Foot

Let me state a certainty. Late Anglo-Saxon England was a nation state. It was an entity with an effective central authority, uniformly organ-ised institutions, a national language, a national church, defined frontiers (admittedly with considerable fluidity in the north), and, above all, a strong sense of national identity.[1]

It may seem extravagant to describe early England as a 'nation-state'. Nevertheless it is unavoidable.[2]

Historians accustomed to thinking about modern states and nations may hesitate over the confidence of these statements and feel themselves more comfortable with the following:

According to whatever standard of political value we make our judgment, the England of the tenth and eleventh centuries will be found utterly lacking in all qualities which make a state strong and keep it efficient ... The principles which underlay its social structure were inconsistent and incoherent. It possessed no administrative system worthy of the name and the executive action of its king was fettered by the independence of his counsellors and rendered ineffective by the practical autonomy of the provincial government into which the land was divided.[3]

The avowed maximum views of eleventh-century statehood are James Campbell's, the two quotations taken from papers published in 1994 and 1995; the second passage may be more surprising to anyone familiar with Sir Frank Stenton's later work. This was Stenton's first book, *William the Conqueror and the Rule of the Normans*, published in 1908 in Putnam's Heroes of the Nations series. In his mature work, Stenton was to prove an energetic defender of the acceptance of the ideal of political unity in pre-Conquest England and of the machinery Old English kings had created for the realisation of that ideal. He had

* I am grateful to Michael Bentley, Michael Braddick, Clare Griffiths and Simon Keynes for discussing these ideas with me and commenting on my argument as it evolved.

by 1943, when his *Anglo-Saxon England* was first published, moved a long way from his early dismissal of the 'weakness of the Anglo-Saxon polity'[4] and was willing then to express greater confidence in the 'power of the state' that lay behind the working of provincial and local government in the late Anglo-Saxon period.

This chapter will explore (or start to explore, for this is very much work in progress) the development of the English historiography of the Anglo-Saxon nation and state over the twentieth century, from the extreme negativity of the early Stenton – 'among so anarchical a people it would be useless to look for any definite political ideas'[5] – to the maximalist position of James Campbell. It has proved difficult to explain how it happened that the word 'state', which, thanks particularly to the work of social and political theorists, has come over this same period to be defined with nuanced precision in ways which pertain specifically to modern political conditions, can be used with such confidence to describe the late Anglo-Saxon polity (which at least superficially appears to have none of the characteristics of a modern state).[6] In all that follows it should be stressed that the discussion will not refer to historians who have used the word 'state' loosely to mean simply the sum of various parts as a stylistic variant on 'polity', 'kingdom' or 'realm', applied particularly to the eleventh-century English kingdom.[7] Rather it is the use of 'state' in a stipulatively defined sense of the political organisation which is the basis of civil government – an over-arching, disembodied network of institutions exercising power over a territorially defined area – on which this chapter will focus.[8]

One might in examining a question of this kind expect to encounter shifting patterns of interpretation between historians, a critical dialectical process of thesis and antithesis; for historical writing is not a seamless process whereby each generation weaves a little more into the interpretative tapestry left by the last. Nor did it seem unreasonable at the outset to anticipate a crude dichotomy between scholars who sought continuities of institution, administration, tenurial arrangements, national sentiment or material culture across the divide of the Norman Conquest and those who argued for varying degrees of discontinuity. What was more surprising (even bearing in mind the significant resistance to theory which characterises this corner of our theory-resistant discipline) was the silence of the literature about the possible meanings of the word 'state' in an Anglo-Saxon context. Equally unexpected was the apparent indifference of those who have written on this subject to ideas about the constructive power of language and its application in a political sphere, implied by their failure to engage with this issue. This is the more remarkable when one considers the related historiography of Anglo-Saxon 'nationhood', where language has played a central role in the development of the argument not just about whether the 'English' imagined themselves to be a distinct community, but about the names by which they articulated that imagination.[9] Before the arguments can be explored in detail, it is necessary to say something about the word and the idea of the state.

I

The main exponent of the maximalist view of the Anglo-Saxon state, James Campbell, has tended to assert the idea of the state as a given without feeling a need to consider the potential disadvantages of his chosen terminology. Since all commentators are agreed that a modern lexicographical definition of the state cannot be applied to pre-Conquest England – where no reflection of a concept of the state is found within contemporary language – the study of the historiography of the Anglo-Saxon 'state' must necessarily involve investigation of conflicting stipulative definitions. Those definitions must, however, be explained and justified if they are to serve an explanatory purpose. For all Campbell's certainty, his case rests ultimately on the assertion that late Anglo-Saxon England was (in some essentialist sense) a state, rather than on any reflection on the definition of the term. Deliberately using a word that has no resonances in a pre-Conquest context is not necessarily unhelpful. Modern conceptual vocabularies can helpfully illuminate earlier societies and reveal aspects of their structures of power that would remain opaque were we to limit ourselves to the language within which contemporaries could have articulated their own ideas. But there are dangers in reifying the state. In large measure the state is, as Philip Abrams has argued, a myth, an ideological construct and a fiction;[10] it is not necessarily helpful to think of the Anglo-Saxon state as a thing.

Although he avoids the problems of definition, Campbell has offered insights into his conception of the state notably in a preoccupation with the level of centralised control manifested in eleventh-century England. The factors that led him to argue that 'the Domesday survey proves England to have been a formidably organised state'[11] were the sophistication of England's economy, notably its monetary economy;[12] the realm's preparedness for war;[13] the existence of a network of agents of the state and of an administrative organisation to control them.[14] It is important to stress at this point that the significance of the institutions and the mechanisms

that Campbell has described should not be denied. The sophistication of
the apparatus of government is indeed remarkable and its extension into
the localities across the English realm argues powerfully for a centralisation
of administrative organisation and for the extension of ideas of proper
government well beyond immediate court circles. What can, however, be
questioned is whether there is also a conception of a disembodied, impersonal 'state' which is separate from the idea of the king. As Kiernan argued
in an analysis of seventeenth-century states, 'a State can be of real significance, can act in some degree formatively on the society over which it
presides, only when it becomes something more than a man or men
exercising personal authority, however acquired'.[15] Can one argue in the
Anglo-Saxon case that any of the institutions or apparatus of government,
or the officials who administered the centralised will, were working
towards an authority distinct from that of the king? Is it not rather the
case that what we have here is a highly developed form of royal government, where the ultimate authority is embodied in the person of the king?
The 'state' – I might prefer to call it the kingdom, or the 'realm' – and its
institutions cannot be imagined without the person of the king in whose
name the agents raised taxes, called men to fight or offered judgement in a
legal process. No contemporary writers provide evidence for a separately
articulated concept of a state, for institutions of power existing independently of the king or operating in the name of an abstract authority (other
than the divine).[16]

   In her reflections on the historiography of medieval states, Susan
Reynolds has argued that this does not matter:

It is also useful to separate the phenomenon of the state from the concept of the
state ... The absence in surviving literature or records of what looks to modern
scholars like 'the concept of the state' or 'the modern concept of the state' is no
argument against the existence of states in the European Middle Ages. Nor, of
course, is the absence of approximations to the word 'state' in its modern sense
(however defined) in any of the relevant languages used at the time. Medieval
writers wrote about politics in a different way from their successors and used a
different vocabulary. Whether this means that they had no concept of the state is
doubtful.[17]

Bearing in mind the markedly different way in which Reynolds has argued
about the unhelpfulness of applying sixteenth-century concepts of feudalism backwards into the Middle Ages, her argument about the state is a little
confusing.[18] There is arguably a considerable danger in applying a term first
deployed in the sixteenth century backwards in to the Middle Ages,
particularly when that idea gets sucked into a Whiggish, teleological view

of the longevity of English political arrangements, as so often it seems to do. Most obviously one might associate such arguments with Edward Augustus Freeman[19] and William Stubbs.[20] Galbraith warned of the dangers inherent in such thinking in 1964:[21]

When we study the origins of states and institutions we are in the unhappy position of knowing the result of the process we are examining and thereby tempted to think that it was implicit in its beginnings. Here it is only necessary to point out that this limited determinism was much increased by the publication of Darwin's *Origins of Species* in 1859. 'The roots of the present' wrote Bishop Stubbs, borrowing the metaphor of evolution and natural selection, 'lie deep in the past', and armed by this analogy our native historians have come near to describing our modern parliamentary constitution as the natural and inevitable outcome of free Teutons imported from the forests of Germany more than a thousand years ago.

Yet some of this teleology is still being articulated by contemporary commentators. Patrick Wormald is no Whig; but in arguing that 'the English kingdom was ultimately the most successful "Dark Age state"'; and 'that England is the world's oldest continuously functioning state' for 'no other European state has existed within approximately its modern boundaries for anything like so long',[22] he hands some hostages to fortune.

Once more there are grounds for perplexity. For Wormald has shown himself to be most sensitive to the significance of contemporary language and exceedingly careful in its use. Consider, for example, his brilliant paper on '*Engla lond*: the making of an allegiance' in which he demonstrates the 'ineluctable if startling fact that the words *Engla-Lond* and *Englisc* were being used in the eleventh century very much as "England" and "English" are used today'.[23] Significantly, this reveals an Anglo-Saxon capacity for and interest in the coining of language to describe changed conditions. When Alfred united the men of Kent, Wessex and Mercia and received their general submission to his rule in 886, his court promoted a new word to define that imagined community: *Angelcynn*. The political novelty of the union of more than one ethnic group under one leader, one law and one allegiance required an innovative language of legitimation.[24] Similarly in the eleventh century, the new term *Engla lond* was coined to articulate the newly conceived territorial space of all England. This sophisticated and imaginative political vocabulary bears witness to the flexibility of English responses to changing situations from the ninth to the eleventh century. The implicit assumption that one should not apply similar arguments to the issue of conceptualising the 'state' is asymmetrical and inconsistent. Had the early English felt a need for a term to denote the over-arching disembodied entity of a 'state' it is hard to believe that they could not have found an appropriate language to express that need. That they were capable both of naming a new territorial realm and of describing the unification of a formerly disunited people we have just seen. Taken together with their ability to discuss the nature of royal power and use complex language to mark its shifting development, this capacity demonstrates the aptitude of the Anglo-Saxons for articulating appropriate vocabularies for contemporary political circumstances. One could go further and argue that their failure to adopt a word to denote an over-arching, impersonal and disembodied governmental machine or expression of political power demonstrates their lack of need for such a word, and hence the lack of a concept of the 'state' in late Anglo-Saxon England.

II

A counter-proposition could be advanced by those historians who prefer to argue that there is only an instrumental relationship between language and things. In this case the 'state' could be taken to have been an entity in Anglo-Saxon England without there then having been a word with which it was described. Yet a state is by definition not a given entity measurable through objective tests, but a construct, a confected scheme of which a variety of elements (an army, an organised bureaucracy, a monetary system etc.) might be held to be characteristic, but which do not themselves prove a state's existence. The notion that a state can be discerned simply from the presence of certain defining characteristics but in the absence of a word for state is unpersuasive. A state is an intangible, constructible only in the mind; if that concept is to be constructed, it must be linguistically conceived.

If one holds that language does not simply reflect back transparently the nature of past societies as if through a mirror, but is in a significant fashion one of the ways in which those societies were constructed, then the absence of a word for 'state' in Anglo-Saxon England may be thought to indicate the absence of a notion of an over-arching structure of statehood, larger than the separate parts of the king, his agents and the various administrative and bureaucratic tools. The Anglo-Saxons had a variety of Latin and Old English words with which to denote kingdoms and royal authority. Bede used the nouns *regnum* and *imperium* both to describe royal power and also with territorial implications, although he most consistently used *prouincia* to denote a kingdom (and also a region within a kingdom).[25] The *Anglo-Saxon Chronicle* consistently uses the noun *rice* to describe the areas over which kings ruled. The same noun was used to describe succession to one of the small, early Anglo-Saxon kingdoms (for example the succession of Æsc to the kingdom of Kent in 488 or Ine to Northumbria in 547) and it was chosen in 1016 to denote the far larger realm that King Æthelred had held 'with great toil and difficulties as long as his life lasted' and which his son Edmund would 'defend stoutly' for the remainder of his own days. Wulfstan of York's tract on political thought known as the 'Institutes of Polity', written c. 1020, provides a carefully considered analysis of the role and responsibility of laymen and ecclesiastics within a Christian nation (*on christenre þeode*),[26] yet those obligations are couched exclusively in terms of a kingdom and its personnel. Lawful kingship is supported by eight columns (including truth and good counsel), and a lawful throne which stands perfectly upright on three pillars: *oratores* (prayermen, who must serve God and intercede day and night for the whole nation, *þeodscipe*), *laboratores* (workmen who supply that by which the entire nation shall live) and *bellatores* (soldiers who must defend the land, *þe eard*, by fighting with weapons). 'Every throne in a Christian nation must stand upright on these three pillars. And should any of them weaken, the throne immediately will totter.'[27] Not only is there no language here of an abstract state, there is no discourse of the state.

When she defined the state, Susan Reynolds qualified the classic Weberian model: 'an organisation of human society within a more or less fixed area in which the ruler or governing body more or less successfully controls the legitimate use of physical force'.[28] It may perhaps be more useful here to consider Michael Mann's definition: 'a centralized, differentiated set of institutions enjoying a monopoly of the means of legitimate violence over a territorially demarcated area'.[29] In relation to seventeenth-century England Michael Braddick has talked very helpfully of the disembodied nature of the state, describing it as 'a mind without a body'.[30] To this one should further add evidence that the members of that society recognised the existence and legitimacy of the body which controlled the use of violence and that that body was distinct from the king himself. As Joseph Strayer suggested, 'a state exists chiefly in the hearts and minds of its people; if they do not believe it is there, no logical exercise will bring it to mind.'[31] Evidence for this abstract conception is, as we have seen, hard to find in an Anglo-Saxon context. Simply announcing that late Anglo-Saxon England was a 'state' is not sufficient.

In a reflexive moment, James Campbell paused to ponder 'how far was there a sense of emotional and ideological commitment to the English state: a "nationalist" commitment? If there was such a commitment, how far down society did it go? To put both questions in crude blunt form: was there a "political nation"; and if so, who was in it?'[32] To answer those questions Campbell looked at evidence for conceptions of Englishness, of the existence of a community of those bound by ethnic origin, a shared history and (all his examples here are taken from the later tenth and eleventh centuries) of belonging to a united realm. His findings are persuasive not about the existence of a conception of the 'state', but rather of a 'nation' (in Benedict Anderson's sense of an imagined community).[33] In the later tenth and eleventh centuries the Anglo-Saxons were a single *gens*, with a common law and customs; they may have had a growing sense of a shared ethnic identity, and those who were able could contemplate a collective history preserved by Bede and in the *Anglo-Saxon Chronicle*. This community happened also to share a common government and to dwell within a single *regnum*,[34] albeit one only recently and perhaps rather insecurely united. There is, of course, a sharp distinction to be made between later and earlier Anglo-Saxon England. As Stubbs observed of the late seventh century, 'There was no English state – no commonwealth, no kingdom of England as yet: there were the eight great kingdoms of the Heptarchy, there were the subkingdoms ...'[35] If following a modern definition of the nation that assumes that the political and national units should be congruent, the English 'nation' only truly emerged at the point at which it found itself united in '*Engla lond*'. But to argue that this can in limited senses be described as a nation is not at all the same as to suggest that 'state' is a useful descriptive label for that polity.[36] Language played a major part in the construction of Alfred's realm, in the making of the united kingdom of England under Edgar in the tenth century and in the re-fashioning of that kingdom and its 'English' people under first a Danish and then a Norman conqueror in the eleventh. There is, however, no discourse that implies those characteristics that one might associate with state-formation. Unlike Professor Campbell, I find the term 'nation-state' entirely avoidable.

The insistence in some quarters on the use of the word 'state' not only fails to separate government or sovereignty from the wider notion of an impersonal state, but also serves seriously to confuse the history of the formation of early states by projecting on to medieval conditions a term that carries the freight of late modern political circumstances. The consequences of this are two-fold. If Anglo-Saxon England is precociously made a state it becomes much more difficult to differentiate this polity and its distinctive features from other polities, contemporary and later. Further, the insistence on the precocity of English governmental organisation tends to reinforce a Whiggish view of continuous development of English institutions, if not from the 'little body of farmer-commonwealths in Sleswick'[37] then from the developed polity of eleventh-century England. It matters still further if historians of later periods assume that an Anglo-Saxonist is using the word 'state' with its modern overtones.[38] Although they located the origins of a unified English state predominantly in the period after 1066, Corrigan and Sayer made substantial use of James Campbell's early work in their book on English state-formation as cultural revolution, identifying several indications of 'Anglo-Saxon state power' and commenting on the legacy on which the Normans and their successors were to build.[39]

III

This chapter began by questioning how historical understanding could have shifted from the primitivism of eleventh-century England painted by Stenton in 1908 to James Campbell's vision of advanced statehood depicted in the 1990s. The story, of course, begins well before Stenton and is particularly to be identified with Stubbs and Freeman, both of whom wrote in a period in which the modern state was not only omnipresent but rapidly developing. In different ways both sought to challenge earlier notions of the degeneracy of the conquered Anglo-Saxons by stressing the nobility of the people and the sophistication of their governmental machine. Stubbs poured scorn on John Milton's clubbing together of Anglo-Saxon rulers of different ages as 'kites and crows', dismissing him as 'a great poet but an execrable historian'.[40] He consigned Carlyle's frequently quoted characterisation of the English as 'a gluttonous race of Jutes and Angles, capable of no grand combinations, lumbering about in pot-bellied equanimity, not dreaming of heroic toil' to a footnote at the end of his lengthy peroration on the glories of the English national character: 'it is seldom remembered in comparing Norman and Anglo-Saxon in point of civilisation, how very little the Norman brought in comparison with what he destroyed, and how very little he brought that was his own'.[41]

Both Freeman and Stubbs, however, dwelt on far more than the nobility and civilisation of the Anglo-Saxon character; each was arguing a case for the continuity of England's history and the longevity of her institutions, particularly her representative institutions, across the apparent caesura of the Norman Conquest. Freeman, in an essay on the continuity of English history, asserted: 'since the first Teutonic settlers landed on her shores, England has never known full and complete submission to the will of a single man. Some assembly, Witenagemot, Great Council or Parliament there has always been. ... From Hengest to Victoria, England has always had what we may fairly call a parliamentary constitution.'[42] The first part of Stubbs's *Constitutional History* traced the process by which an English nation evolved from the separate Germanic peoples who settled in post-Roman Britain and told the story of the gradual unification of the smaller kingdoms into a single state. He, too, concentrated on the constitutional limits placed on the kings and on the significance of the witan in tempering royal power,[43] but he had much to say also about the central role played by the Church in the process of England's unification: 'the unity of the church in England was the pattern of the unity of the state'.[44] By 1066 he perceived that the state was becoming exhausted, although (as James Campbell has noted) what Stubbs called the substructure of English government was to survive the Conquest.[45]

In tracing the historiography of the Anglo-Saxon state from Stubbs to Campbell two themes may be selected for (necessarily brief) discussion: Anglo-Saxon systems of government and administration, and the question of the unity of the late Old English realm. This chapter began with Stenton's remark that eleventh-century England 'possessed no administrative system worthy of the name',[46] and it is striking to what extent the question of administration has dominated the historiography of the Anglo-Saxons over the last century.[47] In an article published in *History* in 1937 R. R. Darlington set out to defend the Anglo-Saxons from the charge of Ferdinand Lot that they were 'a race of barbarians rescued from ignorance and savagery by the Norman conquerors'.[48] Darlington argued that England was indeed strongly contrasted with contemporary European states, but that contrast lay in the extent of its civilisation, the strength of its monarchy and above all in its governmental machinery. He explored the military and administrative function of earls, the representatives of the king in the shires (thegns, reeves and shire reeves), the significance of the emergence of the hundred as an administrative unit and the collection of the Danegeld, a 'national land tax', and the use of written tools in government.[49] He announced the issues on which attention has focused in the past sixty years, ranging from the sophistication of the fiscal organisation of the late Anglo-Saxon realm;[50] the quantity of coin in circulation and the levels of Danegeld and heregeld levied in the eleventh century;[51] the existence or otherwise of a royal chancery responsible for the centralised production of royal charters and, in the eleventh century, writs;[52] the mechanisms for administering justice locally and for dispute resolution;[53] to the role of reeves – shire reeves or sheriffs – in the local administration of the regions and the extent of their obligations to earl or king.[54] Of central significance is the role of law and its administration, in analysis of which Patrick Wormald has been a key figure, contributing to several of the debates about aspects of royal government and administration, but also widening the issue into the question of state-formation, where law-making plays an integral role. For Wormald, the origins of that state are to be found not in the unified late-tenth-century realm but rather earlier, in the time of King Alfred: 'The paradox of Alfred's *domboc* is that this deeply tradition-alist text marks the point when law became the aggressive weapon of a new state.'[55]

It is not difficult to see why an interest in the making of English law can lead to an interest in the longevity of legal ideas and thus why an historian of law may tend towards arguments about continuity. Less immediately obvious are the consequences of historical focus on government and administration, which struck Allen Brown as representing the peculiar contribution of the twentieth century to historical studies. For Brown, this was 'the principal cause of that contemporary up-grading of the Anglo-Saxons', which insisted on 'an exceptional development of gov-ernment both central and local in pre-Conquest England'.[56] The danger here, as Brown saw it, was that the Anglo-Saxons were being over-promoted; their increasing influence should, he urged, be diminished.[57] 'In 1908', he observed in a lecture delivered in the year of the 900th anniversary of the Battle of Hastings,

F. M. Stenton wrote that the apparent unity of Anglo-Saxon England was 'very deceptive', and it does not seem that the more recent concentration upon 'Administrative History' has greatly altered that conclusion. Yet this concentration has undoubtedly obscured the political facts of life in pre-Conquest England, which by themselves seem to point unmistakably to a lack of unity which was to be disastrous. The Danelaw is amongst the foremost of those facts.[58]

A concentration on the alleged precociousness of the Anglo-Saxon governmental machine has indeed imposed an image of unity and uni-formity on the late Anglo-Saxon kingdom which may be exaggerated. Galbraith probably argued this case most vehemently, especially about the extent of the Anglo-Saxon achievement in creating in the tenth century an administrative order of counties, hundreds and boroughs, 'the whole structure articulated by the royal writ addressed to the shire court'. 'With this clue in our hands, Anglo-Saxon history takes on a totally new complex-ion. Instead of a torpid, backward society, is faintly discerned a precocious people, relatively literate and not uncivilized in their own way and their own tongue.'[59] Galbraith's was not, however, a perception universally shared. Writing about British historians and the Norman Conquest in 1946, David Douglas offered a rather different view, doubting the extent of English unity: 'England under Edward the Confessor showed small disposition to unite against the Normans; her political history was dominated by rivalries of the great earldoms; and her social structure was marked above all by the differences which continued to distinguish the several provinces of the late Old English state', namely the Scandinavian element in late Anglo-Saxon society.[60] Others voiced the same uncertainty. In W. L. Warren's eyes, Anglo-Saxon England was a united but not a unified state, not so much de-centralised as uncentralised. Warren has further questioned whether there was any larger unit of management than the shire, and wondered whether there was even really a single 'realm', let alone a state.[61] The separatism of Northumbria within the late Anglo-Saxon polity, whether as a result of its distinctive early history or as a consequence of Scandinavian settlement and the willingness of West Saxon kings to allow its people 'such laws as they best might decide upon', created a political reality that was to endure long beyond the Conquest and cannot easily be explained away.[62]

IV

Arguments about the formation of an Anglo-Saxon 'state' all depend on an understanding that, despite regional differences, the Anglo-Saxons perceived themselves to be one, English, people and that they were governed as a unified realm. Central in the evolution of this analysis has been the work of Sir Frank Stenton. One of the reasons why he seems to have changed his mind between 1908 and 1943, when the first edition of his *Anglo-Saxon England* was published, is that by the 1930s he had come to want to tell a story about how a unified England evolved.[63] Although Stenton has been criticised for pushing that unity too far back into the early Anglo-Saxon era, for trying to see some degree of unification in the so-called *bretwalda* and in the supremacy of the Mercian kings,[64] his conviction of its significance cannot be denied and is stated most clearly at the end of his *Anglo-Saxon England*:

To many historians the last phase of the Old English state has seemed the mere prelude to an inevitable collapse. The more obvious weaknesses of that state – the instability of its social organization, and the excessive power of a small group of wealthy families, have often been taken as signs of impending dissolution. On the other hand, the ideal of political unity was accepted in every part of pre-Conquest

England, and the Old English kings had created a machinery which stronger hands could use for its realization. By law and custom, the powers through which the Conqueror re-edified the English state were inherent in the English monarchy.[65]

It is revealing that when, in her memoir of her husband, Doris Stenton enumerated the projects left undone at Sir Frank's death, she referred to 'the book to be called "The Unity of England", of which he had set out the chapters in his well-worn notebook and had discussed with Mr Sisam, which will never now be written'.[66]

In the last of the series of Oxford seminars on 'The formation of the state', Rees Davies suggested that, without denying the remarkable pre-cociousness of 'the English state', it might prove more profitable to bring the study of the state, 'if we call it such', into the broader arena of the discussion of power generally. Is the state, Davies asked, in fact a tyranny which is oppressing us by forcing us to accept the image which it constructs and projects of itself and in which its history becomes a master narrative, determining our perceptions of continuity of English history?[67] This chapter has argued that the insistence on describing late Anglo-Saxon England as a state (in the absence of an early medieval word for a 'state', or any discourse of the state or its conceptual apparatus) obscures what was distinctive about the exercise of royal power and the governance of England in the early Middle Ages. It may be more profitable to follow the lead of Thomas Charles Edwards who suggested, in relation to early Irish society, that 'there was not a state, distinct from society, but rather a king who was central within society, whose power was effective partly because he deployed the same powers as did other lords, but to a higher degree'.[68] When asking whether or not there was an English 'nation' before the Conquest, one's answer might be rather different. For in this sphere one can find the articulation of a political language used specifically to encompass peoples of different ethnic origin with a recent history of separate lordship. Where this question must remain open is in the universality of the acceptance of that concept of Englishness, not just in the midland, Anglo-Saxon shires of Mercia and East Anglia, but particularly in Northumbria where Anglo-Scandinavian influences were strongest. Evidence for the existence of English national sentiments can be found at various moments in the late tenth and eleventh centuries; consider for example the appeal to a notion of collective identity apparent in the poem commemorating the 991 battle of Maldon;[69] the reluctance of the English to slide into civil war and lay their country open to foreign enemies at the time of the Godwine crisis in 1051;[70] or the identification of prominent early Anglo-Saxon saints as 'national' figures representative of a shared religious heritage.[71] But the way in which we might interpret these factors would look quite different were we able to view them, not from Winchester, but from Durham.

NOTES

1 James Campbell, 'The late Anglo-Saxon state: a maximum view', *Proceedings of the British Academy* 87 (1994), 39–65; reprinted in his *The Anglo-Saxon State* (London: Hambledon, 2000), p. 10.

2 James Campbell, 'The united kingdom of England: the Anglo-Saxon achievement', in Alexander Grant and K. J. Stringer (eds.), *Uniting the Kingdom: The Making of English History*, (London: Routledge, 1995), pp. 31–47; reprinted in Campbell, *The Anglo-Saxon State*, p. 31.

3 F. M. Stenton, *William the Conqueror and the Rule of the Normans* (New York and London: Putnam, 1908), pp. 21–22.

4 Ibid., p. 5.

5 Ibid., p. 8.

6 Interest in looking for the foundations of the state earlier than the sixteenth century is not peculiar to Anglo-Saxonists; see Alan Harding, *Medieval Law and the Foundations of the State* (Oxford University Press, 2002).

7 It is striking that Henry Loyn never found need of the word in his *The Governance of Anglo-Saxon England 500–1087* (London: Edward Arnold, 1984).

8 Compare Michael J. Braddick, *State Formation in Early Modern England, c. 1550–1700* (Cambridge University Press, 2000), pp. 11–20.

9 Susan Reynolds, 'What do we mean by "Anglo-Saxon" and the "Anglo-Saxons"?', *Journal of British Studies* 24 (1985), 395–414; Patrick Wormald, '*Engla lond*: the making of an allegiance', *Journal of Historical Sociology* 7 (1994), 1–24; Sarah Foot, 'The making of *Angelcynn*: English identity before the Norman Conquest', *Transactions of the Royal Historical Society* 6th ser. 6 (1996), 25–49.

10 Philip Abrams, 'Notes on the difficulty of studying the state', *Journal of Historical Sociology* 1 (1988), 82; Philip Corrigan and Derek Sayer, *The Great Arch: English State Formation as Cultural Revolution* (Oxford: Blackwell, 1985), p. 7; Rees Davies, 'The state: the tyranny of a concept?', *Journal of Historical Sociology* 15 (2002), 71.

11 James Campbell, 'The significance of the Anglo-Norman state in the administrative history of western Europe', in W. Paravincini and K. F. Werner (eds.), *Histoire comparée de l'administration (IVe–XVIIIe siècles)*, Beihefte der Francia 9 (Munich, 1980), 117–34; reprinted in James Campbell, *Essays in Anglo-Saxon History* (London: Hambledon, 1986), p. 171.

12 Campbell, 'The united kingdom', p. 33.

13 James Campbell, 'Some agents and agencies of the late Anglo-Saxon state', in J. C. Holt (ed.) *Domesday Studies* (Woodbridge: Boydell and Brewer, 1987), pp. 201–18; reprinted in his *The Anglo-Saxon State*, p. 201.

14 Ibid., pp. 221–2.

15 V. G. Kiernan, 'State and nation in western Europe', *Past and Present* 31 (1965), 21.

16 Compare Quentin Skinner, *Foundations of Modern Political Thought* (2 vols., Cambridge University Press, 1978), vol. II, pp. 353–5: 'the distinctively modern idea of the State as a form of public power separate from both the ruler and the ruled'.

17 Susan Reynolds, 'The historiography of the medieval state', in Michael Bentley (ed.), *Companion to Historiography* (London: Routledge, 1997), p. 120.

18 Susan Reynolds, *Fiefs and Vassals: The Medieval Evidence Reinterpreted* (Oxford University Press, 1994), pp. 1–16.

19 Freeman argued that the 'distinctive character of English history is its continuity': 'The continuity of English history', in his *Historical Essays*, first series (London and New York: Macmillan, 1871; 4th edition 1886), p. 40.

20 Helen Cam, 'Stubbs seventy years after', *Cambridge Historical Journal* 9 (1948), 130.

21 V. H. Galbraith, *An Introduction to the Study of History* (London: C. A. Watts, 1964), p. 6.

22 Patrick Wormald, 'Anglo-Saxon society and its literature', in Malcolm Godden and Michael Lapidge (eds.), *The Cambridge Companion to Old English Literature* (Cambridge University Press, 1991), pp. 19 and 1.

23 Wormald, '*Engla lond*', 10.

24 Foot, 'The making of *Angelcynn*'.

25 James Campbell, 'Bede's *reges* and *principes*', Jarrow Lecture, 1979, reprinted in his *Essays in Anglo-Saxon History*, p. 86.

26 Wulfstan, 'Institutes of Polity', §§2 and 4 in K. Jost (ed.), *Die "Institutes of Polity, Civil and Ecclesiastical"* (Bern: Francke, 1959), pp. 41 and 56; trans. Michael Swanton in *Anglo-Saxon Prose* (London: J. M. Dent, 1993), pp. 188–9.

27 Wulfstan, 'Institutes of Polity', §4 in Jost (ed.), *Die "Institutes"*, pp. 55–6; trans. Swanton, *Anglo-Saxon Prose*, p. 189.

28 Reynolds, 'The historiography of the medieval state', p. 118.

29 Michael Mann, 'State and society, 1130–1815: an analysis of English state finances', in *Political Power and Social Theory* 1 (1980), 166. Quoted by Braddick, *State Formation*, p. 12.

30 Braddick, *State Formation*, p. 20.

31 Joseph R. Strayer, *On the Medieval Origins of the Modern State* (Princeton University Press, 1970), p. 5.

32 Campbell, 'The united kingdom of England', p. 37.

33 Benedict Anderson, *Imagined Communities: Reflections on the Origin and Spread of Nationalism* (2nd edn, London: Verso, 1991).

34 Following Alan Thacker, 'Peculiaris patronus nostrus: the saint as patron of the state in the early middle ages', in J. R. Maddicott and D. M. Palliser (eds.), *The Medieval State: Essays Presented to James Campbell* (London: Hambledon, 2000), p. 2; Susan Reynolds, *Kingdoms and Communities in Western Europe* (2nd edn, Oxford: Clarendon Press, 1997), pp. 254–5.

35 Stubbs, 'The Anglo-Saxon constitution', in Arthur Hassall (ed.), *Lectures on English History by William Stubbs* (London: Longmans, Green, and Co., 1906),

pp. 1–17, esp. p. 10. Compare more recently Thacker, 'Peculiaris patronus nostrus', p. 3: 'seventh and eighth-century England as a whole was not, therefore a state, nor perhaps were most of its numerous component polities'.

36 The opposite case has been argued by Krishan Kumar, who is more comfortable in defining eleventh-century England as a 'state' than he is in seeing this people as a nation: *The Making of English Identity* (Cambridge University Press, 2003), pp. 41–8.

37 J. R. Green, *A Short History of the English People* (London: Macmillan, 1874), pp. 4–5.

38 Harding, *Medieval Law*, pp. 1–2.

39 Corrigan and Sayer, *The Great Arch*, pp. 18–19.

40 Stubbs, 'The Anglo-Saxon constitution', p. 4.

41 William Stubbs, *The Constitutional History of England in its Origin and Development* (3 vols., Oxford: Clarendon Press, 1873–78; vol. I, 5th edition, 1891), pp. 235–6; the quotation from Carlyle's *Frederick the Great* is found at the foot of p. 236.

42 Freeman, 'The continuity', p. 42.

43 For his account of the witenagemot see Stubbs, *The Constitutional History*, vol. I, §§ 51–8, pp. 133–57. On the limited character of kingship, ibid., § 59, p. 158.

44 Ibid., § 90, pp. 266–7.

45 Campbell, 'Stubbs and the English state', Stenton Lecture (Reading: University of Reading, 1989), reprinted in his *The Anglo-Saxon State*, pp. 249–50.

46 Stenton, *William the Conqueror*, p. 22.

47 In this the influence of T. F. Tout seems to have been critical; not so much his own *Chapters in the Administrative History of Mediaeval England: The Wardrobe, the Chamber and the Small Seals* (6 vols., Manchester University Press, 1920–33) which offered only a cursory look at pre-Conquest arrangements, but particularly the spread of his influence via his pupils, perhaps above all through V. H. Galbraith.

48 Ferdinand Lot, *Les invasions germaniques* (Paris: Payot, 1935).

49 R. R. Darlington, 'The last phase of Anglo-Saxon history', *History* 22 (1937), 7 and 9.

50 The Anglo-Saxon financial system which collected the Danegeld was not, Galbraith insisted (quarrelling here with his teacher Tout), 'run from a box under the bed. We must suppose a well-organized and well-staffed Treasury at Winchester for many generations before the Conquest': V. H. Galbraith, *Studies in the Public Records* (London: Nelson, 1948), p. 45.

51 M. K. Lawson, 'The collection of Danegeld and heregeld in the reigns of Æthelred II and Cnut', *English Historical Review* 99 (1984), 721–38; John Gillingham, '"The most precious jewel in the English crown": levels of Danegeld and heregeld in the early eleventh century', *English Historical Review* 104 (1989), 373–84; 'Chronicles and coins as evidence for levels of tribute and taxation in late tenth- and early eleventh-century England', *English Historical Review* 105 (1990), 939–50; M. K. Lawson, 'Danegeld and heregeld once more', *English Historical Review* 105 (1990), 951–61.

52 Florence Harmer, *Anglo-Saxon Writs* (Manchester University Press, 1952); Galbraith, *Studies in the Public Records*, p. 36. Pierre Chaplais, 'The Anglo-Saxon chancery: from the diploma to the writ', *Journal of the Society of Archivists* 3 (1966), 160–76, reprinted in Felicity Ranger (ed.), *Prisca Munimenta: Studies in Archival and Administrative History* (London: University of London Press, 1973), pp. 43–62; Simon Keynes, *The Diplomas of King Æthelred 'the Unready' 978–1016: A Study in their Use as Historical Evidence* (Cambridge University Press, 1980); S. E. Kelly, *Charters of Abingdon Abbey*, Anglo-Saxon Charters, vols. 8–9 (Oxford University Press for the British Academy, 2000–1), part I, pp.cxv–cxxxi.

53 Patrick Wormald, 'Charters, law and the settlement of disputes in Anglo-Saxon England', in Wendy Davies and Paul Fouracre (eds.), *The Settlement of Disputes in Early Medieval Europe* (Cambridge University Press, 1986), pp. 149–68; 'A handlist of Anglo-Saxon lawsuits', *Anglo-Saxon England* 17 (1988), 247–81.

54 W. A. Morris, *The Medieval English Sheriff to 1300* (Manchester University Press, 1927); Judith A. Green, 'The sheriffs of William the Conqueror', *Anglo-Norman Studies* 5 (1983), 129–45; Green, *The Government of England under Henry I* (Cambridge University Press, 1986), pp. 194–214.

55 Patrick Wormald, *The Making of English Law: King Alfred to the Twelfth Century, I, Legislation and its Limits* (Oxford: Blackwell, 1999), p. 429.

56 R. Allen Brown, *The Normans and the Norman Conquest* (2nd edn, Woodbridge: Boydell and Brewer, 1985), p. 57.

57 Ibid., p. 5.

58 R. Allen Brown, 'The Norman Conquest', *Transactions of the Royal Historical Society* 5th ser. 17 (1967), 116. Compare also Brown, *The Normans*, p. 63.

59 Galbraith, *Studies in the Public Records*, p. 36.

60 David C. Douglas, *The Norman Conquest and British Historians*, the David Murray Foundation Lecture, University of Glasgow, 1946, reprinted in his *Time and the Hour: Some Collected Papers of David C. Douglas* (London: Eyre Methuen, 1977), pp. 64–5.

61 W. L. Warren, 'The myth of Norman administrative efficiency', *Transactions of the Royal Historical Society* 5th ser. 34 (1984), 113–14.

62 Compare Frank Barlow, *The Feudal Kingdom of England 1042–1216* (London and New York: Longman, 1955; 3rd edition 1972), pp. 5–6.

63 For discussion of the wartime context in which *Anglo-Saxon England* was finally published see Donald Matthew, 'The making of *Anglo-Saxon England*', in Donald Matthew (ed.), *Anglo-Saxon England Fifty Years On* (Reading: University of Reading, 1994), pp. 111–34.

64 Patrick Wormald, 'Bede, the *bretwaldas* and the origins of the *gens Anglorum*', in Patrick Wormald, Donald Bullough and Roger Collins (eds), *Ideal and Reality in Frankish and Anglo-Saxon Society* (Oxford: Blackwell, 1983), pp. 105–11.

65 Stenton, *Anglo-Saxon England*, p. 537.

66 Doris M. Stenton, 'Frank Merry Stenton, 1880–1967', *Proceedings of the British Academy* 54 (1968), 422.

67 Davies, 'The state'.

68 Quoted by Davies, ibid., 74.

69 Discussed by James Campbell, 'England, *c.* 991', in Janet Cooper (ed.), *The Battle of Maldon: Fiction and Fact* (London: Hambledon Press, 1993), pp. 1–17; reprinted in Campbell, *The Anglo-Saxon State*, pp. 176–7.

70 *Anglo-Saxon Chronicle*, 1051; Campbell, 'The united kingdom of England', pp. 36–7.

71 Wormald, '*Engla lond*', 13.

CHAPTER 6

Exporting state and nation: being English in medieval Ireland

Robin Frame

England was, by medieval standards, an unusually coherent and centralised kingdom, particularly between the late twelfth and fourteenth centuries, the period with which this chapter is concerned. It is not surprising, therefore, that the influence of the crown over the outer edges of the polity should be proportionately strong. This strength is visible in Ireland, to which English law and government were extended between the reigns of Henry II and Edward I. The extension was not of course effective across the entire island, but nor was it restricted to the area around Dublin: the Pale was a concept that appeared only in the early Tudor period.[1] Over much of the east and south, military and political domination was accompanied, on the coasts and in the river valleys, by significant colonisation from Britain. This was the soil in which institutions – which from the time of King John were explicitly described as English – took root. By the middle of the fourteenth century, when the phase of confident expansion had ceased, the settler elites constantly stressed their loyalty to the crown and their Englishness. These qualities had become synonomous.[2]

My subject is the inter-relationship between the extension of the English state and settler identity: between, in other words, 'power' and 'nation'. I shall argue that the latter is comprehensible only if due weight is given to the former. I shall also suggest that there are sufficient resemblances between the medieval Anglo-Irish relationship and later examples of the interplay between colonies and homelands to make conversations between medievalists and modernists worthwhile.[3] Ireland, indeed, displays some features that would enable a classifying mind to assign it, approximately, to Anthony Smith's category of colonial or 'providential frontier' nationalisms – though perhaps without the 'nationalism'.[4] Alternatively, it could be described as a regnal lordship – the king of England was *dominus Hibernie* – which produced its own variety of Englishness. Such conversations have been slow to develop. Two reasons for this merit a brief mention. The first is the telescoped treatment the period receives in general histories of

Ireland, where the English presence tends to be viewed through the spectacles of late medieval contraction and Tudor and Stuart reconquest and plantation. The dominant images are of the shrunken Pale and of a settler population that was 'turning Irish'. These caricatures and elisions of time have left their mark on the few taxonomists of nations and nationalism who have noticed the topic.[5] (The lordship of Ireland lasted from 1171 to 1541, the same length of time that separates Thomas Cromwell from Mr Gladstone or the end from the beginning of Roman Britain: it seems perverse to regard its first 150 years as an overture to preordained decay.) The second obstacle is terminological: the habit in Ireland of labelling the period from 1170 to as late as the fifteenth century 'Norman', 'Anglo-Norman', or 'Anglo-French' – anything, in fact, save 'English'.[6] John Gillingham has recently insisted that the appropriate term is indeed 'English', and this usage is making headway among younger Irish medievalists.[7] Arguments over the point during the twelfth century at which 'Normans' in England became 'English' need not concern us. There is some consensus that the needle was settling on the 'English' side of the meter by the 1170s and 1180s; even on a recent cautious reading, it was firmly fixed there by around 1220.[8] Such a chronology fits with the signs that the Irish enterprise was viewed as English by those who wrote about it in the late twelfth century, and by those in official circles who sought to shape it in the early thirteenth.

I

To begin with the self-consciousness. When King John visited Ireland in 1210, he issued a charter and held a council decreeing that English law should apply there.[9] His reign also saw the first surviving letters patent granting 'English law and privileges' (*legem et libertatem Anglicanam*) to individual native Irishmen.[10] Then in 1216 Magna Carta was transmitted for observance in Ireland. This began the habit of sending new English legislation over for proclamation. Between 1222 and 1246 the government of Henry III responded to requests for clarification of specific legal points by calling to mind the council of 1210, and ruling that law in the lordship of Ireland should be identical to the law of England.[11]

By the late thirteenth century, parliaments attended by the lay and ecclesiastical magnates, and sometimes by knights of the shire and/or burgesses of the main towns, met frequently. Their legislation contains just about everything that might appear on the check-list of the political theorist seeking to define a state.[12] In 1297, for instance, there was an extension of the county system which formed the network of crown government; an ordinance about clearing and maintaining the king's highways; a ruling that all the king's subjects should have military equipment proportionate to their wealth, along the lines of the English Assize of Arms of 1181 and the 1285 Statute of Winchester; there is a territorial sense, embodied in the phrase 'the land of peace'; and a positively Weberian insistence that 'one peace and one war' should apply throughout the country, with all military activity on the marches controlled by sheriffs and other royal agents.[13] In 1299–1300 Irish parliaments agreed taxation for the Anglo-Scottish war, and published ordinances outlawing the substandard continental coins that were circulating in the king's insular dominions.[14]

The question at once arises of how far any of this was effective. Brendan Smith recently described the enactments of 1297 as 'less a practical programme than a declaration of identity through law', a comment singled out as perceptive by more than one reviewer.[15] There has been a small scholarly industry devoted to pointing out the limitations of royal government in Ireland. Writing in 1977, I myself – inconveniently for present purposes – described the country as 'less a lordship than a patchwork of lordships', and English law and government there as 'a thinnish coating over a very un-English set of political facts'.[16] Rees Davies, as usual finding the *mot juste*, has stated that it was one thing to export English institutions, quite another to reproduce a 'political texture'.[17] Comments such as these were partly a reaction against a rather abstract style of institutional history that was influential in Ireland in the middle of the twentieth century. Nobody would argue that the crown had a monopoly of legitimate authority in Ireland; indeed Davies has recently selected it as a prime example of the 'federal' character of power in a pre-modern polity.[18] But, for all the necessary reservations, it remains striking that English systems rooted themselves as firmly as they did. There is plenty of evidence that the state in Ireland was more than an empty shell.

Let us use the obvious measures of jurisdiction and revenue.[19] Around 1300 the shire system stretched from the Ulster borders to Cork and even Kerry. Across this large territory, sheriffs were appointed; judges moved around, hearing criminal and civil pleas; cases flowed to the central courts at Dublin. All this could work only through the involvement of substantial numbers of people at local level – sub-sheriffs, bailiffs of various sorts, jurors, pledges; the panoply of English 'self-government at the king's command'.[20] Admittedly, the governed region contained extensive regalian liberties, which were part of the underpinning of aristocratic power.

But these, unlike the Welsh marcher lordships, were subject to English law; their seneschals accounted at the Dublin exchequer for the profits of pleas reserved to the crown; their lords, even those with strong court connections, had to struggle to ward off intrusions and sequestrations by royal officials.[21]

Like the English 'law state', the Plantagenet 'tax-empire' was vigorous in Ireland at the same period.[22] Financial records reveal the collection of money from lands and custodies, farms of cities, profits of justice, and taxation. They show the exercise of regalian right, which gave the crown income from vacant bishoprics.[23] The wool tax was extended to Ireland, with a customs organisation garnering significant profit from the southern and east coast ports. Edward I's credit systems operated in Ireland, with Italian bankers playing a prominent part in the exploitation of the lordship.[24] At their peak, the revenues of Ireland were not dissimilar in scale from those of the contemporary Scottish kingdom.[25] Throughout the thirteenth century, Ireland was used by the crown for military recruitment and supplies. From the mid-1290s, when the Anglo-Scottish wars began, the energies of government were directed to purveying grain, pork, saltfish, beer and other foodstuffs for armies and garrisons in south-west Scotland. Contributions came not just from the hinterlands of Dublin and Drogheda, but from scores of small towns and royally approved markets upstream from Wexford, Waterford, Cork and Limerick. The capacity of Edwardian government to mobilise and to extract was apparent in Ireland just as in England.[26] It has been argued that the intensity of the demands of the 1290s and early 1300s, coming at a time of poor harvests, harmed the economy. In Ireland, as in England, we encounter the paradox that government was sufficiently effective to damage its own resource-base.

As all this shows, Ireland was firmly attached to the English metropolis. The links included those of administrative routine, such as exchequer audits and judicial appeals and reviews which reached the king's bench, council and parliament. These involved not only comings and goings by officials and messengers, but also the movements of petitioners and agents, as those with interests in Ireland sought to put one over on each other by lobbying in England. This orbit of patronage extended further than the sphere of regular government. Like any new territory, Ireland was initially an asset to the crown; royal grants created ties and habits that endured for generations. Beyond the core settlement areas in the south and east, royal government gave way to aristocratic supremacies. But the perception of aristocratic freedom of action has to be balanced by an appreciation of the continuing ties – through military service, reward and marriage – to the royal court and English aristocracy. Even in northern and western Ireland, those who began as royal agents did not wholly slip the metropolitan reins and disappear into local society.[27] We are encountering a version of the 'administrative maps' and – stretching wider – the 'political highways' that mark out Benedict Anderson's 'imagined communities' of colonial America.[28]

Across the fourteenth century, the reach and effectiveness of English institutions in Ireland was reduced, by economic and demographic catastrophe, and by the inward collapse of settled frontiers as the predatory pasturing and tribute-warfare that characterised Gaelic and marcher society expanded.[29] The clearest symptom of the change is that by the 1360s and 1370s the dominion that had contributed so much to Edward I's wars was being shored up by armies and cash from England.[30] The adverse shift supplies the context for the anxieties about loyalty and identity to which I shall turn shortly. But it is important to retain a sense of the residual strength of English systems during the period when Dublin's control in Ireland receded.

This may be illustrated by three episodes. In 1355 eleven southern and eastern counties responded almost instantly to an order to elect their sheriffs. Each sheriff was to have twenty-four electors, who were also his sureties. We have the names; they reveal the involvement of substantial numbers of gentry families in local government. For instance, tiny, beleaguered Carlow produced twenty-nine sureties from twenty-two families. Remote Kerry contented itself with the required twenty-four; they came from at least fifteen families, including, at the extreme edge of this institutional world, Nicholas and William Fereter from the Dingle peninsula, thrust out into the Atlantic.[31] In 1358, over the same area, county courts were assembled to make grants and appoint assessors and collectors of subsidies to support local defences. We have the names of many scores of those involved.[32] This can be read as a sign of crisis and the partial fragmentation of the 'tax-state'; but it is also evidence of continued interaction between centre and localities, and an example of mobilisation and participation. Finally, as late as 1420–1 representatives of nine counties, together with towns, liberties and dioceses, attended parliaments at Dublin; taxation was agreed; dozens of assessors and hundreds of collectors were appointed. The arrangements were carefully modulated to use the collecting units most appropriate to the individual districts.[33] Moreover, aristocratic, urban and commercial connections still tied Ireland very closely to England. This is apparent in the lordship's sensitivity to English politics, most dramatically during the Wars of the Roses, at the conclusion of which Dublin and Waterford served as bases for the Yorkist pretenders Lambert Simnel and Perkin Warbeck. State power in Ireland was less effective than it had been, but still effective enough to demand responses, arouse hopes, spread contentiousness, and shape the terms of political debate.

Medievalists are often irritated by what they regard as dismissive travesties perpetrated by modernists writing about medieval polities. There is a danger that they will respond by making inflated claims for the power and organisation of the kingdoms and provinces that they now freely refer to as 'states'.[34] Ireland – with its distance from the metropolis, its multiple frontiers, its regional political dynamics, its extended noble kins and large retinues – may seem improbable ground for centralised power and a widespread sense of subjecthood. Yet even in Ireland, the English state bulked large. Participation was, of course, mainly for the elite; but the elite was not a shallow one. English systems depended on the services of men of affairs, in counties and liberties, in their subdivisions (the cantreds and baronies), in towns, in the dioceses and smaller units through which ecclesiastical taxation was arranged. Arguably, too, frontier conditions threw more, not less, governmental responsibility on to local societies. The gentry community of Louth, for example, seems to have gained in solidarity and self-awareness as the county's borders contracted; and its members maintained close contacts with the Dublin government and with England.[35] For the population at large, involvement chiefly meant being mulcted and mobilised. Yet, as in England,[36] their awareness of wider issues should not be underestimated. In Ireland there was the special experience of belonging to threatened communities, which were protected as well as oppressed by representatives of royal authority. Englishness may have been chiefly embodied in the dominant 'horizontal layers' of aristocracy and gentry, leading townsmen and clergy (elements, incidentally, which were not 'segregated' but overlapped and interacted with one another). But a governmental system, which in the heartlands of the lordship was not without 'penetrativeness', 'pervasiveness' and 'infrastructural power', helped in some degree to 'co-opt' those below.[37]

II

How, then, did the settlers perceive and present themselves? John Gillingham's arguments for a swift emergence of a re-modelled Englishness among the Normans does not mean that the subject is foreclosed, in the sense that those who went on to conquer and settle in Ireland were already 'English'. For individuals, families and groups identity was still complex and fluid. Hugh Thomas has recently argued that in the late twelfth century people of mixed ancestry might choose to emphasise either their Norman or their English roots; increasingly more of them more often took the latter option.[38] Intervention and settlement in Ireland had begun in 1169–70 with incursions by mercenary leaders and troops from south Wales. The assertion of control by Henry II in 1171 ensured the participation of a far wider range of beneficiaries, mostly from the western side of England but including men from East Anglia and the Home Counties. Nevertheless, across southern Ireland a significant proportion of the settlers did come from the northern side of the Bristol Channel. Twelfth-century Dyfed was a multi-ethnic, polyglot society. Robert Bartlett's study of its most famous luminary, Gerald of Wales, has brought out just how slippery national labels were in that little world, inhabited by English, 'French', Flemish, and Welsh.[39] These complexities transferred themselves to south Leinster and Munster. This gives added point to the thirteenth-century experience of English law and institutions. In Ireland, as elsewhere in medieval Europe, law corralled the newcomers together, in this case as 'English'.[40] And since English law and government were a daily reality, they gave firmness to what was to remain a fundamental division: between the settlers, who were legally privileged, and the native population, who were not. Increasingly, the Irish could join the club only through explicit, written licences of the sort I mentioned earlier. The boundaries of privilege were defined as 'English', and were closely guarded. Individual grants of English status ensured the co-option of some upwardly mobile Irish into the English system.[41] But they were a small minority. This did not mean that everything was structured around a notionally ethnic divide: those defined as Irish could prosper at manorial level, and to an extent in towns, as chaplains, or as military captains. But their exclusion from official life was total. Ireland lacked anything comparable to the Welsh *uchelwyr*, a native ministerial class that developed into a squirearchy with a stake in the system. The failure to co-opt the Irish elites has since the time of Sir John Davies in the reign of James I been regarded as a fatal weakness of English Ireland.[42] Equally, the ability of English systems to function for so long despite excluding the Irish testifies to the strength of the core settlement areas.

The tendency to draw boundaries and to describe them in a national vocabulary is apparent also in the Church. There was collaboration between the English and reform-minded Irish clergy; but as early as 1217 proposals were made by the authorities in Ireland that the crown should, for security reasons, countenance only non-Irish bishops.[43] In the 1220s the Cistercian Order was riven by factions, which were described in national terms when Stephen Lexington, later abbot of Clairvaux, conducted a visitation of the Order's houses in Ireland.[44] He condemned what he saw as the disorder and backwardness of the native Irish establishments, recommending the removal of unsatisfactory Irish heads of houses, and their replacement by men of 'the other language and people' – a delicacy of phrasing that may suggest an uneasy awareness that he himself was English.[45] Distinctions were never as rigidly applied in the Church as they were in the state. The papacy opposed discrimination between peoples; the king was usually less enthusiastic than the English establishment in Ireland about implementing draconian proposals; Church courts did not make the ethnic distinctions that disfigured royal justice in Ireland. Even so, churchmen were to the fore in formulating xenophobic propaganda against one or other nation. It is hardly necessary to point out that we do not have to await the Reformation to find religious fissures with national resonances.

So legal and institutional demarcations, expressed in national terms, were established during the period when the lordship of Ireland was taking shape and expanding; an age of condescension and confidence verging upon triumphalism. During the fourteenth century the tone changes; we hear shrill voices insisting that they, the king's loyal subjects in Ireland, are 'true English', every bit as English as the 'English born in England', and entitled (in the modern weasel words) to 'parity of esteem' with them. These concerns and terminology appear in legislation, especially in the 1366 Statutes of Kilkenny, and also in the Latin annals kept in Dublin.[46] The statutes sought to organise the defence of the lordship, both militarily and against cultural contamination by the Irish; at the same time they played up the shared allegiance, the shared culture, and the common privileges of the English on either side of the Irish Sea. Such statements raise two questions. Historians often suggest, if only through their choice of metaphors, that the passage of time naturally produced a distancing from England and an increased identification with Ireland.[47] Clearly, it was more complicated than that, both because of the variety of settler environments and experiences, and because specific circumstances might actually reinforce ties with the metropolis. Secondly, being 'English' in the time of King Edward III was not the same as being 'English' in that of King John.

It is not difficult to understand why it was in the fourteenth century, six generations after the arrival of the English in Ireland, that public stress on their Englishness appeared and intensified. There was a sense of increased threat from the Irish, creating a mentality of encirclement in the eroded heartlands. From the start, medieval English Ireland was well supplied with a sense of 'the other'; that aspect of identity now acquired an extra meaning through frontier interactions that were perceived as menacing. Vulnerability in turn produced a heightened sense of dependency on England. Far from lessening, interaction with the homeland intensified. It also posed new problems. In fourteenth-century England political loyalty was convention-ally expressed in national terms. Wars against Scots and French from the 1290s led the crown to play the xenophobic card when seeking military service and taxation.[48] Given this equation of Englishness with loyalty, it is hardly surprising that king's subjects in Ireland, anxious to proclaim their fidelity, get protection, and claim their rewards should do so in words that stressed their English credentials.

Parading of English identity thus took place in particular contexts. It occurred when help was wanted from England. It happened even more when help arrived, for assistance took the form of English governors with their households and retinues, who were competitors with the locals for office and patronage. Declarations of loyalty and claims to Englishness were not the product of leisured musings; they were rhetorical strategies, adopted by political groups.[49] But that is not a reason for dismissing them. It is significant that the vocabulary of nation came naturally. Moreover, historians of England have attributed importance to similar elite tensions – in the middle of the twelfth century between political factions described by chroniclers in terms that (arguably) distinguish between 'Normans of England' and 'Normans of Normandy'; and in the thirteenth between 'native-born' aristocrats and 'foreign' courtiers.[50] There is also much to suggest that the sense of identity expressed at the level of high politics reflected the self-perceptions of local communities, which within Ireland portrayed themselves as islands of English loyalty surrounded by Irish enemies. Nor were such communities always on the defensive. In the 1350s Archbishop Richard FitzRalph of Armagh felt obliged to remind his compatriots in Dundalk and Drogheda that killing native Irish people might not be a felony in English law, but was nevertheless a sin in the eyes of God.[51]

This period saw constant dialogue between the elites of the lordship and the crown. Much of this took place in parliaments and great councils, a feature typical of late medieval polities.[52] Messengers were publicly chosen and briefed; on occasion taxes were raised to fund embassies to England.[53] An establishment, which had a strong sense of ownership of its English

privileges, waved them in the face of kings and their representatives. In 1341
nobles, knights and city mayors met in an assembly at Kilkenny to
denounce a royal revocation of lands and liberties; they brandished
Magna Carta at Edward III.[54] In the 1370s there were heavy demands for
taxation in Ireland as well as England. Resistance in Ireland provoked an
unprecedented summons of Irish representatives to appear in England
before the king's council. County and borough courts in Ireland elected
knights and burgesses with gritted teeth, but denied them the power to
consent to taxation. In an interesting shift of vocabulary, not just County
Dublin but also more distant Tipperary stated that this summons was
contrary to 'the liberties of Ireland'.[55] In 1418 an aristocratic faction headed
by the earl of Kildare and Sir Christopher Preston was in dispute with
the governor of Ireland, Thomas Talbot.[56] Talbot was accused of high-
handedly suspending a parliamentary session because of a security scare.
An attempt was made to continue the meeting in his absence, whereupon
he arrested Kildare and Preston and charged them with treason. Two texts
were found in Preston's possession: the coronation oath, which emphasised
the king's obligation to respect the law, and the political tract *Modus
Tenendi Parliamentum*. The *Modus*, which originated in England, perhaps
with the opposition to Edward II and certainly by the middle of the
fourteenth century, was an attempt to define the rights and procedures of
parliament in the face of rulers who stressed the royal prerogative. By the
1380s it was known in Ireland, where there is indeed more evidence of its
influence on politics than survives in England. It was being used in 1418 as a
guide to the supposed parliamentary proprieties that Talbot was disregard-
ing: the opposition allegedly said that 'it would have been less serious to let
the Irish ravage than to interrupt parliament'.[57]

Such episodes allow us to eavesdrop briefly on the aristocracy, greater
gentry and urban patriciates of eastern and south-coast Ireland. When we
do, we hear things reminiscent of other times and places. Clearly, we are
not in Massachusetts in the 1770s, or among the Irish Commons on
College Green in 1782; yet it would be wrong to dismiss these manifestations as a primitive prefiguring of ideas that deserve serious attention only
when they appear in more modern dress. They belong to a period when
gentry and parliamentary politics in England were prominent and sophisticated.[58] The Preston family had property in Lancashire as well as Ireland,
and Christopher Preston's father, Sir Robert Preston, had been chief justice
of the Dublin Bench and keeper of the great seal of Ireland.[59] England had
implanted in Ireland not just institutions, but a political vocabulary.
Medieval precedents were to figure in later arguments about the rights of

the Irish parliament and political community. For what it is worth, the past that was then imagined and manipulated was far from wholly fictional.[60]

III

This legal and institutional inheritance was one strand in the settlers' sense of their own past. Other strands deserve attention, either because they seem to contribute towards a coherent story, or – perhaps even more – because they do not, and thereby serve as a reminder of the danger of reducing complex and often inconsistent notions to a simplified model. Medieval English Ireland is not rich in surviving literary remains or in discursive political statements. The settlers knew who they were; they had arrived from an identifiable kingdom in the light of documentary day; there was no need for an equivalent of the chronicles that strained to give a shared Frankish identity to the people of varied origins who ended up as the ruling class in the crusader states.[61] Gerald of Wales was by far the most important source of ideas. His *Topography of Ireland* and *Conquest of Ireland* circulated widely in Ireland, where they were to be translated into English and Irish in the fifteenth century. In the early sixteenth, copies of 'Cambrensis' in Latin, English and Irish were in the library of the earls of Kildare.[62] Moreover Gerald shaped other writings. His work underlies what is said about Ireland in one of the two most popular English histories, the *Polychronicon* of Ranulf Higden, a copy of which the Kildares also owned.[63] The so-called 'Dublin' annals, of Cistercian provenance, deal with the later twelfth century largely by cutting and pasting Gerald.[64] He was also used by the compilers of the fifteenth-century Gaelic annals known as 'MacCarthy's Book'.[65]

Gerald explained how and why the English came to be in Ireland, justifying their presence in terms of remoter and of more recent history.[66] The first drew on the fantasies of Geoffrey of Monmouth, who claimed that King Gurguntius of Britain had originally permitted the Irish to settle in Ireland, and that Irish kings had attended King Arthur's court. The recent material cited events within Gerald's own time: the submission of the Irish kings to Henry II without a shot being fired, and the grant of the island to Henry by the papacy. Gerald preserves the text of Pope Adrian IV's letter *Laudabiliter* (1155), which authorised the king to enter Ireland to forward moral reform; he was also aware of endorsements by Pope Alexander III in 1172.[67]

By the fourteenth century all this was common currency. When the Scots invaded Ireland in 1315, their Irish supporters approached the papacy to try to get it to rescind the grant of 1155; they argued, in the document now known as the 'Remonstrance of the Irish Princes', that the English had acted not as benevolent reformers but as oppressors.[68] Counter-petitions, to the pope and the king, from Dublin circles drew very different conclusions from the same evidence. In 1317 Edward II was sent a copy of *Laudabiliter* to remind him of his rights in Ireland, together with a contrary reading of the past.[69] St Patrick had brought Christianity to Ireland; the Irish lapsed from it and fell into internecine wars; because of this, Henry II had come with papal blessing, with troops and with *lawyers* to sort the country out and spread civilisation. If there was a problem now, it was because judges had become soft on crime, failing to enforce the death penalty that the English law of felony demanded. These ideas continued to be repeated and elaborated. In 1420 the Dublin scholar James Young produced an English version of the pseudo-Aristotelian handbook on governance, the *Secreta Secretorum*, for the fourth earl of Ormond, who had just become governor of Ireland. He quoted Gerald's justifications of the English title to the island, adding extra points to back up the case. Chief among these were the fresh submissions made by Gaelic lords to Richard II in 1395.[70] Young's work was re-packaged in a memorandum sent in 1421 to Henry V, to raise his consciousness of Ireland and persuade him to intervene there, now that he seemed to have won the war in France.[71]

We have been reminded that it is one thing to trace views of the past among a narrow group of politicians and propagandists, and quite another to show that they were widely held and reflected upon.[72] But there are signs additional to the scholarly dissemination of Giraldian material that Gerald's account of the origins of the English position in Ireland was familiar. In 1346 a jury of knights and freemen at Tralee in Kerry accused their outlawed lord, the earl of Desmond, of treason. The jury claimed that Desmond had approached the pope requesting that he remove Edward III and appoint Desmond in his place, as papal vicar in Ireland. The earl was said to have alleged 'that our lord the king of England did not have the right to hold the land of Ireland because he had not maintained that land according to the laws of the land, in the manner that Pope Adrian required, but rather he had in various ways changed and annulled those laws and customs'.[73] There is a hint of muddle here that may suggest a living tradition: Adrian had charged Henry II to *replace* immoral Irish laws with ones consonant with Christian standards. Desmond's words (assuming he said any such thing) betray, not an attachment to ancient Gaelic law, but resentment at the failure of Edward's representatives to observe the English customs Henry's successors had established. Desmond had in 1331 suffered arrest and forfeiture by royal ministers; in 1341 he had been associated with the constitutional opposition in Ireland; he was to be forfeited again in 1345. His appeals to the king over the heads of royal officials in Ireland make much of his loss of his legal rights through ministerial envy and malice.[74]

As a founding story, that related by Gerald could hardly be bettered. The English presence in Ireland had a clear historical validation. It was a new, divinely approved, stage in the history of the island, with a Christian moral purpose, to discipline and educate a people presented as barbarous. This past barely connected with Irish historical traditions; it represented a fresh start. It appears a foreshortened affair, beginning only in the events of the later twelfth century. But this was not really so, for it could be viewed against two longer pasts, which were distinct but complementary. On the one hand, the history of the English in Ireland could be conceived as a branch of the longer stream of English history. This sense of time and place is visible in the Latin annals compiled within the lordship. These begin variously with the Creation, the birth of Christ, or the death of the emperor Claudius 'who had conquered Britain'. From there the route to the twelfth century leads primarily through the history of England, its kings, and its churchmen (Augustine, Bede and Dunstan, Lanfranc and Anselm).[75] Too much should not be made of this, since it arose from the re-copying of English annals, some of which had reached Ireland through ecclesiastical contacts well before 1169. Nevertheless, it is clear that annalists working in Ireland found it natural to splice such material to their accounts of the subsequent history of the English in Ireland.[76]

The other past, symbolised by references to Patrick, was that of early Irish Christianity. It is often seen as representing identification by the settlers with their new homeland, visible for example in Arnold le Poer's alleged defence of Ireland in the 1320s as 'an island of saints' against accusations of heresy levelled by Richard Ledrede, the English Franciscan bishop of Ossory. But it has other meanings, and it was certainly not – or not necessarily – associated with 'buying in' to Gaelic culture: indeed Arnold is portrayed as appealing in the same breath to Magna Carta.[77] In the twelfth century, the British Isles were free from hagiographical barriers; cults of Irish saints, notably Patrick and Brigid, were perfectly acceptable in England.[78] No reader of the twelfth-century Life of Patrick by Jocelin of Furness, which was dedicated to the Ulster conquistador John de Courcy as well as to northern Irish bishops, could avoid the message that Patrick the Briton's career belonged to Britain and Europe as well as to Ireland.[79] In Ireland, English-born bureaucrat prelates happily promoted native saints associated with the reputation and rights of their dioceses. Henry of London, archbishop of Dublin (1213–28), whose earlier career lay in the mundane business of King John's administration, and who was hostile to the promotion of native Irish clergy, provided materials for the canonisation of his Irish predecessor, Lorcán Ua Tuathail (d. 1180).[80] Around 1320 the synodal legislation of his successor Alexander Bicknor, a king's clerk and former treasurer of Ireland who was involved in the seamy English politics of Edward II's reign, ordered the strict observance of the feast of Patrick, together with those of Brigid and the other saints of the Leinster dioceses.[81] Rather like the Protestant 'new English' of the seventeenth century, who were to claim to be the heirs of the church of Patrick and Columba, the medieval settlers could see themselves as the true custodians of a Christian Irish past that had disappeared for several centuries into a tunnel of native disorganisation and immorality.

Perspectives such as these – emphasising religious reform, the English title to Ireland, and English law – can be fitted together neatly. However, the most cursory glance at the Statutes of Kilkenny exposes a complication. The people whose views I have been tracing defined themselves not just in relation to England and over against the Gaelic Irish, but also in contrast to 'degenerate' compatriots, who were pilloried as politically unreliable because of their supposed contamination by Gaelic alliances, customs and culture. Lords and kins in that category could dine from very different historical menus. By the fifteenth century some were commissioning bardic poetry and historical compendia which drew heavily on Irish traditions, interlaced with romance motifs.[82] In such productions the 'Franks' (not the 'English' – but, equally, not the 'Normans') could snobbishly take their place as the last of the noble ruling groups who engaged in the successive 'takings of Ireland' by incomers. Such a perspective made sense in the context of regional lordship beyond the zones of direct government, a world in which settler dynasties competed with their Gaelic neighbours in conditions where English institutions were barely relevant. Their sense of the past emphasised ownership justified by the sword and ancestral nobility.[83]

This perspective may be illustrated from bardic poems by Tadhg Óg Ó hUiginn addressed to Walter Burke (d. 1440) and his brother Edmund (d. 1458), successive heads of the Clanwilliam (Mayo) branch of the de Burgh family.[84] Addressing Walter, the poet stresses his bodily perfection. He was chosen by God to rule. The rivers of Ireland, which had been stopped up, gushed forth again at his birth, when his special qualities were recognised by the learned classes. He was a worthy heir to the kingship of Ireland.

Edmund's poem has similar motifs; he is a Foreigner, but 'there is a mingling of all the blood of the Gaoidhil [Gaels] in [his] blushing face'. In structure and tone, and to some extent in content, these are hardly distinguishable from poems written for lords regarded as Gaelic rather than foreign. But not entirely. Edmund is urged to reconquer the whole de Burgh heritage, described as more than half of Ireland. The poet states explicitly that the law of the English king is no longer enforced; might is now the only right. Even so, he refers to the *charter* of Clanwilliam, adding words which suggest that this was no mere figure of speech: 'in their charter is half of Éire – it should be often read – read to them their private documents'. This is followed by an encomium of the first William de Burgh, who came, from Norfolk and the circle of Rannulf Glanville, to Ireland with the future King John in 1185. William is reworked in late medieval Gaelic style: he becomes, ludicrously, 'William Conquer, friend of poets'. But it is admitted that he had received extensive grants from the English king. Moreover, the conceit of being worthy of the high kingship is transmuted into an entitlement to be governor of Ireland under the crown, an office held by several de Burghs between 1228 and 1331.[85]

So, of course, there was not a homogeneous 'English' people in Ireland, with a single sense of its past. Christopher Preston and Edmund Burke inhabited spheres that touched only lightly; they were at the extreme ends of a continuum of aristocratic attitudes. Christopher and his kind would have been appalled by Edmund's Gaelic Irish verses. Edmund, on the other hand, would have found no difficulty in endorsing the past as presented by Gerald. The two men shared a lowest common denominator: consciousness that they were not Gaelic Irish, and a sense of proprietorship that rested not just on the sword, but on English royal documents, sanctioning acquisition. Contemporaries were aware of the discordances. Around 1370 an earl of Desmond penned a Gaelic poem addressed to his ally MacCarthy, in which he spoke of the contradictory pulls of loyalty to his local friends and the expectations of the court of the 'king of the Saxons'. In this context and idiom, he presented the former as overriding.[86] But it is rash to assume that bardic products disclose the secrets of men's hearts whereas petitions and legal proceedings are stereotyped and unrevealing: both dealt in mandarin formulas, and both were aimed at specific audiences.[87]

These examples from the summit of settler society give the merest hint of what must have been a vast range of attitudes and attachments, affected by social standing, education, proximity to – or distance from – Dublin or Waterford or England, inter-marriage (or not) with Gaelic families, the passage of time, the challenge of events, and a multitude of other variables.

Given the nature of the sources, it is easy to build harmoniously proportioned castles in the air and call them 'identities', and all too difficult to be confident of even beginning to understand what individual contemporaries thought and felt. Lesley Johnson has commented that stories about the past were not expressions, let alone determinants, of identity, but 'a forum for ideas'.[88] Colin Kidd, writing about early modern Ireland, has revealed the eclectic way in which men seized upon the various (often contradictory) traditions available to them in order to construct the arguments they required.[89] Nevertheless, it may be possible to locate some firm ground. The power of the English state in the later Middle Ages is visible in its capacity to export laws and institutions, and to some extent a political culture, to a dominion beyond its shores. This served to sharpen the distinctions between settler and native. It also became part of the stock-in-trade of a settler elite, which developed a strong proprietorial interest in its (English) rights and institutions, which it defended against agents of the metropolis. In the bewildering spectrum of attachments and outlooks, this regnalism stands out in sharply defined and comparatively stable colours. Not so long ago, historians might have thought of it as a constitutional tradition; nowadays it is more likely to be labelled an ingredient of what we call an 'identity'. Either way, it was to prove – if I may combine the jargons of horticulture and political sociology – a hardy perennial.

NOTES

1 S. G. Ellis, *Ireland under the Tudors 1447–1603* (2nd edn, Harlow: Addison Wesley Longman, 1998), pp. 70–5. For maps that try to delineate the extent of government at various periods, see A. MacKay and D. Ditchburn (eds.), *Atlas of Medieval Europe* (London: Routledge, 1997), pp. 168–9, and T.W. Moody *et al.* (eds.), *A New History of Ireland*, vol IX, *Maps, Genealogies, Lists* (Oxford: Clarendon Press, 1984), p. 42.
2 On the identity of the 'English of Ireland', see J. F. Lydon, 'The middle nation', in J. F. Lydon (ed.), *The English in Medieval Ireland* (Dublin: Royal Irish Academy, 1984), pp. 1–26; 'Nation and race in medieval Ireland', in S. Forde, L. Johnson and A. V. Murray (eds.), *Concepts of National Identity in the Middle Ages* (Leeds: University of Leeds, Department of English, 1995), pp. 103–24; R. Frame, *Ireland and Britain 1170–1450* (London: Hambledon Press, 1998), ch. 8; and, for a literary approach, T. Turville-Petre, *England the Nation: Language, Literature and National Identity 1290–1340* (Oxford: Clarendon Press, 1996), pp. 155–80. The subject is set in a wider context in R. R. Davies, 'The peoples of Britain and Ireland, I. Identities', *Transactions of the Royal Historical Society* 6th ser. 4 (1994), 1–20, and 'III. Laws and customs', *Transactions of the Royal Historical Society* 6th ser. 6 (1996), 1–23.

3 The case for seeing the development of states and nations as a continuum across the 'medieval'/'modern' watershed is well made by K. J. Stringer, 'Social and political communities in European history: some reflections on recent studies', in C. Bjørn, A. Grant and K. J. Stringer (eds.), *Nations, Nationalism and Patriotism in the European Past* (Copenhagen: Academic Press, 1994), pp. 9–34; and by L. Johnson, 'Imagining communities: medieval and modern', in Forde, Johnson and Murray (eds.), *Concepts of National Identity*, pp. 1–19.

4 Anthony D. Smith, *Nationalism and Modernism: A Critical Survey of Recent Theories of Nations and Nationalism* (London: Routledge, 1998), pp. 193–5.

5 E.g. A. Hastings, *The Construction of Nationhood: Ethnicity, Religion and Nationalism* (Cambridge University Press, 1997), pp. 71–2, 85–6, 92–3; J. Hutchinson, *The Dynamics of Cultural Nationalism: The Gaelic Revival and the Creation of the Irish Nation State* (London: Allen and Unwin, 1987), pp. 50–2.

6 For example, one of the few Irish scholars to use the term 'state' in an Irish medieval context writes of 'the Norman-Irish state' (A. J. Otway-Ruthven, *A History of Medieval Ireland* (London: Benn, 1968), ch. 5).

7 Gillingham's articles, published during the 1990s, are collected in his *The English in the Twelfth Century: Imperialism, National Identity and Political Values* (Woodbridge: Boydell, 2000). See chs. 1, 3, 6, 9, and esp. pp. 150–7. Cf. B. Smith, *Colonisation and Conquest in Medieval Ireland: The English in Louth 1170–1330* (Cambridge University Press, 1999), and S. Duffy, *Ireland in the Middle Ages* (Dublin: Gill and Macmillan, 1997), where chapter 3 is entitled 'Adventus Anglorum'.

8 I. Short, '*Tam Angli quam Franci*: self-definition in Anglo-Norman England', *Anglo-Norman Studies* 18 (1995), 152–75; H. M. Thomas, *The English and the Normans: Ethnic Hostility, Assimilation and Identity 1066–c. 1220* (Oxford University Press, 2003), esp. ch. 6.

9 See G. J. Hand, *English Law in Ireland 1290–1324* (Cambridge University Press, 1967), ch. 1; and esp. P. Brand, *The Making of the Common Law* (London: Hambledon Press, 1992), pp. 445–50.

10 Frame, *Ireland and Britain*, p. 136.

11 *Statutes, Ordinances and Acts of the Parliament of Ireland, King John to Henry V*, ed. H. F. Berry (Dublin: HMSO, 1907), pp. 20, 20–1, 21, 22, 23–4, 24–5, 30, 31–2, 35.

12 On the structure of later medieval states see B. Guenée, *States and Rulers in Later Medieval Europe* (Oxford: Blackwell, 1985), esp. pp. 91–208.

13 *Statutes*, ed. Berry, pp. 194–212. There is a new edition and translation by P. Connolly, 'The enactments of the 1297 parliament', in J. F. Lydon (ed.), *Law and Disorder in Thirteenth-Century Ireland: The Dublin Parliament of 1297* (Dublin: Four Courts Press, 1997), pp. 148–61.

14 *Statutes*, ed. Berry, pp. 212–14, 220–6, 228–36.

15 'Keeping the peace', in Lydon (ed.), *Law and Disorder*, p. 65. See *The Welsh History Review* 19 (1998–9), 346 (R. R. Davies); *English Historical Review* 114 (1999), 690–1 (R. Frame); and *Speculum* 75 (2000), 495–6 (D. M. Korngiebel and Robert C. Stacey).

16 Frame, *Ireland and Britain*, pp. 191, 193.

17 'The English state and the Celtic peoples', *Journal of Historical Sociology* 6 (1993), 13.

18 Rees Davies, 'The medieval state: the tyranny of a concept?', *Journal of Historical Sociology* 16 (2003), 280–300, at 289–90. Cf. M. Mann, *States, War and Capitalism: Studies in Political Sociology* (Oxford: Blackwell, 1988), p. 23.

19 For the paragraphs that follow, see esp. H. G. Richardson and G. O. Sayles, *The Irish Parliament in the Middle Ages* (2nd, edition Philadelphia: University of Pennsylvania Press, 1964) and *The Administration of Ireland 1172–1377* (Dublin: Irish Manuscripts Commission, 1963); Hand, *English Law in Ireland*; Brand, *Making of the Common Law*, chs. 2, 12, 13, 19, 20; A. J. Otway-Ruthven, 'Anglo-Irish shire government in the thirteenth century', *Irish Historical Studies* [henceforth *IHS*] 5 (1946), 1–28; and G. McGrath, 'The shiring of Ireland', in Lydon (ed.), *Law and Disorder*, pp. 107–24. Otway-Ruthven, *History of Medieval Ireland*, ch. 5, provides an overview. For the wider context, see R. Frame, *The Political Development of the British Isles 1100–1400* (revised edition, Oxford: Clarendon Press, 1995), ch. 4, and R. R. Davies, *The First English Empire: Power and Identities in the British Isles 1093–1343* (Oxford University Press, 2000), chs. 4, 6.

20 Cf. A. B. White, *Self-Government at the King's Command* (Minneapolis: University of Minnesota Press, 1933).

21 Hand, *English Law in Ireland*, pp. 113–34; R. Frame, *English Lordship in Ireland 1318–1361* (Oxford: Clarendon Press, 1982), pp. 119–20, 234, 285; B. Hartland, 'Vaucouleurs, Ludlow and Trim: the role of Ireland in the career of Geoffrey de Geneville (*c.* 1226–1314)', *IHS* 32 (2001), 469–71.

22 W. M. Ormrod, 'The English state and the Plantagenet empire, 1259–1360: a fiscal perspective', in J. R. Maddicott and D. M. Palliser (eds.), *The Medieval State: Essays Presented to James Campbell* (London: Hambledon Press, 2000), pp. 197–215, at 198–99.

23 A. Cosgrove, 'Irish episcopal temporalities in the thirteenth century', *Archivium Hibernicum* 32 (1974), 63–71; J. A. Watt, *The Church in Medieval Ireland* (2nd edition, Dublin: University College Dublin Press, 1998), ch. 4.

24 T. O'Neill, *Merchants and Mariners in Medieval Ireland* (Blackrock: Irish Academic Press, 1987), pp. 58–65; M. D. O'Sullivan, *Italian Merchant Bankers in Ireland in the Thirteenth Century* (Dublin: Allen Figgis, 1962), ch. 5.

25 H. G. Richardson and G. O. Sayles, 'Irish revenue, 1278–1384', *Proceedings of the Royal Irish Academy* 62 C (1962), 87–100. Cf. A. A. M. Duncan, *Scotland: The Making of the Kingdom* (Edinburgh: Oliver and Boyd, 1975), pp. 596–9.

26 This is the subject of a series of studies by J. F. Lydon, which he conveniently summarises in A. Cosgrove (ed.), *A New History of Ireland*, vol. II, *Medieval Ireland 1169–1534* (Oxford: Clarendon Press, 1987), pp. 195–204. Cf. J. R. Maddicott, *The English Peasantry and the Demands of the Crown 1294–1341* (*Past and Present*, Supplement 1, 1975).

27 Frame, *English Lordship*, pp. 46–51, and pp. 130–339 *passim*.

28 B. Anderson, *Imagined Communities: Reflections on the Origins and Spread of Nationalism* (revised edition, London and New York: Verso, 1991), pp. 47–65. Cf. John Breuilly's distinction, in modern colonial states, between an 'administrative model' and a system based on alliances and diplomacy (*Nationalism and the State* (Manchester University Press, 1982), pp. 186–94). Both existed, in an overlapping way, in Ireland. See R. R. Davies, 'Lordship or colony?', in J. F. Lydon (ed.), *The English in Medieval Ireland* (Dublin: Royal Irish Academy, 1984), pp. 142–60. The theme is developed by H. B. Clarke, 'Decolonization and the dynamics of urban decline in Ireland, 1300–1500', in T. R. Slater (ed.), *Late-Medieval Urban Decline* (Aldershot: Ashgate Publishing, 2000), pp. 157–92.

29 See Frame, *Ireland and Britain*, pp. 220–39, for the conventions of the 'land of peace' and the 'land of war'. While the contrasts between English and Gaelic rural society were not so wide as to be classifiable as 'agricultural versus pastoral', they were *perceived* as being wider than they were (e.g. R. Bartlett, *Gerald of Wales 1146–1223* (Oxford: Clarendon Press, 1982), ch. 6; Gillingham, *The English*, pp. 3–19). To that extent medieval Ireland fits John Armstrong's model of an interface between sedentary and nomad or transhumance societies (*Nations before Nationalism* (Chapel Hill: University of North Carolina Press, 1982), pp. 41–3, 70–1).

30 See P. Connolly, 'The financing of English expeditions to Ireland, 1361–76', in J. F. Lydon (ed.), *England and Ireland in the Later Middle Ages: Essays in Honour of Jocelyn Otway-Ruthven* (Blackrock: Irish Academic Press, 1981), pp. 104–21.

31 *Rotulorum Patentium et Clausorum Cancellariae Hiberniae Calendarium*, ed. E. Tresham (Dublin: Irish Record Commission, 1828), p. 56, nos. 71–4, 77–8, p. 64, nos. 146–7.

32 Ibid., p. 69, no. 57, p. 71, no. 1, p. 72, nos. 2, 10, 15, p. 73, nos. 35–6, 55, p. 74, nos. 58–9, 64–5, p. 75, nos. 92–3, p. 76, no. 110.

33 *Parliaments and Councils of Mediaeval Ireland*, ed. H. G. Richardson and G. O. Sayles (Dublin: Irish Manuscripts Commission, 1947), pp. 131–91.

34 See the comments of Davies, 'The medieval state', 280–1.

35 Smith, *Colonisation and Conquest*, chs. 6, 7; Brand, *Making of the Common Law*, pp. 37–40.

36 See e.g. D. Carpenter, 'English peasants in politics, 1258–67', *Past and Present* 136 (1992), 3–42; J. R. Maddicott, 'Magna Carta and the local community, 1215–59', *Past and Present* 102 (1984), 25–65.

37 I borrow the terminology of Ernest Gellner (*Nations and Nationalism* (Oxford: Blackwell, 1983), pp. 8–11) and Michael Mann (*States, War and Capitalism*, pp. 1–32).

38 Thomas, *The English and the Normans*, pp. 71–3; also Gillingham, *The English*, pp. 151–2, 153–4.

39 Bartlett, *Gerald of Wales*, ch. 1; I. W. Rowlands, 'The character of Norman settlement in Dyfed', *Battle Anglo-Norman Studies* 3 (1981), 142–57.

40 For general discussion, see P. J. Geary, *The Myth of Nations. The Medieval Origins of Europe* (Princeton University Press, 2003), pp. 126–7, 154, 155.
41 See Hand, *English Law*, ch. 10. Cf. A. V. Murray, 'Ethnic identity in the crusader states: the Frankish race and the settlement of Outremer', in Forde, Johnson and Murray (eds.), *Concepts of National Identity*, pp. 62–4, and Anderson, *Imagined Communities*, p. 145, for the filtered absorption of native individuals into other colonial elites.
42 Sir John Davies, *Discovery of the True Causes why Ireland was never entirely subdued* (1612; repr. J. G. Barry (ed.), Shannon: Irish University Press, 1969), pp. 100–32; Hand, *English Law*, p. 215.
43 J. A. Watt, *The Church and the Two Nations in Medieval Ireland* (Cambridge University Press, 1970), pp. 71–4. For an overview, see B. Smith, 'The frontiers of Church reform in the British Isles, 1170–1230', in D. Abulafia and N. Berend (eds.), *Medieval Frontiers: Concepts and Practices* (Aldershot: Ashgate Publishing, 2002), pp. 239–53.
44 Watt, *Church and Two Nations*, ch. 4.
45 *Stephen of Lexington, Letters from Ireland 1228–1229*, ed. and trans. B. O'Dwyer (Kalamazoo: Cistercian Publications, 1982), nos. 28, 69, 75.
46 *Statutes*, ed. Berry, pp. 430–69, at 436–7, also pp. 417–18 (1357); *Chartularies of St Mary's Abbey, Dublin*, ed. J. T. Gilbert (2 vols., London: Rolls Series, 1884), vol. II, 383, 395.
47 E.g. Lydon, 'The middle nation', p. 11; Turville-Petre, *England the Nation*, p. 169.
48 See e.g. J. Barnie, *War in Medieval Society: Social Values and the Hundred Years War 1337–99* (London: Weidenfeld and Nicolson, 1974).
49 On these disputes, see Frame, *English Lordship*, chs. 7–9.
50 Gillingham, *The English*, pp. 129–40; M. T. Clanchy, *England and its Rulers 1066–1272: Foreign Lordship and National Identity* (London: Fontana, 1983), esp. pp. 241–62.
51 K. Walsh, *A Fourteenth-Century Scholar and Primate: Richard Fitz Ralph at Oxford, Avignon and Armagh* (Oxford: Clarendon Press, 1981), pp. 341–8.
52 Guenée, *States and Rulers*, pp. 172–85; S. Reynolds, *Kingdoms and Communities in Western Europe 900–1300* (Oxford: Clarendon Press, 1984), pp. 308–19; Frame, *Political Development*, ch. 8. Cf. Breuilly, *Nationalism and the State*, p. 359, where dialogue between king and community is presented as a 'first step towards nationalism'.
53 *Parliaments and Councils*, nos. 15, 16, 53; *Statutes*, ed. Berry, pp. 484–6, 562–85; *Rot. Pat. Hib.*, p. 77, nos. 37–9. Committees visiting the king have been described by a historian of the seventeenth century as a 'supplementary institution' (M. Perceval-Maxwell, 'Ireland and the monarchy in the early Stuart multiple kingdom', *Historical Journal* 34 (1991), 286). It was a very old one.
54 Frame, *English Lordship*, pp. 242–61. For Magna Carta, see *Statutes*, ed. Berry, pp. 344–5.

55 M.V. Clarke, *Fourteenth Century Studies* (Oxford: Clarendon Press, 1937), pp. 236, 238. See J. F. Lydon, 'William of Windsor and the Irish Parliament', *English Historical Review* 80 (1965), 252–67. This is an early example of 'slippage' between what might be described as 'the liberties of the king's [English] subjects in Ireland' and 'the liberties of Ireland'; it echoes the Dublin annalist's reference in 1361 to the 'people of Ireland' [i.e., the English] making war against 'the Irish' (*Chart. St Mary's*, vol. II, p. 395).

56 See Otway-Ruthven, *History of Medieval Ireland*, pp. 353–6; 'The background to the arrest of Sir Christopher Preston in 1418', *Analecta Hibernica* 29 (1980), 73–94; N. Pronay and J. Taylor, *Parliamentary Texts of the Later Middle Ages* (Oxford: Clarendon Press, 1980), pp. 117–52.

57 Otway-Ruthven, 'The arrest of Sir Christopher Preston', pp. 79–80. For an important re-evaluation of the *Modus*, which lays emphasis on its influence in Ireland, see K. Kerby-Fulton and S. Justice, 'Reformist intellectual culture in the English and Irish civil service: the *Modus tenendi parliamentum* and its literary relations', *Traditio* 53 (1998), 149–202.

58 E.g. G. L. Harriss, 'Political society and the growth of government in late medieval England', *Past and Present* 138 (1993), 28–57.

59 *Calendar of the Gormanston Register*, ed. J. Mills and M. J. McEnery (Dublin: Royal Society of Antiquaries of Ireland, 1916), pp. ix–xi. Christopher, who went to England in 1375 when he was still under age (*Rot. Pat. Hib.*, p. 93 no. 143), may well have had some legal training.

60 See e.g. C. Kidd, *British Identities before Nationalism: Ethnicity and Nationhood in the Atlantic World 1600–1800* (Cambridge University Press, 1999), esp. pp. 146–81.

61 Murray, 'Ethnic identity', pp. 59–73.

62 *Crown Surveys of Lands 1540–1, with the Kildare Rental Begun in 1518*, ed. G. Mac Niocaill (Dublin: Irish Manuscripts Commission, 1992), pp. 312–14, 355–6; D. Bryan, *Gerald fitz Gerald, the Great Earl of Kildare 1456–1513* (Dublin: Talbot Press, 1933), pp. 268–70.

63 *Polychronicon Ranulphi Higden*, ed. C. Babington and J. R. Lumby (9 vols., London: Rolls Series, 1865–86), vol. I, pp. 328–82. Cf. *Crown Surveys*, 314, 356.

64 *Chart. St Mary's*, ii. 267–76. For an analysis of the annals, see B. Williams, 'The Dominican annals of Dublin', in S. Duffy (ed.), *Medieval Dublin II* (Dublin: Four Courts Press, 2001), pp. 142–68.

65 *Miscellaneous Irish Annals*, ed S. Ó hInnse (Dublin: Institute for Advanced Studies, 1947), pp. x, 46–7, 50–1.

66 *Expugnatio Hibernica: The Conquest of Ireland, by Giraldus Cambrensis*, ed. A. B. Scott and F. X. Martin (Dublin: Royal Irish Academy, 1978), pp. 148–9; *Gerald of Wales, The History and Topography of Ireland*, ed. and trans. J. J. O'Meara (London: Penguin Books, 1982), pp. 99–100.

67 *Expugnatio Hibernica*, pp. 142–7.

68 *Scotichronicon by Walter Bower*, ed. D. E. R. Watt *et al.*, vol. VI (Aberdeen: Aberdeen University Press, 1991), pp. 384–403; J. R. S. Phillips, 'The Irish Remonstrance: an international perspective', *IHS* 27 (1990), 112–29.

69 *Documents on the Affairs of Ireland before the King's Council*, ed. G. O. Sayles (Dublin: Irish Manuscripts Commission, 1979), pp. 99–100 (PRO, S.C.8/177/8820). The text of *Laudabiliter* survives as PRO, S.C.8/177/8818. See also J. A. Watt, 'Negotiations between Edward II and John XXII concerning Ireland', *IHS* 10 (1956), 1–20, at 18–20.

70 *Three Prose Versions of the Secreta Secretorum*, ed. R. Steele (London: Early English Texts Society, 1898), pp. 183–6.

71 *Proceedings and Ordinances of the Privy Council of England*, ed. N. H. Nicolas, 7 vols. (London: Record Commission, 1834–7), vol. II, pp. 51–2. The context is explored in E. A. E. Matthew, 'The governing of the Lancastrian Lordship of Ireland in the time of James Butler, fourth Earl of Ormond, *c.* 1420–1452' (PhD thesis, University of Durham, 1994), ch. 4, esp. pp. 119–20, 143–53.

72 Johnson, 'Imagining communities', pp. 13–14; L. E. Scales, 'Identifying "France" and "Germany": medieval nation-making in some recent publications', *Bulletin of International Medieval Research* 6 (2000), 23–4, 35–6.

73 G. O. Sayles, 'Legal proceedings against the first earl of Desmond', *Analecta Hibernica* 23 (1966), 20, 43–4.

74 *Documents on the Affairs of Ireland*, p. 203.

75 *Annals of Ireland by John Clyn and Thady Dowling*, ed. R. Butler (Dublin: Irish Archaeological Society, 1849), pp. 1–7; *Chart. St Mary's*, Vol.II, pp. 241–80; R. Flower, 'Manuscripts of Irish interest in the British Museum', *Analecta Hibernica* 2 (1931), 330–1; 'Annales de Monte Fernandi', ed. A. Smith, in *Tracts relating to Ireland*, vol. II (Dublin: Irish Archaeological Society, 1843), pp. 1–11.

76 The materials included Henry of Huntingdon (*Chart. St Mary's*, vol. II, pp. 243–63 *passim*) and a Lincoln source. On the process of transmission and the importance of the Cistercian network, see Williams, 'The Dominican annals of Dublin', pp. 142–51. The references to Irish history in these annals concentrate on religious reform and Ireland's links with England and the Continent, themes compatible with the Giraldian view.

77 *A Contemporary Narrative of the Proceedings against Dame Alice Kyteler*, ed. T. Wright (London: Camden Society, old series 24, 1843), p. 17. Cf. Lydon, 'Nation and race', pp. 10–12.

78 R. Bartlett, 'Cults of Irish, Scottish and Welsh saints in twelfth-century England', in B. Smith (ed.), *Britain and Ireland 900–1300: Insular Responses to Medieval European Change* (Cambridge University Press, 1999), pp. 67–86.

79 E.g. John Colgan, *Trias Thaumaturga* (Louvain, 1647; repr., with introduction by P. Ó Riain, Dublin: De Búrca, 1997), pp. 65–70, 86, 101–2.

80 R. Sharpe, *Medieval Irish Saints' Lives: An Introduction to Vitae Sanctorum Hiberniae* (Oxford: Clarendon Press, 1991), p. 28.

81 A. Gwynn, 'Provincial and diocesan decrees of the diocese of Dublin during the Anglo-Norman period', *Archivium Hibernicum* 11 (1944), 82–3.

82 K. Simms, 'Bards and barons', in R. Bartlett and A. MacKay (eds.), *Medieval Frontier Societies* (Oxford: Clarendon Press, 1989), pp. 177–97, at 190–1; J. Carney, in Cosgrove (ed.), *A New History of Ireland*, vol. II, pp. 692–3.

83 R. Bartlett, *The Making of Europe: Conquest, Colonization and Cultural Change 950–1350* (London: Penguin Books, 1993), pp. 90–6.

84 *Aithdioghluim Dána: Bardic Poems from the Yellow Book of Lecan*, ed. L. McKenna (Dublin: Irish Texts Society, 1940), vol. II, pp. 87–93 (poems 36, 37).

85 These are typical of the modifications made by Gaelic poets addressing lords of settler ancestry: cf. Simms, 'Bards and barons', pp. 187, 192.

86 G. Mac Niocaill, 'Duanaire Ghearóid Iarla', *Studia Hibernica* 3 (1963), 17–19.

87 Cf. K. Simms, 'Bardic poetry as a historical source', in T. Dunne (ed.), *The Writer as Witness: Historical Studies XVI* (Cork University Press, 1987), pp. 58–75.

88 'Etymologies, genealogies and nationalities (again)', in Forde, Johnson and Murray, *Concepts of National Identity*, pp. 132–3.

89 *British Identities before Nationalism*, esp. pp. 147–8.

CHAPTER 7

Late medieval Germany: an under-Stated nation?

Len Scales

'Judged purely by its success in creating a nation-state, German history has to be deemed a failure until the nineteenth century.'[1] This familiar view of the historical relationship between power and the German nation gains added significance from the context in which it here appears: in a recent introduction to the political development of late *medieval* Europe. The book's co-authors do, it is true, distance themselves at once from such a narrow perspective. But taken on its own, it seems to encapsulate a piece of well-established common ground among historians of pre-modern and modern Germany – and particularly those writing within the broad Anglophone historiographical tradition. Generally speaking, historians of the modern and the pre-modern nation have been hampered by a failure to pay enough regard to each other's findings and approaches. In the case of Germany, however, the problem has traditionally been, in a way, almost an opposite one, with loosely framed grand narratives and vague, sometimes unvoiced, assumptions and connections being traded freely back and forth between students of different epochs of the German past. Not uncommonly, medievalists have fashioned their accounts with at least half an eye on events far distant in time.[2] Modernists seem at first glance less encumbered, with their bold insistence on the German nation's quintessential modernity. Some are even at pains to declare that there is nothing to say on their subject before, at earliest, the closing years of the eighteenth century.[3] If this sometimes strikes the reader as protesting too much, the suspicion is reinforced by the shades of a more remote German past that have a habit of flitting behind modernist narratives. 'German national consciousness' may have been 'born in the Wars of Liberation from Napoleonic domination', thus emerging 'significantly later' than in neighbouring lands; but the historian who wrote these words still felt the need for an excursion back to the end of the Middle Ages in order to account for this anomaly.[4] Others cover their modernist positions with a parenthetical backward gesture to the effect that 'some form of German identity that one might call national' is here and there to be met with already in more distant epochs.[5]

Why those earlier national stirrings failed in the German case to bear fruit is a question to which medievalists, since their own first nationalist heyday in the nineteenth century, have judged themselves especially well qualified to supply answers. It was the peculiar shape of medieval German political life, and above all the imperial entanglement, which conspired to ensure that Germany 'missed the opportunity for national development' in this crucial formative era.[6] The Germans, on this well-accustomed view, had their place in the ferment of peoples and kingdoms that arose in western continental Europe following the fragmentation of Charlemagne's empire in the ninth century. But a series of colossal outside shocks and self-inflicted false turnings subsequently robbed the Germans of the philosopher's stone that elsewhere in Europe allowed infant political communities to transform themselves into fully grown nation-states.[7] The view of medieval German history as a fateful succession of calamities has for some time now been exposed to a healthy blast of scepticism.[8] But traditional yardsticks and teleologies have died harder in studies addressing the early formation of European states and nations, where we can still read how the Germans in pre-modern times 'failed' to 'achieve' mature state institutions (in contrast to the 'remarkable success' of their French neighbours in the same venture).[9]

But, as readers of Friedrich Meinecke are aware, *Staatsnationen* are not the only nations. The consolation prize of a *Kulturnation* remained a possibility where the framework of the state was wanting.[10] But for the Germans, it is alleged, the medieval legacy proved to be a poisoned one, setting them on that fatal path that led many centuries later to the genocidal nationalism of *ius sanguinis* – into a historical 'toxic waste dump' that, for one medievalist, continues to this day to ooze pollutants into the groundwater.[11] In this chapter I shall argue that this familiar view, of an ethnically and linguistically focused medieval *Kulturnation*, devoid of relationships with power and government, is fundamentally mistaken.[12] I shall also take issue with an assumption often detectable behind both medievalist and modernist accounts of the early history, or pre-history, of European nations, namely that their emergence invariably depended upon the establishment and maintenance of powerful, intrusive and wide-ranging 'state' structures.[13] It concentrates on the decades between the fall of the Hohenstaufen dynasty in the middle years of the thirteenth century and the establishment of an enduring Habsburg presence on the imperial throne in the second half of the fifteenth. This was the period during which, medievalists often contend, the institutions of secular government attained their first mature expression elsewhere in western Europe.[14] In

Germany, by contrast, these two centuries marked, by general assent, the nadir of the medieval *Reich*, viewed as a system of power.[15] But, as will be shown, that disheartening state of affairs did not in fact preclude the articulation of a German identity with a thoroughly *political* character. If medieval nations were 'imagined communities', then relationships with rulership and government were themselves quite capable of being constructed *imaginatively*, in spite of – indeed, sometimes under the direct stimulus of – the all-too-apparent limitations of contemporary structures of power.

I readily concede, at least for Germany, the modernists' claim that the social scope and political consequences of the nation were transformed in the novel circumstances of the nineteenth and twentieth centuries. I do, however, argue against the view, systematically formulated by Jürgen Habermas, that reduces pre-modern political culture to mere 'representation': the one-sided, unchallenged projection of official messages by small, homogeneous ruling elites onto inert populations.[16] Instead, I will suggest that the articulation of German political identities during the late Middle Ages is to a significant degree explicable in terms of the fissured, contested and polycentric character of imperial power in the German-speaking lands. Late medieval Germany may not have known any social formation broad and inter-connected enough to be called a 'public sphere'; but it did know a considerable range and variety of different ('public') spaces, where political ideas were formulated, and where contesting principles sometimes collided. Out of this diversity there emerged a political public for the German nation which, while unquestionably small if measured against modern criteria, displayed greater social breadth and heterogeneity than modernist approaches often allow. Indeed, another of this chapter's contentions is that, while the late medieval German nation was clearly in most respects a lesser thing than its modern successor, there seem few certain grounds for ranking it below the expressions of national identity and solidarity encountered in other European realms of the same period.

The *Kulturnation* was, we have been taught, first and foremost a community of shared speech.[17] Language therefore provides a natural point from which to begin examining the late medieval German nation.[18] Medieval commentators did, it is true, invoke common tongue quite often as a criterion by which the Germans might be identified.[19] We do not, however, need to look far in order to see just how paradoxical such a view was. Late medieval Germany was home to several different written vernaculars, to say nothing of its rich profusion of spoken dialects. When a fourteenth-century scholar, Conrad of Megenberg, made reference to his

German 'mother' tongue, he did not mean some notional universal 'German' language, but specifically the Franconian form of Germanic speech.[20] The paradox was not lost on contemporaries, the chronicler Peter of Zittau wondering at the fact that the Saxon and the Bavarian, neither of whom understood the other, each passed for a 'German' speaker.[21]

It is hard to see how a supposedly common tongue embracing such a Babel of discordant voices could have served as a foundation for collective identity in any society – still less in one as marked by localism and limited communications as was medieval Germany. The explanatory process needs to be reversed. If the various Germanic tongues that were spoken and written within the limits of the *Reich* came over time to be regarded as constituting, at least in some contexts, a single 'German' language, that was the result of processes in which power and rulership had been centrally involved. The earliest developments took place not in Germany but in Italy, where in the course of the tenth and eleventh centuries a number of Latin terms (*Teutonici, Teutones*, and certain derivatives) became current, referring to the northern followers of the Saxon and Salian emperors.[22] Gradually, the new terminology infiltrated writings from north of the Alps, with the Investiture Contest of the eleventh and early twelfth centuries providing a major impetus.[23] 'The Germans' were henceforth, down to the end of the Middle Ages, conceived above all as those speakers of Germanic tongues who were also subject to the emperor.[24]

For Germans, as for other medieval Europeans, what common language represented was not an alternative to a (missing) political identity, but rather one of the elements out of which such an identity was constituted. Language did, it is true, vary considerably in its importance as an element in medieval collective identities, claiming considerable prominence in the articulation of some 'nations', while having only a subsidiary or even a negligible role in others.[25] For literate Germans, the idea of shared language had some utility in demarcating a common identity, though its importance tended to be confined to certain specific contexts, and was never over-riding. What a comparative survey of medieval European realms shows above all, however, is the complexity of language's role: its relative prominence in particular cases in itself tells us next to nothing about the relative cohesiveness, maturity, incipient modernity or long-term future courses of different political communities.

The alleged primacy of language to the early formulation of German identity is thus relatively easily discounted. That, however, is only one of the elements which, it is often maintained, distinguish the course of

German nation-making from that followed elsewhere. The other key determining factor – the relative absence of institutional political foundations – is harder to contest. Bernard Guenée, in a wide-ranging comparative study of late medieval political culture, has made the distinction plain. 'In the birth of French national identity ... a political fact – the existence of a king and a kingdom – was of primordial importance.' In Germany, Guenée goes on, things were different.[26]

The qualities that have led historians to discern in the central and later Middle Ages the formation of a French political nation need only the briefest repetition.[27] Myths of sacrality and Christian mission clustered readily around a dynasty of unusual longevity, within an account of western Frankish kingship which had continuity as well as coherence. Royal saints and miracle-working rituals were accommodated readily in such a framework. The descendants of crusader-kings were able to claim the epithet 'most Christian' without a flicker of irony, even while they defied or manipulated popes, suppressed a crusading order, or taxed their clergy for war.[28] Not just the kings but their land too was a 'holy' one, favoured by God, the special home of Christian piety and learning. The French aristocracy, for its part, established a cultural template for the ruling classes throughout Europe. At the same time, French society was drawn to a focus in a political system of striking coherence and power. A great royal city channelled from early on the material and ideological resources of French rulership. Strengthening threads of power linked the capital with the regions and their populations.[29] A rich, articulate tradition of royalist constitutional theory seems, at least in the estimation of modern scholarship, to have folded out a blueprint for the sovereign nation state by as early as 1300.[30] All the pieces were in place for a story of unshakeable power and success, with even the crises bearing a positive witness. Here, after all, was a monarchical nation-state whose sinews penetrated French society so thoroughly and unmistakably that by the fifteenth century even an obscure teenage girl from the eastern marches could tell who was God's lawful king and her own.

If the long-term course of German history has invited rather different tales from the medieval past, the sorry state of the imperial monarchy has seemed well able to furnish the requisite raw materials. It is hard to imagine a starker contrast. We could start by substituting for good St Louis the Hohenstaufen Antichrist Frederick II. Thenceforward it is down-hill all the way – that is, if we do not opt instead for the alternative view, namely that the fate of the imperial monarchy was effectively already sealed long before that time. The *Reich* had little to show in the way of institutional government. Imperial justice, by the close of the Middle Ages, was hard to get, could not touch the princes, and had little force off the routes of the king's dwindling *iter*. The Empire's ruler could tax only a handful of his subjects, his military resources were puny, and he had few dependable means of making his will known to his subjects, beyond calling to see them in person.[31] There is little here to impress historians of the pre-modern nation-state – especially if they have also imbibed the lesson that what above all made medieval men and women patriotic was the chance to give their bodies to the king's war and their taxes to his coffers, to bear the strictures of his justice and the scrutiny of his officials.

That was not, however, the full extent of the Empire's shortcomings. Where, in Germany, are the miracle-working kings? Where the royal saints? Charlemagne, the most obvious contender, occupies in the medieval German tradition a place too complex to allow him easily to fit the role.[32] Medieval Germany never boasted a temple of monarchy to set beside Paris or Westminster.[33] None of this is surprising when we recall how fully the principle of election by the German princes, established after the middle of the thirteenth century, had obliterated earlier elements of dynastic continuity in the *Reich*.[34] Between Frederick II's death in 1250 and that of his Habsburg namesake in 1493, son followed father on the throne just once.[35] Election helped to encourage the ruler's physical, and in some ways also his ideological, marginality to German political life. For much of the fourteenth century, imperial rulership had its focus in Bohemia. From the fifteenth onwards, its home was in the Austrian duchies of the far south-east. Seen in this way, the period in the 1260s during which Richard of Cornwall affected to rule the *Reich* by remote control from beyond the English Channel seems like only a particularly extreme expression of a distinct constitutional tendency.[36]

If the character of rulership in late medieval Germany seems ill-fitted to nurturing a shared political identity, the traditional conceptual vocabulary of western emperorship appears actively to discourage one. The accustomed terminology in imperial letters and diplomas was, on the whole, Christian and Roman, not German.[37] 'Germany', indeed, had at best only qualified and uncertain significance as a unit of government, within an assemblage of imperial territories that also embraced Burgundy, Bohemia and substantial parts of Italy. A *regnum Alemanniae* is indeed sometimes found in the writings of the chroniclers and, more rarely, in official documents.[38] But it lacks that substance, born of constitutional clarity as well as common repetition, that in the later Middle Ages the 'kingdom of France' or the 'kingdom of England' could command. For some of the time, this nebulous 'German realm' did not even have German rulers. French and English princes were several times candidates for the imperial crown. An English king's brother was actually chosen, as was a king of Castile. The house of Luxemburg, which supplied four of the Empire's rulers, moved in a world of international dynasticism where ethnic categories meant little. Such effort as the Luxemburgs invested in the politics of collective identity was directed more at winning hearts and minds in their dynastic realms than at the *Reich*.[39]

But none of these seeming obstacles was enough to prevent 'the Germans' and their lands from being invoked, in indisputably political ways, in a rich diversity of late medieval writings. Mention of them is not even *especially* rare in documents from the imperial chancery – in which, however, they are mostly confined to the less 'dignified' and formulaic elements. Far more numerous, though, are the references to land and people to be found in vernacular and Latin chronicles and annals, and in the political songs and verses in which the thirteenth and fourteenth centuries were so rich. Easily the fullest and most eloquent formulations of a German political identity come, however, in treatises and pamphlets – often described, misleadingly, as the work of 'publicists' – addressing the character, history, contemporary state and expected fate of the imperial monarchy. These outspokenly imperialist tracts make a telling counterpoint to the relative decline of the *Reich* as a European power between the mid-thirteenth and later fifteenth centuries – the time when most of them were written. Nearly all attest what one treatise-writer, Lupold of Bebenburg, declared was his 'fervid zeal for the German fatherland (*patria Germaniae*)'.[40] What all these different sorts of writing have in common is an outlook which defines German identity mainly in relation to the imperial monarchy, and a view of the Empire which insists on its specifically German roots.

In character, the remarks on the subject encountered in these varied texts cover a wide range, from the programmatic to the off-hand and from the grandiloquent to the workaday. The largest claims were staked by the treatise-writers. Alexander of Roes conjured the full rhetorical span of neo-Roman Christian imperialism, writing of 'the Germans, to whom the government of the world is translated and the direction of the Church committed'.[41] Chroniclers rose occasionally to comparable feats of bombast, with one celebrating the 'world dominion' which pertained to the *Teutonici*.[42] If the Germans ruled the *Reich*, then it could logically be stated that the Empire's home was their lands. In Latin verses, Lupold of Bebenburg had a personified Empire declare that 'I inhabit the Germans' fatherland for my seat.'[43] The fate of those who occupied the imperial throne was therefore the special concern of the German people, and a number of different, sometimes anonymous, versifiers are to be found urging 'Germany' to rejoice at a ruler's election to the Empire or his victories in battle, or to weep at his untimely death.[44] Sometimes, a German identity enfolded the Empire's ruler yet more tightly. For the Strasbourg chronicler Fritsche Closener, writing in the vernacular towards the middle of the fourteenth century, Conrad I (911–18) had been 'the first German *Kaiser*', ruling for seven years 'in the German lands'.[45] Otto I (936–73), meanwhile, was 'the first *powerful* German *Kaiser*'.[46] The ethnic foundation of Otto's rule was emphasised by Lupold of Bebenburg, who told how the Saxon emperor had subjected Italy 'to the power of the rulership and rulers (*regni et regum*) of Germany'.[47] On one influential view (albeit not one which all German writers accepted), Charlemagne himself, historic renewer of the Roman Empire, was an illustrious German.[48] The ethnic variety of the Empire's late medieval rulers, striking to a modern observer, was less evident to contemporaries, who could, when so minded, fashion 'Germans' from the most apparently unpromising materials. 'Thus, Charles IV and his son Wenceslas possessed the *Reich* and were kings of Bohemia; yet they were of German dynasty – and *had to be* of German dynasty.' If the cosmopolitan, Francophone, Slavophile Luxemburgers seem even to the most optimistic view problematical 'Germans', one chronicler at least felt he knew what custom obliged him to see, and duly saw it.[49]

The stage which framed the imperial monarch's routine acts and movements was, despite its lack of firm constitutional structures, often made an explicitly German one. It was to 'Germany', or in vernacular documents 'the German lands', that absent rulers habitually assured their faithful subjects they would shortly come back – a well-established refrain in Charles IV's communications with German recipients.[50] The ruler's visibility on German soil was for some a basic measure of his government. As one chronicler dismissively put it, Richard of Cornwall 'came nowhere in the German lands except to the Rhine, and was in fact impotent in the *Reich*'.[51] As for the ruler's actions when north of the Alps, imperial documents gave these on occasion an explicitly German frame of reference. A letter of Rudolf of Habsburg dealing with the government of imperial Italy signals in addition a clear order of priorities: 'having resolved all things throughout Germany, we are turning our mind to Tuscany . . .'.[52] It was the chroniclers, however, who most often reported the deeds of kings and emperors within a consciously German setting. War and peace, public order and its breakdown, were matters which especially moved them to inflate the monarch's deeds to fill an all-German stage. A Bavarian chronicler, reporting Albert I's victory of 1302 over his princely opponents, explained that henceforth, 'with the spectre of war driven away, ... the security and tranquillity of peace spread through all of Germany'.[53] It is the hyperbolic or generalised note that underlines in remarks like these the binding quality of the 'German' frame of reference: 'all of Germany', not just the handful of regions where the monarch actually went, was held to flourish under a good ruler, or disintegrate into pernicious chaos under a bad one.

The language of *Romanitas* customary in both Latin and vernacular documents from the imperial chancery did admittedly limit in some ways the scope for describing the imperial monarchy as a specifically 'German' institution – especially since it was also adopted by other German chanceries and by many chroniclers and poets.[54] Consequently, we only occasionally find German writers referring to the Empire's ruler, in the terminology habitual elsewhere in western Europe, as 'king of Germany'.[55] But, in sharp contrast, the princes who shared the Empire's rule with their monarch were routinely given an ethnic appellation. This included the electors: contemporary reports commonly recount how the new king and future emperor was chosen by the princes of 'Germany' or 'the German lands'.[56] The language of Germanness may have had few fixed locations in the constitutional vocabulary of the medieval *imperium*.[57] But it was not, on that account, absent from the utterances of the imperial monarchy itself, still less from writings reflecting on the *Reich* or recording the deeds of its rulers. The varied and overlapping language of German identity – *Alemannia, Teutonia, Germania* with a rich array of derivatives in Latin, the abrupt switch to the plural *tiutschiu lant* in the vernacular – is bewildering to the modern observer; but there is little sign that its multiplicity left contemporaries feeling especially troubled or confused (any more than the Inuit appear confused about the nature of snow).[58] Nor does the lack of a distinct, legally bounded sphere of 'German' government seem to have been an insuperable obstacle: writers of various sorts deployed the language of Germanness freely in a range of contexts, without following rigid rules, and clearly felt they knew what they meant with enough precision for their own ends. They did not doubt that the 'German' sphere to which they referred had ascertainable limits – even if many would doubtless have struggled to define them precisely.[59]

We could continue at length heaping up examples in similar vein, expressing aspects of a clearly political conception of German identity.

There seems no obvious reason for supposing them to be either less numerous or less expressive of authentic sentiments, notions and assumptions than equivalent utterances from other European realms. But neither, as modernist critics would justly point out, does the mere accumulation of source references take us very far towards judging the social and political role or consequences of the medieval idea of nation. Any attempt to meet that challenge would need to determine as fully as possible its social location, as well as the social, political and cultural factors affecting its reception. The apparently anomalous relationship between power and identity in late medieval Germany opens up, as will become clear, some suggestive routes down which to explore these problems. First, however, a related question must be addressed: why late medieval views of German identity were able, in the comparative absence of institutional structures or stimuli, to sustain such a close imagined relationship with power and rulership.

To understand this means explaining how an institution with allegedly Roman and Christian foundations and a supposedly universal mission was able to be associated specifically with one people and its lands. This requires in turn two distinct approaches, focusing respectively on the outward characteristics of rulership in the late medieval *Reich* and on the particular and distinctive way in which the ethnic basis of monarchical power was conceived in Germany. One reason why imperial rule was so susceptible to being viewed in a German frame is that it seemed to the outward gaze naturally to fit such a frame. Never was that truer than in the two centuries following the death of Frederick II. Kings and emperors in that period may have exercised only a weak and partial rule in their German territories; but most of them spent more time among their German subjects than in any other part of the *Reich*. The concentration of rulership upon the regions north of the Alps became especially pronounced in the decades after the fall of the Hohenstaufen, during which the number and duration of expeditions into Italy declined.[60] In the same period, the Romance-speaking territories of imperial Burgundy fell increasingly under the sway of the French crown.[61] The remaining imperial properties and revenues lay mainly within the German lands, which also supplied most of the monarchy's servants.[62] The armies which the Empire's ruler led on campaign, depleted though they were, were mainly German in composition, and were so perceived by contemporaries.[63] During the fourteenth century, it became increasingly common for the imperial chancery to address German subjects in their own language – even if there was at first some reluctance to employ the vernacular for recipients outside the High

German heartlands.[64] The main acts in creating the Empire's ruler – election, coronation, and the round of legitimising journeys and occasions that customarily followed – took place on German soil, under the control of German high dignitaries.[65] Indeed, apart from Rome, the main centres of public spectacle and political memory for the *Reich* all lay in Germany. The order of priorities signalled in contemporary comment and sometimes in official documents had an objective basis: Germany was the foundation and starting point for rule of the Empire.

Seen in this way, the relationship between common identity and the framework of rulership in late medieval Germany was in practice closer to the pattern found in other European realms – to the kind of solidarity which Susan Reynolds has termed 'regnal' – than first appearances suggest.[66] Yet viewed from another perspective, it does appear distinctive. By the middle years of the thirteenth century the principle was well established that the whole German people (and not merely its ruler) held in trust the Christian Roman Empire. This idea drew sustenance from traditions tracing Trojan ancestry, first for the Franks, later for the German people as a whole, and thus allowing the Germans to claim blood kinship with the ancient Romans.[67] Another Romanising myth, widely disseminated in writings of the central and later Middle Ages, concentrated on the aid which the ancient Germans had allegedly given Caesar in wresting supreme power from the Senate.[68] Most authoritative, however, was the doctrine that there had at some point in the past taken place a constitutionally binding 'translation' of the Roman Empire to the Germans. This notion gained watertight canon-law foundations at the beginning of the thirteenth century when Pope Innocent III ruled in his decretal *Venerabilem* (1202) that the papacy had transferred the Empire to the Germans in the person of Charlemagne.[69] Thenceforth, according to this widely known and influential text, nomination of the Empire's ruler had lain with the German princes.

The doctrine of the Empire's 'translation' emphasised sharply the ethnic foundations of imperial rule.[70] It provides a key to the language of ethnic identification in which late medieval writers habitually enfolded the main bearers of power in Germany – the princes, the nobility in general, the imperial towns – even as they lauded the *Romanitas* of the monarch. This explicitly German constitutional base was laid open to inspection as never before in the troubled decades after the fall of the Hohenstaufen. At a time of crisis for the *Reich*, it encouraged both the Germans and their neighbours and rivals to scrutinise critically the qualifications of the Empire's bearers.[71] Some German writers now strove to defend their people's hold on the *imperium* in detailed, tendentious accounts of German history and character.[72] They traced a proud tradition, reaching back to Frankish times, of service rendered by 'German' monarchs to Church and Faith. But they also explained why the Germans' innate common qualities, particularly their alleged talent and taste for war, fitted the whole people for the supreme military – more accurately, *political* – charge in Christendom.[73] The matter was now urgent, because Innocent's doctrine made plain that what the pope had transferred once he could transfer afresh, to another, more suitable bearer-people. By the later thirteenth century, rumours were heard in some circles that a new translation was imminent, with the politically ascendant French the likely beneficiaries.[74] In the two centuries that followed, German commentators repeatedly expressed the fear that their people was about to lose the Empire to the French.[75] The dangers in such a prospect were, for patriotic Germans, hard to overstate. Naturally, it imperilled the collective 'honour', and thus the very identity, of the German people.[76] But it also had the gravest implications for the entire Christian commonwealth, since the existence and the specific form of the medieval Roman Empire were, in the eyes of some, embedded within eschatological world-historical schemes.[77] In short, it was argued that tampering with the Empire's constitution risked unleashing on Christian society the lurid terrors of the Last Days.[78]

It is often hard to judge exactly how seriously such beliefs were held. In the hands of imperialist pamphleteers and chroniclers, they were a convenient buttress to arguments defending the status quo. What it seems to me cannot be denied is that there were elements in the political culture of the medieval *Reich* – the 'nationalised' *Reich* of *Venerabilem* and the treatise-writers – that had for their day an unusual potential for social penetration. These elements did not on the whole depend on the strength of the monarchy; indeed, in some ways they fed off its weakness. At the heart of the matter lay a relationship with the Church. It was this more than anything that lent ideas about the Empire an element of distinctiveness in medieval western political culture – the element of urgent controversy and contestation. In making an intermittent enemy of the See of St Peter, the emperors of the central Middle Ages contrived to draw the *imperium* into the fierce spotlight of an institution whose penetrative capacity in medieval society was long without rival.[79] The first shock had come in the Investiture Contest, yielding a precocious crop of what were subsequently to become a familiar accompaniment to imperialism under pressure: 'publicist' tracts.[80] The Hildebrandine message had been for all Christians, regardless of rank; and nowhere did it rouse more troubling echoes than in Germany. But the real transformation came in the thirteenth century.

Frederick II's clash with Rome was not only distinguished by its bitter course and troubling outcome; it also saw novel communications and persuasive media deployed, to touch broader political publics.[81] The Mendicant orders, centrally engaged in the struggle, were a new feature on the European scene. Their milieu was the town, their dramatic growth in thirteenth-century Germany marching in step with the remarkable advance of urbanisation.[82] The Franciscans in particular recruited from middling urban groups – one instance of the expanding audience for the affairs of the 'two powers'. The Mendicants were preachers, with a message attuned to an urban public; but they were also historiographers, whose historical compendia, replete with the sermoniser's improving *exempla*, would feature heavily in any list of late medieval sources for imperial history.[83] Also new was the urgency and febrility of the popular mood. The Mongols, reputedly the biblical scourges of Gog and Magog, menaced Europe in the east, while emperor and pope, in letters dispatched around the West, affected to discern in each other the coming Antichrist. Wildfire rumours took hold and eschatology luxuriated, nourished in some circles by the legacy of the Calabrian prophet Joachim of Fiore.[84] Hopes and fears were further inflamed by the emperor's abrupt and, to many Germans, mysterious departure from the stage in 1250. Meanwhile, excommunications, interdicts and crusading armies, not to mention preaching campaigns, were hurled at Frederick's German partisans.[85] Urban populations were not unmoved. In Strasbourg, Staufer loyalists fell upon the Dominicans, hanging one, casting others in the river. In Oppenheim, a papal crusade preacher was dragged from church to have his nose cut off by a burgher mob.[86]

The point of examples like these should be clear: Frederick's dramatic struggle with the Curia forced people of diverse backgrounds to take sides. Nor were matters allowed to rest with the end of the Hohenstaufen, since contention between the 'two powers' revived in the diminished *Reich* of the fourteenth century, where Ludwig IV ('the Bavarian') for two decades defied the Avignon Curia's wrath. By 1338 papal interdicts, withdrawing the services of the Church from regions loyal to Ludwig, had brought German society to a state of desperation. Dreadful portents were seen, and the Jews attacked.[87] The long arm of the universal Church reached into corners of German society seldom or never touched by the institutions of imperial rule, reminding their denizens that they too were subject to a temporal, as well as a spiritual, head – and that this subjection could have consequences. A co-ordinated wave of protests to Avignon by imperial towns in Germany emphasises the point that papal measures against the emperor potentially affected everyone.[88] By this date, however, the formal establishment of an elective crown had brought its own additional elements of uncertainty and dispute. Alongside the Curia, alongside the rival claimants to the imperial throne, the German prince-electors – in particular, the wealthy Rhineland archbishops – stepped forward as the guardians of constitutional power-bases and sponsors of claims and doctrines of their own.

The constitutional and political *loci* of the late medieval *Reich* were complex, multiple and periodically contested. That fact, usually invoked to account for the Empire's enfeeblement, also helps explain why the imperial monarchy's grip on German minds did not retreat like the institution itself. We can trace on the map a range of different centres, of varying character, orientation, significance and durability, where ideas about the Empire – and, not uncommonly, about its relationship with the German people – were received, interpreted and propounded in writing. The point is substantiated by the imperialist tracts from German pens in which the period is so rich. In contrast to the picture in neighbouring France, these were usually written at centres remote from the ruler's court.[89] Lupold of Bebenburg, for example, was a protégé of the powerful archbishop of Trier, Baldwin of Luxemburg (d. 1354).[90] Especially eye-catching (not to say paradoxical) is the papal Curia's part in giving board and lodgings to German imperialists. Alexander of Roes had a home in a Ghibelline cardinal's entourage, Dietrich of Niem in the papal bureaucracy itself. Conrad of Megenberg finished the first, most frankly Germanophile of his tracts at Avignon.[91]

The diffuse, polycentric character of imperial political culture in Germany can be shown in another way, by looking at the origins of these treatise-writers. Describing them as 'elite' figures is only in the broadest sense defensible: a tight, socially and ideologically homogeneous 'elite' they were not. Their backgrounds, if respectable, were not illustrious. None came from the higher nobility, though ministerial families did supply a number, while others were of substantial burgher stock.[92] If some later protagonists of German nation or of Empire – the peasant's son Celtis, the miner's son Luther, or Nicholas of Cusa, whose father was a Moselle boatman – were to have yet humbler roots, these 'publicists' were scarcely a starry crowd. Geographically as well as socially, they were provincials, rarely blessed with the quality that Peter Moraw has called *Königsnähe*.[93] Treatise-writers, unlike imperial chancery officials, seldom came from the heartlands of the ruler's *iter*: if imperial government moved in Germany with short and leaden steps, the imperial idea drifted far and wide, impelled by other motive forces. Two such writers, Conrad of Megenberg and Lupold of Bebenburg, did admittedly hail from Franconia, where the monarchy remained in the fourteenth century a significant presence.[94] But the Cologne of Alexander of Roes saw the ruler only fitfully, and Westphalia, which nurtured several imperialist writers, was largely cut off from imperial government.[95] Instead, it was primarily personal factors, such as the chances of education, friendship and patronage, that drove these and other Germans to engage with the imperial question.[96] A common framework was provided by the Church's career ladder – a frequent objective for the sons of families such as theirs, with (merely) local standing in town or country. It was through the Church, too, that they mainly encountered the stimuli that called their works into being.

A striking aspect of German writings on the Empire is the inability of their authors to agree on its character or proper constitution. Some writers engaged in explicit, though not always acrimonious, contention with their peers.[97] It is known that treatises served on occasion as the basis for oral exposition and disputation.[98] One reason for such disagreements among the specialists lay in the German monarchy's inability to sustain an authoritative doctrinal centre of its own. Without such a centre, rival perspectives, some reflecting the concerns of competing political groups, were able to interact with and condition one another. To cite just a single example, Alexander of Roes unfolded in his writings a tendentious and partisan account of German history and community, reflecting the outlook and concerns of the Rhineland princes, particularly the archbishops of Cologne.[99] Alexander's view of German identity was shaped by regional patriotism and political partisanship – but also, he makes clear, by acquaintance with other viewpoints, which he was moved to oppose.[100] Space is insufficient here to assess the place of the treatise-writers within German political culture more broadly – though we might observe in passing that Alexander's longest work survives in a full seventy copies, and was drawn on by chroniclers as well as more programmatic thinkers.[101] What should, however, be noted is the unmistakable role of imperial crisis and fragmentation in permitting – indeed, nurturing – contact, contention and exchange of ideas within informal groups of literate Germans. The tangible result was a substantial corpus of late medieval writings, from the pens of writers of varied regional and social origin, reflecting in detail on the nature and historical significance of German political identity.

If 'the Roman eagle' in its 'German feathers' was, as one scholar has put it, by this time 'a dead duck', nobody seems to have told the chroniclers, polemicists and poets of the Empire's German territories – or, we must assume, the patrons and audiences on whom they depended for a livelihood and a hearing.[102] More commonly than the realities of power appear to recommend, it was the Empire that filled their horizon and gave their writings form and significance.[103] Often, it was the imperial monarchy and its deeds that supplied a reason for invoking 'the Germans', their lands, language, institutions or history, and that endowed those concepts with meaning. Late medieval German identity was at its core political: the historian is well advised to leave the *Kulturnation* in the elegant Biedermeier salons where it belongs. What explained and justified being German, to the late medieval mind, was the conspicuous exercise of *power* – in time past and doubtless in time future, if not time present. Not poets and professors, but grim Teutonic warriors had marched south in bloody triumph, rescued popes from their molesters, rebuffed Slav, Magyar and Northman, and carried Christ's Faith abroad at the sword's edge. That the monarchy's power was experienced by literate Germans more as myth, memory, hope and expectation than as institutionalised command and obligation may not have mattered as much as we have been schooled to think. Indeed, it is easy to imagine how for some the idea of supreme sovereign power might have held more appeal than its intrusive reality. Rulership had been present, as fact as well as idea, at the formation of a 'German' political community in the central Middle Ages, and this foundation in legitimate authority and the promise of rule mattered immensely in the centuries that followed. But, once established, the relationship between German identity and imperial power proved sustainable imaginatively, without the umbilical link of mature governmental institutions.

The 'state' may have been weak, but that did not preclude the sustenance, through a range of other channels and media, of a political culture invoking a sense of common 'German' belonging. Those channels became more complex and penetrative, the media more diverse and broadly accessible, between the thirteenth and the fifteenth centuries. For the literate, there was a tradition of historical thought which derived its chronology from the succeeding reigns of Roman emperors, ancient and medieval.[104] The Church, in imperialist thought inseparably bound up with both the Empire and the political claims of the German people, supplied its own, particularly ramified and articulate, networks for communication. Towns provided a new venue and a new, increasingly literate and well-informed, audience for political ideas. The unlettered too might listen – to wild rumour as well as sober report.[105] They could also look at, and thereby register for themselves, some of the host of often 'banal' representations of imperial authority which patterned the German landscape – from the heraldic eagle above the gateway of the *Reichsstadt* via the sculpted and painted monarchs of gallery, clerestory and façade to the scattered fortresses and palaces of Salians and Staufer, or the monumental Roman remains of Trier or Cologne.[106] In absence too, the Empire was widely present.

The monarch's comparative absence was, against this backdrop, as much a conduit to notions of German identity as an obstacle. The Empire was a 'problem', which many felt impelled to discuss. But it was a problem without official solution. The top-down direction of political discourse, the ruler's authoritarian claim to monopolise legitimate thought – for Habermas and his followers keynotes of the pre-modern European order – were unenforceable in Germany. Instead, there arose a multiplicity of voices, some speaking for powerful and contending vested interests, others addressing themselves to the historical curiosity and political self-consciousness of a growing, particularly urban, public of listeners and readers. Among the literate at least, there was contestation about the Empire's history and its nature, focusing attention and debate on the character and historical role of the German people. The late medieval 'German nation', we might say, found its most visible home in the fissures created by crises of legitimate power and authority. If there was no 'public sphere', there were certainly spaces – at great courts, within networks of acquaintance, patronage and common interest, in the towns and, by the fifteenth century, the universities – where elements of a German identity were received, contested and reproduced. It is not clear to me that these local or group-specific communities of sociability and shared culture were, within their limits, in all cases less 'public' than their successors in the eighteenth and early nineteenth centuries.[107]

But the self-same qualities in the German political landscape which facilitated discourse around the theme of German identity also set limits to the scope of that discourse. If the constraining hand of authoritarian rule was lacking among the Germans, so too was the unifying influence of common political institutions, action and experience. Partly in consequence, the most explicit imaginative constructions of 'Germany' and 'Germanness' tended to be made locally, drawing on local perspectives, traditions and resources. Did this make the late medieval 'German nation' a lesser thing than its counterparts in neighbouring, more institutionally unified, European realms? Before answering this question, medievalists will need to be sure that they can trace not merely the documented existence but also the social scope and the material political importance of such allegedly more significant medieval identities. These challenges have still largely to be met, and meeting them will not prove easy. In the meantime, a study of German identity reveals something of the complexity of late medieval 'national' solidarities, the ramified (but sometimes also fractured) publics which they might address, and the diverse, even contradictory, stimuli from which they drew nourishment. It illuminates the need for a model of the historical relationship between power and nation-making more complex and adaptable, and less unilinear, than those commonly deployed by medievalists and modernists alike.

NOTES

1 Daniel Waley and Peter Denley, *Later Medieval Europe 1250–1520* (3rd edn, Harlow: Longman, 2001), p. 83.

2 An extreme example: Geoffrey Barraclough, *The Origins of Modern Germany* (2nd edn, Oxford: Blackwell, 1947).

3 Examples: Harold James, *A German Identity 1770–1990* (London: Weidenfeld & Nicolson, 1989), pp. 1–7; Hagen Schulze, *The Course of German Nationalism: From Frederick the Great to Bismarck 1763–1867* (Cambridge University Press, 1991), p. 43.

4 Liah Greenfeld, *Nationalism: Five Roads to Modernity* (Cambridge, MA and London: Harvard University Press, 1992), p. 277. To describe Greenfeld's approach as a whole as 'modernist' would be misleading; however, her reading of the German evidence broadly corresponds to the modernist position.

5 Brian E. Vick, *Defining Germany: The 1848 Frankfurt Parliamentarians and National Identity* (Cambridge, MA and London: Harvard University Press, 2002), p. 15.

6 Barraclough, *Germany*, p. 299.

7 For some early classic views see Friedrich Schneider (ed.), *Universalstaat oder Nationalstaat: Macht und Ende des Ersten deutschen Reiches (Die Streitschriften von Heinrich v. Sybel und Julius Ficker zur deutschen Kaiserpolitik des Mittelalters* (2nd edn, Innsbruck: Wagner, 1943).

8 John Gillingham, *The Kingdom of Germany in the High Middle Ages (900–1200)*, Historical Association: General Series, 77 (London: Historical Association, 1971); S. Reynolds, *Kingdoms and Communities in Western Europe 900–1300* (2nd edn, Oxford: Clarendon Press, 1997), pp. 289–97.

9 Hagen Schultze, *States, Nations and Nationalism* (Oxford: Blackwell, 1996), p. 24 (German 'failure'); Joseph R. Llobera, 'State and nation in medieval France', *Journal of Historical Sociology* 7 (1994), 361 ('remarkable' French 'success').

10 Friedrich Meinecke, *Cosmopolitanism and the National State* (Princeton University Press, 1970), pp. 9–10.

11 For a view combining some prominent modernist and medievalist assumptions about the course of German history, and invoking the spectre of *ius sanguinis*, see Adrian Hastings, *The Construction of Nationhood: Ethnicity, Religion and Nationalism* (Cambridge University Press, 1997), pp. 108–9. The 'waste dump'

image is in Patrick J. Geary, *The Myth of Nations: The Medieval Origins of Europe* (Princeton University Press, 2002), p. 15.

12 The view remains common in Anglophone scholarship: for a recent reiteration see Geary, *Myth of Nations*, p. 19. For the primacy of language in late medieval German identity see F. R. H. Du Boulay, *Germany in the Later Middle Ages* (London: Athlone, 1983), p. 1.

13 For Germany, the connection is suggested by Sylvain Gouguenheim, 'Les structures politiques', in M. Parisse (ed.), *De la Meuse à l'Oder: l'Allemagne au xiiie siècle* (Paris: Picard, 1994), p. 47: 'Ont manqué à l'Allemagne à la fois le sentiment national et la capacité politique à forger un Etat centralisé'.

14 Michael Jones, 'Introduction', in Michael Jones (ed.), *The New Cambridge Medieval History*, vol. VI (c. 1300–c. 1415) (Cambridge University Press, 2000), pp. 12–13.

15 See e.g. Peter Moraw, *Von offener Verfassung zu gestalteter Verdichtung: Das Reich im späten Mittelalter 1250 bis 1490* (Berlin: Propyläen, 1985).

16 Jürgen Habermas, *The Structural Transformation of the Public Sphere: An Inquiry into a Category of Bourgeois Society* (Cambridge, MA: MIT Press, 1989), pp. 7–8.

17 Meinecke, *Cosmopolitanism*, p. 10.

18 See esp. Peter Wiesinger, 'Regionale und überregionale Sprachausformung im Deutschen vom 12. bis 15. Jahrhundert unter dem Aspekt der Nationsbildung', in Joachim Ehlers (ed.), *Ansätze und Diskontinuität deutscher Nationsbildung im Mittelalter*, Nationes, vol. VIII (Sigmaringen: Jan Thorbecke, 1989), pp. 321–43.

19 For 'German tongue' as a factor uniting different regional communities, see Jansen Enikel, *Weltchronik*, in *Jansen Enikels Werke*, ed. Philipp Strauch, Monumenta Germaniae Historica [henceforth MGH] Deutsche Chroniken 3,1 (Hanover: Hahn, 1891), pp. 532–3.

20 *Das Buch der Natur von Konrad von Megenberg*, ed. Franz Pfeiffer (Hildesheim: Georg Olms, 1962), p. 325; and see Wiesinger, 'Sprachausformung', pp. 334–5.

21 *Die Königsaaler Geschichts-Quellen mit den Zusätzen und der Fortsetzung des Domherrn Franz von Prag*, ed. Johann Loserth, Fontes Rerum Austriacarum: Oesterreichische Geschichtsquellen, I. Abtheilung, vol. VIII (Vienna: Karl Gerold's Sohn, 1875), p. 52.

22 Heinz Thomas, 'Das Identitätsproblem der Deutschen im Mittelalter', *Geschichte in Wissenschaft und Unterricht* 43 (1992), 136–8.

23 Eckhard Müller-Mertens, *Regnum Teutonicum: Aufkommen und Verbreitung der deutschen Reichs- und Königsauffassung im frühen Mittelalter* (Vienna, Cologne and Graz: Böhlau, 1970).

24 Different priorities pertained in those regions of eastern Europe which experienced German settlement, and where law, culture and language were more important than political allegiances in distinguishing 'Germans' from their neighbours. For pertinent examples see Paul Johansen and Heinz von zur Mühlen, *Deutsch und Undeutsch im mittelalterlichen und frühneuzeitlichen Reval* (Cologne and Vienna: Böhlau, 1973).

25 For its evidently small part in France see Bernard Guenée, 'Etat et nation en France au moyen âge', *Revue Historique* 237 (1967), 17–30. For its more important

role in east-central Europe see František Graus, *Die Nationenbildung der Westslaven im Mittelalter*, Nationes, vol. III (Sigmaringen: Jan Thorbecke, 1980).

26 Bernard Guenée, *States and Rulers in Later Medieval Europe* (Oxford: Blackwell, 1985), p. 218.

27 On this subject, see generally Guenée, 'Etat et nation'.

28 On royal saints see Colette Beaune, *The Birth of an Ideology: Myths and Symbols of Nation in Late-Medieval France* (Berkeley, CA: University of California Press, 1991), chs. 1–3; on miracles, Marc Bloch, *The Royal Touch: Sacred Monarchy and Scrofula in England and France* (London: Routledge and Kegan Paul, 1973); for the formula 'Most Christian', J.R. Strayer, 'France: the holy land, the chosen people, and the most Christian king', in T. K. Rabb and J. E. Seigel (eds.), *Action and Conviction in Early Modern Europe* (Princeton University Press, 1969), pp. 3–16.

29 For the role of royal inquisitions in cementing ties to the centre see Jean Richard, *Saint Louis: roi d'une France féodale, soutien de la Terre sainte* (Paris: Fayard, 1983), pp. 280–303.

30 Jacques Krynen, *L'empire du roi: idées et croyances politiques en France xiiie–xve siècle* (Paris: Gallimard, 1993).

31 For assessments of the late medieval *Reich* as a system of government see Ernst Schubert, *König und Reich: Studien zur spätmittelalterlichen deutschen Verfassungsgeschichte* (Göttingen: Vandenhoeck & Ruprecht, 1979); Karl-Friedrich Krieger, *König, Reich und Reichsreform im Spätmittelalter* (Munich: Oldenbourg, 1992).

32 Robert Folz, *Le souvenir et la légende de Charlemagne dans l'empire germanique médiévale* (Paris: Les Belles Lettres, 1950).

33 There was not even an accustomed mausoleum for the bones of the Empire's ruler: Rudolf J. Meyer, *Königs- und Kaiserbegräbnisse im Spätmittelalter: Von Rudolf von Habsburg bis zu Friedrich III* (Cologne, Weimar and Vienna: Böhlau, 2000).

34 On the elective crown, Ernst Schubert, 'Königswahl und Königtum im spätmittelalterlichen Reich', *Zeitschrift für historische Forschung* 4 (1977), 257–338.

35 Wenceslas of Luxemburg, elected in 1376, becoming sole ruler on the death of his father Charles IV, 1378.

36 Björn Weiler, 'Image and reality in Richard of Cornwall's German career', *English Historical Review* 113 (1998), 1119.

37 For the development of this terminology see Gottfried Koch, *Auf dem Wege zum Sacrum Imperium: Studien zur ideologischen Herrschaftsbegründung der deutschen Zentralgewalt im 11. und 12. Jahrhundert* (Vienna, Cologne and Graz: Böhlau, 1972).

38 Schubert, *König und Reich*, pp. 227–30.

39 See generally, Jörg K. Hoensch, *Die Luxemburger: Eine spätmittelalterliche Dynastie gesamteuropäischer Bedeutung 1308–1437* (Stuttgart: Kohlhammer, 2000). For the attitudes of Charles IV, Franz Machilek, 'Privatfrömmigkeit und Staatsfrömmigkeit', in Ferdinand Seibt (ed.), *Kaiser Karl IV.: Staatsmann und Mäzen* (Munich: Prestel, 1978), pp. 87–101.

40 Lupold of Bebenburg, *De Iure Regni et Imperii Rom[anorum]*, cap. xix, in *De Iurisdictione, Autoritate, et Praeeminentia Imperiali, ac Potestate Ecclesiastica*, ed. S. Schardius (Basel: Ex officina Iohannis Oporini, 1566), p. 409.

41 Alexander of Roes, *Memoriale*, cap. 10, in *Alexander von Roes: Schriften*, ed. Herbert Grundmann and Hermann Heimpel, MGH Staatsschriften des späteren Mittelalters, 1,1 (Stuttgart: Anton Hiersemann, 1958), p. 100.

42 *Liber de Rebus Memorabilioribus sive Chronicon Henrici de Hervordia*, ed. Augustus Potthast (Göttingen: Dieterich, 1859), p. 94.

43 Lupold of Bebenburg, *Ritmaticum Querulosum et Lamentosum Dictamen de Modernis Cursibus et Defectibus Regni ac Imperii Romanorum*, in *Politische Lyrik des deutschen Mittelalters: Texte I (Von Friedrich II. bis Ludwig dem Bayern)*, ed. Ulrich Müller (Göppingen: Alfred Kümmerle, 1972), p. 175.

44 Examples in Alfred Ritscher, *Literatur und Politik im Umkreis der ersten Habsburger* (Frankfurt a.M., Bern, New York and Paris: Peter Lang, 1992), pp. 16, 18, 21.

45 *Fritsche (Friedrich) Closener's Chronik*, ed. C. Hegel, in *Die Chroniken der deutschen Städte vom 14. bis ins 16. Jahrhundert* [henceforth *Chron. dt. Städte*], vol. VIII (Leipzig: Hirzel, 1870), p. 34.

46 Ibid., p. 35.

47 Lupold of Bebenburg, *De Iure*, cap. ii, in *De Iurisdictione*, ed. Schardius, p. 339.

48 For medieval German views on Charlemagne see Folz, *Souvenir*.

49 *Chronik des Jacob Twinger von Königshofen*, ed. C. Hegel, in *Chron. dt. Städte*, vol. VIII, p. 422.

50 Examples from Charles's reign in *Urkundenbuch der Stadt Strassburg*, vol. V, *Politische Urkunden von 1332 bis 1380*, ed. Hans Witte and Georg Wolfram (Strassburg: Trübner, 1896), nos. 389, 796, 819, 976, pp. 336, 624, 636, 752.

51 *Sächsische Weltchronik: Sächsische Fortsetzung*, ed. Ludwig Weiland, MGH Deutsche Chroniken, vol. II (Hanover: Hahn, 1877), p. 284.

52 MGH Legum Sectio IV: Constitutiones et Acta Publica Imperatorum et Regum, vol. III, ed. Jacobus Schwalm (Hanover and Leipzig: Hahn, 1904–6), no. 371, p. 353 (1285).

53 *Chronica de Gestis Principum*, in *Bayerische Chroniken des XIV. Jahrhunderts*, ed. Georg Leidinger, MGH Scriptores Rerum Germanicarum in Usum Scholarum, vol. XIX (Hanover and Leipzig: Hahn, 1918), p. 55

54 Koch, *Sacrum Imperium*, esp. pp. 112–13.

55 The term was almost, though not wholly, unknown in official documents: Schubert, *König und Reich*, p. 228, n. 15. It is encountered more frequently (though it is still not common) in narrative sources. Example: *Die Chronik Johanns von Winterthur*, ed. Friedrich Baethgen, MGH Scriptores Rerum Germanicarum in Usum Scholarum (N.S.), vol. III (Berlin: Weidmann, 1924), p. 21.

56 Latin and vernacular examples: *Die Chronik des Mathias von Neuenburg*, ed. Adolf Hofmeister, MGH Scriptores Rerum Germanicarum in Usum Scholarum (N.S.), vol. IV (Berlin: Weidmann, 1924), pp. 10, 46; *Closener's Chronik*, ed. Hegel, pp. 38, 41, 57.

57 There did exist the office of 'archchancellor' for 'Germany' or 'the German lands', held by the archbishops of Mainz. This title, however, conferred no clear role in government in Germany. See Harry Bresslau, *Handbuch der Urkundenlehre für Deutschland und Italien* (2 vols, Leipzig: W. de Gruyter, 1912, 1915), vol. II, p. 518.

58 For the Latin vocabulary see Fritz Vigener, *Bezeichnungen für Volk und Land der Deutschen vom 10. bis zum 13. Jahrhundert* (Heidelberg: Winter, 1901); for the plural vernacular form, Rüdiger Schnell, 'Deutsche Literatur und deutsches Nationalbewuβtsein im Spätmittelalter und Früher Neuzeit', in Ehlers (ed.), *Ansätze und Diskontinuität*, pp. 275–82.

59 As a single example, John of Winterthur explains how Ludwig IV raised an army to repel the pretender Charles of Moravia 'from the bounds of Germany' ('a finibus Alamanie'): *Die Chronik Johanns von Winterthur*, ed. Baethgen, p. 263.

60 Roland Pauler, *Die deutschen Könige und Italien im 14. Jahrhundert: Von Heinrich VII. bis Karl IV.* (Darmstadt: Wissenschaftliche Buchgesellschaft, 1997).

61 See esp. Fritz Kern, *Die Anfänge der französischen Ausdehnungspolitik bis zum Jahr 1308* (Tübingen: Mohr, 1910).

62 For the distribution of imperial properties see Andreas Christoph Schlunk, *Königsmacht und Krongut: Die Machtgrundlage des deutschen Königtums im 13. Jahrhundert – und eine neue historische Methode* (Stuttgart: Franz Steiner, 1988). Even Charles IV's government, heavily concentrated on Prague, relied substantially upon Germans: Peter Moraw, 'Zur Mittelpunktsfunktion Prags im Zeitalter Karls IV.', in Klaus-Detlev Grothusen and Klaus Zernack (eds.), *Europa slavica, Europa orientalis: Festschrift für Herbert Ludat zum 70. Geburtstag* (Berlin: Duncker & Humblot, 1980), esp. pp. 469–80.

63 As a single example, *Chronica de Gestis Principum*, ed. Leidinger, p. 76, for the 'grandis exercitus Alemannorum' in Italy with Henry VII.

64 Helmut Bansa, *Studien zur Kanzlei Kaiser Ludwigs des Bayern vom Tag der Wahl bis zur Rückkehr aus Italien (1314–1329)* (Kallmünz, Opf.: Lassleben, 1968), p. 89; Ivan Hlavaček, *Das Urkunden- und Kanzleiwesen des böhmischen und römischen Königs Wenzel (IV.) 1376–1419*, Schriften der Monumenta Germaniae Historica 23 (Stuttgart: Anton Hiersemann, 1970), p. 88.

65 For Frankfurt elections see Schubert, 'Königswahl'; for Aachen coronations see Silvinus Müller, 'Die Königskrönungen in Aachen (936–1531)', in Mario Kramp (ed.), *Krönungen: Könige in Aachen – Geschichte und Mythos* (2 vols., Mainz: Philipp von Zabern, 1999), vol. I, pp. 49–57. The right of coronation was claimed by the archbishop of Cologne: Franz-Reiner Erkens, *Der Erzbischof von Köln und die deutsche Königswahl: Studien zur Kölner Kirchengeschichte zum Krönungsrecht und zur Verfassung des Reiches (Mitte 12. Jahrhundert bis 1806)* (Siegburg: Schmitt, 1987). For other towns with a ceremonial role see Anna M. Drabek, *Reisen und Reisezeremoniell der römisch-deutschen Herrscher im Spätmittelalter* (Vienna: Geyer, 1964), esp. ch. 1.

66 Reynolds, *Kingdoms and Communities*, p. 254.

67　Werner Goez, *Translatio Imperii: Ein Beitrag zur Geschichte des Geschichtsdenkens und der politischen Theorien im Mittelalter und in der frühen Neuzeit* (Tübingen: Mohr, 1958), pp. 126–7.

68　See Heinz Thomas, 'Julius Caesar und die Deutschen: Zu Ursprung und Gehalt eines deutschen Geschichtsbewußtseins in der Zeit Gregors VII. und Heinrichs IV.', in Stefan Weinfurter (ed.), *Die Salier und das Reich*, vol. III (Sigmaringen: Jan Thorbecke, 1991), esp. pp. 253–7.

69　Goez, *Translatio Imperii*, esp. ch. 7. For *Venerabilem*, Friedrich Kempf, *Papsttum und Kaisertum bei Innocenz III. Die geistigen und rechtlichen Grundlagen seiner Thronstreitpolitik* (Rome: Pontificia Università Gregoriana, 1954), pp. 48–55.

70　The explicitly ethnic reference is already present in Innocent's text: '. . . ad eos [= the electors] ius et potestas huiusmodi ab apostolica sede pervenerit, quae Romanum imperium in personam magnifici Caroli a Graecis transtulit in Germanos' (*Corpus Iuris Canonici*, ed. Aemilius Friedberg (2 vols., Leipzig: Tauchnitz, 1879), vol. II, p. 80). For an example of the infiltration of this ethno-constitutional mode of thought into German historical writings see *Liber de Rebus Memorabilibus*, ed. Potthast, p. 274.

71　Thus e.g. the contemptuous remarks of the Spanish canonist Vincentius, about the pretensions of a people in whose own land 'every hut usurps lordship to itself': Gaines Post, *Studies in Medieval Legal Thought: Public Law and the State* (Princeton University Press, 1964), p. 489.

72　For the role of late medieval crisis in stimulating programmatic writings about the Empire, Herbert Grundmann, 'Politische Gedanken in mittelalterlicher Westfalen', *Westfalen* 27 (1948), 6.

73　Len E. Scales, '*Germen militiae*: war and German identity in the later Middle Ages', *Past & Present* 180 (2003), 49–50 (service to the Church), 51–4 (military qualities).

74　Such rumours were underpinned by eschatological speculation which identified the king of France as the saviour-emperor of the Last Days: Dietrich Kurze, 'Nationale Regungen in der spätmittelalterlichen Prophetie', *Historische Zeitschrift* 202 (1966), esp. 9.

75　Goez, *Translatio Imperii*, pp. 169–70.

76　See e.g. the words of a singer known as Meißner, in verses composed around the middle of the thirteenth century: 'if the German tongue [i.e. the German people] loses its right [to the Empire], its honour will be undermined' (*Politische Lyrik*, ed. Müller, p. 68, no. XIV.2).

77　For the capacity of medieval prophecy to acquire an ethno-political foundation see Kurze, 'Nationale Regungen', 3–9.

78　Thus e.g. Alexander of Roes: *Memoriale*, chs. 11, 13, *Noticia Seculi*, ch. 20, ed. Grundmann and Heimpel, pp. 98, 99, 168.

79　See Heike Johanna Mierau, 'Exkommunikation und Macht der Öffentlichkeit: Gerüchte im Kampf zwischen Friedrich II. und der Kurie', in Karel Hruza (ed.), *Propaganda, Kommunikation und Öffentlichkeit (11.–16. Jahrhundert)* (Vienna: Österreichische Akademie der Wissenschaften, 2002), esp. p. 54.

80 Monika Suchan, 'Publizistik im Zeitalter Heinrichs IV. – Anfänge päpstlicher und kaiserlicher Propaganda im "Investiturstreit"?', in Hruza (ed.), *Propaganda*, esp. pp. 29–30.

81 See generally Peter Segl, 'Die Feindbilder in der politischen Propaganda Friedrichs II. und seiner Gegner', in Franz Bosbach (ed.), *Feindbilder: Die Darstellung des Gegners in der politischen Publizistik des Mittelalters und der Neuzeit* (Cologne, Vienna, and Weimar: Böhlau, 1992), pp. 41–71.

82 John B. Freed, *The Friars and German Society in the Thirteenth Century* (Cambridge, MA: Medieval Academy of America, 1977), pp. 21, 52. There is no scholarly consensus on the size of the urban element in late medieval German society as a whole. According to one well-informed estimate, 16 per cent of the German population was by 1500 living in settlements of more than 5,000 inhabitants: Christian Pfister, 'The population of late medieval and early modern Germany', in Bob Scribner (ed.), *Germany: A New Social and Economic History*, vol. I (1450–1630) (London and New York: Arnold, 1996), p. 43.

83 See e.g. Friedrich Baethgen, 'Franziskanische Studien', *Historische Zeitschrift* 131 (1925), 421–71.

84 For rumour, Mierau, 'Exkommunikation'; for eschatology, Bernhard Töpfer, *Das kommende Reich des Friedens: Zur Entwicklung chiliastischer Zukunftshoffnungen im Hochmittelalter* (Berlin: Akademie, 1964), esp. p. 156; for Joachim, Marjorie Reeves, *The Influence of Prophecy in the Later Middle Ages: A Study in Joachimism* (Oxford: Clarendon Press, 1969).

85 For the role of excommunication in opinion-forming see Mierau, 'Exkommunikation', esp. pp. 69–70; for preaching and crusade, K. E. Demandt, 'Der Endkampf des staufischen Kaiserhauses im Rhein-Maingebiet', *Hessisches Jahrbuch für Landesgeschichte* 7 (1957), 124, 133–4, and Freed, *Friars*, p. 92.

86 For Strasbourg, Freed, *Friars*, p. 160; for Oppenheim, Demandt, 'Endkampf', 133–4.

87 Martin Kaufhold, *Gladius Spiritualis: Das päpstliche Interdikt über Deutschland in der Regierungszeit Ludwigs des Bayern (1324–1347)* (Heidelberg: Winter, 1994), pp. 210, 236.

88 Kaufhold, *Gladius Spiritualis*, p. 219.

89 The 'publicist' circle around Ludwig IV's court in Munich consisted mostly of non-German controversialists enjoying Ludwig's protection: Alois Schütz, 'Der Kampf Ludwigs des Bayern gegen Papst Johannes XXII. und die Rolle der Gelehrten am Münchner Hof', in *Wittelsbach und Bayern: Die Zeit der frühen Herzöge – Von Otto I zu Ludwig dem Bayern* (Munich and Zürich: Hirmer, 1980), esp. pp. 393–4. For French publicists see Krynen, *L'empire du roi*, ch. 2.

90 Katharina Colberg, 'Lupold von Bebenburg', in Kurt Ruh *et al.* (eds.), *Die deutsche Literatur des Mittelalters: Verfasserlexikon* (11 vols. to date, Berlin: De Gruyter, 1978–), vol. V, col. 1075.

91 For Alexander see *Schriften*, ed. Grundmann and Heimpel, pp. 7–10; for Dietrich, Hermann Heimpel, *Dietrich von Niem (c. 1340–1418)* (Münster: Regensbergsche, 1932), ch. 2; for Conrad, Georg Steer, 'Konrad von Megenberg', in Ruh *et al.* (eds.), *Verfasserlexikon*, vol. V, col. 224.

92 Among those of ministerial origin were Lupold of Bebenburg, Conrad of
    Megenberg and the jurist Rudolf Losse (another of Archbishop Baldwin's
    ideological mouthpieces). For Lupold see Peter Johannek, 'Lupold (Leopold,
    Liupold) v. Bebenburg', in *Neue Deutsche Biographie*, vol. XV (Berlin:
    Duncker & Humblot, 1986), p. 524; for Conrad, Steer, 'Konrad', col. 221;
    for Losse, Friedhelm Burgard, 'Rudolf Losse (um 1310–1364)', in *Rheinische
    Lebensbilder*, vol. XIV (Cologne: Rheinland, 1994), p. 49. Dietrich of Niem
    and Gobelinus Persona were sons of leading burgher families, as was in all
    probability Alexander of Roes. For Dietrich see Heimpel, *Dietrich*, pp. 13–14;
    for Gobelinus, Katharina Colberg, 'Person, Gobelinus', in Ruh *et al.* (eds.),
    Verfasserlexikon, vol. VII, cols 411–16; for Alexander, Herbert Grundmann and
    Hermann Heimpel, 'Einleitung', in *Schriften*, ed. Grundmann and Heimpel,
    pp. 2–7.
93 Peter Moraw, 'Die Verwaltung des Königtums und des Reiches und ihre
    Rahmenbedingungen', in Kurt G. A. Jeserich, Hans Pohl and Georg-
    Christoph von Unruh (eds.), *Deutsche Verwaltungsgeschichte* (vol. I,
    Stuttgart: DVA, 1983), pp. 24–6.
94 Steer, 'Konrad', col. 221; Johannek, 'Lupold', p. 524.
95 For the geographical patterns of late medieval imperial rule see Moraw,
    'Verwaltung', pp. 24–31; for Westphalia, Grundmann, 'Westfalen', 5.
96 For the role of these elements in one career see Burgard, 'Rudolf Losse', esp.
    pp. 49–55.
97 For William of Ockham's reaction to the works of Lupold of Bebenburg see
    Jürgen Miethke, 'Wirkungen politischer Theorie auf die Praxis der Politik
    im Römischen Reich des 14. Jahrhunderts: Gelehrte Politikberatung am
    Hofe Ludwigs des Bayern', in Joseph Canning and Otto Gerhard Oexle
    (eds.), *Political Thought and the Realities of Power in the Middle Ages /
    Politisches Denken und die Wirklichkeit der Macht im Mittelalter*
    (Göttingen: Vandenhoeck & Ruprecht, 1998), pp. 207–9. Conrad of
    Megenberg dedicated his *Yconomia* to Lupold of Bebenburg, with whose
    views on the Empire he nevertheless disagreed: Conrad of Megenberg,
    Ökonomik, in *Konrad von Megenberg: Werke*, ed. Sabine Krüger, MGH
    Staatsschriften des späteren Mittelalters 5,3 (II) (Stuttgart: Anton
    Hiersemann, 1977), p. 15.
98 For a public reading of Lupold's treatise at Eichstätt see Miethke,
    'Wirkungen', pp. 207–9.
99 For Alexander's arguments in context of the church of Cologne see Franz-
    Reiner Erkens, *Siegfried von Westerburg (1274–1297): Die Reichs- und
    Territorialpolitik eines Kölner Erzbischofs im ausgehenden 13. Jahrhundert*
    (Bonn: Röhrscheid, 1982), pp. 287–8.
100 For e.g. his controversial views on the Hohenstaufen legacy see Alexander of
    Roes, *Memoriale*, cap. 29, ed. Grundmann and Heimpel, pp. 134–5.
101 Grundmann and Heimpel, 'Einleitung', pp. 40–80, where 63 mss. are listed;
    Jürgen Miethke, 'Politisches Denken und monarchische Theorie: Das
    Kaisertum als supranationale Institution im späteren Mittelalter', in Ehlers

(ed.), *Ansätze und Diskontinuität,* p. 134 n. 53, listing a further six; Jürgen Miethke, 'Das Publikum politischer Theorie im 14. Jahrhundert: Zur Einführung', in Jürgen Miethke (ed.), *Das Publikum politischer Theorie im 14. Jahrhundert* (Munich: Oldenbourg, 1992), p. 8 n. 31, for one more. The manuscript tradition makes clear that there were once other copies besides.

102 J. H. Burns, *Lordship, Kingship, and Empire: The Idea of Monarchy, 1400–1525* (Oxford: Clarendon Press, 1992), p. 97.

103 A phenomenon noted by Peter Moraw, 'Bestehende, fehlende und heranwachsende Voraussetzungen des deutschen Nationalbewußtseins im späten Mittelalter', in Ehlers (ed.), *Ansätze und Diskontinuität,* esp. p. 107.

104 For universal chronicles in late medieval Germany see Peter Johannek, 'Weltchronistik und regionale Geschichtsschreibung im Spätmittelalter', in Hans Patze (ed.), *Geschichtsschreibung und Geschichtsbewußtsein im späten Mittelalter* (Sigmaringen: Jan Thorbecke, 1987), pp. 287–330.

105 Examples of the circulation of rumours about the monarchy: Ernst Schubert, 'Probleme der Königsherrschaft im spätmittelalterlichen Reich: Das Beispiel Ruprechts von der Pfalz (1400–1410)', in Reinhard Schneider (ed.), *Das spätmittelalterliche Königtum im europäischen Vergleich* (Sigmaringen: Jan Thorbecke, 1987), pp. 177–8.

106 For the identity-forming role of 'banal' (i.e. everyday) representations see Michael Billig, *Banal Nationalism* (London: Sage, 1995). For visual representations see Wolfgang Schenkluhn, 'Monumentale Repräsentation des Königtums in Frankreich und Deutschland', in Kramp (ed.), *Krönungen,* vol. I, pp. 369–77.

107 Contrast with the picture drawn by Geoff Eley, 'Nations, publics, and political cultures: placing Habermas in the nineteenth century', in Craig Calhoun (ed.), *Habermas and the Public Sphere* (Cambridge, MA: MIT Press, 1992), esp. pp. 293, 297.

PART III

Routes to Modernity

CHAPTER 8

The state and Russian national identity*

Geoffrey Hosking

On the face of it, Russia appears to refute the modernist account of nation-hood, since there modernisation actually weakened national identity. In the sixteenth and seventeenth centuries the elites and arguably many of the people of Muscovite Rus' had a lively sense of their ethnic identity and of their role in the world. Modernisation, launched by Tsar Aleksei in the middle of the seventeenth century and intensified by Peter the Great in the early eighteenth, actually undermined that identity, as I shall explain below. On further examination, however, I believe it may be possible to rescue at least one version of the modernist approach, that which lays emphasis on the relationship between the state and the political community.

Let us begin with the ethnic myths. By the middle of the sixteenth century the peoples of Muscovite Rus' already possessed the six character-istics which Anthony Smith has posited as constituting an *ethnie*.[1] Following the end of the Mongol overlordship and the collapse of the Byzantine Empire they found themselves living in the only sovereign Orthodox monarchy. They already possessed an agreed generic name, Rus', and Orthodoxy as a marker of their distinctive culture. Their sense of homeland was heightened by the dangers they faced on their various frontiers, and by the success of the princes of Moscow in overcoming those dangers and enlarging the frontiers. A myth of common ancestry and shared historical memories was added during the early sixteenth century by the ideologists of Church and state. When Ivan IV was crowned Tsar (Emperor) in 1547, he claimed the heritage of the Byzantine Empire and also that of the princes of Kiev, with the right to reclaim all the lands of Rus' which had been sundered by the Mongol invasion. If Ivan's ambitions were far-reaching, the Church's were even greater, both for itself and for Tsardom, nothing less than to establish a universal Christian empire: 'In

* The research for this chapter was undertaken while I was the holder of a Leverhulme Research Chair. I am most grateful to the Leverhulme Trust for their support.

the third Rome, which will be the land of Rus', the Grace of the Holy Spirit will shine forth . . . [and] all Christians will finally unite into one Russian realm because of its Orthodoxy.'[2]

The idea of the 'Third Rome' was an intoxicating one. It was especially popular in the Church, and seems to have had considerable resonance among ordinary people. The Tsars, however, were much more cautious about invoking it, partly because it gave too much symbolic power to the Church, and partly because it implied an obligation to conquer Constantinople, something most Tsars were not confident they could achieve. For geo-political reasons, the Tsars took Russia in a different direction. Instead of trying to create a new Christian realm with its focus on the Mediterranean, they gradually assembled a huge empire stretching over northern Eurasia and containing many non-Christian peoples. In such an empire the messianic Christianity professed by the Church was counter-productive, as it provoked uprisings among those newly pacified peoples and made internal peace difficult to secure. Accordingly, though campaigns of conversion were attempted, they were never consistently applied as a policy.[3]

On the contrary, starting in the middle of the seventeenth century the state moved to modernise and discipline the Church, to wean it away from messianic expectations and turn it into an instrument of state policy. In doing so, it split the Church down the middle. Those who rejected the ecclesiastical reforms were anathematised at the Church Council of 1666. These were the so-called Old Believers, who not only survived but increased in numbers right up to the early twentieth century. In my view they did so because they were the bearers of the old Russian ethnic myth, now repudiated by the state in the interests of empire. They regarded both the Tsarist state and the official Church as illegitimate, indeed the work of Antichrist. Their anathematisation meant that a substantial minority of conservative, pious and patriotic Russians were alienated from the established state and religion.[4]

The legitimacy of the Tsarist empire derived from divine right, but it was not messianic, for all that. It rested on Russia's status as empire and great power, and therefore depended on the success of its armies, which from the middle of the seventeenth to the middle of the nineteenth was remarkable. The Tsar was crucial to its symbolism: he was commander-in-chief of the armed forces and father of his numerous and diverse peoples, their ultimate guarantor and unifier.[5]

Not only was the old Russian myth driven underground, but high and low culture were sundered from each other. In the early eighteenth century Peter the Great abolished the patriarchate, subordinated the Church to the secular power and expropriated most of its property. Divided, subjected and poverty-stricken, though still 'established', the Church could no longer function as a guarantor of national culture, even though most Russians, if asked their nationality, would have replied 'We are Orthodox.' In place of a culture resting on the Church, the Tsars deliberately imported post-Renaissance European culture for its elites. They did so because Russia could not be a Eurasian empire without becoming also a European great power and sustaining that status by all possible means, which entailed importing modern science and technology and training a European-educated elite, capable of holding its own in the courts and diplomatic circles of European society. Russian aristocratic salons, academies, universities and publishing houses were powerful centres of a new kind of Russian culture, an imperial, European and largely secular culture, remote from the world of the peasants and the Orthodox Church. So there were really two kinds of Russianness, *russkii* (ethnic, Orthodox) and *rossiiskii* (imperial, Europeanised, largely secular). In Benedict Anderson's sense, the Russian 'imagined community' of print capitalism was *rossiiskii*. The national identity of the elite was cultural and linguistic, but lacked roots in the peasantry and the Church. Bridging this gap was the challenge which faced both the Slavophiles and many of the great cultural figures of nineteenth-century Russia.

The only writer who succeeded in doing so in a manner which suggested an integral national identity was Dostoevskii. In his novels and journalistic writings he expounded his concept of the Russians as a 'holy people', humble and collectivist in spirit, bearing terrible burdens for the sake of their Christian beliefs, and therefore ideally equipped to save Europe from the evils of atheism, materialism and individual egoism. They were a kind of super-nation, endowed with the capacity to provide the conditions in which other nations could develop their own national life without being constrained by Russia's hegemonic role. Led by a strong authoritarian state, the Russians would conquer Constantinople (he wrote many of his articles during the Russo-Turkish war of 1877–8), re-establish Orthodoxy there and thus begin the process of creating universal peace in Europe. Dostoevskii's was the most successful attempt to do what the ideologists of Church and state had not managed: to combine the imperial and the ethnic in a coherent vision which legitimated Russian leadership in Europe. It had great appeal for educated Russians in the late nineteenth and early twentieth century, and again after the fall of the Soviet Union. During the Soviet period, Dostoevskii was officially under a cloud for his anti-socialism (though he was never completely prohibited), but intellectuals continued to find inspiration in his writings, which had unacknowledged similarities with the Soviet ideological attempt to combine great power status with concern for ordinary people. In some respects he might be regarded as the 'shadow' ideologist of the Soviet Union.[6]

Tsarist Russia, then, faced the crises of nation-building with a successful imperial state, but a divided cultural heritage. How did the way it expanded its administrative capacities affect emerging Russian nationhood?

According to John Breuilly, the nation 'does not have a significant pre-modern history'; it is 'a modern political and ideological formation which developed in close conjuncture with the emergence of the modern, terri-torial, sovereign and participatory state'.[7] Furthermore, 'the process which created the modern idea of the state in its earliest form also gave rise to the political concept of the nation'. That is because the powers which the modern state needs to govern effectively, such as taxation, military recruit-ment and law enforcement, could only be achieved 'through a process of negotiation between the ruler and the political community of the core territory under his sway'.[8] That process not only strengthened the ruler but also consolidated the political community and gave it firmer outline – created in effect a potential nation.

Actually Russia – strictly speaking, Rus' – did have a significant pre-modern history, as we have seen. All the same, when it comes to explaining the failure to transform that pre-modern history into the raw material of modern nationhood, Breuilly's account can help us. The key question is that of the political community. Was there such a thing in Russia? Many historians have thought not. The only entity which seems to qualify for the designation of 'institutions of the political community' was the *zemskii sobor*. This was an ad hoc gathering of provincial elites which the Tsar would call from time to time, between the middle of the sixteenth and middle of the seventeenth centuries, when he felt the need of advice or feedback from the localities. There was never a charter which defined its composition or procedures, it was not convened regularly and it had no agreed rights or prerogatives. While it existed, though, it did serve as a channel of communication between the Tsar and the 'best people' of the localities. Far from being strengthened by the modernisation process, however, it was abolished by the first modernising monarch, Tsar Aleksei.[9]

If there was an enduring political community in Russia, we have to look lower down to find it. Because of the enormous size of Russia there was always great difficulty in building the link between local communities and the centre. Russian state-building was a very remarkable and in some respects very successful story. Because of Russia's immensely long and vulnerable frontiers, the Tsars had to accomplish a permanent massive mobilisation of population and resources at a much earlier stage in what might be called the 'natural history' of the state than most European countries. They did so not through institutions and laws, but rather by using the resources available to them: the power of the boyars, later the nobles, in their localities. The resulting process one may call 'the statisation of personal power'.[10]

In recent years research has been abandoning the crude idea of autocratic rule as a form of enslavement of the population. We are coming to see the Russian political system more as a hierarchy of patron–client relationships. The Tsars provided symbolic backing for the personal power of boyars and later on nobles to raise armies, levy taxes and apprehend criminals. This method also had the advantage that it facilitated the assimilation of non-Russian peoples: the agents of the Tsar simply super-imposed themselves on existing tribal and other personal and kinship hierarchies. So the state was constructed, not through building institutions and promulgating laws, but by riding piggy-back on personal bonds.[11] The clearest and most important instance of this phenomenon was serfdom, which arose between the late fifteenth and early seventeenth century. It was never properly defined in law: the fundamental law which supposedly finally consolidated serfdom, the *Ulozhenie* of 1649, did not define in what circumstances someone could be enserfed, nor what duties could be demanded of him thereafter. It merely laid down the fines which could be imposed on fugitive peasants. In other words, it enforced domination without setting any legal limits to it. All the same, it persisted as the backbone of the power structure till the 1860s, when the Tsars abolished it in order to embark on the hazardous process of trying to build proper state institutions and a civil society.

At the lowest level, the social tradition which cemented the system was *krugovaia poruka,* or 'joint responsibility', which implied that the whole community, the *mir,* was responsible for the obligations and also the misdeeds of individuals. *Krugovaia poruka* goes back to the earliest juridical documents associated with the principalities of Rus'. It originally arose as a means of ensuring the provision of criminal justice. Princes and their officials were unable to cope with upholding criminal law over their extensive territories, so they left it to local town and village communities to do so. If a murder or other serious crime was committed, communities had to discover and apprehend the miscreant themselves, or else pay a fine to the prince.[12] Taxation was organised in an analogous way. For princes or even their local officials to determine the amount of tax payable by each household was too cumbersome. Instead, a total levy was imposed on each town or village community, and the distribution of the burden within the community was left to its members. Similarly, when troops had to be raised for a military campaign, each community was required to raise a certain number of recruits, and had to decide for itself which of its members should perform military service.[13]

This procedure meant that vital state functions were accomplished in a personal and informal manner, and that the subjects of law were communities, not individuals or even households. Each urban and rural community held meetings of all heads of households, who took the vital decisions regarding criminal proceedings, taxation and recruitment by mutual negotiation and consensus. They would also elect a *starosta* or elder, who was responsible for ensuring that decisions were carried out and for handling relations between the community and the higher authorities.[14]

Such a system was by no means unique to Russia. English 'tithings', which existed by the early eleventh century, are described by Susan Reynolds as 'groups of surety and mutual responsibility' to which all men over twelve were supposed to belong. There were analogous arrangements in France and elsewhere in medieval and early modern Europe, when poor communications made centralised taxation, recruitment and judicial systems impossible to operate.[15]

The system was effective at advancing the interests of the state, but it was also in many ways beneficial to local communities, especially peasants. It helped them survive in a geographical setting which was at the extreme northern limits of viable agriculture, where survival itself was always at issue. One scholar who has examined the life of peasants in eighteenth-century Tambov province concluded that in a normal year they enjoyed a reasonable level of consumption, not inferior to that in most European countries at the time.[16]

The implications of this system were very far-reaching. It meant that all members of the community, especially the village community, had an interest in ensuring the minimal welfare of each other. If one household suffered a fire, then other villagers would rally round and help the victims re-build their home. If one family had a serious illness during harvest-time, then other families would help them get in the crop. This was common sense, not altruism. For the system to survive, it was vital that each member of the community had enough to live on and a small surplus. If your neighbour's household was indigent, then you would end up having to pay part of his taxes. If your neighbour's sons were unhealthy, then it could be your sons who went off to war instead. For the same reason, many village communities would periodically re-distribute land between households, to reflect family size, the capacities and needs of each family. A large family would be awarded more land, but would pay correspondingly more taxes. As a result 'joint responsibility' became a moral as well as a juridical and administrative concept.[17]

Krugovaia poruka also meant that everyone was intensely interested in everyone else's affairs. If your neighbour drank heavily, or beat his wife or had adulterous liaisons, this could weaken his family and hence his economy, to your disadvantage. Those who fell into long-term helpless poverty were unpopular, since they were a burden to their neighbours, and other villagers would do their best to have them sent off to the army or convicted of a criminal offence and despatched into exile. A *starosta* had extensive powers in this regard, which he might exercise according to his personal feelings. The affluent were also regarded with suspicion, since their relative wealth suggested they were acting illegally, or at least in ways which might jeopardise community solidarity. As a popular saying had it, 'Poverty is a sin against the *mir*; wealth is a sin against God.'[18] Such attitudes encouraged gossip and, worse, denunciation, as villagers tried to rid themselves of burdensome or untrustworthy neighbours.

We may say that *krugovaia poruka* generated some of the most attractive and also the most unattractive features of Russian social life: on the one hand, the tradition of humanity, compassion and mutual aid towards one's fellow-human beings, on the other that of malicious rumour-mongering and denunciation directed against the poverty-stricken, the eccentric, sometimes even against the talented and unusual.

In most countries modernisation eventually undermined and destroyed such institutions. In Russia, on the contrary, modernisation reinforced them. As late as 1861, while emancipating the serfs, Alexander II gave enhanced local government responsibilities to peasant institutions shaped by *krugovaia poruka*.[19] As a result, in the words of Valerie Kivelson, 'Local community and the family remained the key sites for contestation. Patronage networks remained crucial venues for popular aspirations and highly localised public life, interacting with and reinforcing, but posing no competition or opposition to centralised rule.'[20] These were the focal institutions of Russian 'political community', in the sense in which Breuilly uses the term. Obviously, though, political communities so scattered, amorphous and personalised were in no position to 'negotiate' with the ruler or give meaning to the 'political concept of the nation'. Personal hierarchies and joint responsibility impeded the emergence of a modern state, a modern market economy, a civil society and a nation, all of which are mutually dependent on one another.

So much for Tsarist Russia. What about the Soviet Union? Like Tsarist Russia, it was a multi-ethnic empire; but unlike Tsarist Russia, it *was* a messianic state. Its aim was to save humanity by spreading socialism throughout the world. The Bolshevik form of Marxism absorbed the latent messianism of the Russian people: that was what distinguished it from west European Marxism. (One might add that Russian messianism was supplemented in this case by Jewish secularised messianism: the Soviet Union, at least at the outset, should probably be seen as a joint Russian-Jewish project.) Paradoxically, however, that messianism did not take a national form, but was internationalist to the point of Russian self-effacement. The word 'Russia' did not appear in any form in the name of the new state. Russia had no effective political existence within the Soviet Union: there were Ukrainian, Georgian, Kazakh etc. Communist Parties, but no Russian Communist Party. Since the Communist Party was the focus of power and the bearer of the messianic vision, that absence was a peculiarly significant one. It is true that there was a Russian Republic (RSFSR), but like the other republics it had little effective power, and in any case had numerous ethnically named non-Russian 'autonomous' administrative units on its territory, even in regions where Russians were in a majority.[21] The Russian people was dissolved in a higher entity. They were the state-bearers of the Soviet Union, but were also rendered anonymous by the Soviet Union.

The USSR did create most of the characteristics of a nation, as understood by Deutsch, Gellner, Breuilly and the modernists: large industrial cities, a mass education system, a penetrative network of communications and public media, a centralised welfare system, a conscripted army. The language employed as the cement of that system was Russian; the common history and traditions evoked in schools as the shared heritage were mainly Russian. But the potential nation thus adumbrated was not Russia, it was what the leaders liked to call the 'Soviet people'. Actually of course the Soviet leaders were not engaged in nation-building at all: they regarded national feeling as a kind of pubertal disorder, a necessary but regrettable phase in social evolution, which should be got through as rapidly as possible. Their ultimate aim was the creation of an international proletarian community, of which the 'Soviet people' were the forerunners.

At another level, though, the Soviet vision *was* a Russian one. Bolshevism revived elements of the inherited system of Russian myths and symbols dating right back to the sixteenth century: the idea that Russia has a special mission in the world, to practise and disseminate Truth and Justice (*pravda*), based on egalitarianism and the frugal way of life of ordinary toiling people. This was *krugovaia poruka* in modern dress, if you like. By virtue of this special mission, Russians were entitled to exercise patronage or protection over less developed peoples, and also to speak for the poor and oppressed in the developed or 'capitalist' world; this was a form of service to them, what one might call 'the Russian's burden'. Such an outlook was fully compatible with Soviet Communism, and it constituted the practical, working ideology of many Russians employed by the Soviet state.[22] Yet it was also close to Dostoevskii, which is why I consider him the unacknowledged 'shadow ideologist' of the Soviet Union.

So this international mission was in one sense a Russian idea. All the same, it ran counter to the needs and customs of ordinary Russian people. As a modern Russian scholar has put it,

Bolshevism's exploitation of the Russian mytho-symbolic system had ambiguous consequences. On the one hand it ensured that the Communist ideology was convincing, it imparted immense dynamism to all spheres of social life and guaranteed the legitimacy of the new state and its socio-political institutions. On the other hand, the glaring contradiction between the new reality and the *ethnic* interests of Russians in the long run weakened the mobilisational potential of the Soviet mythologems and degraded the imperial mythology.[23]

The relationship between the Soviet state and the Russian people varied greatly during the seventy years or so of the USSR. For the first ten to fifteen years Russian identity was explicitly downgraded, even spurned. Cultural and educational policies deliberately promoted non-Russian languages in the non-Russian republics, so that, for example, in Ukraine all primary school children were taught in Ukrainian, including Russians, Jews and Greeks. 'Indigenisation' (*korenizatsiia*) favoured non-Russians for higher education, and it advanced and promoted local officials to run the non-Russian republics. Non-Russians were given their own ethnically named administrative territories, at all levels, down to the village soviet. Thus in Ukraine there were district and even village soviets which were recognised as Jewish, Greek, Armenian, German, Polish etc. – but no Russian ones, as otherwise whole large cities, such as Khar'kov and Donetsk, would have become Russian administrative regions.[24] The Russians were too numerous, powerful and historically dominant for their own good. (Terry Martin has called this 'the most ambitious affirmative action programme in history'.)[25]

During the 1930s Russia was partially rehabilitated. As early as 1930 Stalin reminded the poet Demian Bednyi that one could not write off all Russians. 'In the past there existed two Russias, revolutionary Russia and anti-revolutionary Russia,' while today's Russian working class was the most advanced in the world. In a later speech he added 'In the past we had no fatherland and could not have one. But now that we have overthrown capitalism, now that power is with us, the people, now we have a father-land, and we shall defend its independence.'[26] By the middle of the 1930s it was not only revolutionary Russia or the working class which was being rehabilitated, but the Tsars who had created and defended the Russian Empire, and had thus made the Soviet Union possible. In the schools Russian victories were once again celebrated, while Ivan the Terrible, Peter the Great and Alexander I were extolled as great leaders.[27]

We should note, though, that this rehabilitation of Russia was entirely imperial, not ethnic. It was, if you like, neo-*rossiiskii*, not *russkii*. Stalin despised ethnic Russia: he continued to pursue policies aimed at the destruction of its two most important aspects, the Orthodox Church and the village commune. Parishes were closed, church buildings sequestrated, priests arrested and not infrequently murdered. Peasant households were herded into collective farms and the most productive farmers exiled to Siberia and Kazakhstan. Nor did *korenizatsiia* cease.

During the Second World War these anti-ethnic policies were moder-ated. Collective farmers were given more scope for trading their produce on the private market. Orthodox Church parishes were re-opened, and in 1943 Stalin reinstated the patriarchate. Censorship was eased in the press, on the radio and in the entertainment of troops at the front, so that ordinary people could express their views more freely. Perhaps the apotheosis of this rehabilitation of ethnic Russia was the publication of Aleksandr Tvardovskii's narrative poem, *Vasilii Terkin.* This account of the front-line adventures of an ordinary Russian soldier from Smolensk oblast' never mentions Stalin or the Communist Party. Its hero is a simple peasant with limited education and no experience of urban life, science or technology. His patriotism is deeply felt, but it is Russian rather than Soviet – or at least the Soviet Union is seen as an extension of Russia. Surveys have shown that this was the most popular reading of Red Army soldiers at the front.[28]

The implications were considerable. This was not just a revival of pre-1917 Russian patriotism, for since the revolution a whole new generation of Russians had grown up and become literate, gaining the most important skill needed to become fully aware of their national identity. During and for a short time after the Second World War we may say that the *russkii* and *rossiiskii*, the ethnic and imperial aspects of Russian-ness, coalesced fully for the first time. This was what made victory possible.[29]

That synthesis did not last long, however. Stalin's concessions to ethnic Russia were rapidly withdrawn. The state's authority over the collective farms was restored, and peasants' recent wartime profits were confiscated in a 1947 currency reform. The re-opening of parishes ceased, and the Church was confined to the performance of weekly divine services; any public manifestation of religious belief, such as processions, Sunday schools, prayer meetings or charitable work, was forbidden.[30] Censorship was fully reinstated, and publication of wartime reminiscences was discouraged, in effect forbidden. Even the meetings of veterans to recall their combat experiences and to offer aid to those in difficulties were subjected to strict party supervision.[31] Where the cultivation of public memory, especially of such traumatic events, is restricted or repressed, then one of the essential components of national consciousness is jeopardised. Memory of the war became part of the official narrative, tightly hedged about and monitored, not available for ordinary people to elaborate in their own fashion. As a result, the close association between the *russkii* and the *sovetskii* was seriously weakened.

Messianism remained, but it gradually changed its nature. For the first twenty years or so after the war, it was still directed towards the future, towards the building of Communism. As that ideal came to seem ever more distant and unreal, however, messianism reoriented itself towards the past. After all, even if it had not built paradise, the Soviet Union unquestionably *had* saved Europe from the apocalypse, from subjection to Nazi rule. Especially after 1964 the centre of gravity of Soviet propaganda shifted from the future to the past, to remembrance and celebration of that great and undeniable victory. Fixated on the past, Soviet official symbolism became ghostly and insubstantial and lost the power to convince young people.[32]

Another feature of old Russia reasserted itself under the Communists and obstructed the formation of Russian national identity. Although the Soviet state assumed and performed many of the functions of a modern state, it did so without generating a political community. The Communist Party functioned as a substitute for such a community, and its conduits of power were largely directed from above through personal channels. At the lower levels, social units re-emerged whose operating principle was *krugovaia poruka*.

Between the 1860s and 1910s civil society, representative institutions and even a measure of pluralist politics, had been emerging. *Krugovaia poruka* was abolished in 1905. But the 1917 revolution abruptly ended that development. Russia was plunged back into unrestricted rule by persons, compounded by the Communist claim to absolute authority in the name of humanity's great future. Both the party and the state in theory ruled through elective institutions, but in practice the nomenklatura appointments system consolidated personal rule by, in effect, creating a monopoly system of patronage. Appointments of responsible staff in all professions were decided by the appropriate party committee on the strength of reports from previous employers, trusted party people and the security police. High-level appointees became patrons who, when they were promoted, took their clients with them, creating what some political scientists have termed *Seilschaften*, evoking the image of mountain climbers roped to each other making their way up the slopes. Observing the rise and fall of these clientele groups constituted the art of Kremlinology. No alternative political parties or genuine elections existed to provide any competition.[33]

Monopoly patronage was supplemented at lower levels by the revival of *krugovaia poruka*. Soviet enterprises, ostensibly charged with achieving the highest possible levels of output, suffered from severe shortages of labour from the 1930s through to the early 1950s, and so had to concede much of the control over the labour process to the workers themselves. As a result they became institutions mainly dedicated to fulfilling the life needs of their major stakeholders, the administrators and workers employed there. The workers would expect to receive pay, housing, medical care, recreation, social security, often basic food supplies as well, provided they exhibited a minimum of productive zeal. The managers received those benefits too and also status, security and the habit of command. Managers and employees were dependent on each other for the continuation of these comfortable arrangements: the managers had to bargain with Gosplan to be assigned undemanding production targets, the employees had then to fulfil those targets. How they did so was no one's business, since in the absence of a market economy, the consumer's needs were not taken into consideration.[34]

As in the village commune, subsistence was ensured by mutual cooperation, but also mutual surveillance, ostensible deference to authority, and agreed traditional work practices. The result was an economy which produced a basic minimum to guarantee a tolerable life for those within the system, but it was hard on outsiders and was unwelcoming to new technology, which threatened to disrupt delicately balanced arrangements. The great difference from the Tsarist regime was that the Soviet enterprise was much more open to penetration by the authorities, especially through its party cell and through the cadres department, which reported to the security police. The tendency of *krugovaia poruka* to generate denunciations was thus intensified.

The same may be said of the communal apartment, which was the basic dwelling unit in the larger Soviet cities from the early 1930s through to the 1960s or 1970s. A bourgeois apartment built before 1917 would be reorganised so that each room contained one family, and all the tenants shared kitchen, bathroom, toilet, hall and corridor. To ensure a minimally harmonious coexistence, they had to combine rudimentary democracy with hierarchy and vigilant mutual surveillance, devising forms of consultation and control over use of the communal areas and facilities, over noise in the early morning and late evening, and such like. Everyone shared a kind of egalitarian poverty, and looked askance on those who deviated markedly from the norm: on the affluent because their relative prosperity suggested underhand, even criminal, behaviour which might endanger their neighbours, the indigent because they would constantly beg, borrow or steal in order to get by. The close proximity in which they all lived ensured that private events were usually known to everyone, and anything unusual or untoward could be reported to the authorities.[35]

Nothing, it would seem, ensures the perpetuation of old habits more than a precipitate attempt to change them. The Soviet Union's headlong modernisation project re-created in a new form the sinews of personal command and joint responsibility which had characterised pre-revolutionary Russian society. Nowhere could the legal institutions and the public arena emerge which are essential to both the modern state and the nation.

In both Russia and the Soviet Union, then, modernisation obstructed the development of a Russian national identity. When dealing with non-Russian national identity, the modernists have a better and simpler case. Non-Russian national movements, as they emerged in both the early and the late twentieth century, represent a clear example of what Breuilly calls 'separatist nationalism'. The paradox is that in many ways their national feelings were deliberately promoted by the Soviet state. As a result, the long-term outcome of the Soviet project, against all the intentions of its leaders, was the creation of something like nation-states. From the late 1930s ethnic identity, recorded on each individual's passport, was a far more important factor in deciding his or her life-chances than social origin. Taken together with *korenizatsiia*, and in the absence from the mid-1950s of state-sponsored mass terror, this 'ethnicisation' of the Soviet Union meant that the non-Russian republics tended to become enclaves for the titular ethnos. The clients of the locally dominant patrons would be appointed to the top jobs, would receive preference in the allocation of education, jobs and housing, and would also control much of the underground, 'second' economy. Incoming Russians, or even long-established Russian settlers, not infrequently lost out in these intrigues.[36] The Russians might be the state-bearing people, but they could no longer dominate the local ethnic political communities.

In reaction to this tendency, in the later decades of the Soviet Union, Russians generated two alternative visions of their own future. The first was an attempt to combine the values of ethnic and imperial Russia into a synthesis. It aimed to rehabilitate and amalgamate the values of the Russian peasant community and those of the Orthodox Church with those of both Russian empires, Tsarist and Soviet. It identified the de-nationalising features of Soviet rule with the Jews, or with the undue influence of 'western bourgeois ideology'. In the final years of the Soviet Union the proponents of such ideas allied themselves with some ideologists of the Russian Orthodox Church, and began to promote a vision of a revived Orthodox Russian Empire, with reformed Communist features, leading the world against the domination of United States imperialism. Once a Russian Communist Party was finally set up, in 1990, this became its ideology, and it was taken over by the leader of the post-Soviet Communist Party of the Russian Federation, Gennadii Ziuganov.[37] Now at last Dostoevskii came into his own.

These thinkers are usually dubbed 'Russian nationalists', but this is acceptable only in the sense in which Krishan Kumar speaks of 'missionary nationalism', the nationalism of a people whose aims transcend the nation, and attempt to transform the international community.[38] The Russian 'nationalists' were really Russian imperialists, who still saw the mission of the Russian people as being not the creation of a nation-state, but continued hegemony in a multi-ethnic state with a worldwide mission.

The continuing weakness of genuine Russian nationalism (as distinct from imperialism) is demonstrated by the fact that even the imperialists' opponents, the Russian liberals, were not really aiming to create a Russian nation-state. They too assumed an all-Soviet framework and anticipated that the democratic reforms they proposed would take effect in the Soviet Union as a whole. During the late 1980s, however, they found themselves in alliance with non-Russian national movements from the Baltic, the Caucasus and elsewhere who shared the same enemy, the autocratic Soviet state, and who wished to establish their own independent nation-states. So the logic of politics impelled them to create at least the outward forms of a Russian nation-state which few of them had envisaged as an ideal.[39]

In the end, then, the decisive confrontation of August 1991 which finally destroyed the USSR was not between Communists and anti-Communists, but between the Soviet Union and Russia, or if you like between those who still saw Russia as empire and those who wanted a new ethnic and civic Russian nation, no longer dedicated to either helping or oppressing non-Russians.

So the Russian Federation emerged almost by accident. It has proved to be a truncated and distorted nation-state. Its legitimacy its still widely contested, especially the separation from Ukraine and Belorussia. Within it both political and economic life are still dominated by personalities and by patron–client networks. Laws, institutions, civil society exist, but are weak and overshadowed. Most Russians are themselves discontented with what they have, so we cannot simply say that this is a Russian form of the nation-state. But whether it is developing into something else is not clear either.

CONCLUSION

Both the Tsarist and Soviet states drew selectively on the existing stock of Russian ethnic myths, symbols and memories in a way which entailed deliberately trampling some of them under foot. In doing so, they brought modernisation and nation-building into conflict. They also jeopardised support for the empire even among the supposedly dominant ethnicity, the Russians. That is why the empire collapsed twice in the twentieth century, and why a proper Russian nation-state still does not exist.

The Russian experience does cast doubt on the necessary connection between modernisation and nation-building. On the whole, though, it confirms Breuilly's view that nationhood rests on a relationship between a modern state and a political community. Rudimentary, personalised forms of the state persisted in both Tsarist and Soviet Russia, and they generated as a mirror-image undeveloped forms of public life and under-developed nationhood.

NOTES

1 Anthony D. Smith, *National Identity* (London: Penguin Books, 1991), p. 21. Smith uses the term 'ethno-symbolic' to describe his approach in his 'Nations and their pasts', *Nations and Nationalism* 2, 3 (November 1996), p. 362.

2 Geoffrey Hosking, *Russia and the Russians: A History* (London: Allen Lane, 2001), pp. 103, 108–9.

3 Andreas Kappeler, *Russland als Vielvölkerreich: Entstehung, Geschichte, Zerfall* (Munich: C.H. Beck, 1992), pp. 34–6.

4 Geoffrey Hosking, 'The Russian national myth repudiated', in Geoffrey Hosking and George Schöpflin (eds.), *Myths and Nationhood* (London: Hurst & Co, 1997), pp. 198–210; S. A. Zen'kovskii, *Russkoe staroobriad-chestvo: dukhovnye dvizheniia 17-ogo veka* (Munich: Wilhelm Fink Verlag, 1970).

5 See Richard Wortman, *Scenarios of Power: Myth and Ceremony in Russian Monarchy*, vol. II (Princeton University Press, 2000), on the importance of

military strength, and on the way the Tsar presented his power as being great because partly *foreign*.

6 Geoffrey Hosking, *Russia: People and Empire, 1552–1917* (London: HarperCollins, 1997), pp. 304–10.

7 John Breuilly, 'The state and nationalism', in Montserrat Guibernau and John Hutchinson (eds), *Understanding Nationalism* (Cambridge: Polity Press, 2001), p. 32.

8 John Breuilly, *Nationalism and the State* (2nd edn, Manchester University Press, 1993), pp. 373–4.

9 L. V. Cherepnin, *Zemskie sobory russkogo gosudarstva v xvi–xvii vv* (Moscow: Nauka, 1978), pp. 55–115; John L. H. Keep, 'The decline of the zemskii sobor', in his *Power and the People: Essays on Russian History* (Boulder: East European Monographs, 1995), pp. 51–86.

10 Hosking, *Russia and the Russians*, p. 92; Mikhail Afanas'ev, *Klientelizm i rossiiskaia gosudarstvennost'* (Moscow: Tsentr kontsitutsionnykh issledovanii, 1997), p. 85.

11 Nancy Shields Kollmann, *Kinship and Politics: the Making of the Muscovite Political System, 1345–1547* (Stanford University Press, 1987); Valerie Kivelson, *Autocracy in the Provinces: the Muscovite Gentry and Political Culture in the Seventeenth Century* (Stanford University Press, 1996).

12 Horace W. Dewey, 'Russia's debt to the Mongols in suretyship and collective responsibility', *Comparative Studies in Society and History* 30 (1988), 249–70.

13 Valerie Kivelson, '"Merciful father, impersonal state": Russian autocracy in comparative perspective', *Modern Asian Studies* 33 (1997), 635–63.

14 V. A. Aleksandrov, *Sel'skaia obshchina v Rossii (xvii–nachalo xix veka)* (Moscow: Nauka, 1976), chs. 2–3; Boris Mironov (with Ben Eklof), *The Social History of Imperial Russia*, vol. 1 (Boulder: Westview Press, 2000), ch. 7.

15 S. Reynolds, *Kingdoms and Communities in Europe, 900–1300* (2nd edn, Oxford: Clarendon Press, 1997), p. 115; Hilton Root, *Peasants and King in Burgundy: Agrarian Foundations of French Absolutism* (Berkeley, CA: University of California Press, 1983); on the decline of such institutions see Jerome Blum, 'The internal structure and polity of the European village community from the fifteenth to the nineteenth centuries', *Journal of Modern History* 43 (1971), 543–76.

16 Steven L. Hoch, *Serfdom and Social Control in Russia: Petrovskoe, a Village in Tambov* (Chicago: University of Chicago Press, 1986), ch. 1; see also David Moon, 'Reassessing Russian serfdom', *European History Quarterly* 26 (1996), 483–526.

17 Jeremy Burds, 'The social control of peasant labour', in Esther Kingston-Mann and Timothy Mixter (eds), *Peasant Economy, Culture and Politics of European Russia, 1800–1921* (Princeton University Press, 1991), pp. 52–100; M. Afanas'ev, *Klientelizm i rossiiskaia gosudarstvennost'*.

18 B. N. Mironov, *Sotsial'naia istoriia Rossii perioda imperii*, vol. 1 (St Petersburg: Dmitrii Bulanin, 1999), p. 330.

19 V. G. Chernukha, *Krest'ianskii vopros v pravitel'stvennoi politike* (Leningrad: Nauka, 1972), ch. 3.

20 Kivelson, 'Merciful father', 663.

21 The history of the RSFSR is aptly summarised in Robert Service, *Russia: Experiment with a People* (London: Macmillan, 2002), pp. 33–44.

22 Vera Tolz, *Inventing the Nation: Russia* (London: Longman, 2001), esp. pp. 94–9, 181–8.

23 Valerii Solovei, 'Russkie protiv imperii', *Svobodnaia mysl'* 12 (2002), 82.

24 Terry Martin, *The Affirmative Action Empire: Nations and Nationalism in the Soviet Union, 1923–1939* (Ithaca, NY: Cornell University Press, 2001), pp. 33–48.

25 Martin, *Affirmative Action Empire*, p. 2.

26 A. I. Vdovin, V. I. Zorin and A. V. Nikonov, *Russkii vopros v natsional'noi politike xx veka* (Moscow: Russkii Mir, 1998), pp. 125–9.

27 David Brandenberger, *National Bolshevism: Stalinist Mass Culture and the Formation of Modern Russian National Identity, 1931–1956* (Cambridge, MA: Harvard University Press, 2002), ch. 3.

28 Geoffrey Hosking, 'The Second World War and Russian national consciousness', *Past and Present* 175 (May 2002), 162–87.

29 Hosking, 'Second World War', esp. 174–8.

30 Elena Zubkova, *Poslevoennoe sovetskoe obshchestvo: politika i povsednevnost', 1945–1953* (Moscow: Rosspen, 2000), pp. 35–7.

31 Nina Tumarkin, *The Living and the Dead: the Rise and Fall of the Cult of World War II in Russia* (New York: Basic Books, 1994), p. 104.

32 Tumarkin, *Living and Dead*, esp. pp. 33–9, 129–36; Hosking, 'Second World War', esp. 186–7.

33 Mikhail Voslensky, *Nomenklatura: Anatomy of the Soviet Ruling Class* (London: Bodley Head, 1984); Thomas Rigby and Bohdan Harasymiw, *Leadership Selection and Patron–Client Relations in the USSR and Yugoslavia* (London: Allen & Unwin, 1983).

34 The emergence of this system is described in Donald Filtzer, *Soviet Workers and Stalinist Industrialisation: The Formation of Modern Soviet Production Relations* (London: Pluto Press, 1986).

35 Il'ia Utekhin, *Ocherki kommunal'nogo byta* (Moscow: OGI, 2001); E. Iu. Gerasimova, 'Sovetskaia kommunal'naia kvartira', *Sotsiologicheskii zhurnal* 1–2 (1998), pp. 224–42.

36 Teresa Rakowska-Harmstone, 'Ethnic politics in the USSR', *Problems of Communism* 23, 3 (May–June 1974), 1–22; Robert J. Kaiser, *The Geography of Nationalism in Russia and the USSR* (Princeton University Press, 1994), esp. pp. 380–91.

37 Joan Barth Urban and Valerii D. Solovei, *Russia's Communists at the Crossroads* (Boulder: Westview Press, 1997), pp. 98–105.

38 Krishan Kumar, 'Nation and empire: English and British national identity in comparative perspective', *Theory and Society* 29 (2000), 575–608. In this article Kumar specifically applies the term to Russia.

39 Mark Beissinger, *Nationalist Mobilisation and the Collapse of the Soviet State* (Cambridge University Press, 2002).

CHAPTER 9

Ordering the kaleidoscope: the construction of identities in the lands of the Polish-Lithuanian Commonwealth since 1569

Robert Frost

> In this sense I can consider myself a typical East European. It seems to be true that his *differentia specifica* can be boiled down to a lack of form – both inner and outer ... he always remains an adolescent, governed by a sudden ebb or flow of inner chaos. Form is achieved in stable societies ... The things that surround us in childhood need no justification, they are self-evident. If, however, they whirl about like particles in a kaleidoscope, ceaselessly changing position, it takes no small amount of energy simply to plant one's feet on solid ground without falling.[1]

Czesław Miłosz, the Nobel prize-winning poet, born in what is now Lithuania in 1911, grew up in the city now called Vilnius during and after the First World War. He became a Polish citizen involuntarily when the city he knew as Wilno was forcibly incorporated into the Polish state in 1919, moving to a Warsaw he neither knew nor loved after Wilno became Vilnius when it was again forcibly incorporated, this time into Lithuania, as a consequence of the Ribbentrop–Molotov Pact. After 1945 he briefly served the Polish People's Republic as a diplomat, before heading for the United States, where he continued to write his poetry in the Polish language that was his native tongue, but which did not necessarily define his national identity.

While he was living in eastern Europe, Miłosz observed at first hand the disjuncture between power, the nation and the state which has, in the modern period, been so evident there; he wrote eloquently of them in his classic autobiographical dissection of the problem of identity, *Native Realm.* For, as Miłosz observed, the problems of state-formation, state power and national identity were particularly acute in the lands of the old Polish-Lithuanian Commonwealth, founded at Lublin in 1569 after over a century and a half of a loose dynastic union between the kingdom of

Poland and the Grand Duchy of Lithuania. For this remarkable political creation was partitioned out of existence by Prussia, Austria and Russia between 1772 and 1795; it disappeared from the European map at the very moment that the French revolutionaries were exporting the doctrine of the Sovereign Nation, One and Indivisible on the points of their bayonets, and Romantic philosophers were seizing on Herder's view of the nation as a mystical, extra-temporal cultural community.

The state which was partitioned between 1772 and 1795 was certainly not, in any modern sense, a nation-state; a multi-national, multi-ethnic polity, its lands were incorporated into the three great empires of nineteenth-century central and eastern Europe. When, however, the political borders set at Vienna in 1815, and solidified in the course of the nineteenth century, evaporated in the cataclysm of 1917–19, it was by no means clear what states should replace them. Woodrow Wilson might talk of 'self-determination'; the problem in eastern Europe, however, was not so much determining the borders between 'nations', over which international statesmen agonised in the years after 1918, as determining what those nations were. For, as Timothy Snyder has recently pointed out, in the absence of statehood between 1569 and 1918, the lands of the old Commonwealth had seen dramatic changes in the ways in which nation and nations were conceived.[2] To understand the bitter struggles over borders and 'nation'-states in eastern Europe after 1918 it is necessary to abandon the simplistic ideas of nationhood peddled by nationalists of the region (and too many scholars elsewhere). Most studies of national identity and nation-building begin with the French Revolution, or at best the Enlightenment. It is true that after 1789 the rapid spread of the idea of the Sovereign Nation brought an intensified need to define the essence of the Nation and to construct a national identity to rally the imagined community, now seen by a growing number of intellectuals as the only valid basis for the state – particularly in eastern Europe, by those who saw it as the only means to challenge the multi-national empires of which they had involuntarily become a part. The case of the lands of the old Polish-Lithuanian Commonwealth, however, suggests that the relationship between 'nation', identity and state power is rather more complex than is often allowed; to grasp this point it is necessary, as Snyder so eloquently demonstrates, to go back before the Age of Nationalism to 1569, if not before.

Poland, as Tadeusz Łepkowski once remarked, was always a country as much divided by borders as defined by them.[3] Eastern Europe was always a land of borders or, more accurately, borderlands – *Marken*, not *Grenzen*. The Polish-Lithuanian Commonwealth at its greatest extent in the seventeenth century included most of modern Poland, Lithuania, Latvia, Belarus and Ukraine, as well as parts of what is now Russia. It thus straddled the great cultural divide between eastern and western Christendom; despite the advances of Catholicism in the seventeenth century, the Orthodox Church remained dominant in much of the Commonwealth's eastern lands, at least at the popular level. By the eighteenth century some three-quarters of the world's Jews lived within its borders, which also contained significant Muslim and Armenian communities. The dominant ethnic groups were of Slavic origin, but if Herder, despite speaking occasionally of the 'Slavian Nations', essentially regarded the Slavs, like the Germans, as one nation with one national character, this was certainly not how the Commonwealth's Slavs saw it, either before or after 1795.[4]

The intense national struggles of the twentieth century in eastern Europe have led many western (and east European emigré) scholars to consider east European nationalism as essentially cultural and ethnic in nature, rather than revolutionary-democratic, to use Hobsbawm's distinction. This dogma led to the view that the multi-national polities of the East, whether the Polish-Lithuanian Commonwealth or the empires which partitioned it, were inherently unstable: the collapse of the Commonwealth, or Austria-Hungary, or, indeed, the Soviet Union, is frequently presented as natural: the explosion of political systems which ultimately can only be held together by force. Yet, despite its slide into political anarchy in the eighteenth century (a state from which it gave some indications of recovery after 1788) Poland-Lithuania had proved one of the more successful and long-lasting states of east-central Europe. Its success was due to the fact that it differed markedly from the composite monarchies so common in medieval and early modern Europe, in which the ruling dynasty frequently provided almost the sole unifying force. For, after the 1569 Union of Lublin, the Commonwealth (*Rzeczpospolita*; *Res Publica*) was a state built from below, by its citizens, not its monarchs; a state whose ruling *szlachta* (noble) elite, which constituted some 6 to 8 per cent of the population, constructed a successful common identity, one that was explicitly national, even if not in a narrow ethnic or cultural way.

The Lublin Union explicitly sought to create a political nation in the sense of an inclusive body of citizens formed regardless of ethnic or cultural origin. This concept was by no means new: already in 1501 the abortive union treaty drawn up in Mielnik had expressed its desire to join Poland and Lithuania in one 'undivided and equal body' to form 'one nation, one brotherhood and a common council'. Such language has often raised the hackles of modern Lithuanian, Ukrainian and Belarus'ian historians, who are prone to interpret it as a manifestation of Polish cultural imperialism and a desire to incorporate the nations of the Grand Duchy of Lithuania into Poland. Yet the idea of a *political* nation of citizens, membership of which was dependent upon recognition and acceptance by the citizen body, not on ethnicity or language, was the only practicable view of the nation in such a culturally and ethnically diverse polity. Following the defeat of the Teutonic Knights in the Thirteen Years War (1454–66) and the incorporation of Royal Prussia into Poland by the Treaty of Thorn (1466), the kingdom of Poland had acquired a large population of German culture. Lithuania was even more culturally diverse: a vast, ill-defined empire it had been created when the pagan Lithuanians, a non-Slavic, Baltic people, swept up the remnants of Kievan Rus', shattered by the Mongols, in the thirteenth and early fourteenth centuries. Although most of the ethnic Lithuanian nobility had converted to Catholicism along with their grand duke Jogaila, elected to the Polish throne as Władysław Jagiełło in 1385, elements of paganism long survived among Lithuanian peasants, while the poorly endowed Catholic Church failed to make any great inroads into the Grand Duchy's Ruthenian Orthodox population, which constituted by far the majority of its inhabitants. The Lithuanian elite was, indeed, heavily influenced by the culture of its Slavic subjects and in the absence of a written language of its own, soon adopted a form of eastern Slavonic known variously as Old Chancery Ruthenian or old Belarus'ian, as Lithuania's language of law and government.

Unions are not beloved of modern nationalists or modern nationalist historians, and it is hardly surprising that the various union treaties drawn up between 1385 and 1569 have been at the centre of an intense debate between Polish, Lithuanian, Ukrainian and Belarus'ian historians, with the Poles broadly taking a positive view, while their eastern neighbours show a marked lack of enthusiasm. Nevertheless, recent attempts by Lithuanian historians to deny that the Union of Lublin succeeded despite the almost unanimous opposition of the great magnates who dominated the pre-1569 Lithuanian political system because of strong support from the lesser Lithuanian nobility, seem misguided. Given the extent of magnate opposition, it is all but impossible to explain the successful consummation of the Union in 1569, and the transfer of the erstwhile Ukrainian territories of the Grand Duchy to the kingdom of Poland as a means to put pressure on the recalcitrant magnates in any other way: certainly the king's envoys had no difficulty in persuading the middling and lesser nobilities of these regions to swear an oath of loyalty to the new constitutional arrangements.

This impression is supported by the rapid acculturation between the political elites of the new Commonwealth which soon brought the assertion of a new, common identity. Already by the early sixteenth century the Polish language and Polish cultural influences were spreading rapidly among the Lithuanian, Ruthenian and German elites of Royal Prussia and the old Grand Duchy. This process accelerated significantly after 1569. The annexation of substantial Ukrainian territories and Podlasie at Lublin opened them up to Polish settlement, which also took place in the relatively sparsely populated remainder of Lithuania, despite various legal attempts to restrict it. By driving an artificial political border through a region dominated by Ruthenian culture the annexations may have weakened its powers of resistance, but one should not underestimate the positive appeal and integrative force of the new post-Lublin citizen nation. Despite the undoubted problems and clashes between Poles and Lithuanians in the early years of the new Union, resentments which certainly festered throughout the long marriage between the two states, the Union continued and was increasingly underpinned by a strengthening common identity which existed above the separate identities of Poles and Lithuanians.[5]

It is important to stress this point, for this process is frequently and inaccurately referred to as 'polonisation', especially by Lithuanian, Ukrainian and Belarus'ian historians. It is true that the Polish language rapidly became the *lingua franca* of citizenship in the new Commonwealth, adopted by German Prussian and Livonian nobles as well as Lithuanians and Ruthenians. For the latter, this was no great problem. Chancery Ruthenian, the official language of the Grand Duchy, was an artificial legal language, not a living tongue. Polish and Ruthenian were to a considerable extent mutually intelligible, and the historian of the early modern period must beware of taking too seriously the boundaries between related languages established by nationalist philologists in the nineteenth century in an attempt to prove the right of their people to take their place among the Herderian cultural nations. In the sixteenth century Ruthenian rapidly gave way. The Third Lithuanian Statute of 1588, itself an attempt by the Lithuanian magnate elite to emphasise the separate political status of the Grand Duchy – some of its clauses explicitly breached the terms of the Lublin Union – was published in three Ruthenian editions (1588, 1593 and 1600); from 1614 every edition was in Polish.[6] The Polish language made steady progress in the local court books; by the middle of the seventeenth century even the Orthodox church was conducting its religious polemics in Polish.[7] Finally, in the late seventeenth century, pressure from the middling and lesser nobility who could no longer understand Chancery

Ruthenian, and could not afford lawyers who did, led to the introduction of Polish as Lithuania's legal language in 1697.

This common identity was based, like all such identities, on a mythologised version of the past, which saw the new political nation, regardless of ethnic origin, as the descendants of the Sarmatian tribes which had successfully resisted conquest by the Roman Empire. Originally, the Sarmatians had been identified as the ancestors of the Slavs as a whole; in the seventeenth century writers increasingly asserted that it was the Polish-Lithuanian nobility which was the true inheritor of the Sarmatian tradition. In 1608 Marcin Paszkowski claimed that the Muscovites were merely a bastard offshoot of the Sarmatians who did not possess a true claim to their ancient territory.[8]

Yet the Sarmatians remained a political not an ethnic nation, despite the widespread adoption of Polish by its members. The Sarmatian nation specifically included the non-Polish Lithuanians and the noble elites of Royal Prussia and Polish Livonia, many of whom were of German descent and some of whom maintained their German identity. It was an ideal which even attracted the burgher elites of the cities of Royal Prussia who were not part of the noble nation although – uniquely in the Commonwealth – burgher representatives did sit in the Royal Prussian *Landtag*.[9] After 1569 the borders of the political nation were thus social, not ethnic, linguistic or economic. Despite the fact that many of the vast numbers of Polish nobles were landless and impoverished, frequently poorer than some peasants, their social status accorded membership of the political nation, although there was growing pressure from the seventeenth century to exclude the propertyless from participation in the local dietines (*sejmiki*) that were the Commonwealth's basic political institution.[10] All that was required was recognition of one's status by the local noble community which could, if in doubt, be tested in the local courts. Outsiders could be accepted into the body of the nation, subject to confirmation by the central diet (*Sejm*) in the form of a decree of *indygenat*. In this way the political nation remained open: many foreigners and not a few peasants were ennobled, alongside Prussian burghers. Under Lithuanian law, all Jews and Tatars, of which there was a sizeable community in Lithuania, who converted to Catholicism were automatically ennobled.

In the seventeenth century this successfully created identity was increasingly built around Catholicism as well as the attachment to the classical, republican tradition with a strong emphasis on the 'Golden Freedom' of the noble citizen which had dominated at the time of the Union of Lublin.

Protestantism – in particular Calvinism, but also anti-Trinitarianism – had spread rapidly among the nobility in the middle of the sixteenth century, but despite significant support from a number of leading magnate families, in particular the Birże branch of the powerful and wealthy Radziwiłł family, the high tide of Protestantism began to ebb in the early seventeenth century. Indirectly, its spread had actually assisted the process of assimilation of the Commonwealth's eastern elites, as many formerly Orthodox noble families ultimately found their way to Catholicism after initial conversion to Protestantism. Orthodoxy was further weakened by the creation of the Uniate or Greek Catholic Church in 1596. The Sarmatian nation was never uniformly Catholic, but its increasingly Catholic nature did much to divorce the noble elite from the rest of the population in the lands of the pre-1569 Grand Duchy of Lithuania.

The triumph of the Sarmatian identity was outwardly expressed in the spread of particular styles of dress and manners. Where the elites of Poland and Lithuania in the sixteenth century had shown some enthusiasm for western fashion, in the seventeenth they increasingly abandoned western dress, which was rejected as decadent and because of its association with a royal court which was suspected of wishing to undermine traditional Sarmatian liberties in the name of western-style absolute monarchy. Polish dress took on a distinctly eastern tinge. Despite their claims to be the eastern bastion of western civilisation and the true inheritors of the western tradition of Roman republicanism, Polish-Lithuanian nobles who lived nearer to Berlin than Bakhchiserai shaved their heads leaving exotic topknots like Tatars and grew bushy moustaches as different from the pointy waxed efflorescences of western fashion as was possible. They dressed in robes and sashes of eastern cloth and decked their walls with oriental rugs. It was a frontier culture in which the importance of the eastern lands which had joined Poland at Lublin was clearly recognised: in the frontier zone between eastern and western civilisation, the Commonwealth created a powerful synthesis that was all its own.

The very success of this invented tradition, however, did much to undermine the political system of which it was an expression. The rejection of the political and administrative models of western Europe, and of the perceived 'tyranny' of Muscovy in the name of Sarmatian republicanism, strengthened latent decentralising forces which left the Commonwealth unable to resist its rapacious neighbours after 1648, when the massive revolt of the Ukrainian Cossacks demonstrated that not all members of the old elites of the Grand Duchy of Lithuania could be accommodated within the Sarmatian nation. By the middle of the eighteenth century, it was clear to many that the Sarmatians could no longer pride themselves on the excellence of their constitution. While some reformers clung to the republican tradition which lay at the centre of the Sarmatian identity, a group of enlightened reformers round the Commonwealth's last monarch, Stanisław August Poniatowski (1764–95), adopted western dress and ridiculed Sarmatism as the benighted doctrine of the conservative petty nobility. After the shock of the First Partition (1772), reformist ideas flourished, but it was not until the Four Year Sejm (1788–92) that the republican reformers and the king's supporters were able to come together sufficiently to pass the Constitution of 3 May 1791, which not only rejected the old, decentralised political system, but also sought to redefine the political nation. In the spirit of the American and French revolutionaries, the Constitution proclaimed that the nation was sovereign, and that the nation consisted of the whole people. This statement was largely rhetorical; in practical terms the old noble citizen body remained the real political nation under the Constitution, but it was radically redefined. If burghers were granted but a limited place in political life and their representatives were only allowed to vote on municipal matters, provision was made for frequent and widespread ennoblement (which meant in effect admission to the citizen body), while landless nobles, some 66 per cent of the total, were formally denied the right to participate in the *sejmiki* and thus effectively removed from the political nation. Yet a political nation it undoubtedly remained: much is sometimes made of the fact that nowhere in the text of the Constitution, apart from the titles of the king, is 'Lithuania' mentioned, but although it certainly introduced common executive organs, thus ending the system by which Lithuania and Poland had separate institutions of government, it did not, as is sometimes suggested, end the separate status of the Grand Duchy.

Quite what all this would have meant in practice is an academic question. The Constitution provoked the final crisis and dismemberment of the Commonwealth at precisely the moment when modern political nationalism was born. Its disappearance was a profound shock to its citizen body; over the next century and a half they and many of their descendants combined nostalgia for the defunct Commonwealth with a burning desire for its reincarnation, though it was by no means clear what sort of national phoenix should rise from the ashes of the old Sarmatian state. Yet if attachment to a political ideal had preceded cultural identification in the old Commonwealth, it was a common cultural identity which survived its collapse. And if it seemed self-evident to those elites that patriots should seek the restoration of the state within the boundaries of 1772, it soon became clear that if the Sovereign Nation, One and Indivisible, was the only true basis for a modern state, as many were prepared to believe after the national disaster of the Partitions, the problem of who might constitute that nation was intrinsically divisive.

One thing was clear. The old, class-based idea of a noble nation was gone forever. The process begun by the Constitution of 3 May was completed after 1795 as the partitioning powers refused to recognise the noble status or political rights of the vast majority of the nobility. The contrast with the position of certain of the wealthier magnates, some of whom had flagrantly co-operated with the partitioning powers before 1795, and who now accommodated themselves rapidly to the new status quo, was glaring. Many of the middling and lesser nobility were instantly radicalised, enthusiastically embracing a new conception of the political nation based on the doctrines of the American and French revolutions. Although Tadeusz Kościuszko, who had fought in the American War of Independence, still made a distinction between the noble nation and the common people when he launched his 1794 rising against the Russians, his Połaniec Manifesto (7 May 1794) called for the abolition of serfdom and the liberation of the peasantry whom he had led to victory at Racławice the previous month. The radical priest Franciszek Dmochowski (1760–1812), a leading figure in the Paris-based Polish Deputation, claimed that the Polish nobility had learned that it could not preserve its freedom unless it shared it with the people in general. Franciszek Gorzkowski (1760–1830), of poor noble background, also called for the peasants to fight for Poland, freedom and equality against national and social oppressors.[11]

Thus the borders of the old noble nation were, in the eyes of the radicals, to be extended to include all the inhabitants of the old Commonwealth. This was also the solution urged by the historian Joachim Lelewel (1786–1861), exiled after the 1830 Rising against the Russians, who associated Polish identity with the cause of freedom. He attacked the wealthy magnates, whom he accused of betraying the Commonwealth and oppressing the common people, urging the extension of political rights to all. He did recognise, however, that there were barriers which needed to be overcome if the common people were to be fully integrated into the political nation which, in talking of the 1791 Constitution, he still identified with the politically conscious nobility. He talked of the rule of the common people (*lud*), but recognised that they were not yet ready to take a full part in government. Nevertheless, he suggested that they shared a potential love of the fatherland and, if inspired with the national spirit, would become politically conscious and able to take their deserved place in political life.[12]

It was a sentiment echoed by the poet Adam Mickiewicz (1798–1855) in his great epic *Pan Tadeusz*, set in 1812, in which one of the characters urges the hero and heroine not just to free their serfs, but to 'make them noble': i.e. to admit them to full membership of the citizen body.[13]

The call for the citizen nation to include the common people did not, however, necessarily represent a narrow, ethnic nationalism, but rather an attempt to embrace not only all social, but also all ethnic groups within the lands of the old Commonwealth, very much in the spirit of Sarmatism. Yet this vertical extension of the political nation to match the horizontal extension which had been so successful in the sixteenth and seventeenth centuries proved easier to conceive than achieve. It was utterly dependent upon the acceptance of the invitation by the common people. If that was not too difficult to envisage in Poland proper, the position was far less clear in the Lithuanian and Ruthenian lands, where, by adopting the Polish language and the Catholic religion, many of the traditional elites, while not considering themselves to be Poles, had created a cultural and, except in ethnic Lithuania, a religious barrier between themselves and the majority of the common people. This was to prove an increasingly intractable problem for the remnants of the old Sarmatian elite in the eastern lands of the former Commonwealth.

For, despite their adoption of the Polish language, the Lithuanian and Ruthenian nobilities had long maintained a dual identity. They were well aware of the differences between the ethnic or cultural nation and the political nation, a distinction famously made by Stanisław Orzechowski when he referred to himself as 'gente Ruthenus, natione Polonus'; a formulation which demonstrates that as early as the sixteenth century the term 'Pole' had two meanings: one referring to the ethnic-cultural nation, and one used more broadly to refer to the political nation of citizens. Nobles in Lithuania or the Ukraine increasingly regarded themselves as 'Poles' in the latter sense, if not the former, and it was this sense of national identity which survived among the old Commonwealth's elites in the early nineteenth century. If high culture was, from the seventeenth century, almost entirely conducted in Polish, this did not mean that landowners could not speak to or identify with their peasants: most Polish-speaking nobles in the Ukraine or Belarus would have understood the *ruski* talked by their peasants without difficulty. In the multi-lingual old Commonwealth, language had been as much a functional matter as a mark of identity; in a land where Jews frequently acted as estate factors and middlemen in the countryside, it was not unknown for nobles to know Yiddish: Teodor Jewłaszewski (1546–c. 1604), a minor noble from Nowogródek in

Lithuania, claimed to be able to write in 'Hebrew', or at least 'in German, since the Jewish Bible is now published in the German [i.e. Yiddish] language.'[14] Many of the German-speaking inhabitants of Royal Prussia knew some Polish, and the urban elites of the province often sent their children into the countryside or to school in Thorn to learn good Polish. German, however, was the language of commerce; as late as the 1880s, many ethnically Polish firms kept their books in German, and Polish lawyers corresponded with each other in German over industrial matters.[15] Miłosz recalled that during the German occupation of 1918, the city of Wilno/Vilnius reverted swiftly to German, the language most widely spoken amongst its older inhabitants; it was his own mother's second language.[16]

Thus for many of the old elite and their descendants in the nineteenth century, the 'Poland' for which they yearned and whose restoration they sought, whether actively or passively, was not an ethnic Polish state, but the old Commonwealth, dominated by a citizen elite which was not based on ethnicity; if it was defined culturally, it was through Catholicism and use of the Polish language. Their vision of the past glorified not Polish conquest of the East, but the consensual extension of the idea of the citizen nation. This is clear in the historical paintings of Jan Matejko (1838–93), who depicted the great moments of the Polish-Lithuanian past, including the baptism of Lithuania, the Union of Lublin and the Constitution of 3 May. The composition of these vast canvasses is suggestive. Where contemporary paintings of Kościuszko's rising, such as that by Michał Stachowicz (1768–1825), depicted the formal swearing of the oath by Kościuszko and his elite associates on Cracow's great Market Square, Matejko chose to illustrate the 1794 battle of Racławice, where Kościuszko led a peasant army to victory over the Russians, thus emphasising the common nineteenth-century radical view that the extension of the citizen nation to the peasantry might well have saved the Commonwealth from its fate. Even more interesting is Matejko's painting of the 1410 battle of Grunwald (Tannenberg), in which the Polish-Lithuanian army defeated the Teutonic Knights. At the centre of the picture is the killing of the Grand Master of the Teutonic Order, Ulrich von Jungingen, by a peasant infantryman (rather than one of the many knights in the painting); what is most striking, however, is that the central figure alongside the dying German is not king Władysław Jagiełło, the man who had instigated the dynastic union of Poland and Lithuania in 1385 and who is relegated to near invisibility in a dark corner of the painting, but his cousin Vytautas (Witold), lauded by modern Lithuanian nationalists as a man who wished to uphold Lithuanian autonomy and break the Union with Poland. Matejko's message, however, was rather different: Poland and Lithuania were strong when they were united, not divided by petty squabbles. Vytautas's co-operation with his cousin saved Lithuania just as much as it saved Poland.

It was increasingly clear, however, that many of the common people in the eastern lands of the old Commonwealth did not regard themselves as Polish in either sense of the word. The spread of the Herderian idea of language as the essential defining characteristic of a cultural nation and the extension of education to wider social groups in the nineteenth century made language a political question, not least because of the policies of Germanisation and Russification launched at various points by the partitioning powers. In the east, where the taxonomic boundaries between varieties of the Slavonic tongues were extremely fuzzy, there was no shortage of individuals attempting to make them clearer. Crushed between the twin cultural Leviathans of Polish and Russian, Ukrainian and – rather later – Belarus'ian nationalists began to re-draw the cultural and linguistic frontiers in order more clearly to assert the separate identity they felt so strongly. If Gogol believed that a talented Ukrainian writer like himself could achieve fame only by writing in Russian, Ukrainian poets such as Ivan Kotliarevsky and, above all, Taras Shevchenko (1814–61) set about constituting, or reconstituting, Ukrainian-Ruthenian as a literary language. After a bitter dispute a modified form of the Cyrillic alphabet was adopted instead of the Latin alphabet based on Polish which had been in use in the old Commonwealth and which some had supported.[17] Various peasant dialects were synthesised with grammatical forms and vocabulary derived from Old Ruthenian and Church Slavonic. Historians, led by the great Mikhailo Hrushevsky, reinterpreted the Ukrainian past, dwelling on the glories of Kievan Rus' and the Cossack revolts against the Commonwealth in order to emphasise the Ukrainian nation's claims to statehood and independence from both. In many respects, however, this emergent Ukrainian nationalism saw Polish, rather than Russian, culture as more dangerous, not least because the noble elites of the Ukraine were still overwhelmingly Polish-speaking. The hostility was reciprocated. Tadeusz Bobrowski, Joseph Conrad's uncle, who grew up among the Polish-speaking elite, found it much easier to relate to the Great Russians than the Ukrainian nationalists, whom he called Little Russians, although he admitted that their character faults were a result of their experiences under Polish and then Russian rule.[18] A similar process took place in ethnic Lithuania, where intellectuals emerged from the half-forgotten Lithuanian peasantry to assert a powerful identity based on the revival of the Lithuanian language, abandoned by the ruling elite half a millennium previously and rescued as a written language by Protestant pastors and publishers in Königsberg. As in the Ukraine, the cultural pressure of Polish was seen as the main threat, and the Lithuanian alphabet, long based on Polish, was abandoned in favour of a system based on Czech.

The fact that these emerging cultural frontiers corresponded closely with class divisions merely accentuated hostility at a time when class was also being asserted, increasingly stridently, as an alternative focus for identification. By the middle of the nineteenth century it was becoming ever more difficult to conceive of the revival of a Poland-Lithuania within its 1772 frontiers which could in any way be based on a conscious political nation with a common political identity. Ethnic, religious and cultural-linguistic identities were proving more attractive. If Kościuszko had proudly proclaimed his Lithuanian identity in the 1790s, and if Mickiewicz's *Pan Tadeusz*, the most famous poem in the Polish language, begins with the immortal line 'Lithuania, my Fatherland!' the dual identity which they and their compatriots had happily maintained with no sense of ambiguity was becoming increasingly difficult to uphold. If in the early nineteenth century members of the Lithuanian *szlachta* were starting to refer to themselves in Orzechowski's terms as 'gente Lituanus, natione Polonus',[19] by 1855 the conservative prince Adam Czartoryski, erstwhile Russian foreign minister and a member of an ancient and distinguished Ruthenian family, had recognised that the choice between territorial and cultural identity might ultimately have to be made, when he observed that 'I am above all a Pole; my whole life gives sufficient proof of that; but I am Ruthenian and Ukrainian.'[20] His Polish identity was winning out over the Ruthenian identity of his forebears.

As the century wore on, conflict between different conceptions of Polish, Lithuanian, Ukrainian and Belarus'ian identity became more frequent. Lithuanian and Ruthenian 'Poles', at first hurt and bemused by the ingratitude of those who rejected the opportunity, as they saw it, for membership of the extended 'Polish' political nation, began to assert their cultural identity more strongly, convinced of the superior civilising mission of the Commonwealth in the east. There were problems even in Lithuania, where at least the *szlachta* and the peasants shared a religion. Although many Polish Lithuanians knew at least some Lithuanian, and sermons were regularly preached in both languages in Lithuanian Catholic churches, by the end of the century Polish cultural activists began campaigning against the use of Lithuanian in church, ostentatiously walking out if a priest dared preach in the language. Lithuanian speakers, on the other hand, complained that Polish priests either did not know, or would not use, their language, accusing them of telling Lithuanians that if they did not understand Polish they should not come to church.[21] An even more bitter battle began over the past. With Lithuanian nationalists presenting their own version of their country's history, one which idealised the pre-Union Lithuanian state, saw Jogaila/Władysław Jagiełło as a traitor and presented the period of the Commonwealth in a luridly negative light, the 'Polish' Lithuanian elite was outraged, particularly since they were themselves cast as traitors for having abandoned the Lithuanian language. The bitterness was only heightened after the First World War as the newly independent states of Poland and Lithuania both laid claim to Vilnius/Wilno. Polish-speaking Lithuanians often found it outrageous to be called 'Poles'; in many respects this was a struggle which paralleled that in Finland between Swedish- and Finnish-speaking Finnish nationalists. As one Lithuanian 'Pole', Michal Juckniewicz, angrily told Lithuanian nationalists: 'Jagiełło Chodkiewicz, Mickiewicz, Piłsudski and I – these are Lithuanians [using the word *Litwini*, the Polish word for Lithuanians] – and you; you are *Lietuvisy* [using a polonised form of the Lithuanian word for 'Lithuanians'].[22]

In the struggle to establish the borders of the new states which emerged from the wreckage of the partitioning powers after 1918, it was by no means easy for Lithuanian or Ukrainian 'Poles' to accept or even consider the surrender of the eastern borderlands of the old Commonwealth: the *Kresy* as they were known in Polish. For the *Kresy* – the term is not used of the western borderlands – were not peripheral regions; in many ways they had long been the dynamic centre of 'Polish' culture. Despite the numerical preponderance of the (ethnically) Polish nobility in the old Commonwealth and the powerful attractive force that Polish culture had exercised, Poland-Lithuania was far from being dominated culturally by the ethnic Polish heartlands. It was the great magnates of the Lithuanian and Ruthenian lands with their fabulous wealth who not only exercised a growing influence over the Commonwealth's politics but also, at their magnificent courts, proved to be among the greatest patrons of Polish culture. Some of these families, such as the Lubomirski, Potocki and Zamoyski, were certainly of Polish origin, but many – the Radziwiłł, the Sapieha, the Czartoryski and their ilk – were of Ruthenian or Lithuanian descent. The magnates of the *Kresy* played an important role in resisting political centralisation in the seventeenth century, not least through the support of Lithuanians in particular for the principle of the *liberum veto*, by which the objection of one envoy could break the proceedings of the Sejm, and which was seen as a useful device to protect Lithuanian interests against the Polish majority in the Sejm.

With this political decentralisation, which made the local sejmik and the noble-run local courts the centre of political life, came cultural decentralisation. Cracow, the ancient seat of Polish royal government, was situated on Poland's south-eastern border far away from Lithuania, and after a fire destroyed the royal castle in the 1590s, Sigismund III (1587–1632) moved the capital to Warsaw, which had already been specified as the location of the Sejm in the 1569 Union of Lublin. Warsaw, however, was still very much a provincial city: it was the capital of Mazovia, a province which had only come back under the Polish crown in 1529, which was dominated by petty and impoverished nobles and which maintained a strong regional identity.[23] The relative impoverishment of the royal court and the deep suspicion in which it was held by many of the szlachta as a centre of alien influence prevented it from becoming more than one of a number of centres of cultural patronage. It was certainly not insignificant, in particular under the Vasas or Augustus II, but the splendid magnate courts of the Radziwiłł, the Zamoyski, the Potocki or the Branicki provided an alternative focus for artists, writers, architects and musicians. Much cultural activity went on in provincial cities; the greatest of these – Wilno, Kiev (to 1648) and Lwów – were all in the *Kresy*.

The cultural influence of the *Kresy* remained powerful long after 1795; indeed, for their elites it was clear that the centre of Polish culture lay not in Warsaw, Cracow or Poznan, but in Lithuania and Ruthenia. It was in these lands that so many of the giants of the 'Polish' literary and artistic world were born: Ignacy Krasicki, Franciszek Karpiński, Adam Naruszewicz, Julian Ursin Niemcewicz, the great Romantic poets Adam Mickiewicz and Juliusz Słowacki, Czesław Miłosz, and Józef Korzeniowski, who made his name outside Poland as Joseph Conrad. It was Wilno, not Warsaw or Cracow, which was the dynamic centre of 'Polish' culture in the 1820s and 1830s and it was at Wilno University (until it was closed in the aftermath of the 1830 rising) that Mickiewicz, Słowacki and Lelewel (born in Warsaw, but with a Ruthenian mother) all studied. Słowacki only ever spent a few brief months in what is now Poland; Mickiewicz never visited it at all. The sons and daughters of the *Kresy* clearly recognised their importance in the world of Polish culture. For Mickiewicz it was Lithuania which represented the most dynamic force in Polish culture; developing Herder's glorification of the Slav national character, he suggested that it was the Lithuanians, called into history by the adoption of Christianity, who had given Polish ideas a wholly new form, and that it was the Lithuanians who would provide the key to solving the problems of the Slavs.[24] The Romantic poets, with Mickiewicz at their head, created an idealised myth of rural life as the essence of the Polish identity, but it was located on the banks of the Niemen, not the Vistula.[25]

It was for this reason that 'Poles' from the *Kresy* fought so passionately for cities like Wilno and Lwów after 1918. It was for them far more than a question of 'cities with a majority Polish population' in the cold words of the Versailles documents. They were fighting to retain cities and regions which were vital to the identity of local elites, who for so long had seen themselves as both Polish and Lithuanian or Ruthenian. Their native realms were not isolated colonies of Polish immigrants, as Lithuanian, Belorus'ian and Ukrainian nationalists sought to depict them, but cultural symbols of a civilisation which had grown and flourished over half a millennium. Long before 1918, however, the ideal of an inclusive political nation which could encompass all the nations of the old Commonwealth lay in tatters. It had been created for a vastly different world; a noble Commonwealth whose cohesive sense of identity had shown signs of cracking even before its final political collapse. The nineteenth century demonstrated that it could no longer provide the basis for a political reconstitution of the state which had disappeared forever in 1795.

Not all Poles were starry-eyed Romantics, however, and this fact had long been recognised. Józef Piłsudski, one of those who saw themselves as Lithuanian as well as Polish, was by 1899 writing in very different terms from those used by Mickiewicz or Lelewel: 'It must be recognised and stated that for many reasons Lithuania is an extension of Poland; thus a huge percentage of its population is Polish, the Polish language [is used] in the towns; there is a huge influence of Polish culture; in a word, Poles are a large formative part of the country.'[26] Piłsudski, like Adam Czartoryski, was in the last analysis Polish; he had accepted the terms of debate set out by the ethnic and cultural nationalists and his political programme was centred around that recognition. He still hoped that a Polish-Lithuanian state could be reconstituted within the borders of 1772, but as a federation of nations, not one political nation in the old style. It was an ambitious scheme, but one which failed to overcome the increasing bitterness between nationalists of different hues. It had to contend with the fiercely narrow ethnic-cultural Polish nationalism of Roman Dmowski (1864–1939) and of the National Democrats (*Endecja*), the political party he founded and led. Piłsudski's ideal of a federal brotherhood of nations was destroyed forever in the battles for Wilno and Lwów at the end of the First World

War. When it came to confrontation Piłsudski was quite sure on which side he stood: he was ultimately prepared to fight for Wilno; as he told Waliszewski, he preferred to negotiate with a revolver in his pocket.[27]

It was a choice that many were forced to make in the turbulent years after 1918. Neither the authorities nor the proponents of cultural nationalism, with their mystic visions, could order the kaleidoscope in the borderlands, where peoples and cultures had for centuries lived side by side, fought, traded, proclaimed their separate identities, intermarried, faded imperceptibly into one another and – occasionally – disappeared, like the Old Prussians. In these areas of mixed populations and mixed loyalties many found it hard to make the choices that seemed so straightforward to the nationalists. Miłosz, brought up in the cultural stew of Wilno/Vilnius/Vilna, scarcely aware as a child of the difference between speaking Polish and speaking Russian, finally chose Poland, and the Polish language in which he wrote his poetry, over the Lithuania which was his fatherland as much as Mickiewicz's. His uncle, Oskar Miłosz, opted for Lithuania, whom he represented at the Versailles talks (where the Polish-speaking diplomats of Lithuania insisted on communicating with their Polish counterparts in French),[28] at the League of Nations, and as ambassador to Paris.[29] Gabriel Narutowicz, first president of the newly independent Poland, who was assassinated by an ultra nationalist in 1922, had a brother, Stanisław, who was a member of the Taryba, the pro-German Lithuanian government, during the German occupation and a signatory of the Lithuanian declaration of independence (16 February 1918). Feliks Dzierżyński, who attended the same school as Piłsudski and was, like him, a Lithuanian Pole of minor noble stock, declared a plague on all the nationalist houses to identify with the class-based internationalism of the Bolsheviks, for whom he established the Cheka. He was by no means the only one of his background to take this route.

The new Polish Republic created in 1918 was neither the broad federation of which Piłsudski had dreamed, a modern reincarnation of the old Commonwealth, nor an ethnic nation-state. Yet, despite the intense minority problems it faced, it never wholeheartedly adopted the narrow nationalism of the National Democrats. Moreover, not all 'Poles' accepted the invitation to join the new nation-state. The *Wasserpolacken* of Silesia and the largely Protestant Masurians of East Prussia, who had lived outside the Commonwealth's borders, were not necessarily pleased at attempts to incorporate them. The German authorities flooded Masuria with good Königsberg vodka in the weeks before the 1920 plebiscite to determine the border between Poland and Germany, and the newly formed *Ostdeutsche*

Heimatdienst kept up sustained pressure on Polish-speaking communities to vote in favour of Germany, but few showed any inclination to opt for a nation-state based on the Polish language community. The leader of the *Mazurski Komitet Plebiscytowy* (the Masurian Plebiscite Committee), founded in June 1919, was the Warsaw-based Juliusz Bursche, General Superintendent of the Polish Lutheran Church. Its propaganda largely met with indifference or outright hostility from local communities. In Lehlesken, near Ortelsburg (Szczytno), the *Altbauer* Johann Gwiazda published his poem, written in Polish, *Protest naprzeciw Polakom* (Protest against the Poles) whose last verse read: 'For 700 years we were Prussians, only now do they want to make out of us Poles, to whom we have bidden farewell, for we bear Prussian names after our forebears.' The Polish-language *Pruski Przyzaciel Ludu* (The Prussian Friend of the People), founded before the war and enjoying a circulation of 50,000, also came out firmly in favour of Germany. In the District of Oletzko, only two people voted for Poland; in Lötzen a mere nine; in Johannisburg fourteen. All these areas had substantial Polish-speaking populations.[30]

Quite what sort of Polish nation-state would have emerged in the nineteenth century had the Polish state survived in its 1772 borders is, to put it mildly, open to question. The absence of a national government capable of gradually broadening the political nation, as the Constitution of 3 May at least suggested was a possible trajectory for the Commonwealth's development, meant that only a political elite was left with a strong consciousness of 'Polishness' in the old sense of a nation of citizens. The partitioning powers deliberately encouraged the development of rival, ethnically based nationalisms to undermine the great social power of the Polish-speaking elites; as the nineteenth century wore on, the inability of those elites to institute a policy of mass education in the Polish language ensured that even those Slavic peasants in the eastern borderlands who could conceivably have been integrated into a broader idea of 'Polish' culture were irrevocably lost, and 'Polishness', even in the eastern borderlands and for szlachta families of Lithuanian or Ruthenian ancestry, increasingly became an ethnic-cultural identity. Poles could no longer be 'gente ruthenus vel lithuanus, natione polonus', but had to become 'gente polonus, natione polonus'. The scouring of the Jews from Poland by the Nazis and their helpers, and the ethnic cleansing instituted by Stalin, created after 1945 for the first time a Polish state which was all but entirely Polish. It excluded, however, the eastern *Kresy*, which had played such an important role in the development of Polish culture, the majority of their remaining Polish inhabitants having been killed or ethnically cleansed between 1939 and 1949.

The power of the nation-state had won out. If the kaleidoscope has finally stopped whirling, and the colours have settled in great blocks; the myriad patterns of a richer past have been irrevocably lost.

NOTES

1 Czesław Miłosz, *Native Realm: A Search for Self-Definition* (London: Penguin, 1988), p. 67.
2 Timothy Snyder, *The Reconstruction of Nations: Poland, Ukraine, Lithuania, Belarus, 1569–1999* (New Haven & London: Yale University Press, 2003).
3 Tadeusz Łepkowski, 'Polska XVIII–XXw.: naród rewolucyjny?' in *Rozważania o losach polskich* (London: Puls, 1987), p. 4.
4 Johann Gottfried Herder, *Outlines of a Philosophy of History of Man* (2nd edn, 2 vols., London, 1803), vol. II, pp. 348–51.
5 For a brilliant account of the difficulties of the years immediately following the Union, see Henryk Lulewicz, *Gniewów o unię ciąg dalszy. Stosunki polsko-litewskie w latach 1569–1588* (Warsaw: Neriton, 2002).
6 Maria B. Topolska, *Czytelnik i książka w Wielkim Księstwie Litewskim w dobie Renesansu i Baroku* (Wrocław: Ossolineum, 1984), pp. 109–10.
7 Frank Sysyn, *Between Poland and the Ukraine: The Dilemma of Adam Kysil, 1600–1651* (Cambridge, MA: Harvard University Press, 1985), pp. 32, 253.
8 Stanisław Cynarski, 'Sarmatyzm – ideologia i styłzycia', in Janusz Tazbir (ed.), *Polska XVII wieku. Państwo, społeczeństwo, kultura* (Warsaw: Wiedza Powszechna, 1974) pp. 272–6. Paszkowski was clearly responding to the claims of the grand dukes of Muscovy, the self-styled 'Tsars of all the Russias', most of which were part of the Commonwealth.
9 For the Sarmatism of Prussian burghers see Karin Friedrich, *The Other Prussia: Poland, Prussia and Liberty 1569–1772* (Cambridge University Press, 2000).
10 See Robert I. Frost, 'The Nobility of Poland-Lithuania, 1569–1795', in Hamish M. Scott (ed.), *The European Nobilities in the Seventeenth and Eighteenth Centuries,* vol. II, *North, East and Central Europe* (Harlow: Longmans, 1995), pp. 183–222.
11 Piotr Wandycz, *The Lands of Partitioned Poland, 1795–1918* (Seattle: University of Washington Press, 1974), pp. 26–7.
12 J. S. Skurnowicz, *Romantic Nationalism and Liberalism: Joachim Lelewel and the Polish National Idea,* East European Monographs LXXXIII (Boulder, CO: East European Monographs Boulder, 1981), pp. 65–7.
13 J. Błonski, 'Les confins. "Paradis Polonais" de Mickiewicz à Rymkiewicz', in Daniel Beauvois (ed.), *Les confins de l'ancienne Pologne. Ukraine, Lithuanie, Bélorussie XVIe–XIXe siècles* (Lille: Presse universitaire de Lille, 1988), p. 62.
14 *Pamiętnik Teodora Jewłaszewskiego nowogrodzkiego podsędka 1546–1604,* ed. T[adeusz]x[iążę] L[ubomirski] (Warsaw, 1860), p. 10.
15 Anthony Polonsky, *Politics in Independent Poland, 1921–1939* (Oxford University Press, 1972), p. 28.
16 Miłosz, *Native Realm,* p. 46.

17 W. Dynak, 'Cultures et nationalité en Galicie Orientale (1772–1918)', in Beauvois (ed.), *Les confins de l'ancienne Pologne*, p. 90.

18 Tadeusz Bobrowski, *Pamiętnik mojego życia*, ed. Stefan Kieniewicz (2 vols., Warsaw: Państwowy Instytut Wydawniczy, 1979), vol. I, p. 212.

19 Juliusz Bardach, 'O świadomości narodowej Polaków na Litwie i Białorusi w XIX–XX wieku' in Bardach, *O dawnej i niedawnej Litwie* (Poznań: Uniwersytet im. Adama Mickiewicza, 1988), p. 201.

20 Quoted by S. Kalembka, 'Les territoires de l'est dans la pensée politique polonaise de 1831 à 1870', in Beauvois (ed.), *Les confins de l'ancienne Pologne*, p. 150.

21 [Juzas Gabrys], *Mémoire concernant la situation de l'église Catholique en Lithuanie. Presenté à sa Sainteté Benoit XV et au Sacré Collège par la délégation du Conseil National Suprême de Lithuanie* (Lausanne, 1918), p. 9.

22 Fr. Walerian Meysztowicz, *Gawędy o czasach i ludziach* (2nd edn, London: Polska Fundacja Kuluralna, 1983), p. 31.

23 Henryk Samsonowicz, 'Przesłanki tworzenia się narodu mazowieckiego na przełomie XV i XVI wieku' in M. Kula (ed.), *Narody: Jak powstały się i jak wybijały się na niepodległość* (Warsaw: Rój, 1989), pp. 146–53.

24 Nina Taylor, 'Adam Mickiewicz et la Lithuanie. Genèse du mythe littéraire' in Beauvois, ed., *Les confins de l'ancienne Pologne*, pp. 70–1,

25 Twentieth-century writers followed in their footsteps, in particular Eliza Orzeszkowa in her classic work *Nad Niemnem* (On the Niemen, 1887–8). Orzeszkowa was the pen name of Gabriela Litwinka (1841–1910), whose very surname meant 'the Lithuanian'.

26 Piłsudski to Leon Wasilewski, 19 November 1899, printed in Leon Wasilewski, *Józef Piłsudski jakim go znałem* (Warsaw, 1935) p. 40.

27 Piłsudski to Wasilewski, 8 April 1919, ibid., p. 175.

28 Though Oskar Miłosz argued with Ashkenazy in Polish: Miłosz, *Native Realm*, p. 30.

29 Ibid., pp. 29–30.

30 Andreas Kossert, *Masuren: Ostpreußens vergessener Süden* (Berlin: Siedler, 2001), pp. 248–54.

CHAPTER 10

Nationhood at the margin: identity, regionality and the English crown in the seventeenth century

Tim Thornton

There is now little doubt that during the early modern period England saw the development of a precocious statehood. It is some years since Patrick Collinson drew our attention to the covenant which sought to ensure continuity in the regime should Elizabeth perish, and since David Norwood highlighted the elements of republicanism in the aristocratic thought of the early seventeenth century. More recently, Sean Kelsey has argued that the interregnum saw creative and effective developments in the ideology and iconography of English republicanism.[1] For our purposes here, all this is significant, but the context of this manifestation of a close alignment between state, nation and power, more or less independent of monarchy, was the complex one of the multi-ethnic British Isles. This chapter seeks to examine the interaction not of English state and English nation, but of English state and nation with the non-English communities of Britain and beyond.

I will be less concerned with Ireland and Scotland, where there has been significant work already on the interactions between power and nation.[2] Rather I want to look at some of the others in this situation who were in some sense territorially defined. All possessed some ethnic, cultural or jurisdictional distinction from the rest of England, in varying measures. Language and Celtic cultural identities mattered in Wales, in Cornwall and in the Isle of Man; Norman-French language and identity in the Channel Islands. Then there were other distinct areas within Britain, such as Cheshire and Durham with their powerful jurisdictional distinction, and Kent, with its lesser jurisdictional identity but stronger sense of cultural and ethnic difference.

These are in some senses anomalies,[3] but they are important, not least because they are anomalies of which modern nations are generally considered to be remarkably intolerant. There is increasing agreement amongst historians that the seventeenth century saw an important step in the development of imagined communities in the nations of these islands.[4] The need

232

to deploy power to fight wars is seen as catalysing these imagined communities, both through the positive aspects of mobilising for action and through the impact of alterity dramatising difference from others, combined with the massive uncontrolled expansion of the print media. This emphasis on developing imagined communities in the seventeenth century, and especially on alterity, tends to go hand in hand with an argument about English imperialism: the English imagined community was the dominant one, and others tended to be imagined for the purposes of defeating or controlling them. Hence Mark Stoyle has recently argued that the English Civil War included a strong expression of ethnic and national tension, with nationalism becoming a significant political factor. Ethnicism, in the sense of a reactive defence of local culture, became evident. According to Stoyle, however, the nationalism which was displayed was a product of, effectively, English imperialism, or of the unscrupulous actions of unrepresentative royalists. Writing of Cornish particularism, he describes it as largely the product of the 'scoundrel' Grenville desperately and ineffectively looking for ways to galvanise support for the king, and of the prejudice and hatred of English commentators.[5] Similarly, he has seen English portrayals of the Welsh accentuating the characteristics of the Welsh nation, even to the point of defining a political agenda of separatism and independence – in order to condemn it.[6] This of course has strong similarities with the internal colonialism thesis of Michael Hechter, whereby difference is cultivated to permit subjection and exploitation.[7]

The extreme example of genocide in Ireland, supported by conceptions of the Irish as sub-human, is often held to lie somewhere towards one end of a fundamental continuum of attitudes of this type. We might recall the powerful argument of John Gillingham that the origins of English imperialism lay in such attitudes to and treatment of the Irish in the twelfth century.[8]

Ultimately these views accord with the overall tendency to doubt the existence of meaningful nations in Ireland, Wales and Cornwall, in the sense of self-identifying coherent communities of relative ethnic and cultural unity. This has been seen, for example, in the historiography of Wales in a tendency to question the coherence of Welsh society, to emphasise the divide between the north and south and the degree to which English towns – Chester, Shrewsbury and Ludlow – were the 'capitals' of Wales.[9] Underlying this is the idea that these nations are imagined communities and they only really begin to be imagined in a meaningful sense in modern times, in the eighteenth century and after.

Contemporary commentators understood a range of possible responses to the ethnic and national challenges posed by war and conquest. One 'J. M.', a scholar of Christ Church, Oxford, provided a thoughtful account of the means towards union in such cases.[10] His models included, at one extreme, the absorption of the power of a territory through a process of assimilation so complete as to result in even the loss of its name – in a sense, the ultimate eradication of its potential nationhood: 'transmutation of names, when the victor doth change the name of the conquered Countrey, and calls it by the name of his own Countrey'.[11] At the opposite end of his spectrum was his preferred solution. He was happy to accommodate difference of dialect, even of language, and diversity in some elements of law; through such an approach, he said, the commonwealth of England had 'made those severall Countries one Nation', following a Roman example.[12]

There are some intriguing signs that even the most extreme form of union postulated by 'J. M.' could have occurred. In the extraordinary days of 1649–50 it might have been that Wales began to disappear completely. Hostility to all aspects of local culture might be combined with, for example, such an approach as in the Act for the Better Propagation and Preaching of the Gospel in Wales, which in its main text does not use the word 'Wales', nor does it refer to a dominion or principality.[13] Wales has become simply a collection of counties distinguished by a common backwardness in religion that is to be rectified.

Yet the concept was not going to disappear. The title of the act betrayed the power of the idea of Wales, since it was known, even in official copies, as the Act for the Better Propagation and Preaching of the Gospel *in Wales*. The very idea of treating Welsh counties in this way implied an underlying assumption of their difference, and one which some commentators immediately latched on to as unacceptable. One of the arguments used by those who opposed the renewal of the act was that Wales was 'many ages sithence happily incorporated into England', with, they argued, the same laws, ecclesiastical and civil.[14]

One crucial factor for those who had to deal with these changes on the local level was that there were concepts to which they could refer in dealing with the larger entity to which they were subjected which did not depend simply on England or Englishness and which supported some diversity. The most obvious of these, and one which of course had a long and controversial history, was Britishness. For the Welsh, who might claim to be in some senses the true owners of the concept, it had an obvious appeal.[15] On the other hand, it might be relatively far less meaningful, as in the case of the Channel Islands, or it might be tainted with suggestions of covert English dominance. In these cases, other options presented themselves. It was possible to refer to the cause of 'parliament' in such a way as to remove an ethnically or nationally descriptive label, however insistently in other contexts it was described as the parliament of England. The term 'commonwealth' also lent itself to similarly non-specific treatment, as – far more vaguely – did the word 'country'.[16]

It is also worth noting that the use of ethnic stereotypes, which might drive an identification of the nation by the imperialist power, was more complex in its impact than might initially appear. If in 1642–3 it helped some, for example, to see all Welsh people as poverty-stricken, ignorant, vain and royalist, things became more complex once significant groups of Welsh supporters of parliament appeared, or at least once opposition to the king within Wales could not be ignored. Even at the time of the most ferocious attacks on the Welsh, for example, in October 1642 the success of 'the well affected party in Wales' was reported, and specifically in Glamorgan against the Marquis of Hertford.[17] Satires might still mock the Welsh in the later 1640s, but as often as not they took the form of attacks by Welsh voices on royalist leaders such as Prince Maurice and Archbishop Williams, or on the king himself.[18] Once the satirised traits became associated with 'well-affected' elements they could become almost terms of endearment, if patronising ones – and they certainly lost the harsh edge of fundamental political and ethnic opposition and hatred. Welshness, within Britishness, for example, might regain its pride: in the attack on Williams it was suggested that a song be sung below his window, including 'The English men both bold and strong, the Scottish stout and hardy, / The valiant Welshmen will be first to take the Papists tardy.' Britishness was the rallying point with this call for unity against the Irish, 'that cut our British Protestants throats'.[19]

That might bring us back to Michael Hechter, and the Welsh patronised and subjected through difference. But to focus exclusively on titles which mock the Welsh, from whatever perspective, is to present only part of the picture. John Taylor, the famous travelling Water Poet, conducted a tour of Wales in 1652 which he published without any hint of pejorative ethnic stereotyping: in fact he was generally most complimentary to the Welsh. He showed regret for the damage caused to the shrine at Holywell by the war, and the lack of food and fodder in Harlech and Barmouth. Yet he was impressed by Caernarfon, and he called the Earl of Carbery's place, the Golden Grove, 'the Cambrian Paradise'. He appended to this an abbreviated version of the David Powel *Historie of Cambria* attributed to Caradoc of Llancarfan.[20] This suggests there was an English market of some kind for a text which celebrated the Welsh and their difference.

We do not have, therefore, the elimination of Wales as an imagined community. Nor do we have something which fits simply into the internal colonial model. We have, equally, only limited attempts to destroy the elements of transacted community, in patterns of jurisdiction and administration, that operated alongside it. Two institutions exemplified Wales's difference: the council in the marches and the courts of Great Sessions. The former had of course been famously unpopular – yet it is important to note that this unpopularity sprang largely from the four English marcher shires under its jurisdiction, Gloucestershire, Shropshire, Herefordshire and Worcestershire, and not from the Welsh ones.[21] The abolition of the Star Chamber jurisdiction of the Marcher Council in 1641, along with Star Chamber itself, cannot straightforwardly be equated with an attack on Welsh jurisdiction and identity. In fact the other elements of the council's jurisdiction were left intact, and it became defunct not by abolition but through a collapse in demand for its services due to the disruptions of war.[22] Great Sessions survived intact, handling the majority of Welsh judicial business, and indeed being ready to take on the work of the Marcher Council after its brief Restoration revival.[23] In August 1655 Major-General James Berry was given charge of Wales as a whole. Although many of his objectives were unacceptable to most of the people he ruled, there are no signs of gross abuse of power, or of ethnically based antipathy. Berry, though not a Welshman, is striking for his emphasis on his love for the Welsh.[24]

At this point it is useful to turn to other cases, to Jersey and Guernsey in the English Channel, and the Isle of Man in the Irish Sea.

In some sense we might expect here an even more ferocious outburst of ethnic hatred, creating imagined communities on the pages of English pamphlets and letters, and setting the scene for a more thoroughgoing eradication of local difference. This is because, if not in the case of Guernsey, then in Jersey and in Man resistance to the forces of parliament was relatively undiluted and remarkably sustained. There were no pockets of local parliamentary support there as there were in Wales, and the islands remained a thorn in the side of parliamentarian operations for nearly a decade.

The role of the Channel Islands as political prisons in the seventeenth century might be expected to have led to particularly forceful denunciation and intervention when the exiles in turn became the victors. Yet we can see an example of how this did not in fact occur in practice, in Henry Burton's reaction to his 'Banishment, and close Imprisonment' in Guernsey: he considered the imminence of doomsday and only in passing referred to the 'naturall taedium of so horrid a solitarinesse', which had inspired his thoughts.[25] William Prynne, a prisoner in Mont Orgueil Castle in Jersey, went even further: his comments, restricted to the castle, constituted a commentary on biblical quotations. He made no unflattering comments, and his praises for his former hosts, Sir Philip Carteret, his wife Lady Anne, and their daughters, were fulsome.[26]

One reason for the lack of English condemnation of Jersey and its people as a whole was the activity of Jersey exiles, especially the parliamentarian bailiff-in-exile, Michel Lempriere. For example, an ordinance was issued voiding Sir George Carteret's actions against them. This ordinance, dated 16 September 1645 and printed the following month, emphasises the loyalty of well-affected persons in the island who had 'notwithstanding the defection of that Island continued firme and stedfast in their Loyalty and Obedience to the King and Parliament'.[27] Ironically, some of the more damning judgements on the island came from one of the prominent royalists who found himself there. Abraham Cowley was primarily aiming at William Prynne in his 'Answer to a Copy of Verses', but in doing so he presented a picture of a relatively primitive island whose main virtues were an absence of bombast and cliché.[28]

After its fall in 1651, in spite of the long-standing resistance of the island, Jersey was not subjected to any significant retribution. Even those most directly associated with the attack on the island tended to speak favourably of the island's people and traditions. For example, Thomas Wright, the 'firemaster' who cut short the siege of Elizabeth Castle thanks to his direct hit with a mortar shell on the magazine, had only praise for the people of Jersey. Wright found the local gentlemen, who offered to raise a collection to help cover his expenses, or to give him free lodging for three or six months, 'very Cordiall'. Carteret, Wright wrote, had needed terror to enforce his will, threatening all the men of one parish with hanging at one point if they did not serve. '[T]he generality of people during my abode there, expressed much love and affection toward the Parliament of England', he recalled. The environment too clearly agreed with him: a place 'of very sweet and pleasant Habitation; the Men and Women are generally courteous, and of a good deportment, the Poorer sort only excepted'.[29]

It was possible in 1651 for pleas to be made to protect the island's culture, society, religion and governmental structures. For example, James Stocall's pamphlet *Freedome. Or, the description of the Excellent Civill Government of the Island of Jersey* described their government as offering 'hitherto (since the Divine Common-wealth of Israel) unparalleld Freedome'. Stocall was the colonel of a regiment of the trained bands of the island. His plea was offered relatively soon after the fall of the island, for the dedication to Lieutenant Colonel Fleetwood is dated 1 March 1651 (i.e. 1652). He emphasised that the people chose their officers, except for the few in the gift of the king or bailiff. The means to justice were 'plaine, common, and easie' and generally free of expense. Offices were already established to cover all the responsibilities necessary for the public good, with the poor and sick, for example, visited 'constantly'. The laws were few but sufficient and known even to the 'very poore silly Women'. Significantly, the islanders' language was proudly defended: it was said that the judicial system operated in the 'naturall Language of the Inhabitants neverthelesse very Maiesticall'. Legal deeds he described as being in 'our naturall tongue'.[30] When these authors spoke of the authority to which Jersey might now be subject, there was remarkably little mention of 'Britishness' or other inclusive concepts. Thomas Wright, firemaster, wrote of the reduction of the island 'unto the obedience of the Parliament', so avoiding any geographical terminology at all.[31] The Jerseymen who wrote a testimonial on his behalf referred to the garrison in Elizabeth Castle as 'the Enemy', and said the castle had surrendered 'to the Commonwealth'.[32]

For royalists too, there might have been a temptation to suggest that Jersey was simply part of England. Yet when Charles, Prince of Wales wrote to the states of Jersey in 1647, commending them on their loyalty, it was a loyalty to the king, 'the Crowne of England', and to the prince himself. The title given to one version of the letter described the island as being *neere the realme of England.* Therefore the identification was with the monarchy, but not as part of the realm itself. Still, one of the prince's objectives in writing was to explain his command to Sir George Carteret to arrest suspects: this was necessary, he said, because 'seditious fugitives of the said Island' were looking for an opportunity to trigger an invasion of that island. Therefore, in a letter which was circulated amongst English opponents and supporters of the prince, it was clear that the island had produced both loyal royalists and supporters of the parliamentary cause.[33] Charles's arrival in Jersey after his father's execution was a key moment for the royalist cause. The choice of a location for his proclamation as king so many months after his father's death had depended in large part on Jersey's close relationship with the monarchy and with England. The prince's own official declaration, issued from The Hague, described how he was 'now safely arrived in a small part of Our owne Dominions, at the Island of Iersey . . . where Our kingly authority takes place'.[34] Yet the notable thing is that the pro-parliamentarian publications drew back from associating these actions with the people of Jersey. For example, one described the landing as 'entertained with many expressions of joy', ironically adding in parentheses 'from the Lord Iermaine' – making the point that the welcome was distinctly thin but coincidentally silently absolving the local population from sharing any of this joy at the royal arrival.[35]

Even that seed of pro-parliamentarian sentiment in exile was not to be found in relationship to the Isle of Man. The island's resistance to the English parliamentary forces was as tenacious as that of any part of Cornwall or Wales. James Stanley, from September 1642 seventh Earl of Derby, went to the island in June 1643 in the face of apparent discontent with his family's regime there. Over the next eight years the island was well fortified, with new forts at Derby Fort on St Michael's Isle and Fort Royal at Ramsey. The Manx militia was developed. The island was used as a base for shipping that might either transport large numbers of royalist troops or simply act as a privateering force against parliamentarian allies. As royalist fortunes faded, the Isle of Man became a resort for increasing numbers of exiles, such as Lord George Digby and Sir Marmaduke Langdale in October 1645. And the manpower and money which supported all this came chiefly from Manx sources.[36]

That apparent resistance to the English had an important context. The geographical position of the Isle of Man meant that it was associated with the north of Ireland and especially with the Scottish Hebridean islands. As such, it was likely to be associated with the ethnically highly distinct Gaelic cultures of the region. Throughout the late medieval and early modern period, in spite of *de facto* English control of Man, the island was seen as being part of Scotland, on both sides of the border.[37] To any Englishman visiting the island, its difference and distance were immediately apparent. In the words of a petition of part of the parliamentary garrison in the island in the 1650s, Man was a strange and remote country.[38] Further, it goes without saying that throughout the seventeenth century the ethnic group most frequently vilified by the English was the Gaelic Irish. It is therefore logical to expect that, if Stoyle is right, the English would have come during the 1640s and 1650s to see the Manx as inferior and beast-like, worthy of expulsion or extermination like the Irish.

Yet this was not the case. There are several reasons for this. First, the hostility of the English was directed not against the Manx *per se* but against the Earl of Derby as their lord. In the summer of 1650, *Mercurius Politicus* commented on Stanley's training of the militia in the island 'where hee rules as *King*, and they say hee hath a *Leaden Crown*, of the same size and metall (no doubt) with that in *Scotland*'. The mocking tone continues: 'It is observed by many, that though the Earls of Derby have had great *Revenues*, and faire Houses, yet their *upper Roomes* have not been very well furnish't, for two or three Generations.'[39] There were special circumstances which supported this choice of target. Derby's power was so all-embracing that there could be no confusion as to where political leadership in the island lay. And Derby was mocked and distrusted not only by parliamentarians, but also by royalists. Many hawks among their ranks had found his attempts at conciliation in Lancashire distasteful, and his advice to the king that the royal standard should be raised at Warrington was turned down, the first sign of the mistrust with which he was viewed at court.[40] So there was no fundamental disagreement on all sides in seeing James Stanley as a worthy target and therefore less temptation to divert fire beyond him on to the Manx themselves.

Second, there was the countess, Charlotte. Although she was not a French Catholic, she was easy to tar with the same brush as had been so effectively used on the queen, Henrietta Maria. In one sense she helped feed this reputation: there is no doubt that she exerted a strong influence in maintaining Stanley resistance to the parliament, both in Lancashire and in the Isle of Man. Her role during the siege of Latham in 1644 is well known: in her husband's absence she commanded her forces through a siege that lasted from February to May, in the face of artillery fire which on one occasion smashed even into her own chamber, until the house was relieved by the forces of Prince Rupert. In fact, while the earl, executed after the Battle of Worcester in 1651, emerges from many accounts as a relatively weak character, a well-intentioned if over-proud martyr for his cause who might be mocked for his empty pretensions, the countess's character concentrated the fire of her enemies throughout the period. In particular, she became associated with atrocity stories in which she allegedly wanted parliamentary prisoners thrown overboard from their captured ships. It mattered little that this story was largely an invention of Robert Massey of Warrington, a man with a strong vested interest in pursuing the countess in an attempt to strip her of her estates.

So if the negative feelings of the English could be focused on the earl and especially the countess, what of the way the English thought about the Manx? Were they simply ignored? The answer to this question seems to be that they were not, and this has significance for our overall argument. For the effect of the war on English attitudes to the small island community of Man was to strengthen an opinion of them as a cruelly oppressed people with a proud and distinct culture, institutions and history. Civil war did not necessarily bring unification and centralisation; it could also foster ideas about the value of protecting minority ethnic groups and their culture and institutions.

We can see this most distinctly in general references to the sufferings of the Manx under the lordship of the Stanleys. When *Mercurius Politicus* mocked Derby in 1650 as wearing a leaden crown, it said that he intended to melt down the crown and use it to make bullets, 'to shoot down that great enemy of Princes, called *The Liberty of the people*'.[41] This almost certainly chiefly refers to pro-Commonwealth prisoners taken to the island, but that at least some of the Manx are intended is implied by an earlier reference to Derby's intent to 'dominere over the people' by using the same leaden crown.

In this reference to liberties being forged into bullets we can see a more specific trend in this writing: towards a greater knowledge of and respect for Manx constitutional structures. There had undoubtedly been in the first years of the seventeenth century a great interest in such questions as the 'royal' title of the lord and the status of the advowson of the bishopric, both in works such as Selden's *Titles of Honor* and in more general topographical publications, especially with Camden's coverage of the island in his *Britannia*, or that in Drayton's *Poly-olbion*. The tone of all this material had been relatively positive, reflecting a general tendency, which might be seen as a characteristic of the 'common law mind', to respect traditional privilege.[42]

This inheritance of respect and interest was not shattered by the war, and from the 1650s a sequence of publications demonstrated that the interest was growing rather than diminishing or being replaced by hostility. Pre-eminent here is James Chaloner's treatise on the island, which appeared in the compilation published by Daniel King in 1656, *The Vale-Royall of England*. Chaloner noted the islanders' affinity to the Scots/Irish of the Hebrides, seen in their language. He speculated that they had once been 'very rude and barbarous', but after the arrival of Christianity had been reformed and 'mixing with the English, they are at this day a very civill People'. They were, he stated, 'ingenuous, in the learning of Manufactures, and apt for the Studies of Humanity or Divinity'.[43] William Blundell too, driven to the island by his uncomfortable position in Lancashire, commented on the Manx gentry as 'truly gentle, courteous, affable' and happy to speak English, which they pronounced 'so naturally as y^t I cou'd not observe any different tone in their pronunciation of our English as is commonly noted, both in the Irish, Scots, and Welsh, and in all strangers'; he followed Speed in reckoning their 'countenance, carriage, apparel, diet, or housekeeping' similar in most respects to the Lancashire gentry's.[44]

Although Blundell described the common people as 'surly, respectless, yea, griping extorters of strangers', he emphasised that they were not prone to the turbulence which some ascribed to the inhabitants of islands, citing their loyalty, most recently to the Stanleys.[45] William Sacheverell's comments on the people were very short but uniformly positive. The Manx, he said, were 'well bodied, and inured to labour; and it is observed that those who are refined by travel, prove men of parts and business. The common sort speak the native language, the gentry better English than in the north of England'.[46] Intriguingly and significantly, Sacheverell added a positive gloss to his treatment of the Manx language. He wrote of original Manx words as 'expressive, and often prettily softened by their abbreviations', and the Manx of the north of the island as being 'least *corrupted* with English' (my emphasis). In general on the language issue, comments tended to be supportive: earlier, Coke and Camden had suggested that as the Manx had peculiar laws so they had a peculiar language.[47] George Waldron compared the keeping of the scriptures out of the Manx tongue to the strategies of the Church of Rome, implicitly ascribing value to the vernacular.[48]

Blundell is specifically keen to exonerate the Manx from allegations of superstition which he says originate from Merrick and his popularisation by Camden. The first is the idea of the women going about in their winding sheets to remind themselves of their own mortality; second, that although highway robbery was unknown, pilfering was common; and third that witchcraft, and specifically selling wind to passengers (as recounted in Ranulph Higden, Gerald of Wales, William Harrison, Caxton and others), was unknown.[49]

Then there is the issue of religion. The men behind the parliamentarian forces ranged in their religious views from Presbyterians, to more radical dissenters such as Independents and Fifth Monarchy Men. As such we might not expect the least sympathy for the Manx, a people whose religion seems to have been highly traditional and still heavily coloured by the practices of Catholicism. Bishop Bridgeman in 1634 had said the clergy in Man were ignorant, there were no schools, and the Manx language was often used in the reading of the Book of Common Prayer; English observers of a variety of religious perspectives made similar comments through the 1650s.[50] Yet even those writing from a potentially hostile viewpoint seem to have recognised, in a rather patronising manner, the quality of Manx religion. Chaloner's belief in the civilising effect of Christianity upon them and their suitedness to the study of divinity has already been noted. He went further in suggesting that they bore 'a great esteem and reverence to the Publique service of God', being seldom absent from church, despite the often lengthy journeys required for their attendance.[51]

So war may not produce a situation in which the particular – here the culture and society of the small island – is targeted as alien and then destroyed. In particular, the English Civil War proved able to nurture a position in which the parliamentarians who were victorious there began to see value in the particular and the different. This was indeed apparent once the island had been seized by the parliamentarians in 1651. There was no doubt that the Commons meant to end any ambiguity about the ultimate control over Man. The ordinance clearly stated that Man was to be considered part of England.[52] On the other hand it was equally clear that it was not the intention of the Commons to interfere with the laws and customs of the island.

In each case, therefore, the evidence suggests a relative absence of hostile stereotyping, and in some sense a striking interest in and respect for the peculiarities of local identity, culture and governance. It might therefore be suggested that the Civil War does not represent a key stage in the advance of English national imperialism, even in the form of an English-dominated Britishness, resulting in either genocide or the types of subjection through difference which Hechter outlined. Rather, it was a key stage in the development of a complex interaction between power and nationhood in these islands, and of a willingness on the part of the English to recognise difference and accommodate it with active concepts of plural nationality.

NOTES

1 Patrick Collinson, 'The monarchical republic of Queen Elizabeth I', *Bulletin of the John Rylands University Library of Manchester* 69 (1987), 394–424; David Norbrook, *Writing the English Republic: Poetry, Rhetoric and Politics, 1627–1660* (Cambridge University Press, 1999); Sean Kelsey, *Inventing a Republic: The Political Culture of the English Commonwealth, 1649–1653* (Manchester University Press, 1997).

2 Scotland, e.g. John Morrill, 'The national covenant in its British context', in J. S. Morrill (ed.), *The Scottish National Covenant in its British Context, 1638–51* (Edinburgh University Press, 1990), pp. 1–30.

3 Of which Susan Reynolds found rulers and communities in the Middle Ages remarkably tolerant: *Kingdoms and Communities in Western Europe, 900–1300*, (2nd edn, Oxford: Clarendon Press, 1997).

4 Benedict Anderson, *Imagined Communities: Reflections on the Origin and Spread of Nationalism* (revised edn, London: Verso, 1991).

5 Mark J. Stoyle, 'The last refuge of a scoundrel: Sir Richard Grenville and Cornish particularism, 1644–6', *Historical Research* 71 (1998), 31–51; idem,

'The dissidence of despair: rebellion and identity in early modern Cornwall', *Journal of British Studies* 38 (1999), 423–44; idem, '"The Gear rout": the Cornish rising of 1648 and the second Civil War', *Albion* 32 (2000), 37–58; idem, '"Pagans or paragons?": images of the Cornish during the English Civil War', *English Historical Review* 111 (1996), 299–323.

6 Mark J. Stoyle, 'Caricaturing Cymru: images of the Welsh in the London Press', in Diana Dunn (ed.), *War and Society in Medieval and Early Modern Britain* (Liverpool University Press, 2000), pp. 162–79.

7 Michael Hechter, *Internal Colonialism: The Celtic Fringe in British National Development; With a New Introduction and a New Appendix* (New Brunswick, NJ, and London: Transaction Publishers, 1999).

8 John Gillingham, 'The beginnings of English imperialism', *Journal of Historical Sociology* 5 (1992), 392–409, reprinted in his *The English in the Twelfth Century: Imperialism, National Identity and Political Values* (Woodbridge: Boydell, 2000).

9 E.g. Glanmor Williams, *Recovery, Reorientation and Reformation: Wales, c. 1415–1642* (Oxford: Clarendon Press, 1987); Philip Jenkins, 'Seventeenth-century Wales: definition and identity', in Brendan Bradshaw and Peter Roberts (ed.), *British Consciousness and Identity: The Making of Britain, 1533–1707* (Cambridge University Press, 1998), pp. 213–35.

10 [M. H.], *The History of the Union of the Four Famous Kingdoms of England, Wales, Scotland and Ireland* (London, 1660).

11 Ibid., p. 42. Earlier, 'a Well-wisher to this Commonwealth' had suggested there were only two options for dealing with Scotland: restraint as a 'distinct Nation', or 'Integration and Incorporation', a gradual process for which he believed Wales provided a model, and which should begin with the destruction of great Scottish families: *The Antiquity of England's Superiority over Scotland. And the Equity of Incorporating Scotland or other Conquered Nation, into the Commonwealth of England* (London: R. Ibbitson, 1652).

12 [M. H.], *History of the Union*, pp. 72–3, 111–13, 138.

13 *Acts and Ordinances of the Interregnum, 1642–1660*, ed. C. H. Firth and R. S. Rait (London: HMSO, 1911), vol. II, 342–8.

14 *Certain Seasonable Considerations and Reasons Humbly Offered, against Reviving the Act, Intituled, An act for the Better Propagation and Preaching of the Gospel in Wales, and Redresse of Some Grievances there* ([London], [1653]). This tract used the argument that geographical distance from London was no more an obstacle than such distance between parts of Wales, citing Swansea and Wrexham (p. 5).

15 It was used powerfully and systematically, at least initially, by the royalists in their attempts to draw on Welsh support: *A Loving and Loyall Speech spoken unto … Prince Charles* ([London], 1642). This is perhaps one reason why 'Britishness' was something mocked in the early anti-Welsh satires, e.g. *Newes from Wales, or the Prittish Parliament Called and Assembled upon Many Good Reasons and Considerations, etc.* ([London], 1642).

16 On Commonwealth, see Kelsey, *Inventing a Republic* (although here as an *anglicist* device, with a strong emphasis on language, e.g. in law, coinage).

17 *A True and Joy full Relation of a Famous and Remarkable Victory Obtained by the Inhabitants of Glamorganshire against the Marquesse of Hartford, and the Cavaleers, Oct. 3, 1642* (London, [1642]).

18 *The true Copy of a Welch Sermon Preached before Prince Maurice in Wales, upon his Departure thence, by Shon up Owen, etc.* ([London], 1642); *The Welsh-mans Propostions [sic] to the Arch-bishop of Yorke, Commander in Chiefe before Conoway Castle in Wales; with their New Lawes, and Orders of Warre, etc.* ([London], 1646).

19 *Welsh-mans Propostions*, p. 5.

20 J. Taylor, *A Short Relation of a Long Journey, made Round or Ovall by Encompassing the Principalitie of Wales, from London* ([London], [1653]); cf. 'Caradoc of Llancarfan', *The Historie of Cambria, now called Wales*, ed. David Powel (London: printed by Rafe Newberie and Henrie Denham, 1584).

21 Penry Williams, *The Council in the Marches of Wales under Elizabeth I* (Cardiff: University of Wales Press, 1958), pp. 215–16; idem, 'The Star Chamber and the Council in the Marches of Wales, 1558–1603', *Bulletin of the Board for Celtic Studies* 16 (1956), 287–97.

22 Caroline A. J. Skeel, *The Council in the Marches of Wales: A Study in Local Government during the Sixteenth and Seventeenth Centuries* (London: Hugh Rees, 1904), pp. 161–2.

23 Glyn Parry, *A Guide to the Records of Great Sessions in Wales* (Aberystwyth: National Library of Wales, 1995); Skeel, *Council in the Marches of Wales*, pp. 166–7.

24 James Berry and Stephen G. Lee, *A Cromwellian Major General: The Career of Colonel James Berry, Illustrated by his Letters and Other Contemporary Documents* (Oxford: Clarendon Press, 1938), e.g. pp. 166–7.

25 Henry Burton, *The Sounding of the Two Last Trumpets, the Sixth and Seventh* (London: printed for Samuel Gellibrand, 1641), A3.

26 William Prynne, *Movnt-Orgveil* (London: T. Cotes, for M. Sparke, 1641).

27 *An Ordinance of the Lords and Commons Assembled in Parliament. For the Making Void all Commissions and Warrants, or other Writings Issued Forth in his Majesties name to Sir Philip Carteret* [or rather, Captain George Carteret], *Governour of Jersey* (London: printed for John Wright, 1645), p. 1. This permitted a relatively smooth transition to the new authority; Cromwell appointed jurats to make up their number, and the whole island was judged to be delinquent (September 1655), but those with estates worth no more than £7 p.a. or personalty no more than £100 escaped penalty even if they had assisted the Carteret regime: A. C. Saunders, *Jersey in the 17th Century* (Jersey: J. T. Bigwood, 1931), pp. 158–65.

28 Abraham Cowley, *The English Writings of Abraham Cowley*, vol. 1: *Poems: Miscellanies, The Mistress, Pindarique Odes, Davideis, Verses written on several occasions*, ed. A. R. Waller (Cambridge University Press, 1905); Arthur H. Nethercot, *Abraham Cowley: The Muse's Hannibal* (London: Oxford University Press, 1931), pp. 91, 115, 118, 128–35; T. Sprat, 'Account', in *The Works of Mr Abraham Cowley*, ed. T. Sprat (London: printed by J[ohn] M[acock] for Henry Herringman, 1668).

29 Thomas Wright, *A Perfect Narrative of the Particular Service Performed by Thomas Wright, Firemaster, with a Morter Piece...* ([London, 1651]).

30 James Stocall, *Freedome: or, the Description of the Excellent Civill Government of the Island of Jersey* (London: printed for Robert Ibbitson, 1651 [i.e. 1652?]).

31 Wright, *Perfect Narrative*.

32 Ibid., p. 5.

33 *The Kings Majesties most Gratious Letter to his Sonne, his Highnesse James Duke of York.... Also a letter from his Highnesse Prince Charles, sent from France, to the Estate and Common Councell of (and Concerning) Jersey...* (London: printed by Moses Bell and Robert Ibbitson, 1647), A3, A4; *Prince Charles his Declaration to the Kings Majesties Loyall Subjects Neere the Realme of England* (London: printed for George Lawrenson, 1647). A key royalist propaganda document, produced in connection with the second Civil War, explicitly located itself as *The Remonstrance of the Inhabitants of the Three Isles of Wight, Garnsey, and Jersey* (London, 1647); yet it had little to do with the aspirations of the ordinary inhabitants of any of them. It harped on English Protestantism, English liberties and the privileges of the English parliament; virtually the only direct reference to any of the islands was an emphasis on their pathetic smallness ('spots of earth in respect of the whole Nation') as an incitement to England and Wales to rebel: pp. 6, 7 and passim.

34 *His Majesties Declaration to all his Loving Subjects in the Kingdome of England and Dominion of Wales* (The Hague: printed by Samuel Broun, 1649), p. 3.

35 *Prince Charles Proclaimed King, and Landed in Jersey with the Duke of York* (London: printed for J. J., 1649), esp. p. 6.

36 J. R. Dickinson, 'The earl of Derby and the Isle of Man, 1643–1651', *Transactions of the Historic Society of Lancashire and Cheshire* 141 (1992 for 1991), 39–76, esp. 52–9, 64.

37 Tim Thornton, 'Scotland and the Isle of Man, *c.* 1400–*c.* 1625: noble power and royal presumption in the northern Irish Sea province', *Scottish Historical Review* 77 (1998), 1–30.

38 *Calendar of State Papers, Domestic Series, 1655,* p. 344.

39 *Mercurius Politicus,* 8 (25 July–1 August 1650), p. 118 (*The English Revolution,* section III, *Newsbooks, no. 5: Mercurius Politicus, 1650–1659* (19 vols., London: Cornmarket, 1971–2), vol. I, 134).

40 Barry Coward, *The Stanleys: Lords Stanley and Earls of Derby, 1385–1672: The Origins, Wealth and Power of a Landowning Family* (Chetham Society, 3rd series, 30, 1983), pp. 169–72.

41 *Mercurius Politicus,* 8 (25 July–1 Aug. 1650), p. 118 (*The English Revolution,* section III: *Newsbooks, no. 5: Mercurius Politicus,* vol. I, 134).

42 John Selden, *Titles of Honor* (London: printed by William Stansby for John Helme ..., 1614); William Camden, *Britannia siue Florentissimorum regnorum* ... (London: per Radulphum Newbery, 1586); Michael Drayton, *Poly-Olbion* (Fourth volume of his *Works*), ed. J. William Hebel (Oxford: Blackwell, 1933), pp. 541–2.

43 James Chaloner, *A Short Treatise of the Isle of Man* (Manx Society, vol. X, 1863), pp. 9–11.

44 William Blundell, *A History of the Isle of Man*, ed. William Harrison (2 vols., Manx Society, vols. XXV and XXVII, 1876–7), XXV, pp. 54–5.

45 Blundell, *History of the Isle of Man*, pp. 56–9.

46 William Sacheverell, *An Account of the Isle of Man* (Manx Society, vol. I, 1859), p. 15: originally published as *An Account of the Isle of Man: its Inhabitants, Language, Soil, Remarkable Curiosities, the Succession of its Kings and Bishops, down to the Present Time* (London: printed for J. Hartley, ... R. Gibson ... and Tho. Hodgson ..., 1702).

47 Humphrey Lloyd and Camden said they spoke Scottish and Irish, Heylin that they spoke half Irish and half Norwegian; Blundell preferred Coke's formulation, 'a compound of mostly Irish, much Welsh, a little English and Scots': Blundell, *History of the Isle of Man*, pp. 60–1.

48 George Waldron, *A Description of the Isle of Man* (Manx Society, vol. XI, 1864), pp. 17–18.

49 Blundell, *History of the Isle of Man*, pp. 61–4.

50 George T. O. Bridgeman, *History of Wigan* (4 vols., Chetham Society, n.s., 15–18, 1888–90), vol. II, pp. 372–3.

51 Chaloner, *Short Treatise*, pp. 10–11. He did note their 'Incontinencie of body, which naturally may be imputed to their eating so much Fish; which is of a flatuous nature' (p. 11). Waldron provides an exception, condemning the tyranny of the Manx Church, the people's 'innate ignorance', and their superstition: Waldron, *Description of the Isle of Man*, pp. 16, 19, 27–9, 48.

52 *CSPD, 1651–2*, p. 22. Although this had a broader implication, it is important to consider the proviso's ambiguity about the association of Man with Scotland, and to acknowledge the direct imperative in 1651: potential Scottish aggression against England.

CHAPTER 11

The nation in the age of revolution

Ian McBride

Since historians are generally engaged in research of a highly specialised kind, and since we are notoriously jealous of our own periods, it may at first seem predictable that an eighteenth-century historian should claim that the modern connection between power and the nation dates from some time in the eighteenth century. Worse still, it may sound as if I am setting out to reinvent the wheel, since the French Revolution has been accorded a pivotal role in the emergence of nationalism by almost every standard work on the subject. In what follows, however, I shall offer fresh arguments in defence of what is, admittedly, a traditional view. By exploring a number of features of nationhood that have so far received relatively little attention, I hope to clarify some of the issues that have divided 'modernists' from their critics in recent discussions of nations and nationalism. Although my focus is on the Irish, who are often cast as honorary Slavs in typologies of nationalism, I shall consider them alongside the 'old' western nations of Britain and France: it is a fundamental premise of my central argument, indeed, that none of them can be understood in isolation.

The approach adopted here is also rooted in the history of ideas, an area somewhat out of fashion among scholars of nationalism since the classic works of Kedourie and Berlin. There is no doubt that the familiar meanings of the word 'nation' were already well established by the eighteenth century when the term might refer to a state, a people or an ethnic community. In Johnson's *Dictionary of the English Language* (1755), a nation is defined as a people 'distinguished from another people, generally by their language, origin, or government'. In Britain the national debt was one of the century's most characteristic preoccupations, and Adam Smith's *Wealth of Nations* (1776) one of its most celebrated works. What was missing, as David Miller has written, was 'the belief that nations could be regarded as active political agents, the bearers of the ultimate powers of sovereignty'.[1] My aim in this chapter is to demonstrate how the concepts of state, sovereignty and nation changed, so that, for the first time, the nation was pushed to the centre of political discourse. The crucial development here was the growing awareness that Europe constituted a states system, based on a common cultural heritage, economic ties and mutual recognition of the principle of sovereignty, all of which distinguished it from the rest of the world. If the eighteenth-century nation became a bearer of sovereignty, it also became a bearer of culture, and a full understanding of its importance, I shall further argue, requires an appreciation of how notions of the self were also changing.

Since there is now a large theoretical literature on the subject, some attempt to clear the ground may be in order.[2] For the purposes of this chapter, the tendency to divide theorists of nationalism into two antagonistic rival schools – modernists and their critics – only serves to obscure the key issues. It is easy to exaggerate their differences, as may be demonstrated by taking two from opposite ends of the spectrum. At one pole can be found Eric Hobsbawm, often regarded as the most provocative exponent of the modernist view. 'The basic characteristic of the modern nation', he announces at the beginning of *Nations and Nationalism*, 'is its modernity.'[3] Eager to combat the notion that national divisions are natural, he echoes Ernest Gellner's insistence on 'the element of artefact, invention and social engineering' in nation-building;[4] like Gellner, he associates nationalism with the emergence of advanced industrial societies in the nineteenth century. In Hobsbawm's view the heyday of nationalism was not until the period between 1870 and 1914, when ruling elites responded to the challenges posed by mass democracy and rapid social change by exploiting national sentiment.

At the other end of the spectrum, Adrian Hastings has demonstrated that a number of medieval and early modern peoples felt that they belonged to a 'nation', and cherished their own distinctively national myths and memories. Stressing the importance of the Bible, and the development of a literary language in the vernacular, Hastings argued that from the early fourteenth century Englishmen felt themselves to be a nation. Evidence to support this view can be found in the work of Rees Davies and Robin Frame on the communities of thirteenth-century Britain and Ireland.[5] There is no longer any excuse for the view that the collective identities of medieval people were confined to localism on the one hand and European Christendom on the other. At the same time, the work of early modernists has shown how myths of national election, based on the Old Testament, were used to portray Protestant nations as chosen peoples;[6] they have also studied classical notions of patriotism, and various 'gothic' myths of ancestral constitutions such as Hotman's

Franco-Gallia (1573) or Grotius' *Treatise on the Antiquity of the Batavian Republic* (1610).

Part of the reason why scholars have been unable to agree on a chronology for the rise of the nation is that they are not always trying to explain the same thing. The assault on Hobsbawm seems misconstrued when we consider that he is really interested in movements that have set out to make or break states according to the principle of nationality. In the early chapters of his book he repeatedly describes his topic as the ways in which the map of Europe was redrawn to respect the territorial claims of national communities – a process that began with the construction of two new great powers, Germany and Italy, and continued with the dismantling of the Habsburg and Ottoman empires.[7] It is possible, of course, to identify self-conscious nations in earlier periods, as Hobsbawm himself recognises in a chapter on what he somewhat grudgingly calls 'proto-national' bonds; their existence, however, did not dictate the political geography of Europe. This is something that Hastings failed to understand. Whilst Hastings conceded that nationalism as a 'formal political philosophy' belongs to the nineteenth century, he nevertheless found in much earlier periods the belief that one's nation needs to be defended 'at almost any cost through the creation or extension of its own nation-state'.[8] How far it would be possible to formulate such a belief, in the absence of 'formal' nationalism, is never explored. Instead, like many other critics of 'modernism', Hastings falls back on examples of xenophobia and expressions of national pride.

A more sophisticated critique of Hobsbawm's position can be found in the voluminous writings of Anthony Smith, who emphasises the importance of pre-existing ethnic and cultural bonds in shaping modern national identities. The quarrel, however, is not about chronology. What Smith really objects to is the 'instrumentalism' that sees everywhere the manipulation of national sentiment by elite interests, while the cultural ingredients of national identities are portrayed as so malleable that ethnicity is deprived of any explanatory force of its own.[9] In fact, although they pull in contrary directions, neither scholar disputes the orthodox view that nationalism was a product of the late eighteenth century. For Hobsbawm, the 'revolutionary-democratic' concept of the nation was crystallised in the early years of the French Revolution: it involved the equation of 'state = nation = people', though without the ethnocentrism of the later nineteenth century.[10] Smith agrees that it was at this juncture that a nationalist doctrine emerged, 'claiming that the world is divided into distinct nations, each with its peculiar character, that nations are the source of political power, ... and that international peace depended on all nations being autonomous, preferably in states of their own'.[11] It is this assumption, that the world is divided into nations, that I want to explore here, beginning with the patriots of eighteenth-century Ireland.

IMAGINING IRELAND: THE REVOLUTIONARY NATION IN THE LATE EIGHTEENTH CENTURY

The most famous of all Irish parliamentary speeches was delivered in the Irish House of Commons on 16 April 1782 when Henry Grattan rose to hail the dawning of a new age of liberty in Irish history. 'I found Ireland on her knees', he began; 'I have traced her progress from injuries to arms, and from arms to liberty.' Identifying himself with the literary patriots of earlier generations, he continued, 'Spirit of Swift! spirit of Molyneux! your genius has prevailed! Ireland is now a nation!' The cause of this jubilation was the so-called 'revolution' of 1782. Trumpeted as Ireland's equivalent of '1688', that year had seen the British government forced to concede legislative independence to the Irish parliament by an unusual combination of parliamentary pressure and the out-of-door agitation of Volunteer companies. Legislative independence, Grattan claimed, was an achievement that rivalled 'those great and ancient commonwealths, whom you were taught to admire', and which future generations would never equal.[12] But what exactly did Grattan mean when he said that 'Ireland is now a nation'?

To begin with, it is better to think of Irish patriotism as concerned with kingdoms rather than with nations in the modern sense. Throughout the eighteenth century, the term 'nation' can be found in general use in a variety of political contexts, yet it is hard to locate writers who articulated the concept with an awareness of the full range of political connotations that we associate with the mature nationalism of the nineteenth century. In appealing to the spirits of William Molyneux (1656–98) and Jonathan Swift (1667–1745), Grattan was invoking a patriot tradition in which national identity was not defined in terms of linguistic or cultural differences but in terms of polity, that is, a specific set of constitutional institutions and practices. No attempt was made by Irish patriots – from Molyneux and Swift to Grattan and Flood – to prove that Ireland was a distinct ethnic or cultural unit. Instead, Molyneux's *Case of Ireland* (1698), the foundational text of the Irish opposition up to 1782, was primarily concerned with historical and legal precedents which were held to prove that Ireland was a self-contained *political* entity, united to England only by a shared allegiance to the crown.[13] Nor did the patriots equate the nation with a sovereign people. When Swift famously addressed his fourth *Drapier's*

Letter to 'the whole people of Ireland', he apparently had in mind all those formal bodies that comprised the *political* nation: the two houses of parliament, the town corporations, the commissions of the peace and the electorate.[14] Although this appeal has puzzled many Irish historians it was in line with early modern usage. In all Thomas Hobbes's works, for example, the term 'people' signifies a legally constituted body or 'civil person', such as the House of Commons, in contrast to the term 'multitude', which refers to a mere aggregate of private individuals.[15]

The spirits of Swift and Molyneux did not inhabit a world of nation-states, but of composite monarchies, dynastic empires, republics, city-states and confederations in which the jurisdictional boundaries were defined by custom and precedent.[16] Like the medieval 'communities of the realm' examined by Susan Reynolds, their notions of legitimacy were 'regnal' in focus rather than national; the ideological task they faced was 'not so much to define, explain or justify the political community, as to define the limits of royal power'.[17] Thus Molyneux's *Case* turned on his interpretation of Henry II's assumption of the overlordship of Ireland. The Anglo-Irish connection was not founded on conquest, as English legal authorities maintained, but on a voluntary declaration of allegiance by the civil and ecclesiastical estates of Ireland; in return, Henry had granted the Irish their own parliament and extended to them the common law. It is true that Molyneux also claimed the rights of an Englishman: even if Henry II had acquired Ireland by conquest, it was only 'the *Antient Race* of the *Irish*' that had thereby lost their rights; the conquerors and their descendants 'retain'd all the Freedoms and Immunities of *Free-born* Subjects'.[18] A further complication arises from the fact that Molyneux and Swift spoke neither for the descendants of the Gaels nor for the 'Old English' – the medieval settlers of Norman origin who had mostly remained faithful to Rome – but for the Protestant newcomers who had dispossessed both older communities under Elizabeth, James I and Cromwell. But questions concerning the nature of the people – as a source of authority or as a community of descent – were not the issue; it was legal origins rather than ethnic origins that determined the relations between the king and his subjects.[19]

In the decades that divided Grattan from the Wood's Halfpence controversy, the term 'nation' had accumulated new connotations as debates on national character, the rise of primitivism in literature, and the new science of political economy all left their marks. We know that the self-image of Irish Protestants had been dramatically transformed, as terms such as 'the English interest in Ireland', which had dominated the literature of the 1690s, were largely displaced by a clear preference for Irish identifications by the middle of the next century.²⁰ In the realm of *political* discourse, however, the basic argument remained the same: it was not that the Irish were culturally distinct from the English, but that legally and historically Ireland was a separate kingdom which possessed certain rights and privileges. Like Molyneux, later generations of Irish patriots continued to cite John Locke's *Second Treatise* on 'the true original, extent and end of civil government', but they did not pursue the radical implications of Locke's ideas on rights of resistance, the dissolution of government and the reversion of power to the people.²¹ If we return to Grattan's speech we find that the Irish revolution consisted of restoring the 'independency of the Irish parliament', so that Ireland secured her liberty 'according to the frame of the British constitution'.²² The ideological alternatives open to Irish patriots were posed by the Dublin barrister Francis Dobbs in 1780 when he insisted that either Ireland was a conquered nation or it was 'a FREE KINGDOM, united with England by long usage, similarity of manners, vicinage, and a common King'.²³

A revealing contrast can be made between Grattan's oratory and the manifesto of the Society of United Irishmen of Belfast, published in October 1791. '*We have no national government*', the latter began, 'we are ruled by Englishmen, and the servants of Englishmen, whose object is the interest of another country.' So great was the weight of English influence in the Irish government that it had disturbed the balance that was essential to 'the preservation of our liberties, and the extension of our commerce'. Although the United Irishmen raised conventional grievances concerning the corrupting effects of government patronage, these were merely symptoms of a disease in the constitution which called for 'a complete and radical reform'. Finally, this endeavour required 'a cordial union among *all the people of Ireland*', and hence the radicals urged that 'no reform is practicable, efficacious, or just, which shall not include Irishmen of every religious persuasion'.²⁴ Each of these principles, drafted by Wolfe Tone, had been anticipated by the radical fringe of the old reform movement, and the United Irish programme was in many ways a crystallisation of ideas that had been widely floated in the 1780s. Never before, however, had these arguments been advanced with such confidence and directness.

It is tempting to think that the United Irishmen's demand for a 'national government' was a deliberate reference to events in France, where the Third Estate had declared itself a National Assembly in the summer of 1789. In the manifesto of the Revolution, *What is the Third Estate?*, Emmanuel Joseph Sieyès had ridiculed the *extase gothique* or ancient constitution. 'The nation exists prior to everything', he claimed, 'it is the origin of everything.'[25] In his classic defence of the French Revolution, *Rights of Man* (1791), Thomas Paine similarly rejected mixed government as an illogical combination of '*this, that* and *t'other*'.[26] 'Sovereignty', he went on, 'appertains to the Nation only, and not to any individual; and a Nation has at all times an inherent and indefeasible right to abolish any form of Government it finds inconvenient.' In a pamphlet of 109 pages the word 'nation' appears more than 170 times.[27] As Lynn Hunt has noted, this key word became the most sacred in the revolutionary lexicon, and worship of the nation was offered as a substitute for the charisma attached to kingship.[28] Recasting old radical traditions in the light of 'Jacobin' doctrines, the United Irishmen also moved towards a concept of representative democracy which opposed popular sovereignty to theories of mixed constitutions and multiple kingdoms that suddenly seemed outdated. By 1798, consequently, the Rev. Thomas Elrington, a fellow of Trinity College Dublin, found it necessary to publish an annotated edition of the *Two treatises* to reclaim the patron saint of whiggery from his own radical admirers: on the right of representation, he retaliated, Locke 'had no idea that he would be interpreted as attributing that power to the multitude'.[29]

More simply, of course, the demand for 'national government' meant the exclusion of English influence. In his seminal pamphlet, *An Argument on Behalf of the Catholics* (1791), Wolfe Tone had announced that there was 'no one position, moral, physical, or political that I hear with such extreme exacerbation of mind as [that] which denies to my country the possibility of independent existence'.[30] This was a remarkable claim, coming at a time when the most advanced Irish radicals confined their objectives – in public at least – to parliamentary reform and Catholic emancipation. Tone had already confided to his close friend Thomas Russell his opinion that separation from Britain would be 'regeneration to this country', though he recognised that such an opinion was 'too hardy' for the contemporary political climate.[31] In an essay 'On the English Connection' drafted in June 1790, he had considered whether Ireland was bound to support Britain in the event of war with Spain over the Nootka Sound dispute. Ireland, claimed Tone, was 'of infinitely greater extent and internal resources than Denmark, or Sweden, or Portugal, or Sardinia [Piedmont], or Naples, all sovereign states'.[32] The references to sovereignty were entirely new. 'What is it that degrades you', he challenged, 'that keeps you without a court, without ambassadors, without a navy, without an army?'[33] In a subsequent pamphlet on the Nootka Sound issue, Tone repeated the classic patriot line on the Anglo-Irish connection as a dual monarchy, but his call for Ireland to assert its 'rank among the primary nations of the earth', like his demand for an independent foreign policy, a navy and national flag, pointed to outright separatism.[34]

The aspiration that Ireland might take its place in a world of nations brings us back to one aspect of the rise of nationalism that has seldom been explored in any detail: the international system within which nations and states interact. Granted, there have been numerous comparative studies of nations and nationalisms identifying common explanatory factors, including the role of warfare. Military competition accounted for an increasing proportion of state expenditure during the eighteenth century, and governments consequently appealed to national interests to justify their actions. Recently, too, historians have demonstrated the importance of international rivalry in the definition of national identities, perhaps the best example being Linda Colley's argument that the self-image of Britons was defined through a series of confrontations with the 'other' of Catholic, absolutist France.[35] What is missing from the discussion, however, is what Anthony Smith describes as the 'interstate network that helps to define a comity of nations'.[36] Theoretical investigations of the nation, even when they are explicitly comparative, tend to work outwards from domestic developments within particular polities; my suggestion here is that we begin with the ways in which power was organised and conceptualised within what contemporaries called 'the political system of Europe', and then work from the outside in.[37]

THE LAW OF NATIONS

As inter-state rivalry intensified after the Reformation, so too did attempts to develop a body of international law capable of regulating the making of war and peace. The origins of a continental state system are usually traced back to the Treaty of Westphalia of 1648, which later diplomatic writers regarded as 'La première assemblée de l'Europe'.[38] The decades after Westphalia saw the increasingly systematic treatment of *jus gentium* by natural law philosophers, most notably in Samuel Pufendorf's *De Jure Naturae et Gentium* (1672). Some aspects of this subject, translated into French as 'le droit des gens' and into English as 'the law of nations', were very old indeed, drawing on the medieval 'just war' tradition and on long-established conventions concerning the privileges of ambassadors.[39] Others were quite novel. Perhaps the most enduring of these was the idea of a balance of power. First given formal recognition in the Treaty of Utrecht of 1713, the concept entered popular usage around the same time, especially in

England, where it had featured in the pamphlet war over the Tory ministry's peace policy in 1710–13. Against the 'universal monarchy' allegedly pursued by Louis XIV, the allies sought to guarantee *le repos de l'Europe* by maintaining a multi-polar world of autonomous sovereign entities.[40] The balance was thus envisaged as a system of weights and counter-weights designed to obstruct the preponderance of any single power and to maintain the stability of the whole.[41]

In part, this new conception reflected changes in the organisation of diplomacy, which was becoming more institutionalised by the later seventeenth century. By 1700 permanent, resident embassies had been established across Europe and foreign offices were taking shape, most clearly in France where specialised departments oversaw the formulation and implementation of foreign policy. At the same time, it has been argued, governments began to insist upon the clear demarcation of borders, where they previously tolerated the existence of hazy frontier zones in which 'the claims and jurisdictions of different rulers and their subjects overlapped and intersected in a complex and confusing way'.[42] The problems posed by ceremonial precedence – the ways in which dynastic status was represented – also began to recede. How was the ambassador conducted to his first audience with a prince? What titles were used? Where was he placed at table? Well into the eighteenth century, such apparent quibbling continued to delay and disrupt inter-state negotiations, though it is noticeable that the representatives at Utrecht in 1713 agreed to enter the town hall *pêle-mêle* and to sit at a round table.[43]

Needless to say, there was little agreement on how the balance of power worked, either in theory or in practice. There was much debate over its origins, whether it was self-regulating or required constant maintenance, and, of course, its implications for contemporary affairs.[44] Baron von Bielfeld, in one of the most methodical enquiries into the international arena, ranked the powers into four categories: those who made war independently (Britain and France); those who possessed significant military force but could fight only with outside support (Austria, Russia, Prussia, Spain); those who were relegated to the status of auxiliaries (the Portuguese, the Swedes, the Dutch); and the lesser states of Germany and Italy. At the same time, he offered an elaborate model of the current balance, which he believed dated from the beginning of the eighteenth century:

Les principales forces qui la tiennent aujourd'hui en Equilibre sont la France & l'Angleterre; & l'on peut envisager, la Maison d'Autriche & le Roi de Prusse comme les poids les plus considérables qui fixent ce même Equilibre, ou qui le rompent selon qui'ils se déterminent vers l'un ou l'autre côté; toutes les autres

Puissances concourrent à le faire pencher plus ou moins, à proportion de leurs forces respectives.[45]

As this description suggests, status continued to be measured by the established criteria of armed strength, territorial extent and population, but it had become accepted by the middle of the century that trade and naval strength were also crucial factors.[46]

The stabilisation of an international balance during the War of the Spanish Succession was regarded as one method of containing warfare; around the same time there appeared a cluster of utopian schemes for an international organisation which would enable Europe to avoid conflict altogether. These included proposals by William Penn (1693), John Bellars (1710), and the Abbé Saint Pierre (1712) for the creation of a federal European council to resolve disputes and maintain peace.[47] All looked back to the Duc de Sully's 'Grand Design' in his *Memoirs of Henri IV* (1638), often republished during the eighteenth century.[48] Saint Pierre's scheme was later edited by Rousseau, who, like Grotius, Pufendorf and Locke before him, had practical experience of diplomacy, having served as a private secretary to the French ambassador in Venice. His interest in war, national defence and inter-state organisation ran through his political writings from his abandoned study of 'Political Institutions', planned in 1743, to the *Considerations on Poland*, his final work. Although his *Social Contract* (1762) concluded by remarking that the external relations of states was a subject too vast for him, Rousseau repeatedly returned to it.[49] For nations, as for individuals, Rousseau characteristically believed that there was no middle way between total union and total separation. If Saint Pierre's federation was 'too good to be adopted', the only alternative, as he counselled the Poles and the Corsicans, was to insulate themselves from the corrupting influence of international politics and trade.[50]

Earlier I spoke of 'inter-state' rivalry, but this was not the terminology employed at the time. Quentin Skinner's classic essay on 'The state' traces the reconceptualisation of the relationship between ruler and ruled that occurred during the Italian Renaissance and the English Revolution, so that subjects now owed their allegiance to an impersonal structure of power rather than a hereditary monarch, and to a single sovereign authority rather than a patchwork of jurisdictions, in which the local competed with the national and the ecclesiastical with the civil. For Skinner it was above all Hobbes who established the state as the 'master noun of political argument'. The term then rapidly spread throughout Western Europe so that by the time of Hume's essays of the 1750s, or Rousseau's *Social Contract* 1762, 'we find the concept of the state and the terms *état* and *state* being put to work in a consistent and completely familiar way'.[51] Arguably, of course, it is precisely this last period that forms the most interesting part of the story. In Britain, above all, political discourse continued to revolve around the ideas of party, common law and the ancient constitution. In the outpouring of pamphlets that accompanied the Glorious Revolution, for example, English propagandists continued to speak of the civil magistrate or the commonwealth, though the notion of a 'supream authority' was sometimes central.[52]

Who then were the individuals that made up international society? The most widely read diplomatic work of the period was *De la manière de négocier avec les souverains* (1716) by the French diplomat François de Callières. The author set out an early definition of the balance of power, explaining 'that all the States of *Europe* have necessary Ties and Commerces one with another, which makes them to be look'd upon as Members of one and the same Commonwealth' so that any significant alteration to one member had the effect 'of disturbing the Quiet of all the others.'[53] Yet his title, translated into English as *The Art of Negotiating with Sovereign Princes*, reflected the dynastic assumptions of the *ancien régime*.[54] The confederation proposals of Saint Pierre and Bellars were based on a league of kings rather than of peoples, even if William Penn's *Essay Towards the Present and Future Peace of Europe* (1693), referred to 'Soveraign Princes and States'.[55] Although the 'sovereigns' who negotiated the eleven bilateral treaties that made up the Utrecht settlement were for the most part monarchs, the actors were referred to variously as 'states', 'nations' and 'peoples'.[56] The international agents, then, were neither the dynastic conglomerations of the early modern period nor the national units of the late nineteenth century, but something in between.

A clearer answer was provided by the Swiss jurist Emmerich de Vattel, whose *The Law of Nations* (1758) was probably the most influential exposition of international relations during the eighteenth century. Vattel set out to define 'the just regulations which ought to subsist between nations or sovereign states',[57] and throughout used 'state' and 'nation' interchangeably. At one point the nation is defined as 'a sovereign state, an independent political society'; elsewhere it is described as 'a moral person' with an understanding and a will.[58] By definition, nations were free and independent, and ought to be left their liberty; no nation had a right to interfere in another's internal affairs. In this sense they were essentially equal: 'a small republic is as much a sovereign state as the most powerful kingdom'.[59] Vattel went on to discuss commercial relations, the naturalisation of subjects, emigration, maritime law, and above all

the legal regulation of war and peace. This conception of an international society comprised of sovereign states was clearly different from
the medieval notions of imperium and papacy, though it owed much to
both.

In general the geopolitical issues that interested Hobsbawm – the
re-drawing of borders, the unification or secession of nations – did not
arise before the 1790s, but there were a number of exceptions. One of these
was Corsica, a colony of the patrician republic of Genoa. Interestingly,
Corsica was cited, together with Ireland, by David Hume as evidence for
his characteristically subversive remark that the provinces of 'free states'
were more oppressed than those of absolute monarchies.[60] From the
1730s the Corsicans were engaged in continual rebellion against their
rich Italian masters, attracting the sporadic sympathy of enlightened
Europe. In the 1760s General Pasquale Paoli, who shifted the struggle
away from the customary privileges of the island's *corporali* towards ideas
of independence and equality, aroused the enthusiasm of Londoners, of
Philadelphians and Dubliners, and won the admiration of *philosophes* such
as Voltaire, Raynal and Mably.[61] Rousseau thought Corsica the one
country left capable of reconciling liberty and the rule of law, because of
the 'valour and steadfastness with which this brave people was able to
recover and defend its freedom'.[62] Its absorption by France in 1768 was
widely denounced as a classic example of the sort of reason-of-state aggression deplored by the *philosophes*. In his *Thoughts on the Cause of the Present
Discontents* (1770) Burke also complained that foreign powers had 'not
scrupled to violate the most solemn treaties; and, in defiance of them, to
make conquests in the midst of a general peace, and in the heart of
Europe'.[63]

Writing from his London exile several years later, Paoli noted that
compassion for the Corsicans had been overshadowed by the fate of 'the
poor Poles'.[64] The dismemberment of Poland, the largest state on the
Continent, marked the first significant breach in 'the modern political
system of Europe', the first of three major partitions.[65] For the American
revolutionary Richard Henry Lee the fate of the Corsicans and the Poles
was doleful proof that European courts maintained 'the assumed right
of disposing of Men & Countries like live stock on a farm'.[66] But the
most spectacular disruption of established borders was the Declaration of
Independence, by which the thirteen colonies claimed the right to
become 'Free and Independent States' acting among 'the powers of the
earth'.[67] Europeans were used to contract theories, but this was contract
theory being put into practice – the dramatic enactment of collective

decision-making – and it encouraged the idea that the nation was prior to political forms, and could create a constitution through its own action. The question of when a people might legitimately secede and establish a state for itself began to be formulated for the first time. Richard Price, in his *Observations on the Nature of Civil Liberty* (1776), analysed what happened when one people had dissolved its political bonds with another, and established its own government. In addition to the United Provinces and the Swiss cantons, he sympathised with 'the brave Corsicans' in their struggle with first the Genoese and then the French. Among other authorities on the subject, incidentally, he cited Molyneux's *Case of Ireland.*[68]

The objective of the American colonists was 'to win the right for their state to enter the society of states as a respectable member, not to overturn it'.[69] The French Revolution, by contrast, was an attack on the international system itself: the renunciation of all wars of conquest in 1790 was the prelude to the Edict of Fraternity promising assistance to 'all peoples who wish to recover their liberty'.[70] In his *Discourse on the Love of Country* (1789), Richard Price distinguished patriotism – the attachment of a people to its constitution – from 'the spirit of rivalship and ambition which has been common among nations'.[71] Paine's classic attack on the hereditary principle contained a similar message. It is seldom noticed that part one of *Rights of Man* begins and ends with the problem of international conflict. Like many of the writers mentioned above, Paine reviewed Sully's 'Grand Design' of 1638 and his conclusion looked forward to a general revolution in Europe, in which the 'intrigue of Courts, by which the system of war is kept up' would be replaced by a confederation of nations.[72] It was this mood that Wolfe Tone hoped to capture in his 'Argument on behalf of the Catholics', in a passage that directly follows his hints on Irish independence:

Where is the dread now of absolute power, or the arbitrary nod of the Monarch in France? Where is the intolerance of Popish bigotry? The rights of man are at least as well understood there as here, and somewhat better practised. Their wise and venerable National Assembly representatives … have … renounced the idea of conquest, and engraven that renunciation on the altar, in the temple of their liberty: in that Assembly, Protestants sit indiscriminately with Catholics.[73]

Already it was clear that the upheaval in France meant not only the fall of absolute monarchy, but a revolution in religion which brought down the confessional barriers that had divided Europe since the Reformation. No less important, a revolution in the international system was beginning which would end the great power warfare which had characterised the previous century.

The development of 'international law' – a term introduced by Jeremy Bentham in 1780[74] – reflected the closer equivalence of nation, people and state during the eighteenth century. It provided a theoretical articulation of the growing assumption that Europeans inhabited a world of nations – of nation-states, that is, separated by precise territorial boundaries, defended by 'national' armies, and capable of being ranked in a hierarchy of greater or lesser powers, where once dynastic houses had disputed the very different order of ceremonial precedence. I want to consider next whether eighteenth-century Europeans, who were learning to take for granted the existence of the national state, might also have understood the notion of a national language, literature or culture. It should be stressed that this is not the same thing as possessing a national *character*. Reviewing a long-running debate, David Hume (1711–76) incisively argued that national characters were derived from 'moral' causes (economic conditions, the nature of government and of public life) as opposed to 'physical' ones (quality of air and climate). The characteristic preoccupation of the Scottish enlightenment was with nations as societies; and Hume was concerned with socialisation, or the 'similitude of manners' that resulted from social interaction.[75] Although Scottish historians and political economists contrasted the 'polished' nations of Europe with primitive peoples, they tended to assume that all societies progressed through the same stages, in which 'manners' differed according to the mode of subsistence.[76] Nations were located on a sliding scale according to their attainment of universal attributes – stable property relations, softened gender codes, politeness; there was no sense that each nation was unique, or that their value lay in their very incommensurability.

'Occasionally', as R. B. McDowell noted in his classic *Irish Public Opinion 1750–1800* (1944), the radical propagandists of the United Irishmen attempted to mobilise popular support by evoking 'the traditional glories of Gaelic Ireland'.[77] Yet McDowell was careful to distance the cosmopolitan, enlightened radicalism of the late eighteenth century from the romantic particularism of the Young Ireland movement or the Gaelic revival, and most historians have agreed with him. The bicentenary of the United Irish movement stimulated new interest in the literary and cultural manifestations of Irish radicalism, however, and the traditional view has been called into question. Most impressively, Mary Helen Thuente's *The Harp Restrung* (1994) has analysed the vast corpus of poems and songs published in radical papers such as the *Northern Star* and the *Press*, and in the various editions of the republican songbook, *Paddy's Resource*. From the celebration of such enlightenment abstractions as 'Freedom' and 'Reason', United Irish poetry came to concentrate on bards, harps, shamrocks, political martyrdom and blood sacrifice – all the images, in short, that we associate with the literary nationalism of Thomas Moore or the Young Ireland poets.[78] Remarkably, the Belfast harp festival of 1792 concluded with Presbyterian ministers and merchants singing 'Ierne United', which told of how the happiness, unity and freedom of Gaelic Ireland was destroyed by the coming of the English. The words were penned by Wolfe Tone himself.[79]

In my own view McDowell was nevertheless right to insist that the United Irishmen never grounded Ireland's right to independence on the fact that the island constituted an ethnic unit.[80] Perhaps the most notable product of their Gaelic enthusiasm was the publication of the magazine *Bolg an tSolair* (1795). Edited by Patrick Lynch, an Irish teacher associated with the Belfast radicals, it contained an Irish grammar, prayers, a glossary and poems selected from Charlotte Brooke's *Reliques of Irish Poetry*. Despite Lynch's boast that Irish was 'the mother tongue of all the languages of the West', and that no language was 'fitter to express the feelings of the heart', only one issue of *Bolg an tSolair* ever appeared. A *Northern Star* editorial on 'The Irish language' focused on the more practical uses of Gaelic: its value for the student of antiquities, especially 'Druidical Theology and Worship', the commercial benefits for merchants and its potential as a medium for the dissemination of republican propaganda. Interest in pre-Norman Ireland no doubt reflected a sense of separateness from England, but there was no explicit attempt to create a distinct cultural personality which might legitimise Ireland's claim to nationhood. The Irish case suggests that Hobsbawm was right when he maintained that the revolutionary nation contained nothing like 'the later nationalist programme of establishing nation-states defined in terms of the criteria so hotly debated by nineteenth-century theorists, such as ethnicity, common language, religion, territory and common historical memories'.[81]

At the same time, it would be short-sighted to dismiss these developments, as some have, as a naïve literary faddishness devoid of any real political significance. For one thing, these dramatic developments were fuelled by a heightened sense of cultural competition that stretched far back into the eighteenth century. Some time ago Gerald Newman described the awakening of English national pride that culminated in the decades around the Seven Years War, and saw the native Saxon 'genius' championed against the cultural dominance of Bourbon France. Beginning with

William Hogarth's protest against the swelling tide of foreign influence, the campaign in favour of domestic art and literature linked dramatists (Samuel Foote and David Garrick), poets and novelists (James Thomson, Oliver Goldsmith, Tobias Smollett), and moralists (the Rev. John Brown) – many of whom, incidentally, were actually Irishmen or Scots. Scholarly activity burgeoned as the Society of Antiquaries was chartered (1751), the British Museum was opened to the public (1759), the Royal Academy was founded (1768) and the first edition of the *Encyclopedia Britannica* appeared (1768–71). The anthems 'Rule, Britannia' and 'God save the King' were popularised during the 1740s. By the 1760s English virtue was given female personification in the figure of Britannia and John Bull had taken shape as 'a very worthy, plain, honest old gentleman, of Saxon descent'.[82] As David Bell has recently shown, this hostility was fully reciprocated by the French.[83]

Of the many developments which made this antagonism possible, three can be sketched briefly. The first was the establishment of French cultural supremacy, related to the enormous prestige of Louis XIV's court at Versailles, and a source of bitter complaint among the Germans and Swiss as well as the English.[84] The Peace of Utrecht marked the triumph of French over Latin as the international language of diplomacy;[85] it was also the recognised language of the international republic of letters.[86] This sense of resentment was as keen and as complex as anti-Americanism is today: 'we are the nation that they pay the greatest civilities to, and yet love the least', noted a French visitor to England in 1747; 'they adopt our manners by taste, and blame them through policy.'[87] Tension was evident even within France itself, where Rousseau presented his decisive break with the *philosophes* as a struggle between simple Genevan virtue and the corrupt sophistication of the French theatre. When he later complained in *Considerations of the Government of Poland* (1772) that 'there are no longer any Frenchmen, Germans, Spaniards, or even Englishmen; there are only Europeans', he was lamenting, as he later made clear, the spread of French taste.[88] He would have understood perfectly John Brown's *Estimate of the Manners and Principles of the Times* (1757–8), which opposed the Grand Tour, insisting that the character of young Englishmen should be formed to 'the *Genius,* of their own *Country*'.[89]

Secondly, the cultural dimensions of Anglo-French hostility were shaped by the literary revolution associated with the impact of sentiment, sensibility and primitivism. Previous generations of Englishmen had praised their own land, their language and character against the historic enemy; but, as Newman indicates, there was a new sense of cultural provocation among writers and intellectuals which meant that national slights were experienced as personal humiliations.[90] Charles Taylor, in an acute exploration of our modern preoccupation with identity and recognition, locates during this period 'the massive subjective turn of modern culture, a new form of inwardness, in which we come to think of ourselves as beings with inner depths'.[91] Like so many of the developments I have been describing, it was most graphically revealed in the writings of Rousseau, who urged his readers to overcome their dependence on the social conventions of commercial society and to re-establish contact with their authentic selves. When Rousseau opened his *Confessions* (1781) with the challenge that 'I may be no better, but at least I am quite different', he announced a new set of criteria that would eventually be applied to nationalities as well as individuals.[92] Paradoxically, the idea of sensibility would not have been possible without the commercialisation of culture, which had centralised the development of 'taste', meaning literary and artistic refinement, as a key index of social betterment.[93]

Finally, the cultivation of politeness brings us to the eighteenth-century public sphere, and most obviously the unprecedented expansion of print culture. It was the growing importance of booksellers, reviewers and readers which enabled the city to replace the court as the centre of literary patronage. This new public – the dwellers of clubs, assemblies and coffee houses whom Addison imagined reading his *Spectator* – came to be recognised as the final arbiter in cultural affairs. As Malesherbes, chief censor in the era of the *Encyclopédie*, confirmed:

A tribunal has been raised independent of all powers and respected by all powers, which evaluates all talents, and pronounces on people of merit. And in an enlightened century, in a century in which each citizen can speak to the entire nation by means of print, those who have the talent for instructing men and the gift of moving them – men of letters, in a word – are, among the dispersed public, what the orators of Rome and Athens were in the midst of the public assembly.[94]

Like Malesherbes, historians have characterised the public sphere as urban rather than courtly, independent and inclusive, and based on reason rather than rank.[95] Equally significant, the public tended to conceive of itself as national. Among the many imitators of the *Spectator* was James Arbuckle's 'Letters of Hibernicus', serialised in the *Dublin Journal* in 1725–6, which complained that lack of public encouragement at home drove men of genius and education out of the kingdom. 'Many an excellent piece has been conceived among our *Hibernian Bogs*', Arbuckle lamented, 'which now passes as the genuine product of *Cam* or *Isis*.'[96]

As I suggested at the beginning of this chapter, scholars are sometimes accused of constructing definitions of the 'nation' to suit their own purposes. It is fitting to close, then, by warning that the processes described above form just one episode in a much longer story. As I have tried to make clear, the Irish patriots of the 1780s and 90s belong to the era of Hobsbawm's 'revolutionary-democratic nation' – an era before the fully fledged ethnocentrism that inspired the nineteenth-century movements of unification and secession, or the integrative nationalism of the peasants-into-Frenchmen variety. On the other hand, this period did not mark the beginning of national consciousness, which, in Ireland and elsewhere, has a much older history. Yet there are a host of specifically eighteenth-century developments – the idea of Europe as a community of independent states, the emergence of the public sphere and the resistance to French cultural hegemony, the collapse of the *ancien régime* – that make it hard to put the accent on continuity rather than change. To suggest that little separates the nation of the 1790s from earlier classical or 'Hebraic' models is to sacrifice analytical clarity. While scholars have shown that national sentiment played a part in the Dutch Revolt (c. 1555–1609), and in the Glorious Revolution of 1688, this is not the same thing as calling the first an expression of 'Dutch nationalism' or the second 'a nationalist revolution'.[97] And while Hastings has shown that fourteenth-century Englishmen thought of themselves as a nation, the real question is what they meant when they did so.

When the United Irishmen thought of Ireland as a nation, they were concerned not just with the legal obligations that existed between ruler and subject, but with the nature and location of sovereignty. To reverse the sentence I quoted earlier from Susan Reynolds, their central problem was no longer defining the limits of royal power, but defining, explaining and justifying the political community. When they imagined Ireland taking its place in a Europe of nations they took for granted the inter-state network that had been forged since the Treaty of Utrecht. By the 1790s it had become commonplace to attribute the superiority of Europe, as Burke did, to its development into a 'vast commonwealth', the components of which were 'distinct and separate, though politically and commercially united' and whose independence was preserved by a balance of power.[98] In their enthusiasm for Gaelic antiquity they were also representative of wider trends. When the *Northern Star* informed its readers that Edward Bunting's collection of Irish music was 'new and decisive proof of the existence of a high degree of civilisation among our ancestors',[99] its editors understood that nations declared themselves not only by embassies but academies, galleries and other public institutions. At the same time, the fact that most of their readers were actually the descendants of seventeenth-century Scottish planters reminds us that the nation was not regarded *primarily* as an ethnic or linguistic unit.

In many ways, these processes are least evident in England. Here, the sense of national consciousness was most developed, but the ideology of nationalism was weakest. With the vital exception of Paine, the references of English radicals to popular sovereignty and the rights of man were tempered by older notions of constitutional balance and the ancient constitution. Yet even in England, less spectacular changes took place. The old Irish patriot tradition, as we have seen, combined loyalty to England's crown with a rejection of her parliament. This distinction, appropriate to the mixed constitution and the composite monarchy, made no sense after 1688, when an increasingly unitary state looked to a unified sovereign, the king-in-parliament. But even the English did not understand their constitution very clearly. Treason continued to be defined by the statute of 1352 as 'compassing and imagining the death of the king', hence the acquittal of Thomas Hardy and the English radicals in 1794. In the following year the notorious Gagging Act expanded the definition of treason, subsuming the monarchy within the unified sovereign of the king-in-parliament, so that an attack on any part of the constitution became an attack on the whole. This is another – characteristically English – manifestation of the transition I have been describing, away from the idea of allegiance as a personal bond between subject and ruler towards something like national sovereignty. Appropriately, in light of the argument I have outlined above, the first victims of the new legislation were the Irish Jacobins of 1798.[100]

NOTES

1 David Miller, *On Nationality* (Oxford: Clarendon Press, 1995), p. 31.
2 The best introduction is now Oliver Zimmer, *Nationalism in Europe, 1890–1940* (Basingstoke: Macmillan, 2003), ch. 1.
3 E. J. Hobsbawm, *Nations and Nationalism since 1780: Programme, Myth, Reality,* (2nd edn, Cambridge University Press, 1992), p. 14.
4 Ibid., p. 10.
5 R. R. Davies, *The First English Empire: Power and Identities in the British Isles 1093–1343* (Oxford University Press, 2002); Robin Frame, *The Political Development of the British Isles, 1100–1400* (Oxford University Press, 1990).
6 Tony Claydon and Ian McBride (eds.), *Protestantism and National Identity: Britain and Ireland 1650–1850* (Cambridge University Press, 1998).
7 For the role of boundary issues in generating nationalism see also Michael Hechter, *Containing Nationalism* (Oxford University Press, 2000).

8 Adrian Hastings, *The Construction of Nationhood: Ethnicity, Religion and Nationalism* (Cambridge University Press, 1997), p. 4.

9 See Anthony D. Smith, 'The myth of the "modern nation" and the myths of nations', *Ethnic and Racial Studies* 11 (1988), 1–26; idem, 'Gastronomy or geology? The role of nationalism in the reconstruction of nations', in *Myths and Memories of the Nation* (Oxford University Press, 1999), pp. 163–86.

10 Hobsbawm, *Nations and Nationalism*, p. 22; on this subject see Istvan Hont, 'The permanent crisis of a divided mankind: "contemporary crisis of the nation state" in historical perspective', in John Dunn (ed.), *Contemporary Crisis of the Nation State?* (Oxford: Blackwell, 1995), pp. 166–231.

11 Anthony D. Smith, 'Nationalism and the historians', in *Myths and Memories*, p. 46.

12 The text is reprinted in Seamus Deane (ed.), *Field Day Anthology of Irish Writing* (3 vols., Derry: Field Day, 1991), vol. I, p. 919. The text of the speech was later revised, but the language is not dissimilar from contemporary pamphlets.

13 William Molyneux, *The Case of Ireland's being Bound by Acts of Parliament in England, stated* (Dublin, 1698), p. 148.

14 Jonathan Swift, *The Drapier's Letters to the People of Ireland against Receiving Wood's Halfpence*, 2nd edition, ed. Herbert Davis (Oxford University Press, 1965), p. 68.

15 See Richard Tuck, *Philosophy and Government 1572–1651* (Cambridge University Press, 1993), p. 312.

16 J. H. Elliott, 'A Europe of composite monarchies', *Past and Present* 137 (November 1992), 48–71.

17 Susan Reynolds, *Kingdoms and Communities in Western Europe, 900–1300*, 2nd edition (Oxford: Clarendon Press, 1997), p. 326.

18 Molyneux, *Case of Ireland*, p. 19.

19 See Colin Kidd, *British Identities before Nationalism: Ethnicity and Nationhood in the Atlantic World 1600–1800* (Cambridge University Press, 1999) for a full exploration of these themes.

20 See David Hayton, 'Anglo-Irish attitudes: changing perceptions of national identity among the protestant ascendancy in Ireland, ca. 1690–1750', *Studies in Eighteenth-Century Culture* 17 (1987), 145–57.

21 Patrick Kelly, 'William Molyneux and the spirit of liberty in eighteenth-century Ireland', in *Eighteenth-Century Ireland* 3 (1988), 133–38.

22 *Field Day Anthology*, vol II, p. 921.

23 Francis Dobbs, *A Letter to the Right Honourable Lord North* (Dublin, 1780), p. 7.

24 'Declaration and Resolutions of the Society of United Irishmen of Belfast', reprinted in Thomas Bartlett (ed.), *Life of Theobald Wolfe Tone* (Dublin: Lilliput Press, 1998), pp. 298–99.

25 Emmanuel Joseph Sieyès, *Political Writings*, ed. Michael Sonenscher (Cambridge University Press, 2003), p. 136.

26 Thomas Paine, *Rights of Man* (with an Introduction by Eric Foner) (Harmondsworth: Penguin, 1984), pp. 140, 143.

27 By contrast, Locke's *Two treatises*, a much longer work, seldom uses the term, and then mostly to describe the division of humankind into nations in the book of Genesis, or the American tribes.

28 Lynn Hunt, *Politics, Culture, and Class in the French Revolution* (Berkeley, CA: University of California Press, 1984), p. 21.

29 John Locke, *Two Treatises of Government*, ed. Peter Laslett (Cambridge, student edition, 1988), p. 373n.

30 [Tone], *Argument on Behalf of the Catholics*, p. 291.

31 Reprinted in *Report of the Secret Committee of the House of Lords* (Dublin, 1793), p. 43.

32 *Life of Theobald Wolfe Tone*, 435.

33 Ibid., p. 436.

34 [T. W. Tone] *Spanish War! An Enquiry how far Ireland is Bound, of Right, to Embark in the Impending Contest on the Side of Great-Britain?* (Dublin, 1790), pp. 31, 42.

35 Linda Colley, 'Britishness and Otherness: an argument', *Journal of British Studies* 31/4 (1992), 309–329.

36 Anthony D. Smith, 'Adrian Hastings on nations and nationalism', *Nations and Nationalism* 9/1 (2003), 28.

37 The quotation is from Edmund Burke, 'Revolution in the political system of Europe', *Annual Register ... for the Year 1772* (2nd edn, London, 1775), p. 2.

38 Abraham de Wicquefort, *L'Ambassadeur et ses fonctions* (1730), quoted in Maurice Keens-Soper, 'François de Callières and diplomatic theory', *Historical Journal* 16/3 (1973), 495.

39 F. H. Russell, *The Just War in the Middle Ages* (Cambridge University Press, 1975); M. S. Anderson, *The Rise of Modern Diplomacy, 1450–1919* (London: Longman, 1993) , ch. 1.

40 Andreas Osiander, *The States System of Europe, 1641–1990: Peacemaking and the Conditions of International Stability* (Oxford: Clarendon Press, 1994), p. 113.

41 The history of international relations theory is still underdeveloped. The most recent study, Jonathan Haslam's *No Virtue Like Necessity: Realist Thought in International Relations since Machiavelli* (New Haven: Yale University Press, 2002), does not live up to its promises. Much better are Richard Tuck, *The Rights of War and Peace: Political Thought and the International Order from Grotius to Kant* (Oxford University Press, 1999), esp. ch. 6; Michael W. Doyle, *Ways of War and Peace: Realism, Liberalism and Socialism* (New York: Norton, 1997), chs. 4–5; see also David Boucher, *Political Theories of International Relations: from Thucydides to the Present* (Oxford, 1998), ch. 11.

42 Anderson, *Rise of Modern Diplomacy*, ch. 2. The quotation is taken from p. 97.

43 Ibid., p. 67.

44 Many of these questions are raised in David Hume, 'Of the balance of power', in *David Hume: Political Essays*, ed. Knud Haakonssen (Cambridge University Press, 1994), pp. 154–60.

45 Baron J. F. de Bielfeld, *Institutions Politiques* (2 vols., The Hague, 1760), vol. II, pp. 84–5, and (quotation) 94.

46 M. S. Anderson, 'Eighteenth-century theories of the balance of power', in Ragnhild Hatton and M. S. Anderson (eds.), *Studies in Diplomatic History: Essays in Memory of David Bayne Horn* (London: Longman, 1970), pp. 183–98.

47 F. H. Hinsley, *Power and the Pursuit of Peace: Theory and Practice in the History of Relations between States* (Cambridge University Press, 1963), ch. 2; see Elizabeth V. Souleyman, *The Vision of World Peace in Seventeenth and Eighteenth-Century France* (revised edition Port Washington, NY: Nennikat Press, 1972), ch. 5 for other projects in the 1740s and 1750s.

48 English translations included *The Memoirs of the Duke of Sully; during his residence at the English Court ... Also, a relation of the political scheme commonly called the Great Design of Henry IV* (Dublin, 1751).

49 Jean-Jacques Rousseau, *The Social Contract and Other Later Political Writings*, ed. Victor Gourevitch (Cambridge University Press, 1997), p. 152.

50 'Abstract and Judgement of Saint-Pierre's Project for Perpetual Peace' (1756), in Stanley Hoffman and David P. Fidler (eds.), *Rousseau on International Relations* (Oxford: Clarendon Press, 1991), p. 100.

51 See Quentin Skinner, 'The state', in T. Ball, J. Farr and R. L. Hanson (eds.), *Political Innovation and Conceptual Change* (Cambridge University Press, 1989), p. 123.

52 Gilbert Burnet, *An Inquiry into the Measures of Submission to the Supream Authority* (London, 1688).

53 François de Callières, *The Art of Negotiating with Sovereign Princes*, translated from the French (London, 1716), p. 7.

54 Ibid. There was another English edition in 1738.

55 William Penn, *An Essay Towards the Present and Future Peace of Europe* (repr. Eastgate, Gloucester: John Bellows, 1915), p. 12.

56 Osiander, *States System of Europe*, ch. 2.

57 Emmerich de Vattel, *The Law of Nations; or, Principles of the Law of Nature: Applied to the Conduct and Affairs of Nations and Sovereigns* (1758; Dublin edn, 1787), p. vi.

58 Ibid., pp. xiii, 1.

59 Ibid., p. 9.

60 'That politics may be reduced to a science', in *David Hume: Political Essays*, ed. Haakonssen, pp. 8–9.

61 Franco Venturi, 'Pasquale Paoli', in idem, *Italy and the Enlightenment* (London: Longman, 1972), ch. 5. James Boswell, *An Account of Corsica, the Journal of a Tour of that Island; and Memoirs of Pascal Paoli* (1768).

62 Rousseau, *Social Contract*, ed. Gourevitch, p. 78 (1762).

63 'Thoughts on the cause of the present discontents', in *Pre-Revolutionary Writings*, ed. Ian Harris (Cambridge University Press, 1993), p. 150.

64 Venturi, 'Pasquale Paoli', p. 148.

65 Edmund Burke, 'Revolution in the political system of Europe', p. 2.

66 David Armitage, 'The Declaration of Independence and international law', *William and Mary Quarterly* 59/1 (January 2002), 49.

67 Ibid., 45.

68 Richard Price, 'Observations on the nature of civil liberty, the principles of government, and the justice and policy of the war with America' (1776), in *Richard Price: Political Writings*, ed. D. O. Thomas (Cambridge University Press, 1991), pp. 30–5, 68, 70 n. 5.

69 David Armstrong, *Revolution and World Order: The Revolutionary State in International Society* (Oxford: Clarendon Press, 1993), p. 42.

70 Ibid., p. 85.

71 Reprinted in *Richard Price: Political Writings*, pp. 178–9.

72 Paine, *Rights of Man*, pp. 35–7; 76–9, 144–7.

73 Tone, 'Argument on behalf of the Catholics', p. 291.

74 Armitage, 'Declaration of Independence', p. 49.

75 Hume, 'Of national characters', *in David Hume: Political Essays*, p. 82.

76 R. L. Meek, *Social Science and the Ignoble Savage* (Cambridge University Press, 1976).

77 R. B. McDowell, *Irish Public Opinion 1750–1800* (London: Faber and Faber, 1944), pp. 208–9.

78 Mary Helen Thuente, *The Harp Restrung: The United Irishmen and the Rise of Irish Literary Nationalism* (Syracuse University Press, 1994), esp. ch. 5.

79 *Northern Star*, 18 July 1792.

80 See my 'The harp without the crown: republicanism and nationalism in the 1790s', in Sean Connolly (ed.), *Whigs, Patriots and Radicals: Political Ideas in Eighteenth-Century Ireland* (Dublin: Four Courts Press, 2000), pp. 159–84.

81 Hobsbawm, *Nations and Nationalism*, p. 20.

82 Gerald Newman, *The Rise of English Nationalism: A Cultural History 1740–1830* (London: Weidenfeld & Nicolson, 1987), p. 116.

83 David Bell, *The Cult of the Nation: Inventing Nationalism, 1680–1800* (Cambridge, MA: Harvard University Press, 2001), esp. ch. 3.

84 For the Swiss see Oliver Zimmer, *A Contested Nation: History, Memory and Nationalism in Switzerland, 1761–1891* (Cambridge University Press, 2003), ch. 2.

85 Anderson, *Rise of Modern Diplomacy*, pp. 101–102.

86 Dena Goodman, *The Republic of Letters: A Cultural History of the French Enlightenment* (Ithaca, NY: Cornell University Press, 1994), p. 21.

87 Newman, *English Nationalism*, p. 79.

88 Hoffman and Fidler, *Rousseau on International Relations*, p. 168.

89 Newman, *English Nationalism*, p. 82.

90 Ibid., pp. 58–9.

91 Charles Taylor, 'The politics of recognition', in Amy Gutmann (ed.), *Multiculturalism: Examining the Politics of Recognition* (Princeton: Princeton University Press, 1994), p. 29.

92 Jean-Jacques Rousseau, *The Confessions … with the Reveries of the Solitary Walker* (2 vols., Dublin, 1783), vol. I, p. 1.

93 John Brewer, *The Pleasures of the Imagination: English Culture in the Eighteenth Century* (London: HarperCollins, 1997), ch. 2.

94 Mona Ozouf, '"Public opinion" at the end of the old regime', *Journal of Modern History* 60, suppl. (September 1988), S9.

95 The best general studies are T. C. W. Blanning, *The Culture of Power and the Power of Culture: Old Regime Europe, 1660–1789* (Oxford, 2002), and James Van Horn Melton, *The Rise of the Public in Enlightenment Europe* (Cambridge University Press, 2001).

96 [James Arbuckle *et al.*,] *A Collection of Letters and Essays on Several Subjects, Lately Published in the Dublin Journal* (2 vols., London, 1729), Vol. I, p. 3.

97 Philip S. Gorski, 'The Mosaic moment: an early modernist critique of modernist theories of nationalism', *American Journal of Sociology* 105/5 (March, 2000), 1435; Steven Pincus, '"To protect English liberties": the English nationalist revolution of 1688–1689', in Claydon and McBride (eds.), *Protestantism and National Identity*, pp. 75–104.

98 Burke, 'Revolution in the political system of Europe', p. 2; Jennifer M. Welsh, *Edmund Burke and International Relations: The Commonwealth of Europe and the Crusade against the French Revolution* (Basingstoke: Macmillan, 1995), p. 70.

99 Ibid., p. 34.

100 Lisa Steffen, *Defining a British State: Treason and National Identity, 1608–1820* (Basingstoke: Palgrave, 2001), ch. 4.

PART IV

Modernity

CHAPTER 12

Enemies of the nation? Nobles, foreigners and the constitution of national citizenship in the French Revolution

Jennifer Heuer

On 26 Germinal Year II (15 April 1794), the Committee of Public Safety banished ex-nobles and enemy foreigners from Paris, maritime towns and military strongholds. These men and women were given only ten days to organise their affairs and leave town – a terrifying situation for those forced to abandon their jobs, homes and support networks. Yet the penalty for disobeying the law was even more alarming: those who stayed after the deadline without having proved that they were good French citizens and non-noble were declared 'outside of the law'. They would be defenceless in the face of the Terror, risking prison or the guillotine.

Hundreds rushed to petition the committee, explaining both why they feared that they would be encompassed by the law, and why they should be exempted from it. Their pleas and the eventual responses – and silences – from the revolutionary government illuminate changing conceptions of membership of the nation. They show both the power of the state in defining citizenship, and challenges to that power even during the most violent moments of the Revolution. They also reveal the profound difficulties contemporaries faced in trying to reconcile new definitions of membership of the nation, which emphasised regeneration and individual adhesion to the state, with the stubborn legacies of older categories of identity and the need to distinguish loyal citizens from dangerous outsiders.

DEFINING THE NATION BY ITS ENEMIES AND ITS RE-BIRTH

The French Revolution is often taken to be a crucial moment, perhaps the crucial moment, in the creation of both the modern nation-state and modern nationalism.[1] Among other innovations, it introduced legal equality among citizens, celebrated popular sovereignty, instituted mass conscription and established territorial homogeneity within the nation. Yet other contemporary developments were distinctly 'un-modern'. Like many later nationalists, especially during wartime, revolutionaries defined membership of the nation partially by opposition to its enemies. However, unlike many of their successors, revolutionaries defined these enemies simultaneously as territorial foreigners and members of a particular social and political community – that of nobles.

Few theorists have considered the relationship between nationality and nobility; modern scholars tend to think about nationalism and national identity more readily in relation to ethnicity, religion or language. Yet foreigners and the 'caste of nobles' were in structurally similar positions during the Revolution: both formed potentially alien bodies within the nation and they were socially and legally conflated. Membership of both groups had also been determined by similar criteria during the *ancien régime*: birth or formal processes of naturalisation and ennoblement, or conversely, the renunciation of citizenship rights and *dérogeance*, the loss of noble privileges. Looking comparatively at how the Germinal laws affected, and were interpreted by, both nobles and foreigners, thus provides us with a window for understanding the extent to which new forms of nationality and citizenship were conceptualised in relation to certain 'premodern' categories.[2] It also illuminates how contemporaries weighed individual claims to participate in the nation against formal titles of inclusion or exclusion.

Judging the citizenship status of both ex-nobles and possible foreigners further reveals contemporary struggles to define how much both the nation and its various inhabitants had been transformed by the Revolution. As William Sewell notes, while nineteenth-century nationalists often imagined the nation as a product of a long historical destiny, revolutionaries viewed it as a dramatic rupture.[3] Contemporaries often heralded this process as one of 'regeneration'. The term had religious, as well as political and social, connotations. Indeed, petitioners regularly described their origins as a 'tache', a term which implied both a stain and original sin that could be washed away by a newly sacralised nation-state.

But there were also fundamentally competing visions of regeneration.[4] In one version, transformation was imagined to be contemporary with the Revolution itself; new men sprang fully armed from the cleansing drama of 1789. A variant on this implied that the Revolution had created individuals who could transform themselves, even if they had not yet fully done so; all those who were willing to renounce membership of lesser groups and identify themselves with the nation could become an integral part of it. A competing, and far less liberal, vision held that the Revolution had only begun the process of regeneration; a legislator or pedagogue – usually embodied in the revolutionary state – was required to direct the process of national and individual transformation. It, and it alone, would distinguish those who had been regenerated from those who had not and who could not be. Those deemed incapable of citizenship were to be expelled – or killed.

All of these visions of regeneration and national belonging appear in the Germinal decree and corresponding petitions. Ex-nobles and alleged foreigners contended that the revolutionary state had given them a new status, that they had transformed themselves, or that despite appearances, they had always been part of the nation. In turn, the government was forced to weigh multiple criteria as it compared various groups of ex-nobles and potential foreigners and debated who could be considered capable of citizenship. Those in power sought both to acknowledge regeneration as the basis of national legitimacy and to purge the republic of its enemies. The new nation was marked by a fundamental tension between an ideology of a fresh start, both individual and collective, and the need to permanently separate citizens from outsiders.

POLICING EX-NOBLES AND FOREIGNERS

The Germinal decree, prompted by Saint Just's reflections on the dangers facing the revolutionary republic, was part of the general arsenal of the Terror designed to purge the nation of its enemies. It not only exiled ex-nobles and enemy foreigners from key locations, it also barred them from holding public office unless given special permission to do so, and excluded them from attending the meetings of revolutionary sections, *sociétés populaires* and *comités de surveillance.* The decree, subsequent amendments and the approximately one thousand surviving petitions[5] provide us with a rare opportunity to explore both how the government of the radical revolution defined the limits of national citizenship and the ways in which ostracised men and women strategically appropriated the language of regeneration to argue for their inclusion in a national community. Many petitions were written personally by men and women terrified that the law might encompass them, as the uncertain grammar and spelling of the letters often poignantly reveal. Some letters were composed or edited by intermediaries trained in legal discourse, but they often retained vivid biographical details.

The Germinal law followed several years of redefining the relationship between 'French' and 'foreigners', as well as between citizens and nobles or aristocrats. Legislators initially aimed to erase differences between different groups within the nation, in the process incorporating nobles and foreigners who supported the Revolution. They eliminated noble privilege in 1789, and abolished nobility itself in June 1790. It was impossible to abolish 'foreignness' – and indeed the abolition of privilege and legal distinctions between citizens made 'foreignness' far more important than it had been before the Revolution. Nonetheless, foreigners who supported the revolutionary cause were welcomed. In August 1792, the National Assembly declared that certain philosophers and freedom fighters throughout the world (including Thomas Paine, Jeremy Bentham and George Washington) were French.

However, with the outbreak of war and the spiral of increasing violence instituted with the Terror, 'foreigners' and 'aristocrats' were increasingly blamed for division and setbacks. Beginning in the winter of 1792, the revolutionary government took a series of measures against ex-nobles, designed to exclude them from the exercise of political citizenship, keep them from 'corrupting' the army, and in general make them more vulnerable to laws aimed at those suspected of counter-revolutionary activity.[6] Similarly, after the Jacobin government became embroiled in war with much of Europe, it increasingly attempted to keep track of foreigners in Paris. It ordered the arrest and confiscation of property of British and Spanish subjects living in France, and in what was probably the most direct precursor of the Germinal decree, proclaimed in August 1793 that subjects of enemy powers who had not been domiciled in France before 14 July 1789 were to be arrested.[7] Yet these measures were limited, even after the Terror was proclaimed the order of the day in September 1793. While repressive laws were applied rigorously to British subjects, such measures were not systematically enforced against other foreigners until the Germinal decree.[8] The decree also appears to have been the first occasion when all ex-nobles faced the prospect of immediate exile and were forced to assess whether they were permanently branded by their former titles.

Policing measures aimed at nobles and foreigners before the spring of 1794 had established a number of important exceptions. Foreigners exempted from earlier laws included those from Liège and Brabant, who, as part of the expanding French empire, were to be regarded as French; so were workers and artists who could get two patriotic citizens to testify on their behalf, and all others who 'throughout their time in France have proved their civic-mindedness and attachment to the French Revolution'. The infamous Law of Suspects of September 1793, which established that anyone could be arrested who was ever suspected of having committed a counter-revolutionary act, focused on 'those former nobles, including husbands, wives and fathers ... who have not constantly demonstrated their attachment to the Revolution'. This declaration conspicuously marked former nobles as suspects, but also provided ex-nobles with a possible means for escaping such identification. The original text of the Germinal decree also allowed for a certain number of exceptions among both nobles and foreigners, primarily those who were too young or old and decrepit to cause real harm or those who were actively useful for the well-being of the revolutionary republic. The National Convention further allowed ex-nobles who were deputies of the Convention to remain in place.[9] But the law made no other provisions for those who could prove their attachment to the revolutionary nation. Indeed, Sophie Wahnich has argued that this decree marked an end to a model of integration through individual political adhesion. She claims that the shift involved a writing back of communal identity before the Revolution to a 'mythical origin' in which foreigners and nobles had not participated. As the revolutionaries of Year II shied away from the idea of a collective social contract that formed the basis of their new society, they also extinguished the possibility of outsiders joining their community through individual 'contracts'.[10]

Wahnich's analysis is based on the debates of the National Convention and particularly on the Committee of Public Safety's proclamation that only immigrants who had been in France before 1789 were to be considered 'French'. The government of the Terror wanted to establish fixed boundaries between virtuous citizens and treacherous outsiders. With the Germinal decree, it seemed to read those boundaries back before the Revolution itself, defending a community of citizens that had existed in nascent form during the *ancien régime*. But the men and women threatened by the Germinal decree challenged this model of national citizenship. Some acknowledged the potential stain of their origin, but argued that it could be easily washed away. Others tried to prove that apparent titles of nobility or foreignness were in fact compatible with membership in a revolutionary community of citizens. Petitioners repeatedly highlighted their own agency both in disassociating themselves from the alien community to which they supposedly belonged and in living and acting as citizens.

Emphasising personal adhesion to the nation made sense for men and women terrified that they would be branded outsiders because of a collective legal status. It was also a logical move given the exceptions in earlier policing measures, and the widespread expectation that good revolutionary citizens should be able to account for their patriotic activities.[11] But the ways in which 'ordinary' men and women strategically argued for their inclusion in the nation highlight key aspects of regeneration and citizenship. They show both the similarities between the position of foreigners and the nobles and their understanding of the role of participation in the state as a means to overcome the past.

ARGUING FOR INCLUSION

By the spring of 1794, most men and women who openly supported nobility and monarchy had fled the radical republic, or been imprisoned or guillotined, while foreigners who were clearly enemies of the revolutionary nation had met similar fates. Those threatened by the Germinal decree often believed in, or at least publicly espoused, revolutionary ideals. Most consulted family, friends, neighbours or their local revolutionary committees to find out if they were included in the decree; they turned to the Committee of Public Safety only if they remained uncertain or dissatisfied with their status. The letters preserved in the Archives Nationales thus represent particularly borderline cases, and ones that revealed the potentially arbitrary nature of the categories that defined outsiders.

Supplicants' questions and pleas were motivated in part by the hope of persuading the government either to issue new exceptions that would include them, or alternatively, to consider their personal circumstances. In so doing, they walked a difficult line between articulating individual and collective identities. Petitioners hoped for group exemptions, but could not identify themselves safely as part of a group, since collective petitions had been outlawed in May 1791. Almost all petitions were signed individually or submitted anonymously. Even when writers referred to other people in similar situations, they usually avoided using the pronoun 'we'.

Petitioners were also often genuinely confused about their positions. Although the decree aimed specifically at foreigners born subjects of enemy powers, the category was more ill defined than it appeared. Many were bewildered by the implications of French territorial expansion. A few, like the seventeen-year-old Russian-born orphan Xaveri, did not even know if their homelands were at war with France.[12] Even immigrants who had been naturalised during the *ancien régime* were far from certain that their letters of naturalisation – granted by a deposed sovereign – assured their citizenship in the revolutionary nation.[13] Alleged ex-nobles similarly puzzled over how Jacobins might understand pre-revolutionary hierarchies. A few supplicants fretted that they might be stigmatised because of their behaviour, like the citizen Prosteau, who feared that he had marked his social aspirations by dressing his servant in livery for fifteen minutes once a year.[14] However, the majority of petitioners – both nobles and immigrants – were terrified that they would be condemned not because of their dress or accent, but because of their ascribed origin, singled out because the paper-work of identity revealed a fatal birthplace or title. They thus sought to prove that their real social and political identity diverged from their apparent legal status.

With only ten days to ward off the threat of exile or the guillotine, petitioners did not wait to find out if they were actually considered dangerous outsiders. Instead, they rushed to prove that they deserved to remain part of the national community. Some maintained that they were not permanently marked by their origin because particular forms of literal and social 'foreignness' were less reprehensible than others, or more com-patible with the new regime. Many tried to show that they had overcome their supposed alien origin, becoming part of the true nation even before the Revolution. They adopted a two-fold strategy, insisting that they had both rejected and been rejected by the communities to which they sup-posedly belonged. Others contended that, whatever their origin, the Revolution itself had allowed them to transcend their roots, either by giving them a new status or by providing them with the opportunity to reveal their citizenship.

Both alleged nobles and foreigners stressed the element of chance that had placed them in an alien community. Supposed nobles lamented that their affiliation with the 'caste' of nobles was due to blind fate, like the businessman Gamaches who described himself as 'excluded for seventy-five years from the caste in which the hazards of birth placed him'.[15] Possible foreigners, particularly men and women born of French parents outside France, similarly maintained that their foreignness was the result of 'unforeseen accident of birth'.[16] The trope of 'accidental birth' had been part of civil law jurisprudence on foreigners during the *ancien régime*.[17] But the idea that origin was 'accidental' also accorded particularly well with arguments for regeneration. If 'foreignness' was a question of chance, not will, then men and women could not be held responsible for their initial membership of an alien community, and could be easily incorporated into the revolutionary nation.

However, men and women could also have excluded themselves from a nascent community of revolutionary citizens as adults, by serving another sovereign, naturalising in a foreign country or being ennobled. The prob-lem was particularly acute for supposed nobles, since government service and social advancement during the *ancien régime* had been deeply entangled with the process of ennoblement.[18] Suppliants thus tried to justify their particular form of nobility, proving that they were not to blame for their titles, or that their apparently indelible 'stain of orign was in fact' recent and could be easily washed away.

Many deliberately took up *ancien régime* justifications for nobility and re-shaped them. This was particularly the case for recipients of the *Ordre de Saint Michel*, the only chivalric order of the *ancien régime* that could be earned through non-military service. As one anonymous petitioner argued: 'only talents and superior merit led to their distinction; it [the order] corresponded to useful talents and to commoners in general; it was accorded to painters, sculptors, doctors, surgeons, engineers, builders and factory directors'.[19] However, petitioners also clearly hoped to emphasise the unusual nature of their titles in order to make their titles acceptable to a radical republican regime based on work and social utility. Other alleged nobles similarly contended that their apparent nobility had been accorded by popular mandate as a reward for their services. Former *échevins*, alder-men who along with mayors had constituted the government of certain cities and towns, were among the most vocal proponents of this vision. They contended that their titles were not a stain that marked polluted outsiders, but a badge of honour, easily compatible with membership of a nation that proclaimed public opinion to be the source of national legitimacy.

Most often, however, petitioners argued that they had not been true nobles because they had held an ennobling office for fewer than the requisite years of service. Venal office provided one of the most frequent mechanisms for social advancement; ambitious men of substance used their savings to purchase offices in the government, which generally awarded personal nobility to the holder after twenty years of service, and hereditary nobility after three generations.[20] Such venal office holders quickly became emblematic of the difficulties of assessing the meaning of nobility during the *ancien régime*, and of using past categories to judge contemporary membership of the nation.

Regardless of their particular forms of foreignness or nobility, men and women also insisted that they, as individuals, should not be counted as part of a community defined by birth because they had acted as French citizens. Petitioners insisted that they had both renounced, and been rejected by, their supposed communities of origin. Indeed, for alleged foreigners, the very act of immigration could be presented as evidence that they had abandoned an alien and repressive community for France. Foreign-born Jews in particular adopted this strategy, like the used-clothes peddler Chayé who argued that not only had he embraced the land of liberty, it was also the only possible community to which he could belong: 'he cannot be considered as a subject of the Emperor because as a Jew he would have been treated as a foreigner at Brody where Jews are only tolerated as slaves. It is only in France that they have a country.'[21] More generally, immigrants – particularly those who had come during the Revolution – often described themselves as 'refugees', suggesting both that they had been chased out of their homelands and that they had gladly abandoned such communities for the revolutionary nation.

Similarly, when supposed nobles reviewed their status before the Revolution, especially those who could not frame their titles positively, they often emphasised that they had been formally excluded from, or cast out of, the system of nobility – but also that they had rejected that system, choosing instead to live as citizens. Many insisted that the caste of real nobles had excluded them, as did Nervet, 'bourgeois de la ville de Perpignan', who claimed that his title referred only to 'a local and illusory nobility, disdained by the nobility of race of this country who neither considered nor admitted him to their caste'.[22] Like foreigners who emphasised their rejection of their homelands, alleged nobles also claimed that they had consciously refused noble titles, rejecting multiple opportunities to register nobility, or abandoning their titles by becoming small-scale merchants and subjecting themselves to *dérogeance*, or the formal loss of noble privilege.

Most often, supposed nobles maintained that they had rejected noble titles and status because they had not 'enjoyed privileges'. Petitioners stressed that they had paid taxes as patriotic commoners – or occasionally that they had not paid the exceptional taxes levied on new nobility who wanted to preserve their titles. They insisted that they had never participated in noble assemblies. Referring to such standard perks of titled distinction emphasised the double nature of their elimination from an alien community. It suggested that petitioners had not been considered sufficiently noble to be part of such a community and that they had deliberately chosen not to partake in the elite and corrupt political organisation of the *ancien régime*.

Few supposed nobles or foreigners described a radical break in their lives between the *ancien régime* and the new republic, as they sought to avoid incriminating themselves for past activities. Instead, they highlighted enduring differences between their ascribed status and their own social position and political actions during both the *ancien régime* and the Revolution. At the same time, however, certain petitioners did invoke the possibility of their 're-birth' with the Revolution itself. Foreigners whose homelands had been conquered by France during the Revolution invoked the idea of regeneration through the state. They beseeched the government to consider that revolutionary legislation had given them a new status, transforming them into French men and women. *Religionnaires fugitifs*, Protestants whose ancestors had fled France after the Revocation of the Edict of Nantes, similarly invoked a 1790 law that granted them full rights of citizenship if they returned to France and took a civic oath.

Some supposed nobles also contended that the Revolution had given them a new status. Men and women who had been born out of wedlock voiced this idea most literally. They worried that the revolutionary government had inadvertently made them into nobles when it give them an unprecedented right to inherit from their families and implicitly recognised them not as bastards without an official status, but as legal descendants of noble relations.[23] Such petitioners argued that they were actually true citizens, having been regenerated or born again, this time legitimately, with the Revolution itself. As Foiselle, self-proclaimed *homme de lettres*, put it, these 'adopted children of the Republic' were 'necessarily born of the new regime'.[24] The revolutionary state had given them both a new birth and a new status as citizens.

In many cases, however, even when petitioners invoked their 'regeneration' through the actions of the legislature, they also implied that they had played an active role in it. They had not simply been given a new status; they had merited and foreseen it. Some proudly proclaimed that they had destroyed their certificates of nobility with the birth of a sans-culotte nation. For example, Jean Esnoult declared that 'I did not wait for the law to order it to burn authentically my parchments with all the disdain inspired by the tyrant who signed them and all the delights that sweet equality can procure in an honest soul'.[25] Several of those accused of criminal nobility in 1794 had been active participants in the Estates General, and emphasised that they had joined with the Third Estate at this crucial moment of the birth of the National Assembly.[26] Their incorporation into the national community was, at least partially, of their own doing.

Others did not point to a dramatic moment of transformation as proof of their status as citizens, but rather to a series of patriotic acts throughout the Revolution. Both alleged nobles and supposed enemy foreigners boasted of being in the National Guard, participating in local assemblies, being present at the *grandes journées* of the Revolution, such as the taking of the Bastille or the declaration of a republic on 10 August 1792, making patriotic donations and generally meriting certificates of civic virtue and the respect of their neighbours. They contended that they had established and proved their citizenship through their repeated acts of patriotism and political adhesion to the revolutionary nation.

Both ostensible foreigners and nobles thus sought to show that apparent titles of exclusion were actually compatible with membership of the revolutionary republic. Some supplicants, particularly alleged nobles, tacitly accepted the idea that there might have been a nascent community of citizens before the Revolution. However, they positioned themselves as part of that community. They underscored their own agency in disassociating themselves from foreign states or the 'caste of the nobility', by immigrating to the land of liberty or disdaining noble assemblies and privileges. Others explicitly used the metaphor of regeneration to argue that the Revolution had made them into good French citizens, but nonetheless emphasised that they had not simply been transformed by the power of the state; they also had a role in their own regeneration. Petitioners repeatedly articulated a model of citizenship that was not one of permanent boundaries between citizens and outsiders, but rather one of voluntary adhesion to the new nation.

THE GOVERNMENT'S RESPONSES

The Jacobin government left many petitions unanswered, in large part because the Germinal decrees were quickly overtaken by the general turmoil of the Terror. However, some responses to individual petitions have been preserved, as has a series of debates and revisions to the original law. In trying to draw clear lines between enemy foreigners or nobles and true revolutionary citizens, the government was forced to consider whether all forms of alien origin were equally staining, how apparent outsiders could be regenerated or recognised as citizens, and whether a circumscribed community of nascent citizens had actually existed before the Revolution.

In their responses, the Committee of Public Safety firmly rejected the idea that ostensible foreigners and nobles could prove their regeneration – or their life-long status as citizens – simply by describing their patriotic activities, or even having others testify to their patriotism.[27] This represented a clear shift from earlier measures. Ex-nobles who were deputies in the National Convention in 1794 could remain in place, but other forms of political participation in the nation, including participation in revolutionary uprisings or in the Estates General of 1789, did not necessarily make former nobles members of the republican nation.[28] Unlike former nobles, those born in foreign countries had been categorically forbidden to represent the French nation on 5 Nivôse Year II (25 December 1793).

Participating, or having participated, in the political institutions of the nation also no longer sufficed to make immigrants citizens. As a particularly astute immigrant, a Jamaican naturalised in France in 1790, pointed out, this policy contradicted other measures of the Terror that were still in place. The National Convention had decreed in March 1793 that those born in foreign countries were to be treated as criminally responsible for abandoning their adopted country, if they had even once 'exercised the rights of citizens in France' and then emigrated, leaving the territory of the revolutionary republic.[29] The Germinal decrees were impossible to reconcile with the March 1793 law unless the government exempted foreign-born men and women who had acted as French citizens, regardless of their birthplace; it did not do so.

Neither ex-nobles nor foreigners could definitively establish their integration into the republican nation by conforming to its social ideals. Following precedents established in earlier policing measures, the Committee of Public Safety did exempt foreign-born manual labourers and retail merchants. In some ways, the exemption for such workers was stronger than it had been previously, as such men and women no longer needed to call upon trustworthy witnesses to establish their social position, as they had in the autumn of 1793.[30] However, it was unclear whether many workers, especially servants, were included in the exemption. More importantly, the Committee quickly established that the exemption applied only to those who had worked with their hands before the autumn 1793 laws against enemy foreigners and who continued to do so, and to small-scale merchants who had been in business since before May 1789.[31] The requirement that foreigners should have opened shop before the opening days of the Estates General seems to suggest that a model of pre-revolutionary belonging or long-term cultural integration was generally replacing one of individual, political adhesion to the new nation during the Revolution itself. But although manual labour appeared the ideal means of regeneration for the parasitic caste of the nobility, the government was even stricter in its application of such exceptions to ex-nobles. Article 8 of the original decree appeared to exempt all small-scale merchants who had set up business before 1789. But within two days of the decree, the government clarified that the exception for both workers and shopkeepers applied only to foreigners.[32] As a few discovered to their horror, it did not necessarily matter if a supposed noble had been living and working as a commoner during the Revolution, or even long before it.[33]

The government did make a serious attempt to respond to petitioners and issued a number of exemptions based directly on individual circumstances.

However, it usually concentrated on the republic's needs, rather than a petitioner's claims to be a productive and loyal citizen. Article 10 of the original Germinal decree allowed the Committee of Public Safety to requisition men and women whose talents were deemed to be particularly useful to the republic. Indeed, the jurist Cambacérès would later take credit for the policy of requisitioning such individuals, claiming that Robert-Lindet had used it to save 1,500 people from banishment.[34] Those granted individual permissions to stay in Paris and other forbidden sites often had jobs that made them beneficial to the nation at war, including employees in the postal system, doctors and self-proclaimed experts in the art of artillery.[35]

But the government also exempted many artists and intellectuals, including the well-known naturalist Lamarck; foreign-born musicians employed by the National Theatre; the widow Paviot and her daughters, responsible for illuminating maps for a national atlas; and the citizen Pangens, who despite being blind was assembling a new dictionary of the French language.[36] In one sense, these requisitions are not surprising: the class of 'former nobles' included many of the educated members of society, while foreigners involved with the arts were particularly likely to have travelled to France's cultural centre despite – or potentially because of – revolutionary upheavals. Such exceptions nonetheless reveal an ironic twist to the government's reluctance to consider voluntary adhesion to a community of citizens. Ex-nobles and foreigners were excluded from the political institutions and centres of the revolutionary republic – but nonetheless permitted to remain part of the national community in order to produce the plays and pictures that shaped the political culture of the new nation.[37]

In general, the Committee tried to respond to petitioners' supplications not by deciding case by case – a practical impossibility given the hundreds of frantic responses to the decree – but by issuing revisions to the law clarifying who was considered to be criminally foreign or noble and by explicitly exempting various categories of people. These changes are particularly revealing of the central government's judgements about whether all brands of alien origin were equally damning; they also reveal a key distinction between foreigners and nobles. In the case of enemy foreigners, the lines distinguishing them from the French were not completely read backwards into the days before the Revolution. However, as we have seen, the government also refused to credit individual foreigners' claims to have regenerated themselves or to have become part of the revolutionary nation through their own initiative. Instead, most exceptions confirmed new groups of 'French' citizens – or at least tolerated outsiders – which had been created by the state earlier in the Revolution. The Committee thus explicitly exempted immigrants who came from conquered territories and who had been pronounced French at the time their homelands were assimilated to France. Another exemption for *religionnaires fugitifs* confirmed a 1790 law that had granted the full rights of citizenship. A third major exception aimed at Dutch political refugees in France. Although they were not considered technically French, they had been welcomed as fellow-revolutionaries in 1790.[38] Most of these categories of transformed foreigners had already been granted exemptions from earlier policing measures.

Since nobility as a whole had been abolished in 1790, it was impossible for the revolutionary government to refer to sub-categories of nobles proclaimed to be part of the nation during the Revolution. Instead, the Committee of Public Safety turned to the *ancien régime*. Couthon originally wanted to extend the definition of 'noble' to include all those who had sought noble titles, proclaiming on 28 Germinal that the law equated with nobles 'those who without being noble according to the ideas and rules of the *ancien régime*, usurped or bought the titles or privileges of nobility, or those who pleaded or fabricated false titles'.[39] Such a definition stressed both the possibility of a nascent community of true citizens and a certain kind of voluntary citizenship – or rather voluntary anti-citizenship – over legal membership in the caste of nobles.

But within a day of the original decree, Couthon reported that 'countless claims' had reached the committee. He had begun to believe that the definition of noble had been extended too far, for 'those who only held for an instant the privileges of an ennobling charge should not be assimilated to those who for centuries outraged the people with their pride and insolence'.[40] In a controversial decision, the government ultimately exempted those nobles whose status was most ambiguous, men and women who had had the title of *écuyer* and those who had purchased a noble office, but only held it for a short period of time.[41] It again emphasised formal status over voluntary belonging, although the exception for *anoblis*, those who had become nobles, was not devoid of moral and political content. Those who had acquired such offices could be seen as most reprehensible, since their nobility appeared to be the result of personal ambition rather than an 'accident' of birth. But they could also be seen as most acceptable, since public service in the *ancien régime* had been intimately tied to the system of ennobling offices. Echoing the claims made by various *échevins*, Robespierre argued that there were ennobling offices that nonetheless 'had useful functions, magistrates necessary to social order'.[42]

Moreover, those who had held an office for a few months or years could be considered as less shaped by the prejudices of the *ancien régime* than the *noblesse de race*. The Committee eventually accepted pre-revolutionary logic: it had taken twenty years for commoners to become nobles, and thus lose their membership in the larger community of citizens – the flip side of the idea contained in the Germinal decrees that twenty years of residence in French territory before the Revolution (or at least before 1794) were required for immigrants to be considered French. There may have been an implicit community of citizens before the Revolution, but the time lag required for *anoblis* to become nobles meant that the boundaries of this community were blurred.

NATIONALITY, CITIZENSHIP AND REVOLUTIONARY REGENERATION

Every attempt by the government to establish definitive boundaries between citizens and outsiders ultimately inspired new questions and pleas. As in the course of the Revolution as a whole, it proved impossible to distinguish clearly between revolutionary citizens and their enemies. The analytical categories of 'nationality' and 'citizenship' can help us understand why it was difficult for the government to establish such divisions. Both terms are anachronisms as regards the Revolution, but we might use 'nationality' to refer to juridical membership in a national community and 'citizenship' as the exercise of political rights.[43] Allegedly foreign petitioners emphasised their legal claims to French nationality when it seemed advantageous to do so. Men and women who had been made French by the state stressed such claims with particular force, whether they had been individually naturalised during the *ancien régime*, or, in the more common case of *religionnaires fugitifs* and those born in conquered territories, collectively proclaimed to be French. Similarly, ex-nobles pointed to official documents, such as letters of *dérogeance*, to prove that they were commoners.

To further their cause, some alleged foreigners emphasised their cultural Frenchness, as did a twenty-five-year-old German woman who declared that 'she never knew her parents or any other Prussians and doesn't speak the language'.[44] But even when petitioners pointed to their long residence and cultural assimilation in France they often reiterated that they had acted as citizens, as did the artist Hubert who proclaimed that his family's ' long residence in France brought them all the rights of French citizens, and all the duties, which they have always zealously fulfilled'.[45] Indeed, both supposed foreigners and nobles repeatedly cited examples of their social, and especially their political, participation in the new republic. While they often tried to rationalise apparent markers of exclusion, they also high-lighted their own agency in 'regenerating' themselves both before and during the Revolution. In so doing, they articulated a model of voluntary adhesion to the revolutionary nation over one of ascribed status or criminal origin – citizenship rather than nationality.

The government was itself caught between conflicting models of national citizenship. The legitimacy of the nation rested on the principle of regeneration and on active participation in the state; many of the members of the government felt compelled to recognise this. In some cases, members of the Committee of Public Safety and the National Convention formally acknowledged the importance of individual adhesion to the revolutionary nation or to an alien community, as when they initially extended the term 'noble' to all those who had assumed noble titles regardless of the formal legitimacy of those titles during the *ancien régime*. At the same time, the fact that ex-nobles were allowed to remain in the National Convention – while they were excluded from other sites of popular sovereignty – suggests that not all apparent outsiders were to be branded by their origin.

But it appeared too easy for men and women to use the language of citizenship and regeneration to claim membership of the nation, and abuse their membership to pervert the course of the Revolution. The central government thus wanted to draw clear lines between citizens and enemies. But such lines could not be drawn while using a model of contractual, political adhesion to the revolutionary nation that suggested that anyone could become part of a community of citizens at any point – and that they could do so of their own volition. The government thus did not auto-matically exempt foreigners or nobles who could prove that they had 'acted as citizens', often turning instead to the criteria of nationality, and attempt-ing to project divisions backwards to a nascent community of citizens that had existed before the birth of the Revolution itself. Yet this community itself proved difficult to define.

In establishing the Germinal decree, the government of the Terror thus sought to mark out and purge the body politic of men and women whose titles of 'nationality' in an alien community branded them as potentially dangerous to the revolutionary community of citizens. Petitioners funda-mentally challenged the closure of a national community, asserting their own acts of citizenship both before and during the Revolution. Wanting to respond to the hundreds of petitions that it received, the government recognised the credibility of some of these claims – while still trying to control who was marked as an outsider. It ultimately proved impossible to reconcile a decree that branded people in terms of their alien and immutable origin with an ideology lauding popular regeneration.

EPILOGUE

The model of contractual, voluntary adhesion to the nation championed by alleged nobles and enemy foreigners would become the model of republican citizenship in nineteenth-century France. Indeed, scholars have frequently, if often simplistically, compared it to an 'ethnic' model of German nationhood.[46] Yet this republican model would also be instituted in a very different way than it had been during the Terror. While the 'nation' was often conceptualised in social terms, 'nationality' and 'nobility' would rarely be thought together again as closely as they were in 1794. 'Pre-modern' and 'modern' categories would also rarely be so closely juxtaposed, in part because the imagined origin and composition of the nation changed. In the immediate aftermath of the Terror, 'regeneration' itself became a suspect word, one that implied destruction rather than stability and essential respect for history.[47] No subsequent political regime would found itself on as dramatic a rupture with the past. Even later revolutionary movements drew on the history of the French Revolution itself, while the Napoleonic era established an administrative continuity in defining nationality which would persist throughout the century. Because later governments did not break publicly and fully with past categories of membership in the nation, as the radical republic of 1794 had done, they also did not need to confront systematically the tensions between the legacies of earlier categories and their own definitions.

The model of contractual adhesion was also limited and re-shaped in other ways. The extreme version of regeneration, in which individuals decided for themselves if they were members of a community of citizens, was never realisable; no government is willing to completely relinquish authority over defining members of the polity. Subsequent regimes openly acknowledged such limits; they praised the reciprocal nature of a contract between the state and would-be-members of the nation, while emphasising the state's role in identifying and selecting those members. Changes in naturalisation law suggest one aspect of this transition: in the *ancien régime*, naturalisation had been essentially automatic if applicants fulfilled the correct procedures and paid enough; in the Napoleonic and post-Napoleonic eras, naturalisation required intense scrutiny of applicants and a real possibility of rejection. Later governments would also perpetuate the revolutionary version of 'republican universalism', in which no group or corporate body (whether that of nobility, or a formally constituted ethnic or cultural community) was supposed to stand between individual and the state. Yet the state would nonetheless repeatedly assert its own ability to identify such groups, often reviving and adapting revolutionary claims to do so in the name of the interests of the nation as a whole.

NOTES

1 One of the most influential formulations is Rogers Brubaker, *Citizenship and Nationhood in France and Germany* (Cambridge University Press, 1992).

2 Few historians have examined the law, and to my knowledge, none has considered the comparative status or reactions of nobles and foreigners. Sophie Wahnich has analysed the text of the law as it pertained to foreigners, while Michael Rapport has briefly explored how it was applied to them. Patrice Higonnet has considered some responses to the law from alleged nobles, but passes over them quickly in a general attempt to assess the role of 'anti-noble ideology' in a revolutionary class struggle. Wahnich, *L'impossible citoyen: l'étranger dans le discours de la Révolution Française* (Paris: Albin Michel, 1997); *Nationality and Citizenship in Revolutionary France: The Treatment of Foreigners 1789–1799* (Oxford University Press, 2000); Higonnet, *Class, Ideology, and the Rights of Nobles during the French Revolution* (Oxford: Clarendon Press, 1981).

3 William Sewell, 'The French Revolution and the emergence of the nation form', in Michael Morrison and Melinda Zook (eds.), *Revolutionary Currents: Transatlantic Ideology and Nationbuilding, 1688–1821* (Lanham, MD: Rowman & Littlefield, 2004).

4 Mona Ozouf, 'Regeneration', in François Furet and Mona Ozouf (eds.), *A Critical Dictionary of the French Revolution* (Cambridge, MA: Harvard University Press, 1989), pp. 781–89.

5 Most documents are in the Archives Nationales (hereafter AN) DIII–373 through DIII–377; a few more are scattered throughout the DIII series. AN AFII 61–2 contain the texts of supplementary decrees and exceptions, judgements on individual cases and some additional petitions and reports.

6 Higonnet, *Class, Ideology and the Rights of Nobles*, pp. 127–8.

7 See AN AD I 87 for the original texts of decrees; for analyses of laws and policies, Wahnich, *L'impossible citoyen*, Albert Mathiez, *La révolution et les étrangers: cosmopolitisme et défense nationale* (Paris: La Renaissance du livre, 1918), and Rapport, *Nationality and Citizenship*.

8 Mathiez, *La révolution et les étrangers*, p. 161.

9 *Archives Parlementaires* (henceforward AP), 88: 621.

10 Wahnich, *L'impossible citoyen*, pp. 231–2.

11 Some petitioners explicitly referred to exceptions in previous decrees, e.g. Lecomte in AN DIII-376. General police measures also often demanded that citizens prove their patriotism; a law which preceded the Germinal decree by a month, 13 Ventôse Year II (3 March 1794), decreed that any arrested person who sought his or her freedom had to describe his or her revolutionary conduct since 1 May 1789.

12 AN DIII–377.

13 Colin Campbell in AN DIII–373 and M. A. Lesvis in AN DIII–376.

14 AN DIII–376.

15 AN DIII–373.

16 Dossier for Marguerite Lynch, AN DIII–376.

17 I am indebted to Peter Sahlins for reminding me of this point. See also Marguerite Vanel, *Evolution historique de la notion de Français d'origine du XVI siècle au code civil* (Paris: Imprimerie de la cour d'appel, 1944).

18 For an analysis of *ancien régime* elites and the mechanisms of ennoblement and social advancement, see Colin Lucas, 'Nobles, bourgeois, and the origins of the French Revolution', *Past and Present* 60 (1973), 84–126 and David Bien, 'Manufacturing nobles: the chancelleries in France until 1789', *Journal of Modern History* 61 (1989), 445–86.

19 AN DIII–373.

20 William Doyle, *Venality: The Sale of Offices in Eighteenth-Century France* (Oxford: Clarendon Press, 1996).

21 AN DIII–373.

22 AN DIII–376.

23 Florence Bellivier and Laurence Boudouard, 'Des droits par les bâtards: l'enfant naturel dans les débats révolutionnaires', in Irène Théry and Christian Biet (eds.), *La famille, la loi, l'état de la Révolution au Code Civil* (Paris: Imprimerie nationale, 1989), pp. 122–46.

24 AN DIII–375.

25 Ibid.

26 Dossier Bastin, AN DIII–373.

27 The one exception, that of 8 Floréal, was for citizens born in countries with which the republic was at war, who had been driven out for having refused loyalty oaths demanded by 'tyrants'.

28 AP, 88: 621.

29 AN DIII–373; Marcel Ragon, *La législation sur les émigrés, 1789–1825* (Paris: Arthur Rousseau, 1904).

30 Compare Article 2 of 6 September 1793 with the Germinal decree.

31 Legislators were concerned that foreigners could otherwise find friends who would 'lend' them stores to exempt them (AP, 89: 30). But while such concerns justified the need for foreigners to have been in business before the Germinal law, they do not explain why such foreigners were required to have opened shop before the earliest days of the Revolution.

32 AP, 89: 30.

33 AN DIII–375.

34 Cambacérès, *Mémoires inédits: Eclarcissements publiés par Cambacérès sur les principaux événements de sa politique* (2 vols., Paris: Perrin, 1999), vol. 1, p. 220.

35 There were occasional exceptions, like that of Madeline Beauvollier, a noble-born girl adopted by a sans-culotte family who was allowed to stay and help her ailing parents: AN AF II–61.

36 Ibid.

37 The Committee of Public Safety did not argue that such men and women helped shape revolutionary political culture, but petitioners presented them-selves as doing so, as did playwright Mercier Lacoste (AN DIII–376).

38 The Committee exempted men and women from the *pays réunis* and Batavian refugees on 6 Floréal Year II (25 April 1794). *Religionnaires fugitifs* were first welcomed on 15 December 1790, and exempted from the Germinal decree on 8 Floréal (27 April). Several Jewish petitioners also tried to take advantage of this exemption, presenting themselves as *religionnaires fugitifs* from despotic nations, but appear to have met with little success.

39 AP, 88: 711.

40 AP, 89: 28–80.

41 AP, 88: 711 and 89: 28–30 and for a summary of the debates on venal office holders, Higonnet, *Class, Ideology and the Rights of Nobles,* pp. 153–4.

42 AP, 89: 30.

43 Gérard Noiriel, 'Socio-histoire d'un concept. Les usages du mot nationalité au XIX siècle', *Genèses* 20 (1995), 4–43; Dominique Godineau, 'Femmes en citoyenneté: pratique et politique', *Annales Historiques de la Révolution Française* 300 (1995), 197–707.

44 Dossier for Guillerault, AN DIII–375.

45 Ibid.

46 See especially Brubaker, *Citizenship and Nationhood,* and Patrick Weil's critique of such comparisons in *Qu'est-ce qu'un Français? Histoire de la nation-alité française depuis la révolution* (Paris: Grasset, 2002).

47 My thanks to Alyssa Sepinwall for this observation, which she explains in further detail in *The Abbé Grégoire, the French Revolution, and the Making of Modern Universalism* (Berkeley: University of California Press, forthcoming).

CHAPTER 13

Nation, nations and power in Italy, c. 1700–1915

Stuart Woolf

HISTORIANS AND THE ITALIAN NATION

The mainstream of the political historiography of European states, from the middle of the nineteenth century to the middle of the twentieth (and often beyond), reads the history of the nation's past through the filter of the final outcome of the nation-state. The 'Prussian school' has attracted particular attention, and indeed it exemplifies the untroubled coexistence of a historicism that exalted the state and the affirmation of a 'scientific' historical methodology in tune with the gospel of positivism.[1] But whether their approach to history was 'Romantic' or scientific, national pride and the certainty of progress constituted central elements in the cultural *habitus* of European intellectuals, which underpinned the writing of the history of the individual states, old as well as new. Although they were more marked in newly unified states, the historians of old national states shared the same convictions, and – like François Guizot or John Seeley – facilely read into them national missions.[2]

In a comparative European context, Italian historiography in this respect is in no way exceptional. From the earliest decades after unification until the fall of fascism, from Nicomede Bianchi and Alessandro Luzio to Pietro Silva and Gioacchino Volpe, historians interpreted the country's history as possessing an unbroken continuity across the centuries, expressed through the presence of an Italian nation, alongside and usually incorporated in the Savoy dynasty, culminating in pre-ordained fashion in a unified independent state (and, for Volpe, in fascism). An aspect of such interpretations, fundamental in the narration of the Risorgimento, was to downplay the intensity of the divisions that set national leaders and movements against each other in their projects and practices, whether over the appropriate method for achieving independence – diplomacy or revolution, liberal reforms or neoguelphism – or over the institutional and administrative form appropriate for the future state – republic or kingdom, centralised or federal. Until after the 1848–9 revolutions, there was certainly no reason for collaboration between the liberal proponents of reforms and the Mazzinians' schemes for republican national unity; at most, by the 1840s Mazzini's intensive propaganda gradually tinged liberal projects with a 'national' colouring. But such incompatibility was played down in the official canon, in which the successful conclusion of the Risorgimento consecrated recognition of the need to overcome differences in the superior cause of national unity. The interpretation of an underlying concord was first expressed fully during the years of Francesco Crispi's leadership of Italy, between the 1880s and the defeat of Adua in 1896. As the canonical version gained substance, the heavy price paid for rivalries and divisions could be brought in as a long-term explanation of Italian history, with Machiavelli and Guicciardini cited as authoritative sources and witnesses of Italy's loss of its political independence.[3]

Throughout nineteenth- and twentieth-century Europe nationalist leaders and movements – from Greece or Belgium to Rumania or Poland – disagreed, usually bitterly, both on how to achieve independence and on the shape that the new state should take. Perhaps the sole exception to so peremptory a generalising statement is Norway, where, in the two decades that were to lead to its independence in 1905, there were differences over the best way to achieve independence, but parliamentary democracy – the institutional form of the state set in place with the passage of sovereignty from Denmark to Sweden in 1815 – was never in question.[4] The projects for independence in the different states were not just competitive but incompatible, as John Breuilly insists, precisely because they embodied political struggles for power.[5] This was certainly true of the Risorgimento and of the post-Risorgimento history of Italy.

The divisions and animosity between the nationalist movements before (or at least until the final passage to) independence were not necessarily more accentuated in Italy than, for example, in Germany. Rather, the differences must be located in the relative strength of the two new states and, consequentially, of the policies that their leaders were able to adopt, once independence had been obtained. In Italy, the 'cultural consequences' of the 1848 revolutions were to widen the basis of support for the different projects and movements, which ultimately was to benefit Cavour's liberal Piedmontese solution and its propagation in the peninsula by the National Society.[6] But the achievement of independence and unity in Italy only momentarily obtained a groundswell of support comparable to that accompanying Bismarck's successive wars; in any case, the unification of Italy under the Savoy dynasty could not be appropriated as an exclusive success by Cavour, given that its territorial achievement in 1860, through the inclusion of the kingdom of the Two Sicilies, was the spectacularly visible success of the swashbuckling republican general Garibaldi.

In the new Germany, Bismarck's power was incommensurably greater than that of Cavour and his successors, as was demonstrated in the *Kulturkampf* and the political exclusion of the socialist party from the body of the nation. The dominant political class in Italy – that of the moderate liberals – was always weaker, not merely in a narrow parliamentary definition of politics, but in the practices of administration and at the level of symbols. The liberals were incapable of transforming their project into reality, not least because their pressing worry over the fragility of the new state conflicted with their liberal ideals.[7] Bruno Tobia has illustrated the telling difficulties in forging a unified nation through the symbolism of monuments. On the one hand, the nation-wide pilgrimage of the people to the memorial to Victor Emanuel II (1884), a remarkable feat of popular mobilisation, appeared to vindicate the assumption that the crown was capable of reconciling and unifying the nation. On the other, the successful obstructionism of the democratic and republican opposition at Milan to the erection of a statue to Napoleon III, Italy's military ally in the successful war of independence in 1859–60, provided a forceful reminder that the struggles of the Risorgimento had carried through into unitarian Italy: the deep emotive commitments of the struggle for independence had been transferred to political parties whose historical memories remained essential to their moral and political patrimony.[8] There is no need to insist further on the multiple structural and political reasons for the weaknesses of the Italian state, compared to Germany, as its politicians, urban elites and intellectuals actively engaged in a prolonged effort of nation-building.[9]

From the earliest years, a sense of disillusion with unified Italy, after the heroic *epos* of the Risorgimento, was a characteristic of the historiography. Denunciation of the 'failure' of Italy to live up to its nascent promise is a recurrent theme that surfaces with regularity, particularly at moments of marked political crisis. In its most extreme forms, disillusion, disgust or despair generated a sort of 'anti-history', the mirror-image of the complacent official teleological narrations, in which Italy's 'destiny' was its failure to live up to successive challenges. Indeed, this negative counterpart to the canonical interpretation could assume the status of an interpretative canon of Italian history, analogous to the historiographical *Sonderweg* whipping-boy applied to Germany.

The fact that such Italian 'anti-histories' can claim a far older genealogy than the *Sonderweg* debate is in itself indicative of the weakness of the

process of formation of the new Italian state compared to Germany: the
Sonderweg reinterpretation of German history is essentially dependent on
the historical experiences of nazism and the two world wars and hence
historiographically only emerged in the later twentieth century. Even
more telling, whereas the *Sonderweg* theme of the peculiarities of the
German path to unity takes the theme back, at the earliest, to the nineteenth century,[10] proponents of Italy's 'failure' argued the case over a
much longer period, as if it was part of the DNA of the Italian nation;
and they could call upon distinguished predecessors, such as Machiavelli,
for whom the presence of the papal state was responsible for Italy's
disunity. The earliest post-unity denunciations – against the 'barbarism'
of the primitive south – carried an implicit denial of the nationalist assumption of the existence of an Italian nation and cast doubt on
the possibilities of creating such a nation (which by definition carried the
connotations of European civilisation and modernity), at least within the
foreseeable future. Periodically, at moments of major crisis, such negative
re-readings of Italy's past re-surfaced – following the aborted semi-military
coup of 1898; with the disastrous defeat of Caporetto in 1917; with the
breakdown of democracy and Mussolini's seizure of power; among dis-
illusioned fascists with the collapse of the regime; with the failure of the
Italian Republic to live up to the ideals of the Resistance.[11] The sense of
an intimate and direct relationship between the past and the present is
unusually strong in Italy, compared to most western countries, and cannot
be separated from the intensity of the antagonisms that have characterised
the political history of united Italy, in which divisive memories persisted,
reinforcing the diffidence and sense of impotence on the occasion of each
new crisis.

Two aspects of the mental assumptions of Italian elites, both during
the Risorgimento and subsequently, merit note. First, whatever the
conflictuality that was an intrinsic part of the Risorgimento, its patriotic
exponents, whether moderate or Mazzinian, imagined and represented
the Italian nation as 'holistic, compact and organicist'.[12] Second, for the
Risorgimento patriots (of all political colourings), as for the critics and
opponents of the successive institutional forms of government (republicans, democrats, socialists, anti-fascists), it was essential for Italy as a
nation-state to progress, if she was to retain (or regain) her place in
Europe, synonymous with civilisation. In this sense, the very concept
of the nation was welded to a broader and more comprehensive ideal,
against which the inadequacies of the Italian people (and/or their governments) were set in relief.

THE CONSTITUENT ELEMENTS OF THE ITALIAN NATION

Until literary theory became influential in cultural studies (from the 1980s), many historians were less sensitive than linguists to the changes in meaning and significance of words and texts, according to context and period. In a recent book that has properly attracted much attention, Alberto Banti has argued a strong case about the Italian nation imagined by Risorgimento elites, on the basis of the memoirs of thirty-three political and cultural figures born between 1783 and 1843.[13] His starting point is the rupture in discourse brought about by the so-called 'Jacobin triennium' (1796–9), when the young Napoleon and his armies brought the French Revolution to Italy. In the eighteenth century, a person's *patria* could be his *paese*, by which was understood his place of birth, or alternatively his region of origin (for example, Sicily or Savoy) or his state (Venice as both city and republic), or again larger territories customarily described as possessing common cultural features, although not constituting a political unit (Italy, Germany). A 'nation' also had different meanings. It could still refer (by now an archaic usage) specifically to family or social origin and descent or, more commonly, by extension, to 'generations of men born in the same province or city':[14] in this latter sense, it had already acquired a collective significance, to describe the customs and practices of a people that distinguished them from other peoples in different territorial areas. There was no necessary coincidence with the territorial boundaries of political states, and the term was employed equally to describe 'nations' within a state (Piedmontese, Neapolitans and so on) and those that included various states (the Italian or German 'nation'). Throughout the eighteenth century, probably starting with the *savant* and historian Lodovico Antonio Muratori (d. 1750), 'nation' (in this instance synonymous with *patria*) also affirmed the recognised presence in the European 'république des lettres' of an Italian cultural community, identifiable through a common language and literature, as in Gian Rinaldo Carli's article 'Della patria degli italiani', published in Pietro Verri's journal *Il Caffè* in 1765.

The brief but extraordinarily intense experience of the Italian democratic republics – which was accompanied, as in France, by an explosion of pamphlets and flysheets – introduced the Revolutionary model of a political nation, 'une et indivisible'. A patriotic sense of the nation was implanted, expressed initially, in the years of Napoleonic rule, by literary figures, poets and writers such as Foscolo and Alfieri, who had lived through the Jacobin triennium. The patriots of the second generation, born between 1815 and 1843, all came from families which had participated

in either the triennium or the immediately succeeding period of
Napoleonic government in Italy (1800–14). As Banti reminds us, literature,
opera and historical paintings were notably influential in the cultural
orientation of nineteenth-century Italian elites.[15] The imaginary nation
common to these patriots (whose political positions ranged from moderate
liberals, like the D'Azeglios or Minghetti, to Mazzini and Garibaldi) was
based on kin, holiness and honour, in a discourse that attracted support
precisely because it interacted with 'other' ideologies, traditionally present
in the education or informal social relations of the youth of good upbring-
ing, and reinforced what normatively was assumed to be compact, holistic
and without divisions.[16]

Across nineteenth-century Europe, inherent in the convictions, discourse and actions of nationalist leaders and movement were two fundamental assumptions: first, that the nation was a reality that had always
existed, so that even if, over the centuries, the people had lost their self-
awareness, it was sufficient to make them (re)gain their national consciousness; secondly that the reality of the existence of the nation gave it an
inalienable right to political independence (or at least to self-government).
I wish to look more closely at the first of these assumptions, in particular at
the constituent elements that were regarded as evidence of the historical
reality of the nation.

In the European context, five such elements – language, historical
memories, territory, religion and common descent (nowadays loosely
referred to as ethnicity) – appear most frequently in nationalist discourse.
Their relative importance varied according to historical and institutional
circumstances, but, once 'coagulated' by that eternal gel of nationalism, the
(inevitable) presence of an Enemy, the sum was greater than its component
parts. Within such a comparative framework, what were the essential
constituent elements of the representation of the Italian nation during
the Risorgimento?

Language has always been central to the claims to existence of an Italian
(as of a German) nation, and properly so, given the literary reputation and
diffusion of Italian since Dante and Petrarch and its adoption in
administrative acts in the majority of Italian states since the late sixteenth–
seventeenth century. By the early nineteenth century, the attribution of
cultural-national overtones to the Italian language, expressed most influ-
entially by Alfieri, was a commonplace: the (bilingual) adolescent Cesare
Balbo cried out in despair at the imposition of French in the public sphere
following Napoleon's annexation of Piedmont (1802), and organised theat-
rical performances in Italian in the family palace.[17] In this assumption

of a national language, Italian patriots were aligned to the tradition of western national states like England, France and Spain, each with an established literary and administrative language, rather than to the 'new' nations of central, Balkan and eastern Europe, where nationally minded philologists and grammarians were obliged to standardise the written language as a necessary preliminary in their struggles for independence. That the majority of Italians did not use Italian habitually – the most recent study proposes 9.5% in 1861, in a population with only 22% literacy[18] – is not so significant, given that the political movements for independence were based on urban elites, for whom language was, at least in this period of Romanticism, one of the most powerful cohesive symbols of national identity. Indeed, at the level of European cultured circles, Italian as a language was a referent for the distinctive identity of its people, which until the late nineteenth century was upheld by the international reputation of Italian opera. Where Italy differed, to the point of throwing doubt on its capacity in nation building, was in the very slow and belated spread of primary schooling after unification, and hence in the persistent unfamiliarity with the Italian language of broad segments of the rural population – as is immediately apparent if Italy is compared to Germany.

History was obviously an equally crucial structural pillars in the edifice of the Italian nation proposed by Italian patriots. On the one hand, there was the double heritage of Rome (classical and Christian) that was claimed as evidence of the continuity and longevity of Italy's existence as a nation. On the other, classical Rome and the Renaissance provided undeniable proof of the leading role played by Italy in the onward march of European civilisation. In the enlightenment formulation of European civilisation, for example in Voltaire, the stages of progress were incorporated in 'nations', not individuals.[19] The ubiquitous visibility of its grand past – the architectural remains of ancient Rome and Magna Grecia, the buildings, paintings and artefacts of its precocious city-states and renaissance, even the medieval cathedrals and monuments that attracted attention with the Restoration 'discovery' of the Middle Ages – amounted to cumulative evidence to present to educated tourists (heirs to the Grand Tour) of the legitimacy of Italians' claim to be a 'historic nation'. Indeed, the contrast between the magnificence of the past and the decadence (and, for the English, the 'Roman' superstitions) of its current state could be put to use to exemplify the standard sequence of nationalist discourse: ancient liberty, foreign invasions and oppression, martyrdom, the right to 'resurrection' (*ri-sorgimento*), even – in its most extreme form, expressed by Mazzini and Gioberti – Italy's 'mission', predestined by reason of its past.

In two respects, the elements and role of history in the self-representation of the Italian nation differed from those of other European national movements. First, Italy's past was quintessentially an urban past – the precocious development of the communes, their transformation into city-states and then into equally urban-centred *signorie*. Contempt for the peasantry reflected the profundity of the division between the city and its *contado* that passed through the centuries.[20] Already expressed in the literary writings of the humanists of the fourteenth and fifteenth centuries, it was only tempered among the modernising liberal landowners of the nineteenth century by charitable compassion and aspirations to mould peasant obstinacy to technical progress through firm guidance. Wholly absent from Risorgimento national discourse is exaltation of the peasantry as the 'carriers' of the original purity and language of the nation, with its accompanying folkloric cult of peasant music, typical of Magyar and many other central European nationalisms. Second – and a logical counterpart to the 'expulsion' of the peasantry from the historical memory – were the exceptionally strong roots of city traditions. Civic identity, as such, was certainly not unique to Italy; it was marked in Germany, and perhaps wherever there had been a cluster of precocious urban economies (for example, in Flanders). What is particular to Italy is the exceptional number of its cities and the apparently uninterrupted sense of civic pride that led Carlo Cattaneo, the democratic leader of the Milan 1848 rising, to describe Italy as a 'country of a hundred cities' and to argue consistently for a federal structure of government (in which cities, rather than regions, would have a primary role).

Territory, so important in many central European nationalisms, was never a significant issue in Risorgimento discourse. The confines of Italy seemed self-evident, whether in terms of physical geography or of the boundaries of the pre-existing states. The issue of the incorporation of minorities within national frontiers forced itself on public awareness only belatedly in Italy, following the First World War. During the Risorgimento, the loss by the Venetian republic of its Adriatic colonial territories does not seem to have aroused particular comment; and the cession of Savoy and Nice certainly outraged the Piedmontese, but not Italian patriots from other regions.

In the European context, religion varied in its importance as an element of national consciousness. In Belgium, Slovakia, Poland or Ireland, for instance, the strong support of the Church or parish priests benefited national movements; where religious faith was divided between churches (as in Germany), its institutional expression was not a significant element, or could be highly divisive, as in the Balkans. In Italy, the role of Catholicism was important in a double sense. On the one hand, it provided the basis for the intense Romantic religiosity of the Restoration, immediately apparent in the biblical imagery (God, martyrdom, chosen people ...) of the language of the patriots. On the other, the uniqueness of Rome as the centre of the universal Church reinforced affirmations of the particular status of the Italian nation. As against this, Italy was the only European country where a national movement asserted itself at the expense of the national Church.[21] The price the new Italian state paid for despoiling the Church of its temporal rule was high: ostracism of the Italian state and boycotting of participation in national elections, which undoubtedly weakened the process of formation and consolidation of a national identity.[22] But, for Italian elites, this never placed in doubt the uniqueness that their nation derived from Rome as the papal see.

Explanations of the origins of the nation were a popular pastime in the Romantic writings of the Restoration, with Walter Scott's novels regarded as a model of historical imagination. For Voltaire, the fall of Rome had marked a prolonged period of regression during the dark ages of barbarian domination; for the Romantics, the ancient world retained its importance for European civilisation, but required the paradigm of a more positive passage from classical to a re-discovered medieval Europe that would also account for the origins of the contemporary nations. The matrix, from which national variants were derived, was a narration of the fusion between the barbarian invaders and the original peoples inhabiting the various regions of the Roman Empire. In Restoration Milan, Carlo Cattaneo, following Gian Domenico Romagnosi, argued for a continuous process of fusion between invaders and existing peoples, as well as of the enduring function of the city as the motor of progress. Alessandro Manzoni, who concurred with Scott's and Augustin Thierry's historical narration of blood and land, genealogical descent and memory, offered a variant, insisting that there had been no mixing of races: the Lombards, in suppressing the original liberty of the Italians, had initiated the secular experience of conquest by foreigners.[23] Germans could claim an additional linkage to the classical world in Fichte's affirmation of the primacy of Germans' empathetic understanding of the ancient Greeks, as language was evidence of the invisible ties that expressed the national soul, and Germans alone had conserved their original tongue against foreign invasions.[24]

Ethnicity is implicit in such discursive narrations of imaginary origins. At the practical level (which, notoriously, may have little direct relationship with discourses about national origins), the very passage of time since the barbarian invasions of Italy can be considered as at least one of the reasons for the absence of the deep ethnic divisions that marked the Balkan territories across the Adriatic. Obviously this is not, by itself, an adequate explanation of the contrasting modern history of these areas on the opposite sides of the Adriatic: in south-east Europe, the shifting Christian–Ottoman frontier and the presence of antagonistic Christian churches are certainly as important as the repeated migratory movements from the Middle Ages to the nineteenth century. But the legacy of a millennium without invading peoples settling in the peninsula meant that nineteenth-century Italy was privileged in the relative homogeneity of the peoples on its territory, with minorities essentially only on the periphery, in Sicily, Sardinia, Friuli and the Valle d'Aosta (and, most recently, in the twentieth century, in the Alto Adige). On the mainland, the Jews alone constituted a different people, most of whom had resided in Italy since the sixteenth and seventeenth centuries (in Rome, since Nero's time); despite the ghettoes and Church anti-Judaism, the integration of Jews in the Italian nation was such that they were disproportionately present and active in the Risorgimento national movements.

If these were the constituent elements of the representation of the Italian nation that in their own right could evoke emotive responses, there was no need to invent an Enemy to draw them together. Spain, France and Austria were successive foreign conquerors. After Napoleon's defeat, Austria was not only an occupying oppressor, but the mainstay and guarantor of the reactionary governments of the various Italian states that opposed not just independence, but all liberal reforms.

NATION AND NATIONS IN UNIFIED ITALY

Nobody would deny that Italy experienced a particularly prolonged process of nation-building. Arguably, the successful construction of a narrative of concord and inevitability – in itself an element of the politics of nation-building – made the weaknesses and difficulties appear more marked. But, from the outset, the liberal elites responsible for unification experienced particularly tight constraints in the process of state building. Brigandage and the military occupation of the south was an immediate and profoundly disconcerting cause for concern.[25] As Banti points out, contemporary commentators did not question that southerners were a part of the Italian nation; they ascribed the appalling conditions in which southern Italians lived to Bourbon misgovernment and corruption. But, beyond the implications for Italy's future that the profound social and economic division between northern and southern Italy made rapidly and increasingly clear, they raised doubts about what was understood by the Italian nation. In a letter to the prime minister, Cavour's proconsul, Luigi Carlo Farini, expressed his shock at his 'discovery' of the Mezzogiorno: 'But, dear friend, what sort of countries are these, Molise and Terra di Lavoro! What barbarism! Anything but Italy! This is Africa: Bedouins, compared to these dolts, are exemplars of civil virtue. What crimes and how many!'[26] The very language, the sense of being confronted by earlier, more primitive stages of society, is reminiscent of that of Napoleon's administrators. Lareintz, intendant of Ragusa in the Illyrian provinces, on coming into contact with the *morlaque* and Albanian clans, exclaimed that they were

semi-savages who can only be contained by their fear of far superior force . . . We have to deal with peoples who are too ignorant, too distant from civilisation and above all too poor to hope to be able to reach perfection suddenly and without shocks . . . their intelligence is not sufficiently developed . . . the methods of healing must be in proportion to the strength of the patient.[27]

The similarity of discourse of these two administrators half a century apart is hardly surprising, since both were based on a mental image of Europe as the culmination of progress and civilisation, to which the French *grande nation* and the Italian nation which had now rejoined Europe equally belonged.

For contemporaries, the rapid degeneration of parliamentary democracy into the clientelistic practices of 'transformism' had aborted any possibility of the 'natural' development of two broad groupings along the lines of the British party system, which was regarded by Italian liberals as an ideal model of modernity;[28] but this never called in question the Italian nation. The historiography of recent decades has increasingly stressed the weaknesses of the process of state-building in Italy. The narrow suffrage, the split loyalties of Catholic voters owing to the papal boycott of the Italian state, and fear of popular upheaval were among the political reasons for such weakness. As Lucy Riall has pointed out, the imposition of political centralisation, despite substantial reservations among liberal moderates and bitter opposition from Cattaneo and other democrats, was closely related to the administrative collapse and popular risings in the south.[29] But, from the outset, the political leadership was incapable of ensuring that its projects or policies would effectively be put into practice across the national territory, whether over the introduction of the new administrative, fiscal and judicial systems, collection of statistical information, the recruitment of literate local officials or the introduction of primary education. The Italian state lacked not only economic resources but also a modern centralised bureaucracy and adequate communication networks: the first generation of prefects saw their task as educative as much as directive of the new order.

The unification of Italy had multiple and contradictory effects on the social groups that constituted the very core of the Italian nation – the urban elites. For it created a wholly new context of power, radical but open to an exercise of influence, interference and negotiation by local notables that was far greater and centrally uncontrollable than had been possible during Napoleon's repeated re-modelling of the political geography of Italy. Compared to the established and habitual pattern of interactions between capital and territory in the previous seven states of the peninsula (eight, if Venetia is included), the nature of the relationships between centre and peripheries was fundamentally altered by the relative distances (and facility or difficulties of communications) from the successive capitals of the new state. Institutionally, the new Italy was a markedly centralised state, as had been those of Napoleon. But, unlike Napoleonic administrators, the liberal political model that legitimated the national case for independence, and the international support it received, required citizen participation and excluded, *a priori*, the authoritarian imposition of the power of the state. The use of the army was the most extreme of measures, only deployed twice: in the very first years of the life of the new state, to enforce unification in the south; and during anti-socialist panic at Milan in 1898. Although prefects and mayors were nominated by the central government, provincial and communal councillors were elected on a broader suffrage than parliamentary deputies.[30] In short, centralisation, rather than allowing a process of state-building imposed from above, encouraged an ever more consolidated relationship of interdependence and interaction, on a continuous basis, between governments and local elites, expressed sometimes (particularly in the south) as resistance, more habitually as compromise and negotiation: on the part of government, not merely to control votes at elections, but to render feasible the enactment of policies in a host of fields; on the part of local notables, as an exercise of power and to obtain personal benefits. Compared to France or Germany, modernisation and industrialisation occurred later in Italy (between the 1880s and the Giolittian years), and with marked territorial disjunctures. Such major processes of change unquestionably exerted pressure on existing social and class relations, to which the rapid growth of the Italian socialist party in northern and central Italy bore witness; but their relative tardiness had given adequate time for patterns of centre–periphery interaction to sink roots, of which clientelism and transformism formed an integral part.

If such is the general context, it is opportune to return to the specific issue of the Italian nation. Debating whether Italians share a national identity has become a popular sport in Italy in recent years, particularly since the political success of a party (the Lega Nord) in breaking the taboo about the inviolability of the Italian nation-state.[31] In historical terms, political unification created the institutional framework and conditions for a prolonged process of nation-building. But, paradoxically, unification also strengthened self-awareness and encouraged the invention of pre-existing self-identifications that could be deployed in the discourse of the public sphere, primarily as an expression of a convergent and inter-dependent relationship with the Italian nation, but also as alternatives to it, that claimed genealogical legitimation in terms of their historical, juridical or linguistic precedence in terms of state, dynastic or territorial usages.

However strong the sense of pride among those who had participated in or supported the political movements that had culminated in unification, this did not produce any automatic abandonment of previous territorial loyalties. In some instances there was a strong and probably growing sense of loss, particularly among the elites of regions – and their capitals – that had played the leading role in the now defunct states. Such was supremely the case for the Piedmontese, who not only forfeited their position as the dominant 'nation' of the former Sardinian state, but were now also deprived of their capital as the price paid by their sovereign to become the king of the new nation-state.[32] (The federal solution imposed by Bismarck a decade later allowed Prussians to have their German national cake without eating Prussia – a further indicator of Italy's relative weakness). The ambivalence about whether the Piedmontese nation had been absorbed within the Italian nation was epitomised by the king himself in his insistence on maintaining his former Sardinian title as Victor Emanuel II and his tendency to speak Piedmontese and French (the two most widely used languages of his former state) rather than Italian.

The Piedmontese had the very substantial compensation of the career prospects opened up by the new Italian state (analogous to the attractions of the British empire for Scots). But for the Sicilians, whose separateness as a nation had been denied with the creation of the Kingdom of the Two Sicilies in 1815 and whose revolution against Naples in 1848 had centred as much on the re-acquisition of their rights as an independent kingdom as on the common Italian cause, unified Italy was increasingly lived as a frustration or a humiliation.[33] For the Piedmontese, as for the Sicilians, the basis for their affirmation of their own identity as a nation – not in contrast to but alongside their membership of the Italian nation – derived from their previous history as a state, or (for the former) as the dominant regional nation among the multiple nationalities typical of a dynastic state. The same was true of Venetians, whose Italian patriotism – both in 1848–9 and after they became part of the Italian nation in 1866 – was suffused with an instinctive sense of the naturalness of their particular identity deriving from the glorious past of their ancestors as privileged citizens (irrespective of class) of the thousand-year-old Republic of Venice.[34] Unification could heighten the intensity of the assertion of regional identity, where previously it had existed among the elite primarily as a generic sense of cultural belonging, based on history or language. The indignant reaction to a proposal made by an excessively enthusiastic (Piedmontese) Italophile that French be replaced by Italian as the official language in the Valle d'Aosta symbolically marks the political birth of a Valdostan nation.[35] In this minute Alpine region, the insistence of the local elite and clergy that the Valdostans were a nation never conflicted with their affirmations of loyalty to the Savoy dynasty and hence to Italy; in practice, such claims were simply ignored – at least until the collapse of fascism – by the Italian ruling class which widely and rhetorically trumpeted the military valour of the Valdostans as proof of their national loyalty. It would be possible (albeit highly artificial) to draw up a spectrum of the emotive appeal now exerted by such pre-existing identities within the pre-unitary Italian states in the early decades of the new Italy: at the opposite extreme to the Piedmontese and Venetians would be the citizens of the former duchies of Parma and Modena or of papal Emilia or the Austrian Veneto; in between, the Romagnols and Lombards.

But unification could also generate contrasting responses, constructing new political identities with a popular base out of opposition to the existence of the upstart 'legal' Italy. In the former Kingdom of Naples, where previously the only 'Neapolitan nation' had been the citizens of the capital, the hitherto reviled Bourbon dynasty became the rallying cry of an anti-unitarian Neapolitan nation that now broadened outwards to include peasants from various areas of the countryside.[36]

It is difficult to gauge the social and cultural implications of such affirmations of regional or local identity, particularly in a country where literary and colloquial reference to one's *paese* were (and remain) common-place in social relations and discourse. It is unlikely that there has ever been an abrupt discontinuity in Italians' pride in their real or adopted birthplace or region. At least since unification, the term *paese* has assumed the eighteenth-century multiple meanings of *patria*.[37] In this 'country of a hundred cities', it is not surprising that, in the early decades of united Italy, civic rather than regional identity was most marked, given that so many Italian towns were imprinted in their architecture and topography with the evidence of their past, whereas provinces had replaced historic regions in the administrative geography of the new Italian nation.[38] From the outset, the urban elites, particularly of the great historic capitals such as Florence, Rome, Milan and Venice, stressed the contribution of their city to the history and culture of the Italian nation, as if they were building bricks in the composite construction of the new nation-state. By the 1880s there was a sense of amicable rivalry between urban elites to demonstrate the essential tie between their civic pasts and national patriotic history, in the revivalist restoration of monuments considered illustrative of the historic high points of their past, in the erection of statues and the renaming of streets to local and national heroes and martyrs.[39] Such demonstrations of patriotic enthusiasm through local identities, which were common to French and German urban elites in the decades until the First World War,[40] were the practical expression of what was seen as the natural and essential relationship of the *petites patries* to the *grande patrie*. Initially, following unification, civic identity, which has been the instinctive assumption of an emotive conviction, soon commuted into the sentimental portmanteau of proper middle-class values; with the added value, in a context of representative democracy, of serving the local elites, whether old or new, as political instruments for obtaining, extending or consolidating their influence and prestige.

Where Italy differed from France or Germany was in the relative weakness of the Italian state. In France, the deep-rooted tradition of state centralisation, reinforced by the Third Republic's effective policies of nation-building, had erased, or at the very least diluted, the regional nationalism of the *ancien régime*, and firmly subordinated pride in civic identity to prefectoral control. In Germany, the Prussian-military-dominated state enveloped and relegated the regional and civic pride that had been guaranteed institutionally by the new federal political structure and socially by ancient urban traditions. In Italy, the relative tardiness in forging a national identity that would be instinctively recognised as superior to that of former, more delimited territories is strikingly clear in the self-identification with their *paese* or region of the vast numbers of Italian emigrants who left the southern and mountainous regions of Italy for the Americas.[41] But among the elites in the decades before the war, included in their common values, alongside family and religion, figured an unusually strong coexistence of different levels of collective loyalties, between *paese*, city, region and Italian nation: at one level, *torinesi* identified themselves as different from other Piedmontese, Venetians from *veneti*, Florentines from Sienese or Pisans, citizens of Palermo from those of Messina and both from Sicilian peasants; at another, when circumstances were appropriate, Piedmontese stressed their differences from Lombards, Tuscans from Umbrians, Neapolitans from Sicilians, northerners from southerners. No contradiction existed between such pride in local identities and the shared sense of forming part of the Italian nation.

Weakness of the state, by itself, nevertheless remains an inadequate explanation. Language and history reinforced and legitimated the expression of regional – and intra-regional – differences between Italians. For a century after unification, Italy was perhaps unusual in the number and continuous usage of its dialects,[42] which in some regions (like the Valle d'Aosta, Alto Adige, Sardinia, Sicily, Friuli or, most recently, the Veneto) were subsequently at the core of their political claims as regional nations. Alongside dialects, the ubiquitous visibility and exceptional importance in the Italian urban landscape and museums of material evidence of Italy's past offered historical support to Italians' conviction of their single and multiple identities, reinforced (in their view) by the canonical European representation of Italy's cultural contribution to civilisation. It needed the First World War and, even more, the insensitive state nationalism of the fascist regime with its insistence on the uniformity of the Italian nation to lead to the emergence of political regional movements – initially in Sardinia after the First World War, with the fall of fascism in other frontier regions of the country – that put to good use their historical and linguistic claims to obtain institutional and material entitlements as 'special regions' in recognition of their particular status as minority nations within the Italian nation.[43] The institutional introduction of regional administrations across the national territory (belatedly, a quarter of a century after their inclusion in the Italian republic's constitution), and the spread of well-funded offices for sponsorship of cultural activities (*assessorati alla cultura*) at all local government levels (communal, provincial and regional) have led, since the 1970s, to the funding of a generalised revivalism of regional and civic cultural traditions – and regional gastronomy – in tune with the exponential growth of tourism. But that is another story.

NOTES

1   Georg Iggers, *The German Conception of History: The National Tradition of Historical Thought from Herder to the Present* (Middletown: Wesleyan

University Press, 1968). For a perceptive recent discussion see Effi Gazi, '*Scientific' National History: The Greek Case in Comparative Perspective (1850–1920)* (Frankfurt am Main: Peter Lang, 2000), ch. 2.

2 François Guizot, *Histoire de la civilisation en Europe depuis la chute de l'Empire romain jusqu'à la Révolution française* (Paris: Didier, 1846); John R. Seeley, *The Expansion of England* (London: Macmillan, 1883).

3 Ilaria Porciani, 'Stato e nazione: l'immagine debole dell'Italia', in Simonetta Soldani and Gabriele Turi (eds.), *Fare gli italiani. Scuola e cultura nell'Italia contemporanea* (2 vols., Bologna: Il Mulino, 1993), vol. I, *La nascita dello stato nazionale*, pp. 385–428.

4 T. K. Derry, *A History of Modern Norway 1814–1972* (Oxford University Press, 1973).

5 John Breuilly, *Nationalism and the State* (Manchester University Press, 1982, 2nd edn. 1993).

6 Lucy Riall, *The Italian Risorgimento. State, Society and National Unification* (London and New York: Routledge, 1994), especially ch. 5; Raymond Grew, *A Sterner Plan for Italian Unity: The Italian National Society in the Risorgimento* (Princeton University Press, 1963).

7 Claudio Pavone, *Amministrazione centrale e amministrazione periferica. Da Rattazzi a Ricasoli (1859–1866)* (Milan: Giuffrè, 1964); Raffaele Romanelli, *Il comando impossibile: stato e società nell'Italia liberale* (Bologna: Il Mulino, 1988); idem (ed.), *Storia dello Stato italiano dall'Unità a oggi* (Rome: Donzelli, 1995); Nico Randeraad, *Authority in Search of Liberty: The Prefects in Liberal Italy* (Amsterdam: Thesis Publishers, 1993); Silvana Patriarca, *Numbers and Nationhood: Writing Statistics in Nineteenth-Century Italy* (Cambridge University Press, 1996).

8 Bruno Tobia, *Una patria per gli italiani. Spazi, itinerari, monumenti nell'Italia unita (1870–1900)* (Bari and Rome: Laterza, 1991); Maurizio Ridolfi, *Le feste nazionali* (Bologna: Il Mulino, 2003), ch. 1.

9 For an excellent recent discussion see Gilles Pécout, *Naissance de l'Italie contemporaine (1770–1922)* (Paris: Editions Nathan, 1997).

10 George L. Mosse, *The Nationalization of the Masses: Political Symbolism and Mass Movements in Germany from the Napoleonic Wars through the Third Reich* (New York: Fertig, 1975).

11 For a discussion of these negative representations of Italian history and, often explicitly, of the Italian people, from Ferdinando Petruccelli della Gattina to Piero Gobetti (the most influential), Giulio Colamarino and Fabio Cusin, see Stuart J.Woolf, 'Risorgimento e Fascismo: il senso della continuità nella storiografia italiana', *Belfagor* 20 (1965), 71–91.

12 Alberto M. Banti, *La nazione del Risorgimento. Parentela, santità e onore alle origini del Risorgimento* (Turin: Einaudi, 2000), p. 204 and passim.

13 Banti, *La nazione del Risorgimento*.

14 'Nascimento, Nascita, Origine, Stirpe, Schiatta', *Vocabolario degli Accademici della Crusca* (1806), vol. IV, p. 254, cit. in Banti, *La nazione del Risorgimento*, p. 5.

15 A. M. Banti and R. Bizzocchi (eds.), *Immagini della nazione nell'Italia del Risorgimento* (Rome: Carocci, 2002).

16 Banti, *La nazione del Risorgimento*, ch. 1 and pp. 199–200.

17 Stuart Woolf, *Napoleon's Integration of Europe* (London and New York: Routledge, 1991), p. 229.

18 Arrigo Castellani, 'Quanti erano gl'italofoni nel 1861?', *Studi Linguistici Italiani* 1 (1982), cited in Banti, *La nazione del Risorgimento*, p. 24.

19 For a fuller discussion see Stuart Woolf, 'French civilisation and ethnicity in the Napoleonic empire', *Past and Present* 124 (1989), 96–120.

20 Antonio Gramsci, *Quaderni del carcere* (4 vols., Turin: Einaudi, 1975), vol. III, pp. 2035–6, 2195.

21 Although the Young Turk movement offers another example – which no doubt confirmed educated and Christian opinion that Turkey was outside Europe.

22 Riall, *The Italian Risorgimento*, pp. 79–80.

23 Martin Thom, *Republics, Nations and Tribes* (London and New York: Verso, 1995), ch. 10; A. M. Banti ,'Le invasioni barbariche e le origini delle nazioni', in Banti and Bizzochi, *Immagini della nazione*, pp. 21–44.

24 Johann Gottlieb Fichte, *Addresses to the German Nation* (1808), trans. T. Jones and E. H. Turnbull (London and Chicago, 1922). It is interesting to reflect that, had Manzoni read Fichte, he would have found that such a theory carried water to his well, although he could never have accepted Fichte's hostility towards the imperialism of the Latin language.

25 John A. Davis, *Conflict and Control: Law and Order in Nineteenth Century Italy* (Basingstoke: Macmillan, 1988), pp. 169–82; Franco Molfese, *Storia del brigantaggio dopo l'Unità* (Milan: Feltrinelli, 1964).

26 Nelson Moe, '"Altro che Italia!" Il Sud dei piemontesi (1860–61)', *Meridiana. Rivista di storia e scienze sociali* 15 (1992), 64; Banti, *La nazione del Risorgimento*, p. 200.

27 Woolf, 'French civilisation', 112–15.

28 Transformism figures prominently in the political historiography of Italy. For a concise and sound introduction see Christopher Seton-Watson, *Italy from Liberalism to Fascism 1870–1925* (London: Methuen, 1967), pp. 51–2, 91–7; for contemporary British views see Stuart J. Woolf, 'English public opinion and Agostino Depretis', *Journal of Italian History* 2 (1979), 218–31.

29 Riall, 'Elite resistance to state formation', in Mary Fulbrook (ed.), *National Histories and European History* (London: UCL Press, 1993), pp. 47–8, 59.

30 P. Aimo, 'Stato e autonomie locali: il ruolo dei prefetti', *Passato e Presente* 14–15 (1987), 211–24; Riall, 'Elite resistance', 61.

31 Gian Enrico Rusconi, *Se cessiamo di essere una nazione* (Bologna: Il Mulino, 1993); Ernesto Galli della Loggia, *L'identità italiana* (Bologna: Il Mulino, 1998); Aldo Schiavone, *Italiani senza Italia* (Turin: Einaudi, 1998); Paolo Pezzino, *Senza Stato. Le radici storiche della crisi italiana* (Roma and Bari: Laterza, 2002); Gaspare Nevola (ed.), *Una patria per gli italiani? La questione nazionale oggi tra storia, cultura e politica* (Rome: Carocci, 2003). For a recent survey in

English see S. Patriarca, 'Italian neopatriotism. Debating national identity in the 1990s', *Modern Italy* 6 (2001), 21–34.

32 Umberto Levra, *Dalla città 'decapitalizzata' alla città del Novecento*, in *Storia di Torino* (9 vols.,Turin, 1997–2002), vol. VII, *Da capitale politica a capitale industriale (1864–1915)* [2001], pp. xix–clxi.

33 R. Romeo, *Il Risorgimento in Sicilia* (Bari, Laterza, 1950; 2nd edn, 1970); Denis Mack Smith, *Modern Sicily after 1713*, vol. III of Moses I. Finlay and Denis Mack Smith, *A History of Sicily* (3 vols., London: Chatto & Windus, 1968), pp. 405–61; Lucy Riall, 'Liberal policy and the control of public order in Western Sicily 1860–1862', *The Historical Journal* 35 (1992), 345–68.

34 Stuart Woolf, *Storia di Venezia. L'Ottocento. 1797–1918*, vol. I of Mario Isnenghi and S. Woolf (eds.), *Storia di Venezia. L'Ottocento e il Novecento* (3 vols. 2002), in *Stona di Verezia* (14 vols. in total, Rome: Istituto Italiano della Enciclopedia Italiana, 1991–2002).

35 Tullio Omezzoli, 'Lingue e identità valdostana', in Stuart J. Woolf (ed.), *Storia d'Italia. Le Regioni dall'Unità a Oggi. La Valle d'Aosta* (Turin: Einaudi, 1995), pp. 161–8.

36 Molfese, *Storia del brigantaggio;* Giorgio Candeloro, *Storia dell'Italia moderna* (11 vols., Milan: Feltrinelli, 1956–86), vol. V, *La costruzione dello stato unitario* [1968], pp. 163–70; Giovanni Sabbatucci and Vittorio Vidotto (eds.), *Storia d'Italia* (6 vols., Bari and Rome: Laterza, 1994–9), vol. II, *Il nuovo stato e la società civile* [1995], pp. 47–8, 531–2. Such is the tenacity of some historical myths that, over a century and a half later, when the exiled Savoys were allowed to return to Italy in 2003, and chose Naples as the location of their first visit, they were opposed by demonstrations of so-called 'neo-borbonic' supporters. *La Repubblica*, 12, 15, 16, 17 March 2003.

37 Pietro Clemente, 'Paese/paesi', in M. Isnenghi (ed.), *I luoghi della memoria. Strutture ed eventi dell'Italia unita* (Bari and Rome: Laterza, 1997), pp. 3–39.

38 A research project on six small walled towns in Tuscany between the sixteenth and nineteenth centuries points strongly towards the uninterrupted transmission of civic identity: Lucia Carle, co-ordinator, with Giovanna Cappelletto, Isabelle Chabot, Francesco Mineccia, Rossano Pazzagli and Paolo Pirillo, *Progetto Identità Urbana in Toscana* (7 vols., Venice: Marsilio, 1996–8).

39 Tobia, *Una patria per gli italiani*; M. Isnenghi (ed.), *I luoghi della memoria* (3 vols., Bari and Rome: Laterza, 1996–7); Umberto Levra, *Fare gli italiani. Memoria e celebrazione del Risorgimento* (Turin: Istituto per la Storia del Risorgimento, 1992).

40 Pierre Nora (ed.), *Les lieux de mémoire* (3 vols. in 7 parts, Paris: Gallimard, 1984–92); Charlotte Tacke, *Denkmal im Sozialen Raum. Nationale Symbole in Deutschland und Frankreich im 19 Jahrhundert* (Göttingen: Vandenhoeck & Ruprecht, 1995).

41 Donna R. Gabaccia, *Italy's Many Diasporas* (London: UCL Press, 2000), ch. 4.

42 Nearly half the respondents to a very recent questionnaire stated that they spoke dialect rather than Italian within the family: Giulio Lepschy, 'How popular is Italian?' in Z. Baranski and R. Lumley (eds.), *Culture and Conflict in*

Postwar Italy. Essays on Mass and Popular Culture (Basingstoke: Macmillan, 1990), pp. 63–75; Lepschy, 'Le lingue degli europei,', in P. Anderson, M. Aymard, P. Bairoch, W. Barberis and C. Ginzburg (eds.), *L'Europa oggi* (1993), pp. 870–2, vol. I of *Storia of 'Europa* (5 vols., Turin: Einaudi, 1993–6).

43 Gaspare Nevola (ed.), *Altre Italie. Identità nazionale e regioni a statuto speciale* (Rome: Carocci, 2003).

CHAPTER 14

Political institutions and nationhood in Germany, 1750–1914

Abigail Green

What did it mean to be German in, say, 1780 and how had this changed by about 1900?

Any attempt to answer this question has to engage with two different kinds of debate about the nature of national identity in Europe between the French Revolution and the First World War. As has so often been remarked, the period between 1789 and 1914 – often known as 'the long nineteenth century' – was the great age of nationalism. Opening with the French Revolutionaries' 'invention' of the nation in the 1790s and closing with the mass nationalist agitation that accompanied the outbreak of the First World War, the nineteenth century witnessed Europe's transition from a continent of undemocratic, dynastic, territorial states to a Europe in which the nation-state, governed through representative institutions, was emerging as the predominant form of political organisation. These changes went hand in hand with socio-economic and cultural modernisation: demographic growth, industrialisation, urbanisation, secularisation, the growth of literacy, increased geographical and social mobility and so on. Some theorists of nationalism, such as Ernest Gellner, Eric Hobsbawm, Benedict Anderson and John Breuilly, have seen these two phenomena as interdependent in different ways.[1] Others, such as Adrian Hastings and Liah Greenfeld, have questioned the extent to which nationalism was an essentially modern phenomenon, arguing instead that it emerged in different cultural and political communities at different times and in different ways.[2] Which of these schools of thought best reflects the German experience? Were German nationhood and/or German nationalism meaningful concepts in 1780, or were they invented afterwards?

Secondly, there is the important debate about the relationship between political institutions and nationhood and, more specifically, the role of the former in engendering the latter. There may have been a German Kaiser and a German Reich in both 1780 and 1900, but these political institutions had virtually nothing in common apart from superficially similar terminology. In 1780, the German Reich was the 'old Reich', the Holy Roman Empire, the '*Heiliges Römisches Reich deutscher Nation*' to give it its proper title. This Reich included Bohemia and Austria, but excluded Prussian Poland. Its Kaiser was the Habsburg ruler of Austria and had been for centuries, except for a brief interlude in the middle of the eighteenth century. In 1900, however, the German Reich was the new 'Kaiserreich', forged in the wars of the 1860s and inaugurated at Versailles in 1871. Unlike the old Reich, the Kaiserreich excluded Bohemia and Austria, but included Prussian Poland, Alsace-Lorraine and Schleswig. Its Kaiser was the Hohenzollern ruler of Prussia, a state which had established itself as a European Great Power only a century or so earlier. How did these far-reaching political changes impact on German national identity?

These questions are complicated by the existence of powerful political institutions below the national level, in the shape of the individual German states. I shall therefore trace the interplay between national and state-based political institutions as a way of addressing questions both about the modernity of German nationalism and about the extent to which it was shaped by existing political institutions. I shall argue that political or civic ideas of nationhood remained predominant in Germany well into the middle of the nineteenth century and that, ironically, only the creation of a 'nation-state' prompted the decisive fusion between political and cultural understandings of the nation in Germany.

The old Reich provided a national framework for German politics throughout the medieval and early modern periods. In the past, historians tended to dismiss the Reich as a stagnant and anachronistic political system, whose excessive fragmentation rendered it incapable of adapting to modernity. This view has been questioned by a new generation of historians, who argue that the Reich was not a modern state and never aspired to be one. Judged on its own terms, however, they claim that the Reich was an effective political and legal order, which provided an institutional framework that promoted cultural, social and political diversity.[3]

Crucially for our purposes, revisionists have questioned the view that the Reich did not inspire 'national' loyalties, and that German nationalism was invented by eighteenth-century intellectuals and developed as a political programme by their nineteenth-century successors. According to Peter Krüger, for instance, the very existence of the Reich meant that the German nation *was* shaped by political decisions, which created a shared history of political and social development within its borders.[4] In particular, Krüger argues that the Emperor, the Reich and above all the Imperial Constitution performed a vital integrative function. They provided a focus for German loyalty for inhabitants of the Reich, but allowed many different forces to coexist alongside it. More recently, Georg Schmidt has argued that German nationhood grew hand in hand with the development of the Reich as a polity.[5] In particular, he notes the role of internal wars in the development of a political rhetoric that drew heavily on the idea of Germanness, and associated specific political values with the institutions of the Reich – above all, liberty.[6]

This kind of *Reichspatriotismus* left its mark both in the propagandistic publications of the Seven Years War and in the plans for reform of the Reich's institutions generated in the last decades of the eighteenth century.[7] *Von dem deutschen Nationalgeist* is perhaps the most famous example of this genre. Writing at the behest of the Austrian government, Friedrich Karl von Moser asserted: 'We are one people (*Volk*), with one name, under one common leader (*Oberhaupt*), under laws which determine our constitution, rights and duties, bound together in the great common cause of Liberty [. . .] a people that could be happy but is in reality much to be pitied.'[8] The link between a collective German identity, political institutions and the idea of 'liberty' is very clear here.

Whether this kind of *Reichspatriotismus* should be seen as nationalism, however, is open to question. If one difference between nationalism and a more diffuse sense of national or ethnic identity lies in the specifically political nature of nationalism, and more precisely its definition of a cultural or ethnic community in political terms, then *Reichspatriotismus* exhibited nationalist characteristics. The work of Moser and others explicitly connected German cultural attributes with the Reich's political institutions and outlined an agenda that would weld the two more firmly together in a genuinely national political order.

If, on the other hand, we see nationalism as a mobilising and legitimising political ideology, then the status of *Reichspatriotismus* is more uncertain. Certainly, *Reichspatriotismus* was a conscious attempt to appeal to public opinion through nationally coloured language, heralding the use of nationalism by social and political elites in the nineteenth century. In the eighteenth century, however, the nature of this appeal was different. First, the audience was far smaller. *Reichspatriotismus* targeted a literate elite; it did not seek to mobilise the masses. Moser stressed the importance of patriotic education in encouraging the young to identify with the Reich, but the young he had in mind were hereditary princes and university students. Implicitly, at least, Moser's nation was restricted to those social groups already engaged in politics. Second, although *Reichspatriotismus* reflected official awareness of the importance of public opinion, particularly in wartime, the arguments of the *Reichspatrioten* were deployed to justify Austrian policy and to bolster the Austrian position, rather than to legitimise the imperial polity in new ways.

In any case, *Reichspatriotismus* represented only one current of German national feeling. Pro-Prussian publicists contested this interpretation of the German past and of the relationship between national identity and political institutions. These writers appropriated German political and historical traditions in the name of Prussian patriotism and the territorial state. Pro-Prussian writers drew on traditional images of France as the hereditary enemy of the German nation and glorified the achievements of Frederick the Great in particular. Like *Reichspatriotismus*, this version of the national past was linked with particular political institutions and strongly associated with liberty. The most prominent of these writers, Thomas Abbt, identified Prussia with the idea of a liberal legal system, and envisaged Prussian expansion as liberating Germany from the papacy, the Habsburg emperor, political impotence and French exploitation.

The polemical publications of the eighteenth century cannot be taken as representative of widespread nationalist feeling. Nevertheless, they do testify to the existence of a generally accepted vocabulary of nationhood amongst educated Germans, and to the potential force of political appeals to public opinion voiced in national terms. At the same time, these polemics demonstrate the fluidity of ideas of German nationhood and the ease with which different groups could appropriate the German past. The existence of competing national narratives means that we cannot talk of a single national political tradition at this time. Arguably the views of both sides simply reflected the realities of Reich and territorial state, rather than any particularly profound fusion of cultural and political identities. *Reichspatriotismus* undoubtedly drew on longer historic and institutional traditions than the new Prussian state patriotism, forged in the crucible of Prussia's struggle for survival in the Seven Years War. But did this necessarily render the former more meaningful in the short term or more lasting in the long term than the latter? To argue that it did is to accept too readily the claims of the *Reichspatrioten* at face value.

This question is central to any assessment of the modernity of German nationalism or the ways in which political institutions shaped German identity. To answer it, we need to explore the legacy of the old Reich after its collapse in 1806 and the viability of Prussian and other forms of state-based patriotism in the years that followed. On the one hand, we need to establish whether Germany's imperial past merely provided a convenient historical justification for the idea of a German nation-state, or whether

Reichspatriotismus represented a meaningful political tradition that shaped the emergent nationalism of the nineteenth century. On the other hand, we need to establish how successfully the German territorial states deployed the German past for their own ends, constructing an invented state patriotism that drew upon a deeper sense of German national identity.

The 1790s and 1800s undoubtedly saw a growing emphasis on the idea of Germany as a *Kulturnation* that existed independently of political institutions, reflecting ideas about nationhood developed by Herder in particular. Yet, as Gerhard Schmidt has argued, this emphasis on culture never entailed the abandonment of aspirations to political unity.[9] Instead, the reverse was true. Nationalists like Friedrich Schiller and Carl Ludwig Fernow hoped that nurturing German culture would make it possible to rebuild Germany as a political power in the future. In other words, the German *Kulturnation* would provide the basis for a new national state.

In practice, most nationalists found it impossible to imagine such a state without groping for imperial precedents. Writing in 1813, Ernst Moritz Arndt declared: '*one* belief, *one* love, *one* spirit and *one* passion must again bring together the whole German *Volk* in brotherly union. They must learn to feel how great, powerful, and fortunate their fathers were in obedience to *one* German emperor and *one* Reich, when the many feuds had not yet incited them against one another.'[10] The strong national feeling voiced by Arndt here is clearly linked to his vision of what one might term a once and future German Empire. In this, Arndt was not alone.[11] The activities of German nationalists during the Wars of Liberation and in the period between the Congress of Vienna and the Karlsbad Decrees testify to the popularity of such views – at least amongst an educated minority. Equally, with its Habsburg president and Confederal diet based in Frankfurt, the German Confederation demonstrated clear continuities with the imperial past. In that the legacy of the old Reich shaped both the realities of German politics and the aspirations of German nationalists, it clearly represented a meaningful political tradition.

Yet the nationalism of this period also drew on religious, racial and cultural elements, which were less obviously connected to Germany's imperial past. This view of nationalism, denounced by Saul Ascher in *Die Germanomie,* prompted anti-semitic polemics but was interestingly rather more tolerant towards the Poles.[12] It fed into the democratic nationalism of the *Burschenschaften.* These currents, which combined nationalism with a more radical political agenda, mark the emergence of nationalism as an oppositional ideology, rather than merely an endorsement of existing political structures and institutions. The radical nationalists' disappointment in the 1815 settlement was two-fold, reflecting both the lack of liberal institutions and the lack of a political framework that met their aspirations for national unity. Yet this rejection of the German present and Austria's reactionary influence should not be equated with a wholesale rejection of Germany's imperial past.

Once again, however, German nationalism of this kind coexisted with other kinds of self-consciously German political identity. During the Napoleonic era and its aftermath, Prussia and the south-west German states embarked on programmes of reform from above, designed to create a unitary state with standardised and meritocratic bureaucratic structures. It is a truism that the Prussian reforms were more radical in socio-economic terms than they were politically, whilst in the south-west German states constitutional reform was more significant than socio-economic modernisation. Ultimately, however, both sets of reforms reflected similar assumptions about the need to mobilise citizens on behalf of the state and the potential role of representative institutions in so doing.

These assumptions demonstrated a new preoccupation with the idea of nationhood amongst ruling elites. Yet the elites took their cue from the French revolutionary 'invention' of the nation as a primarily political entity, rather than from Herder's ideas of nationhood. In his Nassau Memorandum of June 1807, the Prussian reformer Karl, Freiherr von Stein, expressed the hope that representative institutions would prompt 'the awakening of a spirit of community and civic pride, the employment of dormant or misapplied energies and of unused knowledge, harmony between the views and desires of the nation and those of the administrative authorities of the state, the revival of patriotism and the desire for national honour and independence'.[13] In many ways, however, the nation Stein had in mind was Prussian rather than German.

As Matthew Levinger has argued, the idea of the Prussian nation was invoked by various different groups during the Napoleonic era.[14] By and large, it represented an inclusive idea of nationhood as the embodiment of a political community, rather than an exclusive idea of nationhood as an essentially cultural phenomenon. Thus in 1813, Friedrich Wilhelm III called on all his subjects to rise up against Napoleon, irrespective of language or culture – Brandenburgers, Prussians, Silesians, Pomeranians and Lithuanians alike. Yet Friedrich Wilhelm's appeal was tinged with a specifically German nationalism for all that. He linked the victories of the ancient Germans with more recent Prussian achievements, when he recalled 'the time of antiquity, the great Electors, the great Frederick' and urged his *Volk* to rise up against France 'if we don't want to stop being

Prussian and German'.[15] In practice, the government's appeals to Prussian patriotism deliberately exploited German national feeling by presenting Prussia as the defender of German values and traditions. Prussian officials consistently failed to clarify what they meant by the terms 'nation' or 'fatherland' because they recognised that German national sentiment was a more powerful mobilising force than Prussian patriotism.

Potentially, this approach enabled the Prussian government to look beyond a narrowly Prussian constituency in pursuit of its wider political aims. During the negotiations of the Vienna settlement, Prussia deliberately wooed nationalist public opinion in order to strengthen her hand. There are obvious continuities here with the way in which Prussian propaganda during the Seven Years War sought to instrumentalise the German national tradition for its own political agenda. Yet this community of interest proved short lived. The Prussian authorities tolerated Josef Görres's nationalist newspaper, the *Rheinischer Merkur*, when it suited them, but banned it in 1816 when it no longer served their cause. Ultimately, nationalism remained an oppositional ideology, despite the authorities' attempts to instrumentalise German national identity in the name of the Prussian state. They wished to mobilise popular enthusiasm for specific purposes, but not to politicise the people.

Developments in South Germany were not dissimilar. Governments here shared Stein's faith in the ability of representative institutions to generate engagement with the regime. When they introduced constitutions and state parliaments after 1815, however, the motive was not 'national' defence but territorial expansion. Participatory government would, they hoped, promote a sense of unity and encourage the fusion of newly acquired territories with the state's traditional heartlands. How far the civic political communities created through these reforms in south west Germany could be described as 'nations' on the Prussian model is a moot point. Nevertheless, in Bavaria at least the leading minister Montgelas talked readily (and rather tellingly, in French) of the 'nation bavaroise' and of Bavaria as his 'chère patrie'.[16] In Bavaria in particular, state-building during the Napoleonic era went hand in hand with a conscious effort to promote awareness of and engagement in the Bavarian 'nation', above all through education and religious policy.[17]

As in Prussia, however, the Bavarian government recognised that state patriotism had to coexist with German national feeling. In the struggle for public opinion after 1813, Montgelas contested Prussian claims to speak on behalf of the German nation.[18] The officially sponsored Bavarian newspaper, *Allemannia*, poked fun at the festivals and invented rituals of the

German nationalist movement. Yet *Allemania* also argued that the Bavarians, Swabians and Franks were the only real Germans, that Prussia and Austria were 'mixed tribes' (*Völkerstämme*) ruled by 'foreign monarchs'. Consequently, only Bavaria and Württemberg could be seen as 'the holy remainder of the German Reich ('heiligen Reste des teutschen Reiches'), two quite German states'. 'Of all the former members of the *Reich*, only the Bavarian and the Württemberger can say they have a *German* Fatherland.'[19] This view lacked the popular appeal of either the imperial tradition of German nationalism or the Prusso-German symbiosis, but it shows how highly nationally charged terms could be appropriated to promote a variety of agendas and changing political realities.

If we fast-forward to the revolutions of 1848/9, we can see how far these competing interpretations of the national past had succeeded in gaining popular currency. The Frankfurt Parliament of 1848 marked both the emergence of German nationalism as an effective alternative to the existing political order and the failure of its attempt to replace the territorial state as the primary basis for political organisation.

Otto Dann has argued convincingly that before 1848 the memory of the old Reich continued to shape the political aspirations of German nationalists.[20] Geographically the memory of the old Reich meant that nationalists instinctively saw Austria as an integral part of the German nation. Politically, the memory of the old Reich fostered federative rather than unitary nationalism: the desire to preserve the individual German states within a revitalised national political framework rather than to create a centralised nation state.[21] Institutionally, the memory of the old Reich dictated the kinds of solution to the national question initially envisaged by the Frankfurt Parliament: a new imperial constitution, a German emperor and a polity whose borders were those the German Confederation had inherited from its predecessor.

More generally, Brian Vick has underlined how far the nationalism of the Frankfurt parliamentarians reflected an essentially political rather than cultural understanding of nationhood, rooted in existing political institutions. First, Vick argues that for members of Germany's educated elite, the idea of Germany as a linguistically or ethnically determined *Kulturnation* was intimately linked to the idea of the German nation as defined by its political institutions, because the Frankfurt Parliamentarians saw political institutions as an expression of national culture.[22] Second, Vick stresses that during the debates over German citizenship in the Frankfurt Parliament, the consensus was overwhelmingly in favour of defining citizenship pragmatically, rather than in terms of culture. The introductory paragraph of the Basic Rights agreed by the Frankfurt Parliament stated clearly: 'The German people consists of the citizens of the states that form the German Empire', explaining that 'the quality of being a German, through which Reich citizenship is conditioned, is not determined by nationality as tribal relationship (*Stammesverwandtschaft*).'[23] In other words, the Basic Rights present an essentially political view of German nationhood, reflecting the historic traditions of the old Reich and its successor the German Confederation.

In many ways, however, the Frankfurt Parliament marked the moment when German nationalists began to turn away from the imperial tradition. For pragmatic political reasons, the Frankfurt Parliament opted in the end to replace the Austrian-dominated Greater Germany (*Großdeutschland*) of the old Reich with a Prussian dominated Smaller Germany (*Kleindeutschland*). These developments and the subsequent efforts of Friedrich Wilhelm IV to create a *kleindeutsch* national union shaped thinking about the national question. The *großdeutsch/kleindeutsch* debate had not previously featured in national discourse. Now, it was a central concern, highlighting the importance of political realities in shaping the aspirations of the German nationalist movement. Conversely, however, developments at state level remind us that the political institutions of the territorial states were forced to accept national aspirations to some extent.

During the Napoleonic era and its aftermath the words 'nation' and 'fatherland' could be applied either to Germany or, in the case of Prussia and Bavaria at least, to the individual German states. This was still true to some extent in 1848/9. There were two National Assemblies in Germany during the revolution, one in Frankfurt and the other in Berlin. The National Assembly in Berlin testified to the endurance of a civic idea of Prussian nationhood, focused on the Prussian state. Interestingly, however, the term was not applied to the Prussian *Landtag* of the 1850s and 1860s. By and large, Prussian policy during and after the revolution focused on creating a Prusso-German *kleindeutsch* symbiosis at national level. Frederick William IV's Erfurt Union was the most obvious manifestation of this development, but it was certainly not the only one – tacit Prussian endorsement of the *kleindeutsch Nationalverein* after 1859 was a further reflection of this trend.

Of course, Prussian education policy continued to preach the patriotic virtues of loyalty to king and fatherland, in the narrower sense of the words.[24] Nevertheless, there does appear to have been a shift away from an understanding of Prussia as a political community towards a more culturally coloured view of the Prussian state-nation. This indicates the growing influence of German nationalism on policy makers. Prussian treatment of the Walloons of Malmédy, a French-speaking enclave acquired in 1815, provides a striking example of this. Initially, the Walloons were allowed to use French in schools, in courts and as the language of administration when dealing with all levels of government, but this happy situation began to break down in the 1860s.[25] In 1863 von Kühlwetter, Regierungspräsident of Aachen, wrote that he accepted the existence of 'patriotism and German feeling (*deutscher Sinn*)' in the Walloon districts, but added: 'I do not consider the task of turning these areas into a part of the country that is truly and profoundly tied to our fatherland to be complete, so long as the German language has not become the mother tongue of the people (*Volk*) and the language of conversation of the educated classes.'[26] As a result of Kühlwetter's attitudes, the communal authorities of Malmédy had to start using German for all official documents, although this decision was subsequently overturned by the Minister of the Interior.

The tendency to conceptualise officially sponsored state-based patriotic identities in terms of an over-arching German national feeling was if anything more apparent in the medium-sized German states. Bavaria was something of an exception here, for the Bavarian government at least continued to think very much in terms of a Bavarian 'nation'. After 1848, King Max II pursued a conscious policy of encouraging Bavarian national feeling ('Politik zur Hebung des bayerischen Nationalgefühls').[27] In the other medium-sized German states, however, the term 'nation' or 'nationalism' was never used to describe the inhabitants of the state or their patriotic sentiments. In the course of extensive primary research in Hanover, Saxony and Württemberg, I found that government officials thought only in terms of a Hanoverian, Saxon or Württemberg *Volk*. Similarly, government officials always used the adjective *vaterländisch* rather than *national* to denote patriotic feeling or the cultural and historic attributes of the state. Nevertheless, the term 'fatherland' did retain its dual meaning – referring both to the small fatherland of the particular state and the large fatherland of the greater German nation.

The 1850s and 1860s saw concerted efforts by the governments of these states to promote state patriotism through manipulation of the press, and through a range of cultural and educational initatives.[28] Yet propaganda of this kind never questioned the German character or vocation of these states. Instead, it habitually accepted Germany as the primary frame of reference for the individual German states.[29] In this sense, government propaganda tended to reinforce rather than undermine a sense of

Germanness that was clearly deep-rooted, if open to differing interpretation.

Within this framework, however, governments endowed state patriotism with cultural and historic elements. This is most apparent in the portrayal of the Germans as a composite nation, made up of several subnational groups, often loosely identifiable with the different German tribes or *Stämme*. Thus government propaganda sought to emphasise this connection and to portray the German states as the legitimate expression of the German *Stämme*. Typically, the *Neue Hannoversche Zeitung* declared in 1859 that the German 'wants his own customs at home, his own traditions in his towns and his own law in his own country. These customs, these traditions and this law have become deeply rooted over many centuries in the soil of the individual *Stämme*; they are reflected in the dynasties and constitutions.'[30] This emphasis on customs and traditions (*Sitten* and *Gebräuche*) does point to a cultural basis for state identity.

Ultimately, however, government propaganda focused above all on the political institutions of the state in question – notably the dynasty – and the constitution for the 'small fatherland' was an essentially political construction. The governments of these states emphasised their role as meaningful political communities within a wider national unit. This was why the *Neue Hannoversche Zeitung* spoke of law, dynasties and constitutions as well as customs and traditions when stressing the distinctiveness of the different *Stämme*.

It should come as no surprise to find that dynasties and monarchs were absolutely central to the official image of the 'small fatherland' projected in the press, in school text books, and through cultural initiatives. States like Hanover, Saxony and Württemberg were primarily dynastic units and inevitably derived their *raison d'être* from the princely families that ruled them. The role of constitutions, laws and administrative structures in shaping this identity is much more unexpected. In fact, however, state constitutions were central to the idea of the small fatherland and to the efforts of German governments to persuade their citizens that they would be worse off in a more centralised nation-state. In both Saxony and Württemberg, official newspapers published annual articles to celebrate the day on which the constitution had been promulgated, and official accounts of the recent past in school books and other publications also laid great stress on traditions of constitutional government. This emphasis on the constitution highlights the achievements of state-building measures at the level of the territorial state in the first half of the nineteenth century, and the role of political institutions in state-based patriotism. The strength of this patriotism is, of course, open to question. What is clear, however, is that it never posed a direct challenge to German national identity. Instead, it simply offered an alternative political channel through which this national feeling could express itself.

How far was this kind of state patriotism compatible with the German national movement of the 1860s? The success of the Gymnastic, Choral and Sharp Shooting movements during the 1860s indicates that a diffuse sense of cultural Germanness and an unfocused desire for 'national unity' did attract significant public support. Interestingly, these movements were all-inclusive in their imagination of the German nation: Austrians were never excluded. In more narrowly political terms, the Schleswig-Holstein crisis provides evidence of a national consensus amongst educated and politically active Germans, despite bitter differences over the alternatives available. The fact that popular outrage enabled the *kleindeutsch Nationalverein* and the *großdeutsch Reformverein* to unite in a nationwide movement of Schleswig-Holstein committees indicates that members of these organisations ultimately shared the same national concerns and values.

There is no evidence, however, that this national consensus was firmly attached to specific political institutions or structures. Some endorsed *Kleindeutschland* and some *Großdeutschland*, but it is highly questionable whether the *kleindeutsch* party would have rejected a *großdeutsch* solution if it had been a real possibility. Nevertheless, these expressions of national feeling were more than expressions of a loose ethnic identity. We can talk of German nationalism in this context, precisely because nationalists clearly sought a political expression for their national identity in the shape of some kind of nation-state. Nationalism existed as a powerful political current in the public sphere at this time, but it remained curiously lacking in direction.

As a result, German national feeling was in practice open to a wide range of political interpretations, and these interpretations changed pragmatically in line with political developments. This is quite obvious from the behaviour of the nationalists themselves. In 1861, for instance, German nationalists campaigned for a joint *Zollverein* display at the forthcoming World Exhibition in London. They did so not because they really equated the *Zollverein* with Germany, but simply because they recognised that a united *Zollverein* showing was the nearest thing to a national German display that they were likely to get.[31] Equally, during the Prussian constitutional conflict, the *Nationalverein* moved away from its initial support for *kleindeutsch* unification led by a liberal Prussia, and began agitating for reform from below through the individual German parliaments.

At different times, individual German statesmen attempted to exploit German nationalism for their own political ends. Friedrich Ferdinand von Beust, the Saxon Prime Minister, openly wooed the nationalist constituency through his plans for Confederal Reform and his keynote speeches at the nationalist festivals of singers and gymnasts held in Dresden and Leipzig. The Austrians too briefly attempted to assert their leadership of the German national movement through the Frankfurter Fürstentag of 1863. Most famously, Bismarck played the nationalist card from early 1866, when he called for a national parliament, until the creation of the *Kaiserreich* and beyond.

In each case, these policies reflected an awareness of the need to connect German nationalism with political institutions, whether those of the German Confederation or those of the territorial state. This awareness could be taken as an admission of the limited success of existing institutions in generating patriotic feeling. Bismarck finally succeeded in re-establishing the connection between nationalism, state patriotism and German political institutions, but in order to do so he had to transform both these institutions and what it meant to be German.

The bulk of the nationalist movement welcomed Bismarck's nation-state with open arms because it presented a concrete solution to the national problem. They therefore chose to overlook the fact that this new nation-state divided the historic German nation (if such a thing existed) and included significant non-German minorities. By and large, members of the nationalist movement proved willing to attach their nationalist feelings to this new state and to foster a narrower, state-based German nationalism.

The very striking differences between the borders and political institutions of the *Kaiserreich* and the Holy Roman Empire make it easy to argue that this post-unification German nationalism was a new departure, drawing not so much on the traditions of the old Reich as on the Prusso-German symbiosis dating back to the Seven Years War and the experience of territorial statehood in the nineteenth century. Political institutions in the here-and-now, not the political institutions of yesteryear, defined this nation. The nationalism of the *Kaiserreich* may have drawn on a national identity nurtured by the reality of the old Reich and sustained by its memory after 1806, but its acceptability to the National Liberals underlined the weakness of the Reich's legacy and its adaptability to a range of political circumstances.

Yet there is evidence that the nationalists of the *Kaiserreich* did not forget older traditions of Germanness. An awareness of Germany as more than just the *Kaiserreich* survived unification surprisingly intact, despite the strong identification of the National Liberal movement with the new German nation-state. In her study of the German gymnastic movement, for instance, Svenja Göltermann shows that the Austrian gymnasts continued to be warmly welcomed at national gymnastic festivals throughout the *Kaiserreich*.[32] Increasingly, according to Göltermann, the rhetoric of gymnasts at these occasions drew a clear distinction between the political nation and the ethnic people or *Volk*. Crucially, even prominent *kleindeutsch* nationalists shared this vision of a wider German nation that transcended the political borders of the new Germany. In 1871, Treitschke himself declared:

'We Germans have never understood the nationality principle in the raw and exaggerated sense that we would wish to see all German-speaking Europeans belong to our state. ... if in the centre of the world there are two great Empires, the one confessionally mixed and purely German, the other catholic and multilingual, but fertilised by German values – who can say that such a situation is humiliating for German national pride?'[33]

This understanding of the nation appears to have attracted significant public support. Roger Chickering, for instance, has stressed the importance of Germans outside the new German Empire to hyper-nationalist organisations like the General German School Association, the General German Linguistic Association and the Pan-German League.[34] Arguably, therefore, we can see the re-emergence of the imperial tradition in German nationalism as a political movement in the 'nationalist opposition' in Imperial Germany.

On the face of it, the balance between the *Kaiserreich* and this more diffuse sense of German nationhood was very much in keeping with the balance between state-based patriotism and a wider sense of German national identity that had existed before unification. As we have seen, the territorial states were essentially civic political communities, which did not seek to compete with German nationhood on equal terms. Instead, they drew on German political, historical and cultural traditions in order to reinforce state-based patriotism. The difference was, of course, that unlike Bavaria, Württemberg or even Prussia, the *Kaiserreich* claimed to be a nation-state rather than a state-nation. Consequently, the unification of Germany in the name of nationalism totally overturned the existing balance between national sentiment and national institutions on the one hand, and state-based patriotism and political institutions on the other.

Nowhere was this more the case than in Prussia, which had the strongest tradition of state-nationhood. Before 1871, the idea of Prussia remained on the whole politically inclusive, centred on the idea of citizenship.

After 1871 it was no longer possible to be Prussian without being German. This need to nationalise as well as Prussify was neatly expressed by Friedrich Eulenburg in 1872, when he said: 'We must see to it that the Poles become first Prussian and then German, but Prussian and German they must become.'[35] An important manifestation of this was the *Geschäftssprachengesetz* of 1876, which for the first time declared German the official language of the Prussian state.

This policy, which reflected a more cultural understanding of nationhood, marked a significant departure from the political traditions of territorial statehood. It also marked a significant departure from the understanding of German nationhood inherited from the multilingual old Reich, which we saw reflected in the definition of citizenship provided by the Frankfurt Basic Rights. This new, more cultural understanding of nationhood helped to legitimise the new political institutions and state identity of the new *Kaiserreich*. Yet this new understanding of nationhood also undermined the *Kaiserreich* precisely because it was a state-nation and not a nation-state. Inevitably, the new policy of Germanisation prompted greater awareness of cultural and ethnic difference. For the Poles this awareness was also political, taking the shape of a fully fledged nationalist movement. By this time, it was of course too late for the Germans to construct a more inclusive national identity, which focused on the state as a political rather than a cultural community.

NOTES

1 Ernest Gellner, *Nations and Nationalism* (Oxford: Blackwell, 1983); Eric Hobsbawm, *Nations and Nationalism since 1780, Programme, Myth, Reality* (Cambridge University Press, 1990); Benedict Anderson, *Imagined Communities* (London: Verso, 1983); John Breuilly, *Nationalism and the State* (2nd edn, Manchester University Press, 1993).

2 Adrian Hastings, *The Construction of Nationhood: Ethnicity, Religion and Nationalism* (Cambridge University Press, 1997); Liah Greenfeld, *Nationalism. Five Roads to Modernity* (Cambridge, MA, and London: Harvard University Press, 1992). See also the work of Anthony D. Smith, notably *The Ethnic Origins of Nations* (Oxford: Blackwell, 1986), or more recently *The Nation in History: Historiographical Debates about Ethnicity and Nationalism* (Cambridge: Polity Press, 2000).

3 This more generous reassessment of the Reich was first advocated by Karl Otmar Freiherr von Aretin in his monumental *Heiliges Römisches Reich, 1776–1806: Reichsverfassung und Staatssouveränität* (Wiesbaden: F. Steiner, 1967). Since then, such views have become increasingly widespread. A relatively early revisionist perspective is provided by Gerald Strauss, 'The Holy Roman

Empire revisited', *Central European History* 11:3 (1978), 290–312. Both sides of the argument are summarised in John G. Gagliardo, *Germany under the Old Regime, 1600–1790* (London and New York: Blackwell, 1991), p. 363. Also of relevance in this context is Mack Walker's excellent study *German Home Towns. Community, State and General Estate 1648–1871* (Ithaca: Cornell University Press, 1971), which stresses the role of the Reich as an 'incubator' protecting the rights and privileges of these ancient communities.

4 Peter Krüger, 'Auf der Suche nach Deutschland – Ein historischer Streifzug ins Ungewisse', in Peter Krüger (ed.), *Deutschland, deutscher Staat, deutsche Nation. Historische Erkundungen eines Spannungsverhältnisses* (Marburg: Hitzeroth, 1993), pp. 41–70.

5 Georg Schmidt, *Geschichte des alten Reiches. Staat und Nation in der frühen Neuzeit, 1495–1806* (Munich: C. H. Beck, 1999). See for instance his conclusion, pp. 347–354, notably p. 348.

6 See for instance ibid., pp. 350–352. For a summary of Schmidt's argument see also Georg Schmidt, 'Teutsche Kriege. Nationale Deutungsmuster und integrative Wertvorstellungen im frühneuzeitlichen Reich', in Dieter Langewiesche and Georg Schmidt (eds.), *Föderative Nation. Deustchlandkonzepte von der Reformation bis zum Ersten Weltkrieg* (Munich: R. Oldenbourg, 2000), pp. 33–61.

7 On this see Schmidt, but also Wolfgang Burgdorf, '"Reichsnationalismus" gegen "Territorial-nationalismus". Phasen der Intensivierung des nationalen Bewußtseins in Deutschland seit dem Siebenjährigen Krieg', in Langewiesche and Schmidt, *Föderative Nation*, pp. 157–189, and Joachim Whaley, 'Thinking about Germany, 1750–1815: the birth of a nation?', in *Transactions of the English Goethe Society* n.s. 66 (1997), 53–72.

8 Cited after Schmidt, 'Teutsche Kriege', pp. 58–9.

9 See Schmidt, *Geschichte des alten Reiches*, p. 353.

10 Cited after Matthew Levinger, *Enlightened Nationalism. The Transformation of Prussian Political Culture, 1806–1848* (Oxford University Press, 2000), p. 114.

11 See Whaley, 'Thinking about Germany' for further elaboration of this point.

12 See Levinger, *Enlightened Nationalism*, pp. 115–25.

13 Cited after ibid., p. 50.

14 Ibid.

15 Ibid, p. 64.

16 Cited after Wolfgang Piereth, *Bayerns Pressepolitik und die Neuordnung Deutschlands nach den Befreiungskriegen* (Munich: C. H. Beck, 1999), p. 23.

17 On this see Walter Demel, *Der bayerische Staatsabsolutismus 1806/08–1817. Staats- und gesellschaftspolitische Motivationen und Hintergründe der Reformära in der ersten Phase des Königreichs Bayern* (Munich: C. H. Beck, 1983); also the early chapters of Werner K. Blessing, *Staat und Kirche in der Gesellschaft. Institutionelle Autorität und mentaler Wandel in Bayern während des 19. Jahrhunderts* (Göttingen: Vandenhoeck & Ruprecht, 1982).

18 On this see Piereth, *Bayerns Pressepolitik*; also Wolfgang Piereth, 'Propaganda im 19. Jahrhundert. Die Anfänge aktiver staatlicher Pressepolitik in

Deutschland 1800–1871', in Wolfram Siemann and Ute Daniel (eds.), *Propaganda, Meinungskampf, Verführung und politische Sinnstiftung 1789–1989* (Frankfurt: Fischer Taschenbuch Verlag, 1994), pp. 21–43.

19 Cited after ibid., pp. 220–1.

20 See Otto Dann, 'Der deutsche Weg zum Nationalstaat im Lichte des Föderalismus-Problems', in Oliver Janz, Pierangelo Schiera and Hannes Siegrist (eds.), *Zentralismus und Föderalismus im 19. und 20. Jahrhundert. Deutschland und Italien im Vergleich* (Berlin: Duncker & Humblot, 2000), pp. 51–68.

21 The term 'federal nationalism' was first coined by Dieter Langewiesche in 'Kulturelle Nationsbildung im Deutschland des 19. Jahrhunderts', in Manfred Hettling and Paul Nolte (eds.), *Nation und Gesellschaft in Deutschland* (Munich: C. H. Beck, 1996), pp. 46–64, at 48. It is a concept further explored in the contributions to Langewiesche and Schmidt (eds.), *Föderative Nation*. For a different take on the origins of federal nationalism see Maiken Umbach, *Federalism and Enlightenment in Germany, 1740–1806* (London: Hambledon, 2000).

22 Brian E. Vick, *Defining Germany. The 1848 Frankfurt Parliamentarians and National Identity* (Cambridge, MA and London: Harvard University Press, 2002), ch. 1.

23 Cited after ibid., p. 119.

24 On education policy in Prussia at this time, see above all Frank-Michael Kuhlemann, *Modernisierung und Disziplinierung. Sozialgeschichte des preußischen Volksschulwesens 1794–1872* (Göttingen: Vandenhoeck & Ruprecht, 1992). For a more general analysis of German education in the period see Karl-Ernst Jeismann and Peter Lundgreen (eds.), *Handbuch der deutschen Bildungsgeschichte*, vol. III, *1800–1870. Von der Neuordnung Deutschlands bis zur Gründung des deutschen Reiches* (Munich: C. H. Beck, 1987).

25 See Klaus Pabst, 'Die preußische Wallonen – eine Staatstreue Minderheit im Westen', in Henning Hahn and Peter Kunze (eds.), *Nationale Minderheiten und staatliche Minderheitenpolitik in Deutschland im 19. Jahrhundert* (Berlin: Akademie Verlag, 1999), pp. 71–9.

26 Cited after ibid., p. 75.

27 On this see Manfred Hahnisch, *Für Fürst und Vaterland. Legitimitätsstiftung in Bayern zwischen Revolution 1848 und deutscher Einheit* (Munich: Oldenbourg, 1991).

28 Abigail Green, *Fatherlands: State-Building and Nationhood in Nineteenth Century Germany* (Cambridge University Press, 2001).

29 See ibid., pp. 267–71.

30 *Neue Hannoversche Zeitung*, no. 499, 27 October 1859, 'Die deutsche Bundesreform'.

31 On this see Abigail Green, 'Representing Germany? The *Zollverein* at the World Exhibitions, 1851–1862', *The Journal of Modern History* 75 (December 2003), 836–63.

32 Svenja Göltermann, *Körper der Nation. Habitusformierung und die Politik des Turnens, 1860–1890* (Göttingen: Vandenhoeck & Ruprecht, 1998); see for instance p. 223.

33 Cited after Theodor Scheider, *Das deutsche Kaiserreich von 1871 als Nationalstaat* (Cologne and Opladen: Westdeutscher Verlag, 1961), p. 47.

34 Roger Chickering, *We Men who Feel Most German. A Cultural Study of the Pan-German League, 1866–1914* (London: George Allen & Unwin, 1984), pp. 243–5.

35 Cited after Scheider, *Das deutsche Kaiserreich*, p. 26.

CHAPTER 15

Nation, nationalism and power in Switzerland, c. 1760–1900

Oliver Zimmer

In the autumn of 1798, the Minister of the Interior of the short-lived Helvetic Republic lamented that the state of Swiss patriotism left much to be desired.[1] His opinion was echoed in a report he received from the governor of Bern in October of the same year: 'I find no common spirit; the conceptions which exist among our people are too numerous, too inadequate and too vague.'[2] Nearly a century later, the author of an essay on the history of Switzerland's national festivals painted a much more positive picture. In the fifty years since the foundation of the Swiss nation-state in 1848 the Swiss, so he reasoned, had 'become a people'.[3]

On the face of it, these observations seem to confirm what can safely pass as common scholarly wisdom: that the long nineteenth century represents the classic era of nation-formation, a process that strengthened national identity among many of Europe's populations. Yet historians are trained to be sceptical of statements like the ones just cited. Shaped as they are by the perceptions, motivations and ambitions of their producers, they ought not to be taken naively at face value. Thus, if the minister of the Helvetic Republic came to a gloomy assessment of the state of Swiss patriotism, then this may in part reflect the high expectations so typical of members of the new republican ruling class. It also reveals their tendency to equate opposition to the Helvetic regime with disloyalty to 'the nation'. The second statement, on the other hand, conveys a sentiment of patriotic excitement that was rather widespread among Switzerland's cultural and political elite at the turn of the twentieth century.

But while each of the statements quoted above can be deconstructed in this manner, taken together they contain a broader message that deserves further examination. Simply put, the message is that, in the course of the long nineteenth century, the idea of the nation was transformed in significant ways.[4] While until around 1800 it was mainly an educated class of magistrates, educators and professionals who attached political significance to the national idea, by the close of the nineteenth century the concept

enjoyed wide currency. What we witness is not the formation of a consensus regarding the meaning of Swiss nationhood. The definition of
national identity remained highly contested throughout the nineteenth
century, and I shall argue that public contestation was indeed conducive to
the process of nationalisation in Switzerland. Nor did alternative sources of
collective identification (such as class, locality, region, religious affiliation
and gender) lose their grip on people's consciousness. What did happen,
however, was that the nation gained the status of a self-evident cultural
code whose moral authority was no longer in doubt.

In this chapter I shall attempt to explain this transformation through
an examination of the inter-relationship between the nation as a focus
of collective identity and nationalism as an ideological and political
movement whose generic goals are cultural authenticity, national self-
determination and national unity. Nationalism is seen here as pertaining
to collective action, and as such it provides the link to political power, while
the idea of the nation is conceived in terms of a cultural idiom upon which
political actors draw as they construct nationalist arguments.[5] What was
the relationship between the nation as a focus of identification and nationalism in Switzerland between 1760 and 1900? To what extent, if at all, did
modern Swiss nationalism feed on a pre-modern national consciousness?

My argument could be described as qualified modernism: nationalism
did not invent the Swiss nation as a concept or source of collective identity.
But the advent of nationalism in the eighteenth, and its subsequent
modifications during the nineteenth century transformed the idea of the
nation in terms of its meaning, political significance, and social scope. I
distinguish between three phases, each giving rise to a distinctive kind of
nationalism and related discourse of national identity: the period from
1760 to 1798 saw the emergence of nationalism as an *ideological movement*
of educated patriots who used 'the nation' to legitimate demands for
political reform; during the period from 1830 to 1848 nationalism grew
into a *political movement* and the nation became the central frame of
reference in a protracted conflict over the future shape of the Swiss polity;
finally, during the period from 1860 to 1900 nationalism assumed the status
of *normative common sense* in the context of an established nation-state.[6]

DREAMING OF THE WIDER FATHERLAND

The pivotal place of the eighteenth century in discussions about the origins
of nationalism has been confirmed in a number of recent studies. This is
not really surprising to those familiar with the historical literature on the

subject from Hans Kohn onwards. Yet the devil is in the chronological detail. While in the traditionally predominant view the French Revolution opened the chapter of nationalism in world history, new research has demonstrated that the construction of nationalist arguments (if not yet the formation of fully fledged nationalist movements) often pre-dated that event by several decades.[7] Clearly the dating of nationalism's temporal origins largely depends on the definitions we employ. What I take to indicate the beginning of nationalism as an *ideological movement* is the transformation of the idea of the nation from a predominantly descriptive to a dynamic and genuinely political concept. Nationalism is upon us, according to this view, when the 'nation' is used to legitimate projects that are aimed at the creation of new political communities. In Switzerland this stage was reached in the 1770s, when a group of reform patriots began to invest the nation with their expectations regarding the creation of a Confederate state.[8]

Although this dynamic and explicitly political use of the national idea was not wholly absent before the eighteenth century, the available evidence suggests that it was as yet little developed. In the sixteenth century, for example, Swiss humanists employed the 'nation' and related concepts in order to defend the Swiss Confederation against accusations from the German Reich. Such accusations multiplied both during and immediately after the Swabian War of 1499. Although this early modern application of the concept of the nation was politically significant – the term was used, after all, to legitimate the Swiss Confederation as a separate (and, in many ways, 'deviant') political community within an imperial political framework – its social impact was limited. It was but a small Confederate elite that took part in the controversy with representatives of the German Empire.[9] The same cannot be said of the Confederate myth–symbol complex which appeared for the first time in the Confederate chronicles of the late fifteenth and early sixteenth centuries. Centring on the liberation legends of Wilhelm Tell and the Oath of the Rütli, it amounted to an increasingly popular narrative of communal self-description. Yet although the medieval liberation myths were undoubtedly more widely diffused than the national idea, their impact was for the most part restricted to regional political campaigns. Even where the liberation myths were used to legitimate insurgent action, they did not inspire a genuinely 'national' movement. The Swiss Peasant War of 1653, triggered as it was by a fiscal crisis and largely confined to the countryside of Lucerne and Bern, offers a case in point.[10]

It was not until the late eighteenth century that the concept of the nation began to be invoked as a moral weapon in pamphlets and speeches to highlight perceived deficits of state-institutional existence. Most of these broadsides were directed against the constitutional and political status quo. The fact that the Old Swiss Confederation was a relatively loose conglomeration of states now appeared as the prime cause for the lack of national consciousness among the wider population. The Swiss, so many patriots contended, had a 'dual fatherland'. Their collective loyalties were split between individual state or region and nation. Not that the existence of sub-national loyalties was brandished in the style of the French Jacobins, who had equated regional attachments with a hated 'federalism': most Swiss patriots of the 1770s and 1780s accepted that locality and region provided a valuable, even indispensable, source of identification. Yet their aim was to shift people's loyalties away from the locality and towards the 'general fatherland'. Thus in 1786, the Helvetic Society declared that it would have realised its purpose only if it succeeded in 'bringing together the multitude of strengths that is contained in the individual states in a way that will enrich the national genius'.[11]

As this critique of the status quo carried certain risks for the individuals concerned, it had to be justified in moral terms. This explains why the Swiss patriots, to use Quentin Skinner's splendid phrase, marched backward into battle.[12] Historicism offered the most potent means to invest their project with moral authority. It was from the Confederation's alleged historical origins, symbolically expressed in the medieval founding myths, that they expected moral guidance and spiritual regeneration. Allied to this was a conspicuous move away from the neo-classical patriotism prevalent in previous decades. Thus in 1775, Joseph Anton Felix Balthasar wrote that he did 'not reprimand those whose aim it [was] to make our youth acquainted with the peculiar deeds of Caesar or Scipio', only to add that what was 'far more beautiful and worthy of praise [was] to tell the Confederates about the history and the lives of their forefathers' and 'the origins of the Swiss Confederation'.[13]

Crucially, from the 1770s onwards this ethno-historicism became interwoven with a debate about 'national character' in which the hegemony of cosmopolitan values was identified as the root cause of national decline. 'What do we gain', one patriot asked the assembled members of the Helvetic Society, 'if we know how numerous the French armies are, how many duchies there are in Germany, how far away Moscow is ... in one word, what the whole world around us looks like?' His answer was unmistakably clear: 'Unless we know more about our own strength and power we will remain aliens in our own fatherland, ignorant of its history and the evolution of our state.'[14] What would the nation benefit, another interrogated his fellow-patriots, if Swiss youths spent their days 'dancing in the anterooms of kings' in the morning and having 'lunch every afternoon with a dragoon-captain and three comedians?'[15] In this climate, open admiration for foreign works of philosophy and literature attracted suspicion. As another patriot lamented: 'As things stand in our Confederation, you will not come across many homes where you cannot find, along with the most recent products of Gallic slipperiness, the sort of German novels and plays which leave you in the dark whether the hero or heroine is to be taken as a model to be emulated or, quite to the contrary, as an abhorrent example.'[16] The obsession with the preservation of 'national character' that manifests itself in these debates had practical consequences. At its 1782 meeting, the Helvetic Society decided to depart from its existing membership policy by restricting the status of foreigners to that of honorary membership without the right to vote.[17]

Most historians have used functional arguments to explain the eighteenth-century preoccupation with 'national character'. Many have drawn inspiration from Frederik Barth's work on the reproduction of small groups through the maintenance and continual reconstruction of a symbolic boundary vis-à-vis other communities.[18] In the words of Linda Colley: 'men and women decide who they are by reference to who and what they are not. Once confronted with an obviously alien "Them", an otherwise diverse community can become a reassuring or merely desperate "us".'[19]

But how persuasive are such arguments? While negative stereotypes have undoubtedly shaped the definition of national identities, it is hard to see how ordinary men and women could acquire any notion of the 'other' in the absence of any idea of their own 'self'. Although negative stereotypes greatly reinforced the contours of Swiss nationhood in the late eighteenth century, they did not, in themselves, create it. Rather, the two narratives that had underpinned the Confederate self-image since the sixteenth century – a more elitist one centred on the 'nation', and a more vernacular one focused on the Confederate founding and liberation myths – prepared the ground from which the anti-cosmopolitanism of the 1770s and 1780s would spring. It was this early modern cultural legacy, politicised in the historicist patriotic revival of the mid-eighteenth century and re-shaped to fit a new purpose, that fostered the kind of national self-centredness without which the identification of the 'international' with 'contamination' and with subversion of 'national character' would have made little sense. Where ethno-historicism lacked clear political connotations, as seems to have been the case in eighteenth-century Germany, anti-cosmopolitan tendencies

remained comparatively weak. It was precisely the prevalence of cosmopolitanism over national sentiment – a sentiment he found in England, the
Swiss Confederation, the Netherlands and Sweden – that the German
writer Friedrich Carl von Moser criticised in his 1765 pamphlet *Von dem
deutschen Nationalgeist.*[20]

But these more cultural aspects of nationalism need to be assessed in the
context of the political motivations and intentions of relevant carrier
strata and movements. For, ultimately, the fact that the emergence of a
self-conscious national movement in Switzerland from the 1770s was
inextricably linked with a language of cultural authenticity and national
self-determination finds its explanation in the motivations of the patriot
reformers. Hence, at their very first annual gathering in 1762, the patriots of
the Helvetic Society promulgated as their *raison d'être* the incorporation of
the Confederation's 'different parts into a single coherent body'.[21] Their
aim, in other words, was the creation of a single Swiss state. From their
point of view, French cosmopolitanism directly undermined their state-
building ambitions; they perceived it as a force that threatened to divert
scarce resources and urgently needed attention from the domestic state-
building project. Thus, to a large extent it was such genuinely practical
concerns that inspired the painting of the gloomy scenarios in which an
alien cosmopolitanism was undermining the culture and character of the
nation. It was considerations of this kind, at any rate, that lay behind the
plan to set up a political academy for the education of Bern's young
patricians. The debate accompanying this project contains numerous
examples, such as the following, in which the possible effects of receiving
a foreign education were painted in the darkest colours:

> When the youth steps into the world, he moves outside the sphere delimited by his
> compatriots' eyes, and even his parents are no longer able to supervise him. The
> first ideas he is acquainted with will be imparted by foreign sophists; his young
> heart develops without any appreciation for his fatherland, without enthusiasm for
> his place of birth, of that noble national pride which is the virtue of the true
> republican ... When he returns home, the young republican, the future business-
> man or magistrate who was educated abroad to serve his fatherland, will be a
> foreigner in his own land.[22]

ENEMIES WITHIN AND WITHOUT

Between 1798 and 1848, Swiss nationalism was transformed from an
ideological movement of the educated to a political movement of considerable popular appeal. As the democratic *Landbote* exclaimed after a

majority of cantons had approved the new constitution in the autumn of 1848: 'On the evening of 12 September, with a series of cannon salutes and bonfires, the Swiss people solemnly declared to the peoples of Europe: "We have become an independent nation."'[23]

Yet at the beginning of this second phase of nation-formation are revolution and foreign occupation. In March 1798, the Swiss Confederation (along with the Low Countries, Milan and the Kingdom of Naples) became one of France's 'sister republics', established to con-solidate her contested rule on the Continent and to spread the mission of the French Revolution.[24] Within a few weeks, the Helvetic Republic had replaced the loose confederation of cantons that had existed for several centuries. The first nation-state in Swiss history was committed to the concept of the one and indivisible nation first elaborated by the French revolutionaries. As it was put in the opening paragraph of the French-imposed Helvetic Constitution: 'The unity of the fatherland and the interest of the nation will henceforth take the place of the weak bond that used to connect the large and small localities ... in a rather haphazard fashion.'[25]

In reality, the period from 1798 to 1803 was marked by continuous civil war, interrupted only by brief spells of relative tranquillity. Particularly during the last two years of the Republic, the experience of external interference, of occupation and economic depression, provoked an ideologi-cal response that drew on a glorified image of the popular democratic assemblies common in central Switzerland.[26] It needs emphasising, how-ever, that neither the popular rhetoric of direct democracy nor the wide-spread anti-republican activity was on the whole driven by grassroots nationalism. A few educated voices aside – Johann Caspar Lavater's pamphlet against the French Directory offers a case in point[27] – opposition to the new order was not justified primarily on nationalist grounds, at least not in the sense in which the term was defined at the outset of this chapter.

This failed experiment with centralist republicanism was succeeded by two decades of conservative restoration during which Switzerland was returned to a loose confederation of cantons. It was not until the 1830s that liberal and radical groups would successfully challenge the political status quo. By the end of 1831 eleven Swiss cantons, representing more than two thirds of the Swiss population, had introduced liberal or democratic constitutions. For liberals and democrats, these successes in the cantons were merely the start signal for a federal constitutional reform, and they used the meetings of the Confederate Diet to pursue their ambition. The first attempt at transforming the constitutional status quo failed in 1833 due to the resistance of a coalition of conservative and French-speaking cantons. It would take the Civil War of 1847 for the liberal mission of closer political integration to succeed with the creation of the *Bundesstaat* in 1848.

As important as the outcome of the constitutional conflicts of the 1830s and 1840s was the extent to which they transformed traditional patterns of social communication. Politics, during the years of conservative restoration still largely the preserve of small, educated circles, had begun to capture the wider population. An 1833 Austrian report had it that in Switzerland 'so-called public opinion', rather than the 'voice of the educated' was 'the decisive arbiter' in political affairs. It was the legitimacy of this principle, the report concluded, that accounted for the rapid decline of traditional authority and the strength of the radical movement.[28] Many Swiss contemporaries made similar observations. 'The main reason why I cannot escape from politics', the conservative Jeremias Gotthelf maintained, 'is because today politics is everywhere.' 'In fact', he continued, 'what characterises radicalism is that politics permeates the lives of every estate, ravaging the holy sphere of the family and decomposing Christian faith.'[29]

This politicisation of the public sphere, in part a consequence of the extension of the franchise in the liberal and radical cantons, went in tandem with a massive expansion of the political press.[30] During the 1830s, Switzerland became a country with one of the highest densities of newspapers in the world.[31] There was one newspaper for every 21,800 Swiss in 1848, while in Prussia in 1845 there was one for every 360,000 inhabitants.[32] In 1848, there were more than 110 newspapers in Switzerland. Of those, 32 (29 percent) were liberal, 31 (28 percent) radical, 10 (9 percent) belonged to the 'juste milieu', 12 (11 percent) subscribed to a Catholic-conservative and 2 (2 percent) to a socialist world-view. In addition, there were 2 (2 percent) newspapers that embraced the cause of German republicanism, while 21 papers (20 percent) did not follow a specific political creed.[33] Not only had Switzerland witnessed a proliferation of newspapers in the wake of the July Revolution, but the political press also became more 'national' and populist in content and style.

Numerous popular associations and a burgeoning festival culture contributed their part to the nationalisation of the public sphere. Well before the founding of the federal state in 1848, various popular associations pursuing an overtly national agenda were founded. The most important were the Confederate Shooting Association (founded in 1824), the Confederate Gymnastic Society (founded in 1832) and the Confederate Choral Association (founded in 1842). Not only did these national associations provide an organisational focal point for hundreds of regional and local societies, they also served to concentrate the minds of their members on the national cause. The Confederate Choral Association, for instance, stated as its purpose the 'promotion and embellishment of the folk song movement, the awakening of higher feelings for God, Liberty and Fatherland, and the bringing together of the friends of the arts and of the Fatherland'.[34] Their annual festivals amounted to huge national celebrations attended by hundreds of active participants and thousands of visitors.[35]

The various manifestations of vibrant patriotism notwithstanding, differences of ideology, motivation and strategy remained strong. Particularly during the early 1840s, the divisions between liberals and radicals appeared to pose a permanent obstacle to constitutional progress at federal level. What was decisive, however, was that nationalism supplied the competing political factions with a common political language and morality. The moderate liberals used the language of unification nationalism to legitimate their calls for constitutional progress (above all the rule of law and a number of basic individual rights) and tighter institutional (including economic) integration at the federal level. This project, they argued, was an embodiment of the progressive spirit that the modern age demanded; better still, it was also in the interest of 'the nation'. Radicals and democrats, on the other hand, while sharing some of these views and ambitions, embraced a somewhat different brand of nationalism. Radical associations in particular placed the stress on popular sovereignty and national self-determination, reflecting their task of mobilising those sections of the public that had social grievances, and demanded the extension of participation rights.[36]

Involving mass mobilisation in the name of the 'common fatherland', the civil war of 1847 undoubtedly strengthened national sentiment and increased the moral pressure in favour of a national parliament. The fact that tens of thousands of citizen soldiers had served in the Federal Army vindicated those who claimed that a 'national will' did in fact exist. In a lengthy editorial, the democratic *Landbote* insisted that it was the 'sentiment of unity and common nationality' that had 'rescued Switzerland from great danger'. The war against the troops of the Catholic *Sonderbund* had been the starkest demonstration in favour of the broadest possible form of democratic representation: 'What we demand, therefore, is nothing more than that the people, the nation, be directly represented.'[37] The left-liberal *Schweizer-Bote* concurred. 'The consciousness of belonging to one nation' had become the view of the majority. This majority, so its editors concluded with a broadside against Catholic conservatives and moderate liberals alike, would 'no longer endure having its rights curtailed by a stubborn minority'.[38] In the end, the majority of democrats and left-liberals supported the bicameral solution on the US model while conservatives and extreme radicals opposed it.[39]

The explosive international constellation that developed after the victory of the liberal-democratic coalition in November 1847 reinforced the moral pressure on those who continued to oppose the establishment of a national parliament. Thus in late March, the left-liberal *Schweizer-Bote* began to outline a vision that could be seen as a *Kulturkampf avant la lettre*. In an extensive article on the constitutional debate, its editors declared that those who continued to oppose the 'joyful rise of the entire nation' were 'enemies of a better future'. When the popular referenda of August and September 1848 revealed that the bulk of opposition to the new constitution came from Catholic cantons, the same newspaper doubted the capacity of Swiss Catholics for national loyalty.[40]

It was thus a series of contingent events and processes (rather than economic motives or institutional needs produced by an abstract modernity)[41] which favoured the temporary blurring of the ideological boundaries that under 'normal' circumstances might well have driven a wedge between the nationalist visions of liberals, democrats and radicals. In the context of increasing domestic tension between Protestant and Catholic-conservative cantons and external threats, the nationalist language of the moderate liberals, with its emphasis on the national interest, and that of democrats and radicals, with its insistence on the sovereignty of the nation, coalesced into a broad-based political programme.

THE DYNAMICS OF CONFEDERATE NATION-FORMATION

The establishment of the Swiss *Bundesstaat* in 1848 produced the institutional conditions and socio-political dynamics that were to shape the process of nation-formation in the late nineteenth century. Reducing the actual complexity of the historical situation for a moment, we might say that what characterised this process was a controversial attempt to increase the federal state's influence and power in the name of social progress and national integration. The result was a contest over nationhood in which one of the central issues that nationalism raises – that concerning the loyalty of the population to the nation – appeared in a new light. Whereas before 1848 the concept of national loyalty had served as a rhetorical device for the exclusion and stigmatisation of those who opposed the creation of a federal state based on a liberal constitution, in the second half of the century it was increasingly perceived as something that should be cultivated and developed. From the 1860s onwards, liberals and radicals grew more confident in their ability to turn former opponents into loyal supporters of the nation-state. Their ambition was to forge a mass public culture that would transcend existing boundaries of class and religion and reduce differences in economic performance and social mobility.

In the scholarly literature this drive for institutional standardisation and cultural uniformity is usually described as 'nation-building', with the state and its personnel appearing as the agents of 'modernisation'. The national messages disseminated via a modern communication infrastructure (roads, railways, schools and integrated markets), so the argument runs, will gradually increase the national awareness of the inhabitants living within the same territorial-political unit.[42] Functional explanations of this kind possess an intuitive plausibility. Who can seriously doubt that accelerated social change is likely to foster the need for the symbolic re-structuring of social relations via public ceremony and ritual display, or that state elites will periodically seek to enhance social cohesion by promoting nationalist doctrines? Nor is it deniable that modern ('capitalist' or 'industrial') societies require dense networks of communications and efficient means of transport. In fact, after a protracted start the construction of railways in Switzerland was finally boosted in the latter part of the nineteenth century, culminating in the opening of the line through the Gotthard in 1882. Switzerland's occupational structure, too, underwent a profound change in the second part of the century. Whereas in 1850 approximately 54 per cent of the working population was occupied in the agricultural sector, this figure had decreased to 42.4 per cent by 1880, falling to a mere 31 per cent in 1900.[43] The density of communication, too, progressed yet further, aided by the proliferation of newspapers and private associations, as well as the introduction of the popular referendum at the federal level in 1874.[44]

Yet for all its undoubted merits, the nation-building school offers an excessively top-down account of modern nationalism. For Switzerland's path towards the modern mass nation was not tantamount to a process of institutional penetration and cultural diffusion. Nor can it be satisfactorily analysed in terms of a state-induced attempt at ideological manipulation. There has been no shortage of critical engagement with explanations of this sort. Perhaps the most important critique developed in the early 1990s, when historians studying particular regions began to stress the multiplicity of human identity, albeit with different emphases. Some portrayed national and sub-national identities as existing side by side in a relatively unproblematic fashion. Others have described their relationship as one of tension and conflict.[45]

While this 'regional turn' has no doubt added historical nuance and texture to the study of nations and nationalism, it nonetheless raises its own set of problems. We may readily concede, for example, that the arrival of the nation-state did not mark the death knell of sub-national allegiances. But the emphasis on the plurality of identities evades rather than offers an explanation for the kinds of dynamics that the nationalising state unleashed in the second half of the nineteenth century. At the centre of these dynamics is the complex interaction between the nation-state and what is commonly described as civil society.[46]

From such a perspective, the nationalisation of society appears neither as a process of top-down cultural diffusion nor, conversely, as a phenomenon that dissolves in the face of a plurality of rampant regionalisms. It was precisely because national loyalty had assumed such a central role in the moral economy of the modern nation-state that the regions and localities had little alternative but to engage (rhetorically and otherwise) with national institutions and state-led cultural initiatives. Even those opposing state policies could no longer afford to justify their grievances by reference to local and regional interests alone. Increasingly, deviant views had to be formulated in 'national' terms.

But the moral pressure exerted by the federal state and its supporters was not the only factor driving the localities and regions into the national arena. Equally important was the fact that the nation-state became an essential source of status and prestige. The historical regions and localities in particular began to compete for status, prestige and recognition within this new frame of reference – not just for economic resources and political influence. In concrete terms, this competition between the nation-state and its constituent parts frequently took the form of a contest over public culture and institutions. It was through such contests that men and women were drawn into a modern public sphere and directly and explicitly engaged with the concept of nationhood. Two examples can serve to illustrate the nature of this process.[47]

Education, particularly elementary education, was perhaps the field in which this contest became most visible. Switzerland's liberal middle classes were in agreement that a strong and internationally competitive state depended on a well-educated populace. One of their principal ambitions was therefore to draw the population into the schools, and to ensure that attendance rates remained consistently high. There were external as well as domestic factors that drove this ambition. Among the former, the victory of the German states over France in 1870 weighed particularly heavy. That France's defeat had to be attributed, at least in part, to the alleged superiority of German education quickly emerged as a European consensus. This view was echoed in a Swiss government report advocating educational reform.[48] From the late 1860s onwards, moreover, private associations and pressure groups had begun to urge the federal government to initiate a nation-wide reform. Between March 1871 and March 1872 the federal authorities received twenty-eight petitions in favour of making primary schools compulsory and free of charge, combined with calls for a more stringent regime of assessment and control. These demands were largely realised in the constitutional reform of 1874. Article 27 of the Swiss Constitution made the provision of 'sufficient primary education' the responsibility of the cantons. In state-run elementary schools, education was to be offered free of charge, and pupils had to be accepted irrespective of religious affiliation. The federal state reserved the right to take measures against cantons that failed to re-organise their education system in accordance with these regulations.[49]

Significantly, however, the Swiss constitution did not enable the federal authorities to introduce a common curriculum for elementary schools; the sovereignty of the cantons remained largely intact in this area. But the federal government did not give in easily. In 1875, it added a paragraph to the existing military legislation. It stipulated that every recruit would have to undergo an examination in general knowledge, focusing on the following four areas: reading; essay writing; written and oral arithmetic; the history and constitution of Switzerland. The results of these annual tests would be evaluated on a score from 1 (very good) to 5 (very poor).[50] By publishing the results in the form of detailed league tables, the Federal Bureau of Statistics exposed the cantons' individual performance and turned the annual pedagogic examinations into a public event. In the Bureau's first report in 1875, the publication of the results was justified as follows: 'We need to know the standard of our people's education. A thorough and adequate assessment of the situation will appeal more to an education-hungry people than nice phrases about our marvellous progress.'[51] Once introduced, the tests served as a basis for cross-border comparisons. Pondering the results of the first annual examinations, the journal of the Protestant-dominated Swiss Teachers Association noted that only the best cantons could 'compete with such states as Württemberg, Baden, Sachsen and the Rhineland'. In 'some of our cantons', its editors concluded, 'the state of primary education is as desolate as in some of Prussia's eastern provinces or in Upper and Lower Bavaria'.[52]

On the face of it, the educational debate impelled by the pedagogic tests was highly technical. It was focused on the practical aspects of the annual examinations, the rankings above all, and on specific measures designed to improve the status quo. But these more technical aspects were soon overshadowed by a broader normative discussion concerning the role of elementary education in the modern nation-state. As one contemporary observed: 'People are eager to scrutinise the league tables with the individual cantons. In fact, these league tables have become the mark sheets on which public opinion judges not just the individual recruits but the cantons themselves.'[53] Most importantly, however, from the outset the contest over education was infused with patriotic rhetoric. As early as 1878 the official periodical of the Swiss Teaching Association announced that primary school reform was part of the country's national mission. Those cantons that had managed to improve the state of primary education were praised for their patriotism, while those perceived as either indifferent or openly hostile to educational reform were brandished as violating the national cause.[54]

The controversy surrounding the establishment of a national museum – the *Landesmuseum,* as it would soon be called – offers another instructive example of a competitive debate over nationhood in which federal authorities, the governments and populations of different cantons and towns as well as political parties and private associations took part. After it had first been raised in circles not directly linked to the federal government, the idea of a national museum began to gain wider currency when it entered the debate of the federal parliament in the early 1880s. In July 1883, Salomon Vögelin, a member of the National Council, clergyman and professor of art history, proposed the founding of a museum that would 'express the national idea in all possible directions'. A typical advocate of a liberal nationalism who wished to see the state's role in the field of cultural policy strengthened, Vögelin declared that national patriotism was more than the 'sum of the patriotism of the twenty-five cantons'. Turning against the opponents of a state-led cultural policy, he argued that 'twenty-five local collections' did 'not yet constitute a national museum'. While national museums had been created in Germany, France, the Netherlands, England, Denmark, Italy, Spain and Russia, Switzerland still lacked a comparable institution.[55] Initially, however, Vögelin's proposal for a national museum met with resistance from the defenders of cantonal autonomy. A specially appointed parliamentary commission concluded that what was urgently needed was not a national museum but the passing of new legislation to prevent the sale of nationally significant antiquities to foreign art dealers.[56]

Once raised in parliament, however, the idea of a *Nationalmuseum* proved hard to remove again from the public agenda. Ironically, it was its opponents who did most to keep it alive in the public mind. In 1885, two Catholic-conservative members of the Council of States submitted a proposal that in many ways represented a counter-initiative to Vögelin's idea. Instead of founding a central national museum, the two politicians encouraged the federal government to support the cantons in their efforts to 'preserve historic buildings' and 'antique collections'. Arguing that Switzerland's history, at least up until 1848, was essentially the sum of the 'history of the cantons', they insisted that a federal museum would have to confine itself to the post-1848 era. In contrast to Vögelin and his liberal allies, they painted a positive picture of the numerous local museums, which, they insisted, were manifestations of a vibrant patriotism that benefited the nation as a whole. Although this conservative intervention enjoyed some public support, the liberal-radical majority in parliament and in the media was in favour of a national museum. So was the Federal Council, which explicitly rejected the vision of the Swiss past underpinning the conservative initiative. Switzerland's history as a nation, the government declared in a report to parliament on 14 June 1886, began neither in 1798 nor in 1848. Although these dates represented milestones in the nation's history, this was equally true of 'the heroic battles' that the Confederates had fought in the late medieval period. They too represented 'national' rather than merely 'cantonal' events. The report concluded with an open declaration of support for Vögelin's plan to create a national museum, and with an invitation to potential applicants to submit their bids.[57]

By the summer of 1888 four contenders had put themselves forward in what would become a fierce competition: Basel had made the start on 7 March, Bern submitted its bid on 31 May, while Zurich and Lucerne followed suit on 12 and 14 June respectively. The federal government swiftly proceeded to appoint a panel of foreign experts whose brief it was to produce a report. The ensuing parliamentary and public debate quickly came to centre on the main contentious issue, the location of the future museum, and here a veritable contest erupted in the spring of 1888. One newspaper likened the competition over the National Museum to the quarrel over Homer's place of birth which had for so long preoccupied the city-states of ancient Greece.[58] Given the advantages they offered in terms of existing infrastructure and ease of access by railway, Bern and Zurich quickly emerged as favourites. From the summer of 1890 the contest between these two towns was fought out in parliament and in the

editorials of the political press. The two federal chambers could not agree
on the issue. In the Council of States, Zurich prevailed largely due to the
support it received from representatives of Catholic cantons who were
suspicious of the politically more radical Bern. But in the National
Council, Bern received eleven votes more than Zurich. Yet the relatively
clear support for Zurich in the Council of States put considerable pressure
on the larger chamber to fall in line. When in a fourth ballot a majority of
delegates again voted for Bern, the supporters of Zurich's candidature
accused the Bern members of the National Council of putting their canton
before the interests of the nation. At last, in the summer of 1891, a final
ballot confirmed the decision of the Council of States in favour of Zurich.
It would take until 1898 for the *Landesmuseum* to open its doors to the
public, attracting more than 170,000 visitors in the first few months of its
existence.[59]

Concluding on a broader conceptual and methodological note, this
chapter has emphasised three points. First, and most basically, I have
suggested that it is eminently useful to distinguish between nationalism
as an ideological and/or political movement and the nation as a focus of
collective identification. The distinction allows us to separate cultural
codes or idioms, which for most of the time are too self-evident to many
people to become a topic of public debate, from explicit, action-related
ideologies employed by particular movements to address particular problems. To put it deliberately crudely for the sake of clarity: nationalism is
active and driven by collective expectations, while the nation is passive and
rooted in the status quo.

Secondly and closely related, I have restricted the use of the term
'nationalism' to those cases where the idea of the nation is employed to
legitimate the construction of new kinds of political community (whether
this involves the destruction of the political status quo or its partial
reformation) rather than merely to describe or justify existing ones. If we
apply the latter, weaker definition, as some scholars suggest we should, then
nationalism as a phenomenon is clearly much older than the eighteenth
century, while nationalism as an analytical concept loses its analytical force.
In Switzerland, the first explicit demands to create a new (i.e. more closely
integrated) political community in which the word 'nation' (and the
cognate term 'fatherland' as well as the various elements of the ethno-
historicist liberation narrative) played a central role were made in the 1770s.

My final point was to stress that the obvious need for some basic
working definitions, which as ideal types are necessarily static, should not
prevent us from recognising the dynamic nature of the phenomena we

study. Historically, both the idea of the nation and nationalism as an ideology and movement were subject to change, reflecting significant transformation in the social, political and technological structure of a given society. In Switzerland it was in the two decades before the French Revolution that nationalism emerged as an *ideological* movement, whose central ambition of closer national integration and constitutional reform was most forcefully pursued by the Helvetic Society. Yet it was not until the constitutional conflicts of the 1830s and 1840s that a more populist and democratic idea of the nation began to capture the public to an extent that allows us to speak of nationalism as a *political* movement. And it was only with the creation of the *Bundesstaat* in 1848 that we witness the rise of a nation-building nationalism that triggered a contest over the shaping of public culture and institutions. Ironically, it was in and through these public controversies between the nationalising state and civil society (and not as a result of an ideological consensus) that the national idea got solidified into a moral common sense.

NOTES

1   *Aktensammlung aus der Zeit der Helvetischen Republik (1798–1803)*, ed. Johannes Strickler and Alfred Rufer 16 vols. (Bern, 1886–1911, Freiburg 1940–66), vol. III, p. 268. Subsequently cited as ASHR.

2   *ASHR*, vol. III, p. 529.

3   M. Bühler, 'Die Nationalfeste', in P. Seippel (ed.), *Die Schweiz im neunzehnten Jahrhundert* (Bern: Schmid & Francke, 1900), p. 352.

4   The transformation of the nation and of nationalism in the course of the long nineteenth century may represent an obvious question. But it is a question too easily ignored in a discussion sometimes restricted to what might be termed the 'emergence' of these phenomena. In many of the general historical accounts, as well as in much of the theoretical literature, for example, these changes, and their possible causes, are not really explored.

5   On the distinction between 'ideology' and 'cultural idioms', see Theda Skocpol, *Social Revolutions in the Modern World* (Cambridge University Press, 1994), p. 204.

6   The focus of this chapter is thus above all on basic formal changes in the use of the national idea over the long nineteenth century. For an article that is more specifically concerned with the nature of national identity and nationalism during the same period, see Oliver Zimmer, 'Circumscribing community: Swiss nationalism in the long nineteenth century', in Mark Hewitson and Timothy Baycroft (eds.), *Nationalism in Europe 1789–1914: Civic and Ethnic Traditions* (Oxford University Press, forthcoming). The view adopted in this essay, which sees nationalism as a problem-solving ideology that is itself subject

to change, owes much to John Breuilly's essay, 'Nationalism and the History of Ideas', *Proceedings of the British Academy* 105 (2000), 187–223.

7 On the debate over nationalism's temporal origins in some classic works, see Anthony D. Smith, *Theories of Nationalism* (2nd edn, London: Duckworth, 1983), ch. 2. For recent research on the eighteenth century, see in particular David A. Bell, *The Cult of the Nation in France: Inventing Nationalism, 1860–1900* (Cambridge, MA: Harvard University Press, 2001); Gerald Newman, *The Rise of English Nationalism: A Cultural History 1740–1830* (New York: St. Martin's Press, 1997); Oliver Zimmer, *A Contested Nation: History, Memory and Nationalism in Switzerland, 1761–1891* (Cambridge University Press, 2003), ch. 2. See also the essay by Ian McBride in this volume.

8 Koselleck's concepts are eminently useful here. Nationalism as an *ideological movement* seems most likely to arise where the gap between experience ('Erwartungsraum') and expectation ('Erwartungshorizont') is increasingly perceived as unbridgeable. Reinhard Koselleck, *Vergangene Zukunft. Zur Semantik geschichtlicher Zeiten* (Frankfurt: Suhrkamp, 1989).

9 For an exploration of this early modern discourse of Swiss nationhood, see especially Thomas Maissen, 'Weshalb die Eidgenossen Helvetier wurden. Die humanistische Definition einer *natio*', in Johannes Helmrath, Ulrich Muhlack and Gerrit Walther (eds.), *Diffusion des Humanismus. Studien zur nationalen Geschichtsschreibung europäischer Humanisten* (Göttingen: Wallstein, 2002), pp. 210–49. On the constitutional development of the Swiss Confederation, see Hans Conrad Peyer, *Verfassungsgeschichte der alten Schweiz* (Zurich: Schulthess Polygraphischer Verlag, 1978); Roger Sablonier, 'The Swiss Confederation', in Christopher Allmand (ed.), *The New Cambridge Medieval History*, vol. VII (Cambridge University Press, 1998), pp. 645–70.

10 This is the theme of Andreas Suter's study, *Der schweizerische Bauernkrieg von 1653. Politische Sozialgeschichte – Sozialgeschichte eines politischen Ereignisses* (Tübingen: Bibliotheca Academica, 1997).

11 *Schweizerisches Museum* (1786), 69.

12 Quentin Skinner, 'Some problems in the analysis of political thought and action', *Political Theory* 2 (1974), 295–6.

13 Joseph Anton Felix Balthasar, *Historische und moralische Erklärungen* (Zurich: Orell, Gessner, Fuesslin, 1775), preface. Focusing on debates and prize competitions of the Académie Française and other manifestations of patriotic discourse, David A. Bell has identified a similar transition from classical to 'national' role models in the cult of great men that acquired such prominence in late-eighteenth-century France. See Bell, *Cult of the Nation*, p. 122.

14 *Verhandlungen der Helvetischen Gesellschaft* 1765, 27. Subsequently cited as *VHG*.

15 *VHG* 1769, 30–1.

16 *VHG* 1782, 78–81.

17 *VHG* 1783: 11. The decision to restrict active membership to citizens of Swiss cantons did not, however, result in a decline in the number of foreign visitors.

See Ulrich Im Hof and François de Capitani, *Die Helvetische Gesellschaft. Spätaufklärung in der Schweiz* (2 vols., Frauenfeld: Huber, 1983).

18 Frederik Barth (ed.), *Ethnic Groups and Boundaries* (London: Allen & Unwin, 1969).

19 Linda Colley, *Britons: Forging the Nation, 1707–1837* (London: Vintage, 1996), p. 6.

20 Quoted from the article 'Volk, Nation, Nationalismus, Masse', in Otto Brunner, Werner Conze and Reinhard Koselleck (eds.), *Geschichtliche Grundbegriffe. Historisches Lexikon zur politisch-sozialen Sprache in Deutschland* (8 vols., Stuttgart: Klett, 1992), vol. VII, p. 310.

21 *VHG* 1763, 36–37.

22 *Schweizerisches Museum* I (1787), 187–8.

23 *Der Landbote* 38 (21 September 1848).

24 Stuart J. Woolf, *Napoleon's Integration of Europe* (London: Routledge, 1991), p. 15. For popular responses to French rule see, for example, Otto Dann and John Dinwiddy (eds.), *Nationalism in the Age of the French Revolution* (London: Hambledon, 1988); T. C.W. Blanning, *The French Revolution in Germany: Occupation and Resistance in the Rhineland, 1792–1802* (Oxford University Press, 1983).

25 Cited after *ASHR*, vol. I, p. 567.

26 The Helvetic Republic is discussed in Zimmer, *A Contested Nation*, ch. 3.

27 See Johann Caspar Lavater, *An das Directorium der Französischen Republik* (Zurich, 1798).

28 'Mémoire über die Lage in der Schweiz' (27 August 1833). Cited in Luzius Lenherr, *Ultimatum an die Schweiz. Der politische Druck Metternichs auf die Eidgenossenschaft infolge ihrer Asylpolitik in der Regeneration* (Bern: Peter Lang, 1991), p. 40.

29 Cited in Rémy Charbon, *'O Schweizerland, du schöne Braut'. Politische Schweizer Literatur 1798–1848* (Zurich: Limmat Verlag, 1998), p. 9.

30 See Albert Tanner, 'Das Recht auf Revolution. Radikalismus – Antijesuitismus – Nationalismus', in Thomas Hildbrand and Albert Tanner (eds.), *Im Zeichen der Revolution. Der Weg zum Schweizerischen Bundesstaat* (Zurich: Chronos, 1999), p. 63. For a testimony of the influence of newspapers on the world-view of the rural population, see the diary of Johann Ulrich Furrer, *Schweizerländli 1848. Das Tagebuch eines jungen Sternenbergers* (Stäfa: Rothenhäusler Verlag, 1998).

31 Christoph Guggenbühl, 'Pressefreiheit als "Quelle der Wahrheit". Zur Entstehung politisch-publizistischer Öffentlichkeit in der Schweiz, 1798–1848', in Andreas Ernst *et al.* (eds.), *Revolution und Innovation. Die konfliktreiche Entstehung des schweizerischen Bundesstaates von 1848* (Zurich: Chronos, 1998), p. 225.

32 Thomas Christian Müller, 'Switzerland 1847/49: a provisional, successful end of a "democratic revolution"', in Dieter Dowe, H.-G. Haupt and D. Langewiesche (eds.), *Europe in 1848: Revolution and Reform* (New York and Oxford: Berg, 2001), p. 229.

33 These figures are based on Franco Luzzato, 'Mediale Konstruktion des liber-
    alen Nationalismus im Vorfeld der Bundesstaatsgründung', unpublished
    MPhil thesis, University of Zurich (1996), p. 24. For a comparative assessment
    of pre-revolutionary forms of communication, including the role of the press,
    see Jonathan Sperber, *The European Revolutions, 1848–1851* (Cambridge
    University Press, 1994), pp. 55–63.

34 Cited in Rudolf Braun, *Sozialer und kultureller Wandel in einem ländlichen
    Industriegebiet im 19. und 20. Jahrhundert* (Zurich: Chronos, 1999 [1965]),
    p. 328.

35 Tanner, 'Das Recht auf Revolution', pp. 118–19.

36 Zimmer, *Contested Nation*, pp. 129–32.

37 *Landbote* 12 (23 March 1848); 1 (6 January 1848); 21 (25 May 1848).

38 *Schweizer-Bote* 37 (25 March 1848).

39 The most vocal advocates of the bicameral solution were the French-speaking
    cantons, while the liberals of the German-speaking cantons tended to favour a
    single national parliament. This was discussed in an article entitled 'Die
    deutsche und die französische Schweiz', *Neue Zürcher Zeitung* 233 (20
    August 1848).

40 *Schweizer-Bote* 37 (25 March 1848) and 106 (2 September 1848).

41 Interestingly enough, the strongest challenge to economic determinism has
    come from economic historians such as Hans-Jörg Siegenthaler and Margrit
    Müller. Müller has gone so far as to deny the existence of a 'national economic
    interest' for the period 1830–48. What did exist, she argued, was disparate
    economic interests and ambitions of individual cantons, which hindered rather
    than favoured the drive for constitutional reform at the federal level: Margrit
    Müller, 'Nationale Einigung aus wirtschaftlicher Notwendigkeit', in
    Hildbrand and Tanner (eds.), *Im Zeichen der Revolution*, pp. 91–112. The
    first systematic critique of functionalist accounts of the 1848 settlement can
    be found in Hans-Jörg Siegenthaler, 'Supranationalität, Nationalismus und
    regionale Autonomie. Erfahrungen des schweizerischen Bundesstaates –
    Perspektiven für die europäische Gemeinschaft', *Traverse* (1994), 117–140.

42 See the seminal historical account by Eugen Weber, *Peasants into Frenchmen:
    The Modernization of Rural France, 1870–1914* (Stanford University Press,
    1976). For theoretical elaborations, see Karl W. Deutsch, *Nationalism and
    Social Communication* (2nd edn, Cambridge, MA: MIT Press, 1966); Ernest
    Gellner, *Nations and Nationalism* (Oxford: Blackwell, 1983). For a more
    instrumentalist account, see Eric Hobsbawm and Terence Ranger (eds.), *The
    Invention of Tradition* (Cambridge University Press, 1983). The best critical
    examination of these theories is Anthony D. Smith, *Nationalism and
    Modernism: A Critical Survey of Recent Theories of Nations and Nationalism*
    (London and New York: Routledge, 1998), esp. chs. 1–4.

43 In the late nineteenth century, only Britain revealed a considerably lower
    degree of agricultural occupation than Switzerland. See Jean-François
    Bergier, *Wirtschaftsgeschichte der Schweiz. Von den Anfängen bis zur
    Gegenwart* (Zurich: Benziger, 1983), pp. 111–12, 225–6.

44 On these developments see Roland Ruffieux, 'Die Schweiz des Freisinns (1848–1914)', in Beatrix Mesmer (ed.), *Geschichte der Schweiz und der Schweizer* (Basel: Helbing & Lichtenhahn, 1986), pp. 661–3.

45 For these different approaches, see Celia Applegate, 'A Europe of regions: reflections on the historiography of sub-national places in modern times', *American Historical Review* 104 (October 1999), 1157–82.

46 This draws on Norbert Elias's conception of society as figurations of inter-dependent actors. See his work *Über den Prozess der Zivilisation: Soziogenetische und psychogenetische Untersuchungen* (2 vols. Frankfurt: Suhrkamp, 1976), vol. I, preface.

47 For a more thoroughly documented statement of this argument, see Zimmer, *A Contested Nation*, ch. 5. See also the contributions of Abigail Green and Stuart J. Woolf in this volume. Both authors draw on examples that point to the importance of competition between the nationalising state and its con-stitutive parts.

48 See the report by the Swiss Councillor Numa Droz, *L'Art. 27 de la Constitution Fédérale et l'instruction primaire en Suisse. Rapport au Conseil Fédéral Suisse par le Département Fédéral de l'Intérieur* (Bern, 1878), pp. 5–8.

49 See Lucien Criblez, 'Der Bildungsartikel in der Bundesverfassung vom 29. Mai 1874', in L. Criblez, C. Jenzer, R. Hofstetter and C. Magnin (eds.), *Eine Schule für die Demokratie. Zur Entwicklung der Volksschule in der Schweiz im 19. Jahrhundert* (Bern, 1999), p. 348. See also Hans von Greyerz, 'Der Bundesstaat seit 1848', in *Handbuch der Schweizer Geschichte*, vol. II (Zurich: Berichthaus Verlag, 1980), p. 1113.

50 See the following reports: *Art. 27 der Bundesverfassung und der Primarunterricht in der Schweiz. Bericht an den schweizerischen Bundesrath vom eidg. Departement des Innern* (Bern, 1878), p. 68; *Regulative für die Rekrutenprüfungen und die Nachschulen* (13 April 1875).

51 Eidg. Statistisches Bureau (ed.), *Ergebnisse der Rekruten-Prüfung in der Schweiz im Jahr* 1875 (Zurich, 1876), p. VII.

52 *Schweizerische Lehrerzeitung* 14 (1 April 1876), p. 116.

53 *Landbote* 31 (5 February 1882).

54 Catholics and Protestants opposing the federal *Schulartikel*, the conser-vative *Schwyzer-Zeitung* complained, were portrayed as 'enemies of the fatherland': *Schwyzer Zeitung* 91 (15 November 1882).

55 *Die Errichtung eines schweizerischen National-Museums. Rede, gehalten im schweizerischen Nationalrath, den 9. Juli 1883, von Salomon Vögelin* (Uster: J. Weilenmann, 1883), pp. 4–5.

56 *Bericht des Bundesrates an die Bundesversammlung vom 25. November 1884*, 3 Spalte.

57 'Botschaft des Bundesrathes an die Bundesversammlung vom 14. Juni 1886'.

58 *Landbote* 56 (6 March 1888).

59 See *Jahresberichte Schweizerisches Landesmuseum Zürich* (Zurich: Orell Füssli, 1892–1900).

CHAPTER 16

Nation and power in the liberal state: Britain
c. 1800–c. 1914*

Peter Mandler

The ancient historiographical tradition that held that the British state was different from European norms has been challenged in the past generation by Gramscian and Foucauldian perspectives, which have tended to suggest that power constructed the nation in Britain just as in the rest of Europe, only not so palpably through the agency of the state, but rather through a cultural 'hegemony' or a 'master narrative' or a discursive rather than institutional 'governmentality'.[1] In this chapter I want to try to reinstate the gist of the traditional argument, while responding to and – to a certain extent – incorporating these newer perspectives. Liberalism did involve a distinctive configuration of power, one in which power was more widely diffused throughout society, and not concentrated in the state. It also entailed, partly as a consequence, a distinctive pattern of national belonging, one which was not so attached to or generated by the state. Especially before the First World War – though also enduringly – nation and state remained more distinct than in many other modern polities, to the extent that national belonging could be explicitly defined as independence from (or even opposition to) the state.

I

Historians often argue that the British state did not engage in the strenuous nation-building characteristic of other European polities because it did not need to. There is a good deal of truth in this, but only in certain ways, about which we must be precise. There is, first of all, the view that the modern British state benefited from a long pre-modern period of nation-building, in which most of the crucial work was done before the eighteenth century.[2]

* I am grateful to the participants in the 'Power and the Nation in History' conference for their helpful comments on the oral version of this chapter, and to Phil Harling for very penetrating observations on an early written version.

As a qualified 'modernist', I think this argument can only be taken so far. The long continuity of institutions, for example, only looks like successful nation-building after the fact. Up until 1792 the French monarchy could claim the same antiquity as the English, as could other European dynasties and nobilities. In certain ways, Burke's insistence on the special and sacred continuity of English institutions was only possible – and was certainly of new significance – after the continuity of other countries' institutions had been ruptured. It also required a certain lapse of time, permitting memory to dissipate or blur, after Britain's significant discontinuities – 1649, 1688, and, for Scotland, 1707.

The four-nations perspective reminds us how new, in fact, most British institutions were at the beginning of the nineteenth century. Even where British institutions represented the extension of English practices to other nations, as in the special and important case of parliament, they had a job of integration to perform that was still under way (or, in Ireland, only just beginning) in 1800. The four-nations perspective also modifies our traditional view of England as a small, compact, insular, well-integrated (i.e. monoglot, easily travelled, single-market) kingdom: England was never an island, Britain was not particularly small or compact, monoglot or easily travelled, and the single market was still being hammered out contentiously in 1800.

This is not to deny that England itself benefited from an unusual degree of homogeneity, nor that the Union with Scotland (and, later, Ireland) was aimed at extending that homogeneity to the rest of the British Isles – but this homogeneity or integration was not necessarily a manifestation of nation or a creature of the state. Early commercialisation and urbanisation, and unusual degrees of physical mobility, undoubtedly facilitated high levels of social and economic integration. Movements around the British Isles had long preceded the modern period, such that almost a third of the Irish population in the early eighteenth century was of Scottish or English descent.[3] Commercialisation and urbanisation accelerated this movement. By 1800 most parishes had, as Roy Porter has observed, more 'movers' than 'stayers'.[4] One sixth of the entire population had experienced life in London.[5] The resulting degree of cultural integration was striking: thus the famous difference between the population of France, of which less than 20 per cent was 'fully conversant' with the language of the Parisian elite in 1790, or the population of Italy, of which only 2–3 per cent was fluent in the language of the Turin elite in 1870, and the population of the United Kingdom, of which perhaps 80 per cent was fluent in the language of the London elite in 1800 (that is, nearly 100 per cent of the English, Cornish having just died out; nearly as many of the Scots; 50 per cent of the Irish; and even in Wales perhaps a third).[6] No wonder the French and Italian regimes needed state schools more than the British.

The point here is that such integration was achieved without significant impetus from or association with the state, and possibly without extensive national identification. This highly mobile, increasingly monoglot people experienced its cultural integration as a freedom from the impediments of a particularist or authoritarian state; it did not necessarily experience thereby a positive Englishness or Britishness and it certainly didn't associate much of its national consciousness with the state. If we consider the plebeian identities famously identified by E. P. Thompson, 'the rights of the free-born Englishman' naturally come first to mind in this connection. These were not, however, the terms in which the Scots or the Irish expressed their rights, except some self-identified Englishmen in Ireland, and in fact it was a distinctive feature of the British state that it kept the legal rights of the Scots and the English largely distinct. Amongst the English, these rights were as likely to be expressed in and through the context of local community institutions – the parish, the petty sessions, the borough – as in nation-state terms. Very often, too, they were expressed as a barrier of self-protection against fellow-citizens and against the power of the state, rather than as an affiliation with the state. 'The meanest English plough-man studies law, /And keeps therefore the Magistrates in awe', Daniel Defoe wrote in 1700, as part of his definition of 'that het'rogeneous thing, an Englishman'.[7] 'The stance of the common Englishman', as E. P. Thompson himself put it, 'was not so much democratic, in any positive sense, as anti-absolutist. He felt himself to be an individualist, with few affirmative rights, but protected by the laws against the intrusion of arbitrary power.'[8]

As Bob Shoemaker has pointed out, in the most urbanised settings (at first, principally London), rights were not even likely to be expressed through or in the local community, but rather through an increasingly individuated sense of self, and 'new collectivities' formed out of these selves from the bottom up, 'such as voluntary societies and class'.[9] Shoemaker shows that Londoners made decreasing recourse to the law to defend their honour over the course of the eighteenth century, a sign in his view that 'honour' was defined less in communal terms and thus also that 'rights' to go to a common law were less useful. Instead, he suggests, Londoners turned for identity and support to those new collectivities, the most powerful of which were religious in nature – already well established by 1800, as Thompson showed, as providing primary plebeian identities.

Here, too, the Union left Scottish and English state Churches entirely distinct, and, *pace* J. C. D. Clark's view of eighteenth-century England as an *ancien régime*,[10] within England the picture was one of considerable religious pluralism, so that identities were forged variously as Christian or Protestant but not necessarily as English or state Protestant. After 1830, state intervention to bolster the cultural purchase of religion worked through this plural structure, amounting to virtual concurrent endowment of the separate Churches of England, Ireland and Scotland, and also the Catholic, Methodist and dissenting churches, mostly by means of state funding of denominational schools and colleges. Out of these plural religious identities sprang the great nineteenth-century panoply of associational identities – political, moral, philanthropic, as well as gender and class. Already by 1800 the English were best known amongst foreigners for their fissiparousness: they had the homogeneity of the market-place, 'the nation of shopkeepers', buying, trading, shifting, changing, not the homogeneity of common values and traditions supposedly characteristic of other nations.[11]

Thus by 1800 we do have across the United Kingdom, yet not wholly defined by the United Kingdom, an increasingly well-integrated, monoglot, physically mobile, commercialised and urbanised people. This people was already displaying many of the qualities of the ideal-type liberal subject as hypothesised by the Foucauldians, defined as 'free', not requiring artificial constraints or visible discipline, but having internalised the invisible disciplines of liberalism; nucleated, neither dependent upon nor much connected to kin or neighbours or fellow-citizens; self-reliant, making diminishing demands upon public institutions and diminishing recourse to the law; and civil, tolerant of (or merely uninterested in) the activities and differences of the rest of society and obedient to the minimum set of common rules that policed such peaceful coexistence in large, densely packed numbers. Each of these characterisations could be and has been challenged: for example, the Foucauldians' liberal subject rarely engages in the collective solidarities of associational life that were such an integral part of British society at this time. For the moment, I offer this ideal-type picture simply as a way of conceding that the supposed modernising motives for nation-building were rendered unnecessary in Britain by early modernisation, but largely outside of a nation-state context.[12]

Now, in 1800, of course, Britain was fighting the last and by far the greatest of its great eighteenth-century wars, its state was taking a quarter of GNP (more than it would again until the First World War), and a new sense of Britishness was building up in the process described by Linda

Colley.[13] Let us acknowledge some criticisms of Colley – that she exaggerates the integrating power of Protestantism across the four nations, and that she smoothes out what was in fact a cyclical and not necessarily cumulative process; the American War, for example, was one of the least popular wars in British history and a source of division as much as unity. Nevertheless, we must also acknowledge that wartime nation-building, when British elites undertook it, was devastatingly successful precisely because of the degree of integration already prevailing in British society and economy. On the crudest level, as John Brewer, Thomas Ertman and Martin Daunton have shown, the British 'fiscal-military state' was able to extract vastly more of the nation's resources than any of its continental rivals; this fiscal success was owing not only to Britain's wealth but also to the efficiency of the interaction between tax payer and state; and this efficiency was owing at a basic level to the taxpayer's *trust* in the state.[14]

What did that trust mean, and what does it say about the extent of identification with both nation and state? This is not a simple question. A complex apparatus entailed many different kinds of trust. There was trust in the processes of tax assessment and collection, facilitated by local rather than national administration of the tax system. There was trust in the public credit markets, which encouraged investors to lend to the state on the security of future taxes. There was trust in the honest and efficient handling and expenditure of public monies. Above all, there was trust in the objects to which that expenditure would be directed – principally war against France – and equally importantly the objects to which that expenditure would not be directed – the infringement of liberty. To employ Michael Mann's terms, the British state was weak in 'despotic power', and for that very reason strong in 'infrastructural power'.[15]

Something of the same sort can be said of forms of identification with state and nation, moving beyond the bottom line of willingness to pay taxes. The kinds of patriotism identified by Colley – willingness to fight, identification with the monarchy and the military – were mostly circumscribed by the same limited purposes, and defined similarly by the same absences. This very militaristic patriotism was, as Colley argues, couched in official propaganda as 'a crusade for freedom against the forces of military tyranny'.[16] It was calculated to appeal to a people traditionally suspicious of royal, military or indeed any kind of executive power, and which relied on those checks and balances implicit in the idea of the 'King in Parliament', but importantly it also came from the heart of a political elite that had itself only a limited interest in the nationalisation of power. We may disagree about whether this elite disposition was a matter of ideology or self-interest – whether, in the way I have already suggested, the needs of power were already quite adequately served by the construction of a liberal subject. But we cannot ignore the crucial convergence between popular and elite hostility to the concentration of power in the hands of a centralised state. There was also a parallel degree of convergence in an unwillingness to associate the people collectively with the national military effort (the kind of modern nation-building in which France and America were already specialising). While the parliamentary elite was, unsurprisingly, perfectly happy to memorialise its own martial virtues in medals, monuments and paintings to heroic generals and admirals, there were no tributes to the people *en masse* (and fewer even to allegorical figures such as Britannia) as there were in France, America or indeed Prussia. The diarist Joseph Farington was rather shocked to see that all ranks were included in a memorial tablet that he espied at the Invalides during the Peace of Amiens.[17] But there is also evidence that popular sentiment was equally averse to such displays, condemned as Jacobinical if too nationalist, 'Old Corruption' if too oligarchic. More popular than Britannia was the symbol of 'John Bull', who in this period metamorphosed from bumbling squire to grumbling tax payer, oppressed by the parliamentary elite's dreams of national glory.[18] Even the parliamentary elite's self-commemoration had to be hidden in the crypt of St Paul's, where it remains today; if, as has been suggested, it amounts to a 'British Pantheon', it is a Pantheon that vividly reveals the differences between British and French nation-building.[19]

Of course a great deal could be justified by or hidden amongst the costs of war. Elite and popular convergence around the minimal nation-state is more strikingly evident in the rapid dismantling of the fiscal-military state in the years immediately after the peace of 1815, and the strict limits within which the resulting laissez-faire state was able to engage in further acts of nation-building.

II

It seems to me one of the most extraordinary facts of modern European history that, uniquely among the major states of Europe, the expenditure of the British state in the nineteenth century did not grow but shrank. Even if we take the immediate post-1815 levels (rather than higher wartime levels) as our baseline, we can still say that British state expenditure grew more slowly than that of any other major European state – up 50 per cent by 1880, versus 400 per cent for France, 300 per cent for Austria, Sweden and

Belgium.[20] The disparity remains if we compare not absolute levels of expenditure but expenditure per capita or as a proportion of GNP.[21] By 1880, central government was taking 6 per cent of GNP in Britain, 12 per cent in Austria, 13 per cent in France. Some of this disparity derives from varying distributions of responsibility between central and local government. The British did prefer to pass as many responsibilities as possible down to local government, an ideological decision which itself testifies to a nation/state disjunction.[22] Still, taking account of different central–local balances, all public expenditure in Britain amounted to 9 per cent of GNP compared with 13 per cent in Germany, 16 per cent in France. Predictably, only the United States, of the major states, took substantially less than Britain.[23] Borrowing another of Michael Mann's apt generalisations, nineteenth-century states in general found it difficult to keep pace with the rate of growth of the peoples and economies they were alleged to be controlling or constructing.[24] The difference was that the British state deliberately fell behind, not because it couldn't keep up, but because it didn't want to.

Expenditure can tell us only so much. Among other objections, these calculations ignore the base-rate issue (Britain's voracious fiscal-military state started from a high base); they ignore highly variable population and GNP changes; above all, they only measure the nation-building activities that cost money.[25] Let us focus instead on the most intensive nation-building activities in which states engage, those things that turn 'peasants into Frenchmen'.

Of these by far the most important is education. Here the British followed their distinctive pattern until around 1870. Almost alone of the major European states, they had no state schools; state funding for education was channelled through schools run privately by religious societies. This would have long-term effects upon national consciousness, lasting well into the later period of state education. As late as the First World War, few classrooms had the flags or maps that are supposed to provide the foundation for the 'banal nationalism' of the modern citizen; they had instead bibles and religious tracts, and accordingly many early-twentieth century schoolchildren recalled in their memoirs that they had long thought 'their country' was the Holy Land.[26] As before, I do not claim that this privately run religious education gave no sense of national consciousness, only that what sense of national consciousness it engendered was loosely if at all connected to the state.

What of the more culturally symbolic acts of nation-building? I am thinking here of the invention and/or cultivation of national history, traditions, culture and landscape by state institutions, normally at a more elevated social level but still with heavily freighted symbolic value for the imagining of the national community. No effort at all was made on a United Kingdom basis to develop this national symbolism (with one key exception which I will come to shortly). National institutions *were* developed on a four-nations basis – for example, National Galleries for England (1824), Scotland (1850) and Ireland (1854), or Public Record Offices for Scotland (as early as 1789), England (1838) and Ireland (1867). Separate systems of higher education were maintained. It cannot be said however that the institutions of the four nations were impressive by European standards; they performed rather like the four national football teams of the United Kingdom do today in relation to the single teams of Germany, France or Spain. There was little official patronage of national history, either through the universities or, still less, through purpose-built research institutions. In the matter of its cultural patrimony, Britain suffered from the survival of its monarchy in its current semi-private, semi-public form. Royal collections and institutions were never nationalised, as they were elsewhere, both in republican regimes (as in France) and in constitutional monarchies (as in the German states, where royal collections became formally public in the course of the nineteenth century). British cultural institutions had to be created from scratch by parliament, which was sparing with its funding and tight in its control.[27]

Parliament itself was, of course, that key exception to the general rule that no United Kingdom institutions were created in this period. The Scottish and Irish parliaments were merged into the English, and very grand and expensive new quarters were built for them (though only because, fortuitously, the medieval palace of Westminster burnt down in 1834). These new buildings were, exceptionally, larded heavily with national symbolism, from their basic architectural form (a canny blend of historicist styles) down to the nationalist frescoes that adorned the interior, carefully patterned after German models. As with the 'British Pantheon' in St Paul's, the parliamentary elite was always happier to accord national status to itself than to any rival social actors. Furthermore, the fire of 1834 had coincided with an unusual period of state-sponsored nationalism in Britain, beginning with the Reform Act of 1832 and ending with the revolutions of 1848. It seems unlikely that anything so grand or so explicitly national would have been built after a fire in 1824 or 1854, as witness the more modest (and deliberately non-national) rebuilding of government offices in Whitehall around the latter date.[28]

The monarchy was another 'new' United Kingdom institution, and as Linda Colley has shown one which had in the pre-1815 belligerent period taken its nation-building responsibilities unusually seriously. However, George IV's attempts to push this nationalising strategy into the post-war period came unstuck on his own personal unpopularity and parliamentary opposition to undue monarchical self-assertion, as witness the Queen Caroline affair and the check delivered to the royal reconstruction of the West End of London. The Victorian compromise represented a partial retreat from this nationalising strategy. The crown created few of its own national institutions, preferring to offer 'patronage' to bodies, especially philanthropies, already legitimated by civil society. Those quasi-royal institutions already in existence, such as the Royal Academy of Arts, took a lower profile or followed a parliamentary lead. Victoria offered herself less as the embodiment of and more as the mirror of the nation, a semi-public, semi-private role which, contrary to the Gramscian interpretation, did not necessarily entail a 'mystification' rendering her *more* powerful. When contemporaries spoke of Britain as a 'crowned republic' – Tennyson's words – they were articulating this sense of a nation and a crown in partnership.[29]

III

What forces were inhibiting the state sponsorship of nation-building in nineteenth-century Britain? Most obviously, many of the ulterior goals of European nation-building had already been achieved, or were being achieved by market rather than state-based mechanisms in place at the beginning of the period. A very large part of nineteenth-century European state activity, for instance, was devoted to building up state infrastructural power that the British state already had, or, more simply still, to building up a national communications infrastructure – road, post, railway and telegraph networks. Much of the disparity between British and other European state expenditure in the nineteenth century arises from this difference, that more of the communications infrastructure and the personnel needed to run it were in state hands on the Continent. The Prussian state in 1911 drew half of its revenues from its railway enterprise.[30] Conversely, some of the growth of the British state at the end of our period derived from the fact that its high levels of integration led to more use of those parts of the infrastructure that the state did own; for example, it had by far the highest postal flows in Europe.[31]

Most of the rest of the state's nation-building activity was devoted, in Eugen Weber's classic formulation, to an internal *mission civilisatrice*: nation-building not for its own sake, but to make citizens with state-friendly internal norms.[32] Here again the British state found most of its work had already been done for it. It could communicate with its people; it could, for its limited purposes, rely on their trust or at least co-operation; it could, at least after 1848, expect the general maintenance of social order with relatively low levels of domestic police or military presence. Although towards the end of the century there was concern in elite circles that some of the new collectivities, notably class (though also party), were in danger of providing alternative power-centres to rival the state, in practice the state's responses to these threats remained limited. State education, introduced in 1870, was locally controlled until 1902. At that point there was a more concerted effort to build national consciousness and to attach it to the state, in the rash of so-called 'national efficiency' movements and campaigns around the time of the Boer War. But this spasm was short lived and decisively short circuited by the Liberal landslide of 1906, after which state activity re-focused on welfare reforms with a less explicitly nation-building mission.[33]

There *was* a development of national consciousness in Britain over the course of the nineteenth century, but it was mostly not sponsored by the state, and its core values continued to work against state-sponsored nation-building. An increasingly homogenised people across the four nations – with a burgeoning sense of cultural enfranchisement motored by the communications revolution and by social and political stability – did have a set of collective identities, some of which cut across the nation, but others of which took a national form. 'The people' was one; 'the English people' (or sometimes the Scottish or Welsh peoples, but rarely the British people) was another;[34] after the middle of the century, the 'Anglo-Saxons' was another, actually more multi-national version.[35] The growth of these national identities was undoubtedly stimulated by elite *under*-provision of national consciousness, especially in the increasingly anomalous exclusion of most men from the franchise, and it was initially democratic movements – against post-Napoleonic repression, for the Great Reform Act, for the People's Charter – that propelled national consciousness forwards.

While fuelled by the demand for political franchises, this new national consciousness was not defined by them. As much recent scholarship has sought to demonstrate, British democratic radicalism from Peterloo to Chartism was dominated not so much by a desire to capture the nation-state for the people as by a desire to throw it off and blow it up. The nation-state was 'Old Corruption', 'the Thing', a 'system' of blood-suckers, parasites and plutocrats. From this point of view, parliament could either be the saviour of the people or, depending on how far one felt it was enmeshed with 'Old Corruption', part of the problem. Similarly, the reform of parliament as achieved in the 1830s could be interpreted either as a belated (but still welcome) legitimation of the nation-state or as a shriving, a purification, or indeed as a new source of oppression. Debate over these crucial questions raged in elite as well as popular circles throughout the 1830s and 1840s. Ultimately, the events of 1848 were decisive in discrediting a statist and even, for many people, a parliamentary understanding of the nation.[36]

The emerging Victorian discourse of national consciousness came to revolve around the Englishman's capacity for *self*-government. This theme began to dominate discussion of English national consciousness in the 1830s and 1840s, in parallel and to some extent in competition with, in popular circles, Chartist and, in elite circles, 'liberal Anglican' alternatives.[37] It drew, of course, upon older national and religious discourses of liberty, but from the 1840s became less defensive – aiming not to keep the magistrates in awe but to make the Englishman his own magistrate – and also more firmly collective and explicitly national. The free-born Englishman was coming into his own. Whether exercised individually, in the family or perhaps in the local democracy of the parish or (stretching the point) the borough, the capacity for self-government both captured the distinctive quality of the English and counterposed it to the organs of the central state, including, on occasion, Parliament.

Though it could be (and was) used to argue for further enfranchisement, as a recognition of the '*nation*' (that is, the people), it could be (and was) also used to argue for the essential irrelevance of the nation-*state*. An extreme and provocative version of this argument was regularly offered in the middle of the nineteenth century by radical advocates of parochialism like Joshua Toulmin Smith, who took as the fundamental principle of the English Constitution that 'the will of the folk and people is the only foundation for the authority of any in whose hands any public functions may, for any time being, be lodged', and that almost by definition this will could only be clearly expressed through local, face-to-face consultation. In such a view, parliament had no special value: 'Its authority is not, like that of the folk and people, self-derived and inherent.' Indeed, it could pose special dangers: 'When Democracy, in the shape of universal suffrage, erects an oligarchy, the nation is, as has been seen in France, as much subjected to an irresponsible and burthensome yoke as if a Dictator ruled or an hereditary aristocracy governed.'[38] Less controversially, but to much the same effect, Samuel Smiles polemicised against reliance upon great leaders, national institutions or Acts of Parliament in the 1866 edition of his bestseller *Self-Help*: it was rather 'the spirit of self-help, as exhibited in the energetic action of individuals . . . in all times . . . a marked feature in the English character, that furnishes the true measure of our power as a nation'. 'The vigorous growth of the nation has been mainly the result of the free energy of individuals . . . counteracting from time to time the effects of errors in our laws and imperfections in our constitution.'[39]

This conviction prevailed widely across many levels of society in the second half of the nineteenth century, reinforced by the sense of British distinctiveness at a time when much of the rest of Europe seemed to have fallen under the spell of 'bureau and barrack'.[40] Though normally voiced in a language of Englishness, it was equally accessible to – and nearly as popular among – the Scots and the Welsh (but not the Irish, as grew clear at the end of our period). Its independence from the institutional manifestations of the state meant, in fact, that it was ideally suited as a form of national consciousness for a multi-national kingdom and, indeed, for an empire. This 'ethnocentric liberalism', as I would call it, was therefore only partially 'national'.[41] It still burnt fiercely in the hearts of many – perhaps most – electors in 1906, when it was partly responsible for the check to more statist manifestations of national consciousness. Though no longer unrivalled, it continued to shape English and British national consciousness at least until the Second World War. When commentators (foreign as well as domestic) distinguished – as they did frequently – between English 'patriotism' and continental 'nationalism', they were not only making a partisan defence of English goodwill and pacific intentions; they were also asserting their preference for a national unity that had emerged organically in and from civil society over a national unity orchestrated by the state.[42]

During and after the Second World War, and to an extent before it, the British state became more like its continental counterparts, and in some ways more ambitious than they. But that twentieth-century process was not, I would argue, motored primarily by a drive for national integration. Much of the pressure for state intervention in social and economic organisation arose, in fact, out of working-class impatience both with 'ethnocentric liberalism' and with the empty rhetoric of patriotism, which expressed a real national unity without effecting any gains in social equality, for which state action was necessary.[43] The lesson of the twentieth century, at least for Britain, may be that the state grew stronger while national consciousness weakened. This process is a corollary (though not necessarily a consequence) of the nineteenth-century process, during which the state was weakened while national consciousness may have grown stronger.

NOTES

1 Robert Colls and Philip Dodd (eds.), *Englishness: Politics and Culture 1880–1920* (London: Croom Helm, 1986); Mitchell Dean, *The Constitution of Poverty: Toward a Genealogy of Liberal Governance* (London and New York: Routledge, 1991); James Vernon, *Politics and the People: A Study in English Political Culture, c. 1815–1867* (Cambridge University Press, 1993); Mary Poovey, *Making a Social Body: British Cultural Formation 1830–1864* (Chicago and London: University of Chicago Press, 1995), esp. ch. 3; Catherine Hall, Keith McClelland and Jane Rendall (eds.), *Defining the Victorian Nation: Class, Race, Gender and the Reform Act of 1867* (Cambridge University Press, 2000).

2 Liah Greenfeld, *Nationalism: Five Roads to Modernity* (Cambridge, MA: Harvard University Press, 1992); Adrian Hastings, *The Construction of Nationhood: Ethnicity, Religion and Nationalism* (Cambridge University Press, 1997).

3 R. F. Foster, *Modern Ireland 1600–1972* (London: Viking, 1988), p. 14.

4 Roy Porter, *English Society in the Eighteenth Century* (Harmondsworth: Penguin, 1982), p. 54.

5 E. A. Wrigley, 'A simple model of London's importance in changing English society and economy, 1650–1750', *Past & Present* 37 (1967), 49–51; considered if anything an under-estimate by Leonard Schwarz, 'London 1700–1840', in Peter Clark (ed.), *The Cambridge Urban History of Britain*, vol. II: 1540–1840 (Cambridge University Press, 2000), pp. 653–4.

6 David Vincent, *The Rise of Mass Literacy* (Cambridge: Polity, 2000), pp. 138–9; Gearóid Ó Tuathaigh, *Ireland before the Famine 1798–1848* (Dublin: Gill and Macmillan, 1972), p. 157; Keith Robbins, *Nineteenth-Century Britain: England, Scotland, and Wales, the Making of a Nation* (Oxford University Press, 1988), p. 31. See also V. E. Durkacz, *The Decline of the Celtic Languages* (Edinburgh: Donald, 1983).

7 Daniel Defoe, 'The true-born Englishman' (1700), in *The True-Born Englishman and Other Writings*, ed. P. N. Furbank and W. R. Owens (Harmondsworth: Penguin, 1997), pp. 35, 43.

8 E. P. Thompson, *The Making of the English Working Class* (1963; Harmondworth: Penguin, 1968), p. 87.

9 Robert B. Shoemaker, 'The decline of public insult in London 1660–1800', *Past & Present* 169 (2002), 97–131, esp. 125–30.

10 J. C. D. Clark, *English Society 1660–1832: Religion, Ideology and Politics during the Ancien Regime* (2nd edn, Cambridge University Press, 2000).

11 Paul Langford, *Englishness Identified: Manners and Character 1650–1850* (Oxford University Press, 2000), p. 280.

12 My interpretation here would probably appear too Weberian or functionalist to a Foucauldian: but their own interpretations often appear that way to me,

too, differentiated only by the rhetorical insistence that the liberal subject does not emerge organically from the modernisation process but is 'constructed' by 'power' (see e.g. Dean, *Constitution of Poverty*, pp. 214–15).

13 Philip Harling, *The Modern British State: An Historical Introduction* (Cambridge: Polity, 2001), pp. 42, 149; Linda Colley, *Britons: Forging the Nation 1707–1837* (New Haven and London: Yale University Press, 1994).

14 John Brewer, *The Sinews of Power: War, Money and the English State, 1688–1783* (New York: Alfred A. Knopf, 1989); Thomas Ertman, *Birth of the Leviathan: Building States and Regimes in Medieval and Early Modern Europe* (Cambridge University Press, 1997), pp. 208–23; Martin Daunton, *Trusting Leviathan: The Politics of Taxation in Britain, 1799–1914* (Cambridge University Press, 2001), ch. 1.

15 Michael Mann, *The Sources of Social Power*, vol. II: *The Rise of Classes and Nation States, 1760–1914* (Cambridge University Press, 1993), p. 59; Brewer, *Sinews of Power*, p. xx.

16 Colley, *Britons*, pp. 310–11.

17 Nicholas Penny, '"Amor publicus posuit": monuments for the people and of the people', *Burlington Magazine* 129 (1987), 793–800.

18 Miles Taylor, 'John Bull and the iconography of public opinion in England c. 1712–1929', *Past & Present* 134 (1992), 93–128.

19 Holger Hoock, *The King's Artists: The Royal Academy of Arts and the Politics of British Culture, 1760–1840* (Oxford University Press, 2003), pp. 257–76.

20 Philip Harling and Peter Mandler, 'From "fiscal-military" state to laissez-faire state, 1760–1850', *Journal of British Studies* 32 (1993), 59.

21 Cf. calculations in Mann for per capita central government expenditure at constant prices, 1820–80 (*Sources of Social Power*, p. 365): Britain down 10 per cent, France up 200 per cent, Austria up 100 per cent, United States up 200 per cent. I exclude Prussia/Germany only because its borders and its balance between central and local expenditures changed too dramatically over the period. I exclude local government expenditure because my focus here is on the nation-state; but the quantitative picture does not look all that different.

22 Daunton, *Trusting Leviathan*, ch. 9, shows how this worked in practice, until the fiscal machinery of local government cracked under the pressure towards the end of the nineteenth century.

23 Mann, *Sources of Social Power*, p. 366. I cannot find any support (even in his own statistics) for Mann's later contention (ibid., 376–7) that British civil and military expenditures per capita were *higher*, although he appears to be basing his comparison on 1910 figures, by which time the disparities noted above were closing: cf. ibid., p. 379.

24 Ibid., pp. 368, 370.

25 Although a similar result is given by another quantitative comparison, the proportion of the population in the civil service in 1880: roughly 0.3 per cent in Britain, possibly 0.7 per cent in Germany, 0.9 per cent in France, 1 per cent in Austria. Military personnel account for about another 1 per cent in all countries. Ibid., p. 393.

26 Jonathan Rose, *The Intellectual Life of the British Working Classes* (New Haven and London: Yale University Press, 2001), pp. 340, 351–2; Michael Billig, *Banal Nationalism* (London: Sage, 1995).

27 Peter Mandler, 'Art in a cool climate: the cultural policy of the British state in European context, 1780–1850', in T. C. W. Blanning & H. Schulze (eds.), *Unity and Diversity in European Culture c. 1800* (British Academy, forthcoming).

28 Emma Winter, 'German fresco painting and the new Houses of Parliament at Westminster, 1834–1851', *Historical Journal* 47 (2004), 291–329; cf. M. H. Port, *Imperial London: Civil Government Building in London, 1851–1915* (New Haven and London: Yale University Press, 1995).

29 Frank K. Prochaska, *Royal Bounty: The Making of a Welfare Monarchy* (New Haven and London: Yale University Press, 1995); idem, *The Republic of Britain, 1760–2000* (London: Allen Lane, 2000).

30 Mann, *Sources of Social Power*, p. 388.

31 Vincent, *Rise of Mass Literacy*, pp. 19–21.

32 Eugen Weber, *Peasants into Frenchmen: The Modernization of Rural France, 1870–1914* (Stanford University Press, 1976).

33 G. R. Searle, *The Quest for National Efficiency: A Study in British Politics and Political Thought 1899–1914* (Oxford: Blackwell, 1971); J. H. Grainger, *Patriotisms: Britain 1900–1939* (London: Routledge and Kegan Paul, 1986), esp. pp. 168–206; Aaron L. Friedberg, *The Weary Titan: Britain and the Experience of Relative Decline, 1895–1905* (Princeton University Press, 1988); Stephen Heathorn, *For Home, Country, and Race: Constructing Gender, Class, and Englishness in the Elementary School, 1880–1914* (Toronto: University of Toronto Press, 2000).

34 Patrick Joyce, *Visions of the People: Industrial England and the Question of Class, 1840–1914* (Cambridge University Press, 1991); Peter Mandler, *The English National Character: The History of an Idea from Edmund Burke to Tony Blair* (forthcoming), chs. 2–3.

35 On the multi-national appeal of 'Anglo-Saxonism', see Colin Kidd, 'Teutonist ethnology and Scottish nationalist inhibition, 1780–1880', *Scottish Historical Review* 74 (1995), 45–68, and 'Race, empire, and the limits of nineteenth-century Scottish nationhood', *Historical Journal* 46 (2003), 873–92.

36 Philip Harling, *The Waning of 'Old Corruption': The Politics of Economical Reform in Britain, 1779–1846* (Oxford: Clarendon Press, 1996); Gareth Stedman Jones, 'Rethinking Chartism', in *Languages of Class: Studies in English Working-Class History 1832–1982* (Cambridge University Press, 1983), 90–178; Peter Mandler, *Aristocratic Government in the Age of Reform: Whigs and Liberals 1830–1852* (Oxford: Clarendon Press, 1990); cf. James Vernon (ed.), *Re-reading the Constitution: New Narratives in the Political History of England's Long Nineteenth Century* (Cambridge University Press, 1996), and Hall, McClelland and Rendall, *Defining the Victorian Nation*.

37 The national dimensions of Chartism are still relatively under-explored; on elite thinking about nationality in this period, see H. S. Jones, *Victorian Political Thought* (Basingstoke: Macmillan, 2000), ch. 2.

38 J. Toulmin Smith, *Local Self-Government and Centralization . . . Including Comprehensive Outlines of the English Constitution* (London: John Chapman, 1852), pp. 18–19, 21–22, 23, 58.

39 Samuel Smiles, *Self-Help* (1866; Oxford University Press, 2002), pp. 19, 20, 37.

40 Bernard Porter, '"Bureau and barrack": early Victorian attitudes towards the Continent', *Victorian Studies* 27 (1983–4), 407–33; J. P. Parry, 'The impact of Napoleon III on British politics, 1851–1880', *Transactions of the Royal Historical Society*, 6th ser., 11 (2001), 147–75.

41 Cf. the idea of 'missionary nationalism' in Krishan Kumar, *The Making of English National Identity* (Cambridge University Press, 2003).

42 Mandler, *English National Character*, ch. 5.

43 This represents my interpretation of some recent work on 'national identity' in the Second World War: see e.g. Steven Fielding, Peter Thompson and Nick Tiratsoo, *'England Arise!' The Labour Party and Popular Politics in 1940s Britain* (Manchester University Press, 1995); John Baxendale, '"You and I – all of us ordinary people": renegotiating "Britishness" in wartime', in Nick Hayes and Jeff Hill (eds.), *'Millions Like Us'? British Culture in the Second World War* (Liverpool University Press, 1999), pp. 295–322; Sonya O. Rose, *Which People's War? National Identity and Citizenship in Wartime Britain 1939–1945* (Oxford University Press, 2003). Each of these is distinctive, but they all offer a critique of the quasi-Gramscian arguments of Angus Calder, *The Myth of the Blitz* (London: Cape, 1991).

Index